MORALITY AND THE MARKET
IN VICTORIAN BRITAIN

MORALITY AND THE MARKET IN VICTORIAN BRITAIN

G. R. Searle

CLARENDON PRESS · OXFORD
1998

Oxford University Press, Great Clarendon Street, Oxford OX2 6DP
Oxford New York
Athens Auckland Bangkok Bogota Bombay
Buenos Aires Calcutta Cape Town Dar es Salaam
Delhi Florence Hong Kong Istanbul Karachi
Kuala Lumpur Madras Madrid Melbourne
Mexico City Nairobi Paris Singapore
Taipei Tokyo Toronto Warsaw
and associated companies in
Berlin Ibadan

Oxford is a trade mark of Oxford University Press

Published in the United States by
Oxford University Press Inc., New York

British Library Cataloguing in Publication Data
Data available

Library of Congress Cataloging in Publication Data
Searle, G. R. (Geoffrey Russell)
Morality and the market in Victorian Britain / G. R. Searle.
p. cm.
Includes bibliographical references and index.
1. Capitalism—Great Britain—History—19th century. 2. Great
Britain—Moral conditions. I. Title.
HC255.S43 1998
330.12'2'094109034—dc 21 97–48954
ISBN 0–19–820698–4

1 3 5 7 9 10 8 6 4 2

Typeset by Graphicraft Typesetters, Ltd., Hong Kong
Printed in Great Britain by
Biddles, Guildford & King's Lynn

*In memory of Roger
Virgoe (1932–96)*

Preface

IN October 1994 the then Foreign Secretary, Douglas Hurd, wrote a newspaper article in which he mused out loud about the proper scope and limits of the free market in public life:

We admire capitalism because it feeds us, clothes us, and gives us a material comfort which no other system can match. It enables individuals to make the choices they prefer in life, and fits well the diverse and flexible nature of democracy. A community which denies capitalism is a dull and doleful place, as the historical record makes clear. But capitalism without the community is an empty husk. Capitalism does not on its own possess some supreme moral quality, regardless of its consequences for people. It is a technique rather than a religion. . . . The market can only deliver its promise within a social and political context.[1]

The utterance was clearly meant as a warning against the excesses perpetrated by those doctrinaire free traders in Hurd's own party who were seeking to establish the primacy of the market in all areas of national life.

Capitalism strikes even many of its admirers as morally repulsive if its principles are taken to extremes. But where is the line to be drawn? How can the market be 'moralized' without its effectiveness being blunted?

As many Conservatives in the late 1980s and 1990s struggle to rediscover what their mid-Victorian forebears learned through painful experience, this book sets out to examine the ways in which, a century and a half ago, intelligent middle-class Britons who broadly sympathized with the development of a commercial society grappled with the problem of how the logic of the market could be reconciled with what they took to be their irreducible religious, moral, and social duties.

This study focuses upon the 1830–1870 period because it was then that 'individualism', *laissez-faire*, and free enterprise capitalism were supposedly at their apogee. To go beyond that point in time would involve the introduction of a host of doubts and qualifications appropriate to the more troubled and complex world of late Victorian Britain: years which saw the development of socialism, the revival of protectionism, and the emergence of a new collectivist outlook on life, all of which, in their different ways, assigned a creative role to the state. But in mid-Victorian Britain, with the Repeal of the Corn Laws a heroic moment of liberation, the principles of market liberalism enjoyed more support than they had ever done in the past or than they were ever to do in the future—until perhaps the rise of 'Thatcherism'.

But even in these years of innocent optimism the practical application of market values proved capable of arousing disquiet, controversy, and genuine

---

[1] D. Hurd, 'Charting the clear blue water', *Guardian*, 12 Oct. 1994.

perplexity. In fact, the country's most intelligent citizens devoted a great deal of energy to searching for intellectual approaches which would enable them to combine economic efficiency with morality. The story of this quest, with all its successes and failures, is one that deserves telling.

However, the middle years of the nineteenth century cannot be studied in isolation. For no generation, even one confronting a set of unprecedented challenges, starts its thinking afresh, and many of the problems encountered by the Victorians and the strategies that lay at hand for coping with these problems, had been inherited from the past. Take, for example, the issue of how the other-worldly asceticism of Christ's teaching, with its stern warnings about material wealth as the source of corruption, could be made compatible, if at all, with contemporary social and economic arrangements. This dilemma was as old as Christianity itself. It had exercised the schoolmen and it had agitated Protestant 'reformers' in sixteenth- and seventeenth-century Europe long before the Victorian churches started worrying about it.

Indeed, as Keith Thomas has recently remarked, the 'application of the Ten Commandments to daily life had never been a straightforward business' and it 'did not grow easier with the passage of time', since 'traditional maxims about buying and selling or lending or borrowing appeared archaic as the economy diversified and credit became universal'.[2] Hence the need for 'casuistry': the application of natural or divine law to particular cases where there was doubt or ambiguity.

Thomas's thesis is that by the start of the nineteenth century there had been 'a shift from a conception of morality as the application of divine laws to human affairs to the idea of it as the simple love of God and pursuit of goodness', morality being essentially simple and accessible to what Adam Smith calls 'the man within the breast'.[3] Even so, the seeming misfit between religious truth and the maxims which regulated everyday commercial life persisted,[4] and, as future chapters will show, casuistry (in fact, if not in name) continued to play an important role in public life.

Another inheritance from the past was the debate over the desirability or otherwise of 'commercial society'. Discussion of this subject had begun in earnest when the Revolution Settlement of 1688 led to the emergence of a financial system centred upon the National Debt. This had resulted in the creation of a large class of bond-holders, whose interests were defended, at the level of central government, by an alliance between the aristocratic Whig governing class and those working in the financial and commercial markets.

Throughout the eighteenth century this alliance had aroused the ire of the 'country' opposition, who invoked a 'republican' concept of 'virtue', derived from a study of classical literature, which condemned the mere pursuit of wealth as

---

[2] K. Thomas, 'Cases of Conscience in Seventeenth-Century England', in J. Morrill, P. Slack, and D. Woolf (eds.), *Public Duty and Private Conscience in Seventeenth-Century England: Essays Presented to G. E. Aylmer* (Oxford, 1993), 30. [3] Ibid., 51–2.
[4] See Ch. 2.

productive of effeminacy, luxury, and corruption. Against these evils, said the 'country' opposition, the sole protection was the public-spirited citizen, willing and able to defend the *patria* by force of arms.[5] This, too, was a line of argument which carried over into Victorian Britain, admittedly in modified forms. Conversely the social and moral advantages of a 'commercial society' which had been identified by the thinkers of the 'Scottish Enlightenment' also continued to be stressed.

One figure from the eighteenth century made a crucially important contribution to mid-Victorian debate: Adam Smith. In fact, the *Wealth of Nations*, first published in 1776, became the bible of most mid-Victorian free traders, just as it was to be venerated by the Radical Right over one hundred years later. If only for that reason, Adam Smith will often make an appearance in these pages.

How closely this 'Adam Smith' resembles the historical figure who earlier lectured at Glasgow and Edinburgh Universities is a moot point. In recent years many intellectual historians have seen their main task as being one of recovering the *intentions* of powerful and original thinkers whose meaning has subsequently been distorted, simplified, or falsified. Writing from this perspective, Donald Winch has written an important study of Adam Smith, with the aim, as he puts it, of expounding 'the historiographic problems involved in establishing necessary conditions for the recovery of meaning from texts considered within historical and linguistic contexts'. Winch goes on to say that this has led him to understand 'how the application of what are basically nineteenth-century perspectives to what is quintessentially a work of the eighteenth century not only introduces various artificialities and anachronisms, but obscures important features of Smith's project'.[6]

The purpose of my study is fundamentally different. I am only indirectly concerned with the 'authentic' aspects of Smith's work: it is the later falsifications and distortions which interest me rather more.[7] Nor does this study set out to provide an intensive examination of a small number of illustrious individuals. Although some of the major thinkers of the age, John Stuart Mill and Herbert Spencer, for example, as well as a host of lesser but well-known writers, like Thomas Chalmers, Harriet Martineau, and Samuel Smiles, figure prominently in its pages, little will be said about how well their texts cohere. For example, the much debated *Adam Smith Problem* (the issue of how to reconcile Smith's *Wealth of Nations*, which emphasizes 'self-love', with his earlier *Theory of Moral Sentiments*, which extols

[5] W. D. Grampp blames this on the influence of a classical education: the Athenians permitted trade but gave agriculture pride of place ('Classical Economics and its Moral Critics', *History of Political Economy*, 5 (1973), 372–3).

[6] D. Winch, *Adam Smith's Politics: An Essay in Historiographic Revision* (Cambridge, 1978), 164–5. Winch acknowledges as his models the intellectual historians, John Dunn, Quentin Skinner, and John Pocock.

[7] There is anyhow much to be said for the recent view of the *Wealth of Nations* as 'a canonical text for Victorian liberalism', a work which was 'after all, rather more Gladstonian in character than it has lately been fashionable to admit' (J. Robertson, 'The Legacy of Adam Smith: Government and Economic Development in the *Wealth of Nations*', in R. Bellamy (ed.), *Victorian Liberalism: Nineteenth-Century Political Thought and Practice* (London, 1990), 19–20, 35–6).

'benevolence') cannot detain us long here.[8] Nor is the book given over to an elu-
cidation of the subtle shifts of belief which took place during the long writing
careers of, say, Malthus, Martineau, Mill, Spencer, and Smiles.[9]

Educated mid-Victorians sought enlightenment as they faced the conflicting claims
of conscience and self-interest, religion and political economy. As we shall see,
when they turned to the revered 'canonical' texts, whether sacred (like the New
Testament) or 'secular' (like the *Wealth of Nations*), they seldom found the clear
and unequivocal guidance which they craved. And so, confronted by a whole array
of practical difficulties, each raising its own kind of contentious ideological issue,
intellectuals, journalists, businessmen, and MPs painfully argued out their differences, sometimes reaching a broad consensus, sometimes failing to do so. What
provides the subject-matter of this book are the intellectual strategies that materialized from such debates, whether these strategies were formulated in highly
abstract language or whether they emerged, incidentally, from the cut and thrust
of polemical exchanges.[10]

My approach has led me to make heavy use of the following sources: the political and economic writings of the day, both books and pamphlets; contemporary
periodicals; parliamentary debates; and the deliberations of the Social Science
Association. For it is in these forums that we can best observe the development
of the thought processes that eventually fed into policy-making.

A final word of caution. This book is not yet one more contribution to the
swelling literature on the 'critics of capitalism', be they 'sages', radical prolet-
arians, or socialists. In other words, it is not primarily dealing with people who
were blankly and irreconcilably hostile to the theory and practice of modern commercial society. My main protagonists are intelligent middle-class Victorians who
admired the economic achievements of their day, saw no viable alternative to some
version of the market philosophy which had made these achievements possible,
but who suffered uneasy consciences.

Pride of place goes to men and women on the Radical-Liberal end of the political spectrum: notably businessmen, dissenters, Radical MPs, and, in particular,
utilitarians and political economists. This cast of actors has been deliberately
chosen because, by concentrating on those who set out with a strong commitment
to securing the sovereignty of the market, we can most clearly explore the dilemmas that arose when this objective clashed with traditional morality. In other words,

---

[8] This issue only excited scholarly interest in the closing years of the 19th c., Smith being known
for most of the Victorian period solely as the author of the *Wealth of Nations* (J. Evensky, 'The Evolution
of Adam Smith's Views on Political Economy', *History of Political Economy*, 21 (1989), 143).

[9] For a subtle account of the development of Malthus's thought, see D. Winch, *Riches and Poverty:
An Intellectual History of Political Economy, 1750–1834* (Cambridge, 1996). On the ambiguous relationship between Samuel Smiles's early writings for the *Leeds Times* and the later books, see A. Tyrrell,
'Class Consciousness, Leeds Politics, and the Self-Help Creed', *Journal of British Studies*, 9 (1970),
102–25.

[10] The historians whose work I have found most suggestive are Boyd Hilton and Brian Harrison,
to both of whom I owe an obvious debt.

the weaknesses and limitations of economic liberalism, as well as its strengths, are likely to stand out clearly if studied from the viewpoint of educated Victorians who favoured that creed—more clearly, certainly, than if seen through the lenses of those who were hostile to it, or lukewarm or equivocal in their support.

The attempt to 'moralize' the market failed in many respects, but the intellectual energy that went into the search for a solution of the dilemmas brought about by economic growth casts a vivid light on the workings of the mid-Victorian 'mind'. It also has an obvious relevance to our own troubled times.

Acknowledgements

In writing this book I have accumulated many debts. First, I must thank the University of East Anglia, which, through its grant of study leave and provision of other facilities, has speeded up its completion. I am also grateful to the staff of the many libraries which I have used in the preparation of the book, especially Cambridge University Library.

Many friends and colleagues have helped by reading early drafts and by making constructive suggestions. I would particularly like to thank the following: Professor Colin Davis, Dr Terry Jenkins, Dr John Charmley, Dr John Greenaway, Dr Roger Munting, and Dr Steve Cherry. Dr Matthew Carter rendered invaluable assistance by checking the many references and citations. Needless to say, I am wholly responsible for any errors that remain.

Finally, I would like to acknowledge the support and encouragement which I have received from my wife, Barbara.

G. R. S.

Norwich
May 1997

Contents

I

Introduction

From the first days in which political economy rose from the region of empirics into those of science, a covert war has been waged as to how far it expresses the whole truth in regard to social wellbeing. The great laws which it defines stand up like rocks amidst the wild waves of theory, and compel them to retire, yet natures in whom love and reverence predominate insist on supplementing their shortcomings by a higher principle.

(Bessie Rayner Parkes, 1865)[1]

For my part, I think that Capitalism, wisely managed, can probably be made more efficient for attaining economic ends than any alternative system yet in sight, but that in itself it is in many ways extremely objectionable.

(John Maynard Keynes, 1926)[2]

It might seem strange that anyone in 1926 could have expressed so much confidence in the efficiency of capitalism. But Keynes believed that the unemployment then ravaging the Western world could be removed by the application of human intelligence. At the same time his belief in the necessity and utility of modern capitalism was accompanied by a realization that in many ways it was, as he himself put it, 'absolutely irreligious, without internal union, without much public spirit, often, though not always, a mere congeries of possessors and pursuers'. Capitalism, thought Keynes, had therefore to be 'immensely, not merely moderately, successful', if it was to 'survive'.[3]

Over a period of two hundred years or more many have broadly endorsed Keynes's position. True, in the first half of the nineteenth century some admirers of the new industrial system wondered whether its expansion could indefinitely continue, even fearing that it might prove to be a brief transient episode.[4] 'The accumulating policy of Dr Adam Smith', warned the clerical economist Thomas Chalmers in 1844, would 'at length give way, before the doctrine that capital has its limits as well as population'; and such a realization, he argued, 'would induce a far more healthful state of commerce than it is possible to maintain with the distempered overtrading of the present day'.[5] Chalmers was here following in the footsteps of

---

[1] B. R. Parkes, *Essays on Woman's Work* (London, 1865), 160.
[2] 'The End of Laissez-Faire' (1926), in J. M. Keynes, *Essays in Persuasion* (London, 1933; first pub. 1931), 321.   [3] Ibid., 306–7.
[4] Boyd Hilton, *The Age of Atonement: The Influence of Evangelicalism on Social and Economic Thought 1795–1865* (Oxford, 1988), 65–6.
[5] T. Chalmers, 'The Political Economy of the Bible', *North British Review*, 2 (1844), 52.

Thomas Malthus, who had earlier warned about the economic, as well as the spiritual, dangers produced by overinvestment and gluts.

However, even in the opening decades of the last century, Ricardo had argued against such pessimistic prognostications,[6] and after 1850 confidence in an expanding capitalism revived. Subsequently, it is true, this confidence was dented by the onset of the Great Depression in the 1870s, by Jevons's gloomy observations concerning the possible exhaustion of coal stocks in 1865, and again, a half century later, by the impact of the interwar depression. Nevertheless, the superiority of capitalism over all alternative economic systems, *from the point of view of maximizing production*, has not often been questioned.

Socialists, one might protest, have always taken a different line. It is certainly true that central to Marxism is the belief that capitalism will inevitably collapse under the weight of its own contradictions. Moreover, many socialists have put their faith in 'planning': the turn-of-the-century Fabian Society, for example, saw unregulated capitalism as both wasteful and inefficient. And this sort of critique also attracted large numbers of supporters in the 1930s (and later in the 1960s).

But probably the socialists' most effective ploy has always been, not so much to censure capitalism for its inefficiency, but to castigate it for being morally obnoxious. As the essayist W. R. Greg sarcastically observed in his defence of capitalist enterprise, socialists sought to substitute 'the noble, Christian, and pacific principle of concert and co-operation' for 'the selfish, mischievous, and wicked one of competition'.[7] The Christian Socialist Wilfrid Richmond, writing in 1890, was therefore surely right to identify as 'the distinctive feature of modern Socialism . . . its appeal to the principles of justice and mutual help as the principles which should regulate economic life'.[8]

Undoubtedly one reason why co-operation, as an alternative to individualistic capitalism, won so much respectful attention during the mid-Victorian years was not so much its purely economic advantages as the fact that, resting on altruism and benevolence rather than on greed and acquisitiveness, it seemed to be a morally superior mode of activity. John Stuart Mill, a leading economist of the classical school, was much influenced by these considerations: 'We hope the time is coming', he once wrote, 'for more rational modes of distributing the productions of nature and of art, than this expensive and demoralizing plan of individual competition, the evils of which have risen to such an enormous height'.[9]

Those attempting a moral justification of capitalism mainly rested their case on the alleged benefits flowing from commercial and industrial growth. One thinks of Macaulay's famous encomium on Progress in his Essay on Francis Bacon, which

---

[6] S. Hollander, 'Ricardo and the Corn Laws: A Revision', *History of Political Economy*, 9 (1977), 45.
[7] W. R. Greg, *Essays on Political and Social Science, contributed chiefly to the Edinburgh Review* (London, 1853), i. 516.   [8] W. Richmond, *Economic Morals: Four Lectures* (London, 1890), 18–19.
[9] Anonymous article of 1833, cited in F. E. Mineka, *The Dissidence of Dissent: The Monthly Repository, 1806–1838* (Chapel Hill, NC, 1944), 277.

characteristically blurs the frontier between technological advancement and the *growth of liberty*.[10] When in 1886 Samuel Smiles compared 'modern' society favourably with society a hundred years earlier, he, too, linked commercial and technological progress to an improvement of morals and manners,[11] and such a conflation was regularly made by *The Economist*.[12]

In fact, as the historian Brian Harrison has shown, there were many Victorians who confidently predicted that commerce would 'banish superstition, ignorance, war, and brutality', supersede slavery by introducing a contractual relationship between employer and employee, facilitate peaceful intercourse between the peoples of the world through the spread of trade, and promote the sobriety and literacy upon which modern industry depended.[13]

Yet few mid-Victorians felt able to strike a totally optimistic note when discussing modern commercial society. They had two grounds for anxiety. The first had to do with the human and social costs of 'progress': the hardship endured by the labouring people huddled together in the new manufacturing centres. Many critics came forward to denounce the exploitation of the poor and the soul-destroying monotony of their existence, as well as the polluted, dangerous, and ugly urban environment in which they were trapped.

Those not directly injured by the harshness of industrial society sometimes felt deeply about the wrongs inflicted on their fellow citizens, especially once their initial complacency had been broken down by first-hand contact with the lives of the deprived. The factory movement of the 1830s and 1840s provides an instructive example of a motley group of outside well-wishers—paternalistic landowners, Anglican clergymen, and even a handful of 'enlightened' factory owners—coming to the support of the exploited northern operatives.

The resulting 'Condition of England' question has already generated an enormous historical literature. Only two of its features merit attention here. First, it is noticeable that concern for the urban underclass was seldom confined to their *material* hardships, nor even to fear of the social and political consequences of doing nothing. More often the emphasis fell on the *moral* degradation produced by bad living conditions, an emphasis especially marked in the sensationalist literature of the 1880s stimulated by the publication of Andrew Mearns's *Bitter Cry of Outcast London* (1883). But much of the mid-Victorian literature of protest similarly explores the links between depravity and deprivation and between sin and suffering.

---

[10] T. B. Macaulay, 'Francis Bacon' (July 1837), in id., *Critical and Historical Essays*, 2 vols., Everyman edn. (London, 1907), ii. 375–6.

[11] S. Smiles, *Thrift* (London, 1886), 224–8. So did Harriet Martineau; see *The Moral of Many Fables* (London, 1834), 6–8, 140–4.

[12] 'The First Half of the Nineteenth Century. Increase of National Well-Being', *The Economist*, 25 Jan. 1851, pp. 81–3, and 'Scientific, Educational, and Moral Progress of the Last Fifty Years', ibid., 1 Feb. 1851, pp. 109–11.

[13] B. Harrison, 'Philanthropy and the Victorians', in id., *Peaceable Kingdom: Stability and Change in Modern Britain* (Oxford, 1982), 230.

This leads on to the second kind of anxiety about capitalism—an anxiety which, by its very nature, even improvements in living standards could do little or nothing to alleviate. The problems of the new industrial society, it was often argued, were only the external manifestation of a more deep-seated *spiritual* malady, resulting from a changed perspective on life. Indeed, as the scope of market transactions widened in the 1840s and 1850s, with the repeal of the Corn Laws, the Navigation Acts, and the Usury Laws, it became commonplace to associate all these 'reforms' not just with the development of a system of manufacturing industry based on factory modes of production, but also with the spread of the ideology of 'political economy'. The critics denounced this way of looking at the world as pernicious because they thought it reduced labour to the status of a marketable commodity, something which seemed to involve a blatant departure from older notions of a 'moral economy'.[14]

In the attacks on the mechanistic individualism of the age, Samuel Taylor Coleridge was an early and eloquent prophet. 'The Spirit of Commerce', he conceded, was 'capable of being at once counteracted and enlightened by the Spirit of the State, to the advantage of both', but he warned of the 'consequences of the Commercial Spirit *un*-counteracted and *un*-enlightened, wherever Trade has been carried to so vast an extent as it has in England'.[15] 'We are . . . a busy, enterprizing, and commercial nation', argued Coleridge, and this disposition had engendered habits which predisposed men 'to look at all things thro' the medium of the market, and to estimate the Worth of all pursuits and attainments by their marketable value'.[16]

Thomas Carlyle, in 'Signs of the Times' (1829), carried on the attack, lashing out at his two bugbears: the utilitarians and the political economists, groups which he tended to fuse together in the heat of his anger. Men, he complained, had 'grown mechanical in head and in heart, as well as in hand'.[17] ' "Make money; and don't bother about the Universe!" '—this, he later fumed, was the philosophy of the likes of M'Croudy (his nickname for the economist J. R. McCulloch): it was, he raged, a philosophy 'reckoned a quiet, innocent and rather wholesome notion just now; yet clearly fitter for a reflective pig than for a man'.[18]

Now, we will see in a later chapter that utilitarianism and political economy were really somewhat different ideologies. But both, in their nineteenth-century form at least, took the calculating individual as the unit of their analysis, with Adam Smith's higgling 'economic man' bearing some resemblance to Bentham's

---

[14] In Ireland, too, 'objections to political economy, and especially to *laissez-faire*, were overwhelmingly moral' (T. A. Boylan and T. P. Foley, *Political Economy and Colonial Ireland* (London, 1992), 142).

[15] 'Blessed are ye that sow beside all Waters!' (1817), in R. J. White (ed.), *The Collected Works of Samuel Taylor Coleridge*, vi, *Lay Sermons* (London, 1972), 195, 223.

[16] Ibid., 189. See the discussion in C. Gallagher, *The Industrial Reformation of English Fiction, 1832–1867* (Chicago, 1985), 21. On Coleridge's 'romantic' critique of political economy in general and of Malthus in particular, see D. Winch, *Riches and Poverty: An Intellectual History of Political Economy in Britain, 1750–1834* (Cambridge, 1996), ch. 11.

[17] T. Carlyle, 'Signs of the Times', *Edinburgh Review* (1829), in G. B. Tennyson (ed.), *A Carlyle Reader: Selections from the Writings of Thomas Carlyle* (Cambridge, 1984), 37.

[18] T. Carlyle, 'Hudson's Statue', in id., *Latter-Day Pamphlets* (1858; first pub. 1850), 241.

hedonistic citizen armed with his felicific calculus through which he sought to maximize his own pleasure/happiness.

Concern was specifically expressed at the great emphasis currently being placed on the role of *competition*. 'All are sedulously trained to buy cheap and to sell dear', Robert Owen complained, 'and to succeed in this art, the parties must be taught to acquire strong powers of deception; and thus a spirit is generated through every class of traders, destructive of that open, honest sincerity, without which man cannot make others happy, nor enjoy happiness himself'.[19] Charles Kingsley, in tract and novel, continued the indictment of what he called 'the brute natural accidents of supply and demand'.[20] The spirit of the present age, sneered the novelist, Peacock, was 'the spirit of buying and selling . . . regulated by no more enlightened or extensive views that those which [regulate] the dealings . . . in coffee, treacle, and fish-sauce'.[21]

Even more than political economy, utilitarianism seemed a subversive creed— not just because of its close associations with political radicalism, but also because it denied the importance of local custom and tradition. In that sense utilitarianism could be viewed as a faithful reflection of contemporary economic developments which, in transforming the social landscape, were also effacing some of its best-loved features.

Acquisitive individualism was also widely mistrusted because it conflicted with a number of traditional social codes like Tory paternalism. But it was Christianity which constituted the main difficulty. As we shall see in the next chapter, strenuous attempts were made to harmonize the new science of political economy with religious truth, but it was not easy for those soaked in the New Testament to embrace it whole-heartedly. 'Thou shalt not covet; but tradition | Approves all forms of competition', wrote Arthur Clough sardonically in his 'New Decalogue'.

Similarly utilitarianism offended many pious Christians because it seemed so *flagrantly* at variance with the spirit of the Sermon on the Mount: how could Bentham's injunction that individuals should calculate the probable *consequences* of their actions possibly be reconciled with Christ's commendation of the lilies of the field?[22] In *Middlemarch* George Eliot invites her readers to admire Dorothea Brooke, whose nature, we learn, 'was entirely without hidden calculations either for immediate effects or for remoter ends',[23] a woman who 'disliked this cautious

---

[19] R. Owen, *A New View of Society and Other Writings*, ed. G. D. H. Cole (New York, 1963), 122, cited in Gallagher, *Industrial Reformation*, 14. See also C. C. Ryan, 'The Fiends of Commerce: Romantic and Marxist Criticisms of Classical Political Economy', *History of Political Economy*, 13 (1981), 82.

[20] C. Kingsley, *Alton Locke: Tailor and Poet* (London, 1895; first pub. 1850), p. cvii.

[21] W. D. Grampp, 'Classical Economics and its Moral Critics', *History of Political Economy*, 5 (1973), 371.

[22] It was not only the New Testament which utilitarianism seemed to be contradicting. Consider, for example, Eccles. 11: 1–6.

[23] G. Eliot, *Middlemarch*, Penguin edn. (London, 1965; first pub. 1871–2), ch. 5, p. 74. However, Eliot's own attitude towards Dorothea's 'Theresa-complex' is ambivalent, and some critics contest the idea that she is at the moral centre of the novel.

weighing of consequences, instead of an ardent faith in efforts of justice and mercy, which would conquer by their emotional force'; 'what do we live for, if it is not to make life less difficult to each other?', Dorothea was wont to ask.[24]

Stefan Collini has argued that what he calls 'the Culture of Altruism' was central to Victorian life.[25] Whereas in the eighteenth century it was possible for theorists to accept that 'benevolence' and 'self-love' would never perfectly tally, by Victorian times, claims Collini, it became common to assume the existence of a strenuous struggle between 'egoism' and 'altruism' in which the latter would hopefully triumph over the former.[26] The Victorian 'Sages', he shows, all derived much of their influence as moralists from their reputation as uncompromising devotees of altruism and from their high-minded rejection of any shabby compromising of this ideal.[27]

The pervasiveness of such an ideology, with its accompanying cult of 'character',[28] was certainly widespread. Indeed, according to one recent authority, even Victorian *Liberals* were 'haunted by this ethos of egoistic, possessive individualism and strenuously battled against it', so eager were they to demonstrate that Liberalism was no 'narrow economic doctrine'.[29]

Now, it is arguable that all these *moral* anxieties proved to be more long-lasting than concern over the living conditions of the urban poor—and possibly more influential, too. For by the end of the nineteenth century, social segregation had made it possible for the well-to-do to avoid contact with poverty in its most stark forms for months on end. By contrast, commercial greed, and its consequences, affected nearly all members of the Victorian middle class, directly or indirectly.

This became a particular problem with the growing separation of management from ownership, a process further stimulated and encouraged by the legalization of limited liability during the 1850s. A dramatic expansion of the share-owning public ensued, and the facilities for speculation naked and unashamed enormously increased. Moreover, during the 1850s and 1860s a series of commercial failures and financial panics revealed how extensive was wrongdoing at all levels of society, from dishonest company directors down to embezzling clerks.[30]

Many moralists derived great satisfaction from the widespread loss of savings resulting from the speculative manias which periodically swept the country: they saw in this a salutary punishment for human greed. And such revelations were eagerly exploited by the Victorian 'Sages' (Coleridge, Carlyle, Ruskin, Arnold) and

[24] Ibid., ch. 72, p. 789.
[25] Stefan Collini, *Public Moralists: Political Thought and Intellectual Life in Britain, 1850–1930* (Oxford, 1991), ch. 2.   [26] Ibid., 65–7.
[27] Collini notes that Gladstone recommended Mill (a pivotal figure in this thesis) to the electors of Westminster in 1868, not by referring to his intelligence or knowledge, but by emphasizing that 'his presence in the House of Commons has materially helped to raise and sustain its moral tone' (ibid., 169).   [28] Ibid., 97. See the more extended discussion in chs. 2, 3, 11.
[29] R. Bellamy, 'Introduction', in R. Bellamy (ed.), *Victorian Liberalism: Nineteenth-Century Political Thought and Practice* (London, 1990), 2.   [30] See Ch. 5.

later by the pioneers of socialism.[31] Attacks on 'Mammonism' as the besetting sin of the age also provided a popular theme for Victorian novelists, journalists, and sermonizing clergymen. Anthony Trollope, writing in the mid-1850s, was not alone in identifying *dishonesty* as the prevalent characteristic of the age.[32]

It was in vain that the political economists pointed out that all the evils of contemporary society could hardly be laid at their own door. The principles of this infant science, they protested, had only recently been revealed and, in some cases, had not yet been seriously put into practice: 'Economists affirm, and with perfect justice', wrote Greg, 'that the existing wretchedness of England is directly traceable to ignorance, neglect, and systematic *violation* of the principles of political economy'.[33] Richard Cobden took a different tack, attributing the unpopularity of political economy to well-meaning but tactless exponents of the new science like Edwin Chadwick who had frightened 'ignorant people' and done 'infinite injury to the benign truths of Adam Smith'.[34]

But such protestations were widely ignored. Instead, as Catherine Gallagher puts it, 'the ideology most often associated with the industrial bourgeoisie, laissez-faire entrepreneurialism, [was] on the defensive . . . from its inception'.[35] In fact, the dominant middle-class response to the development of capitalism—seen, for example, in the greatest contemporary writer, Charles Dickens—was neither approval nor rejection, but ambivalence.

The central predicament for such people was how to reconcile their economic convictions with their ethical principles, the new world-view which had emerged to explain modern society with the social values which they had inherited from their ancestors. For example, trading in human beings, or in pornographic literature, or in addictive drugs could surely never be justified? This in turn led on to a search for appropriate 'boundaries', so that the realm of the market could be separated from the enclaves sheltering family, morality, and religion.

It thus became incumbent on those who broadly accepted what we would now call 'capitalism' to justify their preferences, a task which clearly involved establishing the parameters of the market and laying down ground rules which would prevent or mitigate abuses. What came of these attempts forms the subject matter of the rest of the book.

---

[31] See the anthology edited by E. Jay and R. Jay, *Critics of Capitalism: Victorian Reactions to 'Political Economy'* (Cambridge, 1986).

[32] See Trollope's strictures (written 1855–6) in N. J. Hall (ed.), *Anthony Trollope, The New Zealander* (Oxford, 1972), 211. He explores the theme further in his novel, *The Three Clerks* (Oxford, 1989; first pub. 1857), 395 and *passim*). The two most powerful indictments of 'Mammonism', both dating from the mid-1850s, are Thackeray's *The Newcomes* (London, 1855) and Dickens's *Little Dorrit* (London, 1855–7).

[33] My italics. Greg, 'English Socialism', in *Essays*, i. 476–7. As Collini argues, Liberal theorists like Mill, Fawcett, and Spencer also made much of the 'distorting' effect of hereditary and landed privilege, which served them as an alibi, enabling them to claim that the principle of free competition had never yet been given a fair trial (Collini, *Public Moralists*, 183).

[34] Cobden to Bright, 5 Nov. 1855, cited in D. Read, *Cobden and Bright: A Victorian Political Partnership* (London, 1967), 4.   [35] See Gallagher, *Industrial Reformation*, p. xv.

2

Capitalism and Christianity

An affection for riches, beyond what Christianity prescribes, is not essential to any extension of commerce that is at all valuable or legitimate; and, in opposition to the maxims that the spirit of enterprise is the soul of commercial prosperity, do we hold, that it is the excess of this spirit beyond the moderation of the New Testament, which, pressing on the natural boundaries of trade, is sure, at length, to visit every country, where it operates with the recoil of all those calamities, which, in the shape of beggared capitalists, and unemployed operatives, and dreary intervals of bankruptcy and alarm, are observed to follow a season of overdone speculation.

(Thomas Chalmers, 1820)[1]

Trading without capital is dangerous; but without principle, it is what insurers call 'doubly hazardous', as it affords no sufficient guarantee for good faith . . . The worldly man of business has none but worldly safeguards; his bills want endorsement; whatever trust may be reposed in him must be in the man alone. There is no means of trusting God in His servant.

(Revd J. B. Owen, 1855)[2]

In *Hard Times*, Dickens's satire on the factory town is principally directed at two targets: political economy and utilitarianism, which, following Carlyle, he conflated and presented as the typical creeds of the modern age. The theme of the novel is the way in which both violate the sanctities of morality and religion, it being taken for granted that they are secular, materialistic creeds, at war with 'fancy', imagination, conscience, family affection, and other spiritual values.[3]

Yet nearly all the early pioneers in the field of academic economics were clergymen, among them the pivotal figure of the Reverend Thomas Malthus.[4] The books of another Anglican divine, Archbishop Whately, may well have commanded a wider audience than the writings of any other political economist of the age.[5] Indeed, Boyd Hilton goes so far as to claim that the influence on early and mid-Victorian

---

[1] T. Chalmers, *The Application of Christianity to The Commerce and Ordinary Affairs of Life, In A Series of Discourses* (Glasgow, 1820), pp. v–vi.

[2] J. B. Owen, *Business Without Christianity* (London, 1855), 12–14.

[3] Even the friends of 'political economy' often admitted the truth of the charge of philistinism. Thus the *Edinburgh Review* wrote of Whately, perhaps unjustly: 'Of poetical feeling or appreciation he had barely a scintilla' ([H. Merivale], 'Archbishop Whately', 120 (1864), 399).

[4] S. G. Checkland, 'The Advent of Academic Economics in England', *Manchester School of Economic and Social Studies*, 19 (1951), 70.

[5] P. Mandler, 'Tories and Paupers: Christian Political Economy and the Making of the New Poor Law', *Historical Journal*, 33 (1990), 103.

governments exercized by the famous classical economists pales into insignificance compared with the influence of Evangelical churchmen like Thomas Chalmers —especially when 'liberal Tory' ministries were in office.[6] In the 1820s in particular, there was, as one contemporary observed, 'a rage for Christian economics'. Of what did this consist?

CHRISTIAN ECONOMICS

In the eighteenth century there was no such thing as an autonomous, secular field of study called economics. Economic speculation was still inextricably intermingled with natural science, ethics, and religion. Economics, in short, was a sub-branch of 'natural theology', and was so treated by its most famous exponent, the Anglican cleric, Dr Paley, author of a famous book bearing that title, published in 1801.

Paley and the earlier theologians in whose footsteps he was treading set out to demonstrate the existence and goodness of God. This they did by claiming that God had not made Himself intelligible to the human race only through Revelation. For God at the Creation had endowed humans with the faculty of Reason through which they could comprehend the workings of Nature and thereby achieve a partial understanding of the Divine Mind. Reason was thus a moral intuition by means of which *all* mankind, whether or not individuals had received the blessings of the Gospel, could distinguish between right and wrong. But Reason also threw light on the handiwork of God the Creator. Through a study of the wonders of the natural world and a grasp of the 'laws' by which it was governed, Reason could grasp that the Creator was an intelligent and purposeful Being.

But a study of the nature of *humankind* and an understanding of the laws of *social* behaviour, too, enabled God to be worshipped with greater devotion. In Richard Whately's words, since anatomy and physiology furnished 'a most important portion of Natural-Theology . . . it might have been anticipated, that an attentive study of the constitution of Society, would bring to light a no less admirable apparatus of divinely-wise contrivances, directed no less to beneficial ends'.[7]

Beliefs of this kind could be harnessed to a wide range of religious and political purposes. They formed the bedrock of 'deism', which dismissed Revelation as superstition, but they were also used by clergymen like Paley and Whately to underpin Christianity. Such beliefs could similarly be put to different social and political uses, depending upon the way in which 'natural law' was interpreted.[8]

---

[6] B. Hilton, *The Age of Atonement: The Influence of Evangelicalism on Social and Economic Thought, 1795–1865* (Oxford, 1988).

[7] R. Whately, *Introductory Lectures on Political Economy: Delivered at Oxford, 1831* (London, 1847), 80.

[8] For example, Paine, the Deist, thought that God, the First Cause, had made all men equal —a position which he developed into an attack on all political and religious establishments (I. Harris, 'Paine and Burke: God, Nature and Politics', in M. Bentley (ed.), *Public and Private Doctrine* (Cambridge, 1993), 34–62).

But, as Frank Turner has shown, since the late seventeenth century 'natural theology' had been particularly closely associated with a justification of contemporary
economic arrangements.[9]

Distinctions in social rank and wealth, for example, were said to fit in with
God's plans for the world, because they stimulated competition by appealing to
the ambitious and by providing work-incentives to the labouring poor, which in
turn led to the development of meritorious traits of character: 'In a religious view',
Paley concluded, 'privation, disappointment, and satiety, are not without the most
salutary tendencies'.[10] Some 'natural theologians' even argued that God gave
human beings different faces, so as to reduce the incidence of commercial fraud!
The exploitation of coal was also seen as an expression of the Divine plan.[11] Thus,
to quote Turner, Paley 'sought to demonstrate not only that science did not endanger religion but also that science and natural theology positively embraced contemporary commercial values'. The revolution in France in 1789 gave renewed
urgency to this attempt at reconciling religion with science.[12]

However, as Boyd Hilton has shown, the propensity of eighteenth-century
Enlightenment thinkers to portray Nature in all its forms as the expression of
a benevolent Mind was largely displaced by a more gloomy view of God's Providential design once political economy started to be taken up by conservatives,
whose natural pessimism had been intensified by the revolutionary disturbances
in France. In addition, the Evangelical Revival highlighted the Fall and dramatized the role of evil in the world, leaving theologians with the task of explaining
'the apparent discrepancies in nature' and the way in which 'God wrought ultimate Good out of apparent Evil'.[13]

Out of this climate of opinion there emerged Thomas Malthus's *Essay on
Population*, the first edition of which was published in 1798.[14] Writing under the
shadow of Jacobinism, Malthus, an Anglican clergyman, intended his essay to undermine the 'irreligious' doctrine of human perfectibility as propagated by the likes
of William Godwin and Condorcet through a demonstration that population
growth was doomed to press up against a world of finite resources: economic prosperity could never feed the growing population which it had stimulated because
population grew in geometric ratio, while the resources needed to sustain it only
increased in arithmetic ratio. Malthus thus portrayed human beings as locked
into a life-and-death competitive battle. As Donald Winch observes, in this way

---

[9] F. M. Turner, 'The Secularization of the Social Vision of British Natural Theology', in id., *Contesting
Cultural Authority* (Cambridge, 1993), 102–4.   [10] Cited ibid., 108.
    [11] Ibid., 102–3.   [12] Ibid., 104–5.
    [13] B. Hilton, 'Chalmers as Political Economist', in A. C. Cheyne (ed.), *The Practical and the Pious:
Essays on Thomas Chalmers (1780–1847)* (Edinburgh, 1985), 143.
    [14] The following is an oversimplified account of Malthus, though it probably corresponds quite
closely with what a later generation of admirers and critics believed him to have said. See D. Winch's
Riches and Poverty: An Intellectual History of Political Economy in Britain, 1750–1834 (Cambridge,
1996), pt. 3. Winch, more than most other commentators, stresses the 'progressive' aspects of Malthus's
teaching.

Malthus added 'the fear of falling in the social scale to Smith's assumptions concerning the restless desire for individual improvement as part of the motivation necessary to sustain commercial society'.[15]

The necessary outcome of this struggle, Malthus declared, was that both population growth and prosperity would quickly be checked by famine and war —a gloomy conclusion lightened in subsequent editions, where 'moral restraint' was also mentioned as a possible mitigating factor. Mankind, being placed in a 'probationary state' (a phrase first used by the eighteenth-century theologian, Bishop Butler), needed to *struggle* in this harsh environment if it were to realize God's plans for the world.

Malthus's 'principle of population' was originally intended to refute the doctrine of human perfectibility to which the French Revolution had given currency, thereby encouraging a due Christian humility. But the Malthusian doctrine aroused bitter antagonism even among the orthodox. Many pious Christians and the tender-hearted were alike offended by Malthus's ill-chosen phrase about there being too many guests at Nature's feast—a phrase which helped to associate political economy as a whole with misanthropy. 'It is difficult to reconcile the idea of human immortality with the idea that nature wastes men by constantly bringing them into being where there is no room for them', Henry George was later to write.[16] Thus, not only did Malthus contribute to Ricardo's 'iron law of wages', but, by seeming to present competition as something *feral*, he helped pave the way for the later Social Darwinian view of the world.[17]

Paley, who was basically an optimist, managed to incorporate Malthus's population principle into his *Natural Theology*. But it took a number of other Christian apologists writing in the first two decades of the nineteenth century to build up a convincing 'theodicy' around the population principle. Here the crucial advance was made by Bishop Sumner, who linked the 'principle of population' with the traditional theological defence of God's purpose in establishing inequality of ranks and fortune.[18] Sumner, following Malthus's lead, also argued that God was seeking, through scarcity, to stimulate human adaptability and moral exertion,[19] an idea taken up and developed by Thomas Chalmers, the Scottish Evangelical divine who emerged as the chief exponent of 'Christian economics' in the opening three decades of the nineteenth century.

[15] Ibid., 260.

[16] H. George, *Progress and Poverty* (1884), quoted in R. Ledbetter, *A History of The Malthusian League 1877–1927* (Columbus, Oh., 1976), 90.

[17] R. M. Young, 'Malthus and the Evolutionists: The Common Context of Biological and Social Theory', *Past & Present*, 43 (1969), 109–45. Needless to say, this is a distortion of what Malthus really meant.

[18] A. M. C. Waterman, *Revolution, Economics and Religion: Christian Political Economy, 1798–1833* (Cambridge, 1991), 163.

[19] Cheyne (ed.), *Practical and Pious*, 144. See also R. A. Soloway, *Prelates and People: Ecclesiastical Social Thought in England 1783–1852* (London, 1969), 107–16; Winch, *Riches and Poverty*, 238–9; Waterman, *Revolution, Economics and Religion*, 165.

In Chalmers's hands, however, the concept of 'moral restraint' became transformed. Malthus had almost casually introduced the term into the second edition of his *Essay* as a factor *mitigating* the operation of the population principle. But Chalmers turned it into the central concept in a moral drama in which the Church played a vital role.

For Chalmers contended that the clergy, in preaching the Gospel, indirectly fostered the habits which strengthened prudence and so allowed the human race to escape from the population trap. 'If we seek to reform or to ameliorate either their condition or their habits, it is altogether by another sort of moral dynamics being brought into operation', he wrote: hence the importance of a 'Christian education' and of a 'moral and religious training'.[20] The masses, Chalmers insisted, could be left in total ignorance of political economy provided that they were brought into contact with

the lessons of the Gospel; and so [were] made to participate in the humanizing and enlarging influences of that Christianity which, wherever it takes effect, is sure to tell generally on the intellect and taste, as well as on the principles of men—investing all their higher faculties, the reason, and the understanding, and the conscience, with a more efficient control over their inferior propensities and instincts of their merely animal nature.[21]

There was thus a 'harmony . . . between what an enlightened science pronounces to be true, and an enlightened Christianity (by which we mean no other than the Christianity of the Bible) pronounces to be right and good'.[22] By this ingenious line of argument Chalmers was able, *as a political economist*, to mount a case for a Church Establishment, on the ground that an educated clergy which upheld high standards of morality and civilization thereby enriched the national community.[23]

'Those who would divorce Theology from Science, or Science from Theology, are, in effect if not in intention, the enemies of both', Chalmers once declared.[24] When writing in this way, as well as when extolling the wonders of divine 'adaptation', Chalmers resembles Malthus less than he does Paley, with whom he shared a somewhat complacent belief in a harmonious and beneficent universe. Unlike Malthus, for example, Chalmers tended to *conflate* political economy and morals[25]—as, in a famous passage in his *Bridgewater Treatise* of 1833, where he wrote of an 'inseparable connection between the moral worth and the economic comfort of a people', which demonstrated that 'political economy [was] but one grand exemplification of the alliance, which a God of righteousness hath established, between prudence and moral principle on the one hand, and physical comfort on the other'.[26]

[20] T. Chalmers, 'The Political Economy of the Bible', *North British Review*, 2 (1844), 7.
[21] Ibid., 7–8.   [22] Ibid., 13.
[23] On Chalmers's hostility to competition between different religious bodies, see Ch. 11.
[24] Chalmers, 'Political Economy of Bible', 3.   [25] Winch, *Riches and Poverty*, 248–9.
[26] T. Chalmers, *On the Power, Wisdom and Goodness of God as Manifested in the Adaptation of External Nature to the Moral and Intellectual Constitution of Man* (London, 1853; first pub. 1833), 248–9.

Starting off from these premises, Chalmers sought to justify private property and inequalities of rank and wealth as necessary elements in the divine economy by arguments which the eighteenth-century natural theologians, as well as Sumner, had made commonplace. He also reasoned that commercial growth multiplied contacts between peoples, increased their mutual inter-dependence, and so contributed to moral improvement:

It is, indeed, an animating thought, amid the gloom of this world's depravity, when we behold the credit which one man puts in another, though separated by oceans and by continents; when he fixes the anchor of a sure and steady dependence on the reported honesty of one whom he never saw, when, with all his fears for the treachery of the varied elements through which his property has to pass, he knows, that should it only arrive at the door of its destined agent, all his fears and all his suspicions may be at an end. We know nothing finer than such an act of homage from one human being to another . . . nor do we think that either the renown of her victories, or the wisdom of her councils, so signalizes the country in which we live, as does the honourable dealing of her merchants.[27]

Such a line of argument neatly intermeshed with the older, secular case supporting 'commercial society'. 'To most eighteenth-century defenders of Whig civilization', Professor Pocock notes, 'the rise of commerce and the rise of polite culture went together, under the name of "the progress of the arts", and required to be defended together, against those who hankered after the austere republicanism of Spartan or Roman antiquity'.[28] Commercial society, seen from this perspective, was unequal but progressive, unvirtuous but just—as Adam Smith himself had maintained.[29]

Many Christians also celebrated the development of commerce as part of God's design for propagating the Gospel throughout the world. In his *Considerations on the Alliance between Christianity and Commerce*, the Evangelical divine, Richard Raikes, presented the 'general propensity to barter and exchange' as 'the great motive to intercourse between different countries', arguing that

this disposition, which is implanted by the Author of Nature, we may consider as co-operating with another and higher part of the divine economy; and in consequence we may venture to affirm, that, in the present state of things, miracles having ceased, Christianity, without Commerce, could not attain its purpose, or duly influence the minds of man.[30]

Yet, influenced by the Evangelical temper of the day, Chalmers and Raikes put more of an emphasis upon man's sinfulness than the eighteenth-century Whigs had done. And from this both men were led to the recognition that commerce,

[27] Chalmers, *Application of Christianity*, 30.
[28] J. G. A. Pocock, *Virtue, Commerce and History* (Cambridge, 1985), 210.
[29] I. Hont and M. Ignatieff, 'Needs and Justice in the *Wealth of Nations*: An Introductory Essay', in I. Hont and M. Ignatieff (eds.), *Wealth and Virtue: The Shaping of Political Economy in the Scottish Enlightenment* (Cambridge, 1983), 1–44. See also G. Claeys, 'The French Revolution Debate in British Political Thought', *History of Political Thought*, 11 (1990), 73.
[30] R. Raikes, *Considerations on the Alliance between Christianity and Commerce* (1806; reissued 1825), 17–19. See the discussion in D. Turley, *The Culture of English Antislavery 1780–1860* (London, 1991), 180.

for all the blessings it bestowed, was also multiplying the opportunities for fraud and dishonesty. So Chalmers favoured a moderate extension of commerce, but only if it were tempered by Christian principle; and Raikes laid down rules for the guidance of merchants, one of which stipulated that no commerce could be advantageous which contradicted the principles of Christianity or which evidently tended to the corruption of morals.[31]

As Boyd Hilton has explained, 'the Evangelical economists [also] drew a parallel between the tendency of population to outstrip food supply and the tendency of capital to outstrip demand'. Financial crises were portrayed as a necessary check on wilful 'overtrading', and business failures as a providential warning to the nation to cleave to 'true commerce' but to fly from evil 'speculation'. Chalmers thus saw bankruptcy as a mechanism for eliminating *immoral* traders, unlike the secular Ricardo who thought its value lay in weeding out the *inefficient*.[32]

But the divine purpose would not be realized if human beings impertinently interfered in the natural operation of natural law. Therefore, like Malthus before him (but far more recklessly), Chalmers urged the total abolition of the poor laws, believing that they not only led in the long run to more rather than less human misery, but that they also frustrated God's plans. The outcome, Chalmers asserted, had been a horrendous increase in pauperism—'an emphatic demonstration for the superior wisdom of nature which is never so decisively or so triumphantly attested, as by the mischief that is done, when her processes are contravened or her principles are violated'.[33] A few years later Nassau Senior went down the same track when, in condemnation of the old poor law, he wrote: 'There never was a better illustration of the quiet truths, that in Morals, as well as in Political Economy, the laws of nature are wiser than those of man'.[34]

These were precisely the grounds on which Chalmers proclaimed the virtues and necessity of free trade:

The philosophy of free trade is grounded on the principle, that society is most enriched or best served, when commerce is left to its own spontaneous evolutions; and is neither fostered by the artificial encouragements, nor fettered by the artificial restrains, of human policy. The greatest economic good is rendered to the community, by each man being left to consult and to labour for his own particular good—or, in other words, a more prosperous result is obtained by the spontaneous play and busy competition of many thousand wills, each bent on the prosecution of his own selfishness, than by the anxious superintendence of a government, vainly attempting to medicate the fancied imperfections of nature, or to improve on the arrangements of her previous and better mechanism.[35]

[31] Raikes, *Christianity and Commerce*, 20.
[32] Hilton, 'Chalmers as Political Economist', in Cheyne (ed.), *Practical and Pious*, 146–9. He also argues that Malthus's underconsumptionism was really a theory of *overproduction* (150–1).
[33] Chalmers, *On the Power, Wisdom and Goodness of God*, 224. However, on Malthus's qualifications of this harsh view of the poor laws, see Ch. 8.
[34] Anon (Senior), 'Poor Law Reform', *Edinburgh Review*, 74 (Oct. 1841), 33.
[35] Chalmers, *On the Power, Wisdom and Goodness of God*, 238.

Taken in isolation, such passages closely resemble the advocacy of free trade made a decade later by the likes of Richard Cobden, who, as Goldwin Smith observed in his obituary, 'distinctly saw and deeply felt that commerce was the material basis on which Providence had ordained that a community of a higher kind should be built'.[36] But they were rooted in a coherent *religious* view of the world, from which political economy later became at least partially detached. How did this process of disengagement occur?

THE DECLINE OF CHRISTIAN ECONOMICS?

Specialists are divided over how and why Christian economics collapsed, if, indeed, it ever did so completely. Professor Waterman, for example, thinks that this whole way of examining economic phenomena quite quickly lost its credibility after 1832, when the disappearance of the Jacobinical threat, coupled with the emergence of a reforming, but responsible, Whig administration, removed its original *raison d'être*.[37] Hilton, on the other hand, locates the change much later, in the 1850s and 1860s, and attributes it to the waning prestige of the Evangelical doctrine of the Atonement and to the consequent replacement of Chalmers's 'God of Righteousness' by a 'God of Mercy'—a development which encouraged Christians to take a more humanitarian view of the world and to reject the notion of God-inspired inexorable laws.[38]

Both explanations are plausible, but there may also be more matter-of-fact explanations for the decline of 'Christian economics', which had, after all, been a highly unstable compound from the very start. In particular, attempts to vindicate contemporary economic arrangements by presenting them as elements in the divine plan had always been contentious, since the existence of so much poverty and suffering seemed to mock the notion that the universe was either harmonious or could possibly have been created by a benevolent God. In fact, to square the social and political *status quo* with justice, both Malthus and Chalmers had been obliged to invoke immortality: for, as Frank Turner puts it, 'only with the balancing of moral accounts in the hereafter of eternity did their ethical teaching become bearable for the overwhelming majority of their countrymen'.[39] In other words, economics as a branch of 'natural theology' had never been entirely autonomous, since it ultimately depended upon Revelation.

It was the problem of reconciling 'natural theology' with the generally accepted Christian message which led Chalmers to outline what he called 'the political economy of the Bible' in an attempt to demonstrate that, say, Malthus's population

---

[36] G. Smith, 'Richard Cobden', *Macmillan's Magazine*, 12 (1865), 91.
[37] Waterman, *Revolution, Economics and Religion*, 255.   [38] Hilton, *Age of Atonement*, pt. 3.
[39] Turner, 'Secularization', 109–10.

law was consistent with biblical authority. In practice, this involved the citation of often quite obscure biblical passages, often blatantly taken out of context. 'Suitable' texts like the Parable of the Talents (Matthew 25: 14–40) were reproduced *ad nauseam*, while Christ's many recorded utterances which seem flatly at variance with the 'lessons' of political economy—to take the most famous examples, the Sermon on the Mount and the Parable of the Good Samaritan—tended to be glossed over.

When an inconvenient Biblical text proved impossible to ignore, recourse was had to historical relativism: Malthus, for example, explained away the biblical maxim, 'be fruitful and multiply', by differentiating between historical epochs, each of which had its own separate needs.[40] The problems of an advanced commercial society, it was argued, had made the divine wisdom of an earlier age inapplicable. 'In the days of Christ, and in the circumstances of his land', wrote W. R. Greg, 'it may be that alms-giving was one of the most prompt and certain means of doing good, and was unattended by any of those mischiefs which invariably follow and surround it here. It is not so now.'[41] The Reverend Richard Raikes pursued another strategy, claiming that 'every precept of the Gospel, rationally interpreted', contributed to the present as well as the future happiness of man—from which he deduced that 'if any passage seems to require what is destructive of Commerce in general, we have reason to suspect that it is misinterpreted or misapplied'![42]

Greg, an unbeliever, was unusual in being prepared to criticize, head-on, the Sermon on the Mount and other of Christ's sayings.[43] Greg particularly disliked the doctrine of the forgiveness of sins, which, he complained, had 'encouraged millions—feeling what a safety was in store for them in ultimate resort—to persevere in their career of folly or crime—to ignore or despise those natural laws which God [had] laid down to be the guides and beacons of our conduct'.[44] Rather unconvincingly, Greg represented his views as an attempt to rescue the *essential* truths of Christianity from the errors perpetrated by the 'orthodox', rather than as a total repudiation of Christianity as such.[45] But this was a risky line to take in a Protestant country peopled by practising Christians, most of whom were both knowledgeable about the Bible and prone to read it 'literally'.

If Protestant fundamentalism was one enemy, so, too, was Tractarianism, with its emphasis on the supremacy of Church authority and on the need to subordinate secular knowledge to Christian dogma, a commitment which, of course, it

---

[40] Winch, *Riches and Poverty*, 243 and fn. 33.

[41] Anon [Greg], 'Charity, Noxious and Beneficent', *Westminster Review*, 59 (1853), 80. Martineau deployed a similar argument: 'Almsgiving, however appropriate an act of benevolence in so peculiar a polity as that of the Jews, is not a virtuous deed at present, if it can be proved to create more misery than it relieves' (H. Martineau, 'On the Duty of Studying Political Economy', id., *Miscellanies*, 2 vols. (Boston, 1836), i. 275–6, 279, 281).   [42] Raikes, *Christianity and Commerce*, 23.

[43] R. J. Helmstadter, 'W. R. Greg: A Manchester Creed', in R. J. Helmstadter and B. Lightman (eds.), *Victorian Faith in Crisis: Essays on Continuity and Change in Nineteenth-Century Religious Belief* (London, 1990), 187–222.

[44] W. R. Greg, *The Creed of Christendom; Its Foundations and Superstructure* (London, 1851), 267.

[45] Helmstadter, 'Greg', 219–20. See, in particular, Greg's remarks in *The Creed of Christendom*, 270.

shared with Roman Catholicism. John Henry Newman, in *The Idea of a University*, accordingly attacked political economy as 'a science at the same time dangerous and leading to occasions of sin, . . . if studied by itself, and apart from the control of Revealed Truth'.[46] Indeed, political economists blamed the strength of Catholicism for the slow spread of their beloved 'science' in Ireland, Nassau Senior, for example, complaining that the Irish were the 'tools' of priests who remained 'ignorant of the economical laws on which the welfare of the labouring classes depends'.[47]

There was yet another obstacle to surmount. The prestige of political economy, like that of natural science, depended upon its claim to make the world a more intelligible place, and this it could only achieve if its practitioners were committed to a disinterested search for truth. But, for the most part, what inspired the Christian apologists for political economy was a sense of the importance of not allowing this infant branch of knowledge to be monopolized by the godless. Thus in 1825 Henry Drummond endowed a Chair of Political Economy at Oxford because he was alarmed at the 'ignorance prevalent with respect to the true principles of political economy', rather than because he wanted to commemorate the 'Scotch school of economists'.[48] In a similar spirit, Whately, the holder of the chair of Political Economy at Trinity College, Dublin, gave priority to contesting the prejudice 'that seems to have been based on the hypothesis that [its] study was very unfavourable to religion, and a check to charity'.[49] In an article in the *Edinburgh Review* (September 1828) Whately elaborated on this point: 'Those who avow their dread of the pursuit of knowledge of any kind, as likely to be injurious to the cause of religion, forget that the acknowledgement of such a feeling, or even a bare suspicion of its existence, does more harm to that cause than all the assaults of its adversaries'.[50]

In his account of 'Christian economics', Waterman is anxious to acquit its advocates of prostituting their religious convictions. On the contrary, he argues, clergymen like Chalmers and Whately provided an economic basis for Christian theology, not merely a Christian basis for political economy. In other words, political economy was, if anything, 'bent' to fit the theology, rather than vice versa.[51]

[46] Cited in Checkland, 'Academic Economics', 67.

[47] T. A. Boylan and T. P. Foley, *Political Economy and Colonial Ireland* (London, 1992), 7.

[48] Cited in M. Francis and J. Morrow, *A History of English Political Thought in the Nineteenth Century* (London, 1994), 112.

[49] Cited in S. Rashid, 'Richard Whately and Christian Political Economy at Oxford and Dublin', *Journal of History of Ideas*, 38 (1977), 148.

[50] Ibid., 150. This forms the main theme in Whately's *Introductory Lectures*, delivered at Oxford University in 1831.

[51] A. M. C. Waterman, 'The Ideological Alliance of Political Economy and Christian Theology, 1798–1833', *Journal of Ecclesiastical History*, 34 (1983), 244. However, the Malthus of the first edition of the *Essay on Population* stands accused by Waterman of theological crudity (*Revolution, Economics and Religion*, 107). See the discussion in E. N. Santurri, 'Theodicy and Social Policy in Malthus' Thought', *Journal of History of Ideas*, 43 (1982), 315–30. Winch thinks that Chalmers ultimately brought the alliance between political economy and Christianity into disrepute through his exaggerations (*Riches and Poverty*, 387).

It is certainly questionable whether any Christian political economist other than Malthus made a major contribution to the subject that was of lasting interest to its secular adherents. In any case, with the growing specialization of political economy from the 1820s onwards, the role of clergymen and bishops was probably bound to become peripheral to a realm of knowledge that was steadily acquiring a more and more technical character. If for most of the nineteenth century Adam Smith was the most quoted economist, this may be because he was also the most intelligible.

It is also worth bearing in mind Frank Turner's larger argument about Victorian intellectual life: that academic disciplines tended to emancipate themselves from religious control when their lay practitioners succeeded in achieving professional autonomy through the establishment of their own organizations and journals. Political economy had reached this point by the 1830s, with the creation of the Political Economy Club in 1821 and the endowment of several university chairs in the subject. And though one of the earliest chairs, that of Dublin, may have been held by a cleric, Richard Whately, a more typical incumbent was J. R. McCulloch, Professor of Political Economy at King's College, London, who has been dubbed the first professional economist.[52]

Paradoxically, some of the clerical exponents of 'Christian economics' themselves gave a boost to this development. Thus the Noetics, a group of Fellows at Oriel College (all of them in Holy Orders, obviously), drew a sharp distinction between description and prescription.[53] One of their number, Whately, explicitly discriminated between religious or moral truths, on the one hand, and historical or physical truths, on the other, a discrimination which allowed him to separate the 'theoretical' from the 'practical' dimensions of political economy, its scientific from its ethical elements. Political economy, he modestly declared, could be narrowly defined as the science of exchange—no more and no less. This position even led him to deny that Adam Smith had judged all actions by reference to wealth; if Smith *had* done this, he was not writing in his capacity as a political economist, Whately argued.[54]

By drawing a boundary in this way between 'positive' and 'normative' economics, the Noetics were able to insulate their Christian beliefs from some of the more disquieting aspects of political economy. (Admittedly, Whately took little notice of his own axioms, his writings on political economy being full of controversial polemics.[55]) But an additional consequence was the uncoupling of economics and

[52] D. P. O'Brien, *J. R. McCulloch: A Study in Classical Economics* (London, 1970), 15.

[53] R. Brent, 'God's Providence: Liberal Political Economy as Natural Theology at Oxford 1825–62', in Bentley (ed.), *Public and Private Doctrine*, 85–107. On the Noetics, see Winch, *Riches and Poverty*, 372, and Mandler, 'Tories and Paupers', 86–91.

[54] Whately, *Introductory Lectures*, 5–6. He thought the pursuit of wealth was helpful to society, albeit dangerous to the individual, and argued that economic laws revealed the existence of an omniscient and benevolent mind at work (ibid., 16–18, 46–51). See the discussion in Rashid, 'Whately', and Brent, 'God's Providence'.

[55] Thus Whately wanted small children taught the reasons for inequality of condition and of wealth (Whately, *Introductory Lectures*, 186–8). Perhaps in political economy, one man's polemical propaganda is another man's uncovering of objective scientific law.

religion, with the former increasingly developing as an independent field of study. David Hume's attacks a century earlier on 'the naturalistic fallacy' (the illegitimate derivation of an 'ought' from an 'is') thus belatedly bore fruit. But this meant that the attempt to 'tame' political economy by incorporating it into a Christian framework of belief began to to break down, leading to a situation in which David Ricardo could describe political economy as 'a strict science like mathematics'.[56]

CHRISTIAN RESIDUES

Yet Christian economics, far from being *entirely* displaced by the more materialistic rival versions of that subject, indirectly exercised considerable influence for decades to come. Whatever was being said at the Political Economy Club or written up in specialist journals, not only popular but even educated opinion on political economy remained highly coloured by Chalmers and Whately well into the middle of the nineteenth century. Even Paley's *Natural Theology* continued to be a staple of the university curriculum and a 'people's edition' of the work came out as late as 1837.[57] Chalmers, in particular, long enjoyed a high reputation. In 1852 John Lalor, dismissing Ricardo as 'much over-rated', saluted the Scotsman as 'the man who began that baptism, so to speak, of political economy into Christianity'.[58] Chalmers it was who also helped to convince the conscience-racked Gladstone that 'the system of modern industry' was not 'fundamentally and essentially at variance with the principles of the gospel' and that 'religion and Christian virtue, like the faculty of taste and the perception of beauty, [had] their place, aye and that the first place, in political economy, as the means of creating and preserving wealth'.[59] How interesting, too, that Chalmers's *Bridgewater Treatise* was re-issued in a new edition in 1854: a testimony to its enduring reputation.

Moreover, belief in some kind of providential design manifested by the laws of political economy also underlay, often as an unstated assumption, many of the formulations presented by the more secular writers and politicians of mid-Victorian Britain. Feeling under an obligation to produce their own 'theodicy', many of the political economists had resort to a watered-down version of 'Christian economics'. This is particularly the case with that assiduous popularizer of political economy,

[56] Cited in Winch, *Riches and Poverty*, 286. Ricardo put it to Malthus (who strongly dissented) that the political economist's duty was 'to tell you how you may become rich, but he is not to advise you to prefer riches to indolence, or indolence to riches' (ibid.).
[57] N. C. Gillespie, 'Divine Design and the Industrial Revolution: William Paley's Abortive Reform of Natural Theology', *Isis*, 81 (1990), 226. Whately was preparing a new edition of Paley's *Moral Philosophy* in 1857–8 (E. J. Whately, *Life and Correspondence of Richard Whately, DD* (London, 1875), 339).
[58] J. Lalor, *Money and Morals: A Book for The Times* (London, 1852), p. xvii.
[59] H. C. G. Matthew, *Gladstone: 1809–1874* (Oxford, 1988; first pub. 1986), 76–7, citing 'Course of Commercial Policy at Home and Abroad', *Foreign and Colonial Quarterly Review*, 1 (Jan. 1843), 252.

Mrs Marcet. Diversity of rank and condition, argued Mrs Marcet, was 'productive of much general benefit, as it is that state of society best calculated to stimulate the industry, and bring into action the various faculties of mankind'.[60] Her
defence of 'commercial society' also proceeded along traditional lines.[61] On the
population question, Marcet cites Paley, but her treatment of the question is really
an optimistic rendition of Malthus, as extended by Sumner:

Remember that you must consider the tendency of population to press upon the means of
subsistence as a measure necessary to rouse our exertions; it is a law of nature, wisely calculated to call into activity the various powers of man. It is to this pressure that we owe
the appropriation of land, and the consequent diversity of ranks and conditions which
we have observed to be so essential to the progressive improvement of society; it is the
foundation-stone of the great structure of civilization, and the means by which scanty
tribes of wandering savages have been transformed into populous nations of civilized beings.
If then it produces want and wretchedness in ill-governed states, it feeds millions of industrious happy beings in a well-constituted society, and as civilization and education gain
ground, the evil will always diminish and the good increase.[62]

Harriet Martineau, who started off her writing career as a Unitarian, similarly
drew upon traditional Christian precepts in her advocacy of political economy.
The Parable of the Talents came in for especial praise: 'it is good political economy, and they who wish it may plead a gospel sanction for its pursuit'.[63] True,
she also included what is probably a sly dig at Chalmers:

We are not among those who mix up moral questions with political economy, as if they were
not only connected but identical. We do not speak of demand and supply and heavenly-
mindedness in the same breath, or bring exchangeable value into immediate connexion with
filial piety.[64]

But at other times Martineau sounds a rhapsodical note that brings Chalmers clearly
to mind:

Social institutions are the grand instruments in the hands of Providence for the government of man, and no labors can be more worthy of the disciple of Providence than that of
deducing the will of God from the course of events—of ascertaining the Divine signature
by which institutions are sanctioned or prohibited.[65]

---

[60] Mrs Marcet, *Conversations on Political Economy: In Which The Elements of That Science Are Familiarly
Explained* (London, 1839; first pub. 1816), 73.
[61] Caroline, the pupil, is initially worried about the injurious effects which the division of labour
have on the mental faculties of industrial workers, but her governess convinces her that it enriches
social intercourse and promotes diffusion of knowledge (ibid., 67–70), an argument also found in Adam
Smith.   [62] Ibid., 137.
[63] Martineau, *Miscellanies*, i. 285.
[64] Ibid., 277. As a Dissenter, Martineau would not have been an unqualified supporter of Chalmers.
[65] Ibid., 283–4.

J. R. McCulloch, often presented as an early proponent of a new secular political economy, also had a strong sense of providential design which allotted rewards and punishments to individuals according to their deserts.[66]

Residues of these older beliefs frequently surface, too, in the lay sermons of Samuel Smiles later in the century. For example, in *Self-Help*, Smiles quotes approvingly from Chalmers's famous observations about how the 'implicit trust' that bound together the commercial world could be seen as testifying to the existence of a higher morality.[67] Traces of Chalmers can also be found in such passages as these: 'We cannot escape the consequences of transgression of the natural laws, though we may have meant well. We must have done well. The Creator does not alter His laws to accommodate them to our ignorance.'[68]

Moreover, one of Smiles's central ideas is that human life has been designed as a 'trial' with the aim of strengthening character. 'Precepts and instructions are useful so far as they go', wrote Smiles, 'but, without the discipline of real life, they remain of the nature of theory only. . . . To be worth anything, character must be capable of standing firm upon its feet in the world of daily work, temptation, and trial.'[69] For, he added:

If there were no difficulties, there would be no need of efforts; if there were no temptations, there would be no training in self-control, and but little merit in virtue; if there were no trial and suffering, there would be no education in patience and resignation. Thus difficulty, adversity, and suffering are not all evil, but often the best source of strength, discipline, and virtue.[70]

Obedience to the law of labour, thought Smiles, was 'not only in conformity with the Divine will, but also necessary for the development of intelligence, and for the thorough enjoyment of our common nature'.[71]

Even more common was the blurring of the boundary between the 'natural' and the 'God-given', usually for the purpose of deprecating unwise legislative interference. This was a staple in the rhetoric of the Anti-Corn Law Leaguers. For example, Archibald Prentice called the Corn Laws 'an impious attempt to intercept, for the profit of a few, the gifts which God has bestowed for the benefit of all',[72] and Cobden himself often spoke in the same sense, referring without any embarrassment to the 'sacredness' of the free-trade principle. To buy in the cheapest and sell in the dearest market, he once said, was merely to carry out 'to

---

[66] 'The great bulk of mankind must look for their advancement to . . . the blessing of Providence on their industry, perseverance, and economy, and to nothing else' (J. R. McCulloch, *Considerations on Partnerships with Limited Liability* (London, 1856), 26).

[67] S. Smiles, *Self-Help: With Illustrations of Conduct and Perseverance* (London, 1910; first pub. 1859), 337. 　　[68] S. Smiles, *Thrift* (London, 1886), 25.

[69] S. Smiles, *Character* (London, 1871), 343.

[70] Ibid., 350. On Smiles's belief that success was often achieved through failure, see ibid., 352. All this formed part of Smiles's sense of the existence of a divine mystery (ibid., 371).

[71] Smiles, *Thrift*, 6. For Smiles's application of these beliefs to cases of commercial 'failure', see Ch. 5.

[72] Cited in M. J. Turner, 'Before the Manchester School: Economic Theory in Early Nineteenth-Century Manchester', *History*, 79 (1994), 232.

the fullest extent the Christian doctrine of "Doing to all men as ye would they should do unto you" '.[73] Harriet Martineau, too, denounced all restrictions on trade as 'a sin in government'.[74]

Finally, the case of Herbert Spencer is revealing. Another Unitarian by upbringing, he spent much of his formative years living with his uncle, Thomas, an Anglican clergyman with a strong belief in the depravity of man and the consequent need for a harsh, deterrent poor law. Herbert Spencer's early debt to his uncle is very evident. In fact, a youthful production like 'The Proper Sphere of Government' (1843) so closely resembles Thomas Spencer's pamphlet, *Objections to the New Poor Law Answered* (1841) that whole passages could easily be transcribed from the one to the other without producing any sense of incongruity.[75] Even in the slightly later *Social Statics*, a much more individual work, Herbert Spencer was still anchoring his moral theory in the 'Divine will'.[76]

BUSINESS EVANGELISM

The links between capitalism and Christianity were also important because few apologists for capitalism felt that reliance on market principles would *automatically* produce a morally beneficial outcome. The search was thus on for a 'moralized capitalism'; and in this quest an important role was played by committed Churchmen. For although many secular intellectual writers continued to insist— some robustly, some wistfully—that, in time, economic progress would generate the higher level of moral responsibility needed for its own long-term success, most Christians approached the problem from the other end. The laws of the market might indeed emanate from God. But the human beings who regulated their conduct by these laws were inherently sinful.[77]

Hence the moralization of economic life would only be achieved through a *prior* effort of the moral will. One clergyman vividly delineated 'the perils, mischiefs, and miseries of engaging in business without Christianity' and likened such a

---

[73] Cited in G. R. Searle, *Entrepreneurial Politics in Mid-Victorian Britain* (Oxford, 1993), 303.

[74] H. Martineau, *The Moral of Many Fables* (London, 1834), 113.

[75] Herbert Spencer can write: 'by allowing the wicked to take advantage of the right held out by the [old] poor law, we not only annul the just punishment awarded to them, but we also take away the most effectual prompter to repentance and improvement' (J. Offer (ed.), *Herbert Spencer: Political Writings* (Cambridge, 1994), 21–2). There is evidence that Thomas helped his nephew compose the 'Proper Sphere' (D. Wiltshire, *The Social and Political Thought of Herbert Spencer* (Oxford, 1978), 21).

[76] However, he abandoned this approach in his later writings: see J. Meadowcroft, *Conceptualizing the State: Innovation and Dispute in British Political Thought 1880–1914* (Oxford, 1995), 71. On both Spencers, see the further discussion in Ch. 8.

[77] See E. J. Garnett, 'Aspects of the Relationship Between Protestant Ethics and Economic Activity in Mid-Victorian England', D.Phil. thesis (Oxford, 1986), for an important analysis of the response of evangelical Anglicans and Nonconformist divines.

reckless enterprise to setting out on an unknown sea without a compass.[78] Indeed, commercial life, churchmen believed, was only possible at all because of mankind's God-given faculty for distinguishing truth from falsehood, a faculty which the country's religious leaders had constantly to nurture.[79]

Here the dominant figure was once again Chalmers, who found much in the commercial world 'to magnify the wisdom of the Supreme Contriver' but 'also much in it to humble man, and to convict him of the deceitfulness of that moral complacency with which he looks to his own character, and his own attainments'.[80] Chalmers saw with dismay the introduction of 'a certain quantity of what may be called shuffling, into the communications of the trading world—insomuch, that the simplicity of yea, yea, and nay, nay, is in some degree exploded'.[81] It was therefore the duty of the Christian Church to preach righteousness to the wicked.[82] 'In other words', Chalmers concluded, 'the virtues of society, to be kept in a healthful and prosperous condition, must be upheld by the virtues of the sanctuary.'[83]

Chalmers's writings gave a powerful impetus to the work of 'business evangelism'. Just as there were Christians who acknowledged a calling to 'save' fallen women, so there were Christians who targeted businessmen exposed to the myriad temptations that surrounded them: the sins of sharp practice, covetousness, pride, arrogance, luxury, worldliness, and indolence.[84] The prime task for these evangelists was to combat the common notion that Christianity had little relevance to the workaday world of business. Religion, complained one Unitarian clergyman, was 'not expected in the market, the exchange, the warehouse or the workshop. These are not the places to which men in general think of taking their religion with them.'[85] Other clergymen gloomily agreed: 'It has been too much the custom to maintain a distinction between the pursuits of commerce and those of religion, as if the affairs of trade and speculation could have no sort of affinity with the cultivation of personal holiness in the fear of God', wrote the Revd Robert Bickersteth.[86] 'Are we about to have magnificent chapels as a sort of adjunct to the

---

[78] Owen, *Business Without Christianity*, 3.   [79] Cited in Turner, 'Secularization', 116.
[80] Chalmers, *Application of Christianity*, 76–7.
[81] Ibid., 225. These words were often echoed: for example: 'If you penetrate into the recesses of commerce, you frequently detect a low and shifting standard of equity—you discover that a thousand practices are connived at, and pass current in business, which, when weighed in the balances of the sanctuary, are found utterly wanting' (H. Stowell, *A Model for Men of Business: Or Lectures on the Character of Nehemiah* (London, 1854), 8–9).   [82] Chalmers, *Application of Christianity*, 173–4.
[83] Ibid., 141.
[84] Such anxieties were rife during the speculative mania of the 1840s: see J. Garnett and A. C. Howe, 'Churchmen and Cotton-Masters in Victorian England', in D. J. Jeremy (ed.), *Businessmen and Religion in Britain* (Aldershot, 1988), 72–94. See also E. J. Garnett, ' "Gold and the Gospel": Systematic Beneficence in Mid-Nineteenth Century England', in W. J. Sheils and D. Wood (eds.), *The Church and Wealth*, Studies in Church History, xxiv (1987), 347–58.
[85] J. Seed, 'Unitarianism, Political Economy and the Antinomies of Liberal Culture in Manchester, 1830–50', *Social History*, 7 (1982), 21.
[86] Revd H. A. Boardman, *The Bible in the Counting-House: A Course of Lectures to Merchants* (London, 1854), introd., p. vi.

warehouses of large mercantile firms?', asked a Mancunian Wesleyan: 'One building in which *business* shall be most diligently done, and another in which *worship*
shall be most properly "performed"?'[87]

Ministers of religion devoted to this work regularly cited Nehemiah 5: 16,
'But so did not I, because of the fear of God'. The moral of this favourite text,
according to the Evangelical clergyman, Hugh Stowell, was that the Christian
businessman

must endure to be accounted a fool, and to be pitied as too scrupulous for success. He must
esteem the reproach of Christ greater riches than all the treasures of earth. When he sees
competitors prospering by doubtful expedients, or hears them glorying in their equivocal
gains, his reflection and his joy will be—'So did not I, because of the fear of God'.[88]

Another clergyman wrote: 'Never was it more necessary for saints to "condemn
the world" by secular integrity, to give a nobler example for it to follow, to bring
a spirit from above to bear on its pursuits. May we be able to say, "So did not I,
because of the fear of God!".'[89] To these Christian moralists, what mattered above
all else was the purity of a businessman's *intentions*: 'What a man *is* in his
Counting-house, or on the Exchange, in the midst of his mercantile pursuits
—*that* he is in the house of prayer, in the closet of devotion—in the sight of
Him who will judge him at the last day.'[90]

But though the purpose of these sermons was to save the businessman from
succumbing to the evil pressures which surrounded him, Christian moralists also
argued that, especially in subordinates, a rigid, even obstinate, adherence to religious principle and a sensitive conscience were to be cherished as an indication of
utter honesty. For example, the clerk who refused in any circumstances to work
on a Sunday was likely to be more scrupulous in other business matters than employees of a more 'worldly' bent.

Ultimately the Christian evangelists fell back upon the proposition that, even
in this world, unrighteousness would incur an appropriate punishment—
bankruptcies and the like being viewed not so much as a sign of God's anger with
those directly affected, but as divine retribution on a society which had strayed
from the straight and narrow—a divine manifestation from which sinful men would,
at least for a while, draw the needful lesson. Conversely, in the words of the Revd
Joseph Owen, 'honesty *is* the best policy, but piety is the best principle'.[91]

---

[87] Garnett, 'Gold and the Gospel', 348.
[88] Stowell, *Model*, 18. On the background to Stowell's exhortations, see Garnett and Howe,
'Christians and Cotton-Masters', 73, 83.
[89] A. J. Morris, *Religion and Business: Or Spiritual Life in One of Its Secular Departments* (London,
1853), 65, 70. The text was also cited by W. H. Lyttelton, *Sins of Trade and Business: A Sermon* (London,
1874), 1.   [90] Stowell, *Model*, 1–2.
[91] Owen, *Business Without Christianity*, 38. On the effectiveness or otherwise of these admonitions,
see Ch. 11.

CONCLUSION

There was no one Christian approach to the social problems created by urbanization and industrialization, just as there was no single Christian perspective on political economy. To the many churchmen who disliked all these innovations, the
New Testament provided a rich storehouse of texts demonstrating the immorality of the new materialistic creed.[92] Even some of the clergymen whose tracts and
sermons have been quoted above clearly viewed the modern commercial world
with no particular favour,[93] while others supplied an account of it so lurid that the
Christian reader, concerned to safeguard his immortal soul, might well have supposed that the only safe course was to avoid a business career altogether.

But among Evangelicals, in particular, business life was usually viewed more
positively—as a 'vocation' in which the committed Christian might legitimately
display his principles, whether as employer, trader, or even investor. According
to one divine, though there were those who embarked on commerce 'as a reputable kind of larceny', the occupation was a highly respectable one for those who
had a 'divine calling' to follow it.[94] Dangerous the commercial world might be,
but the Christian merchant was voluntarily submitting himself to a *salutary trial*,
from which, despite all temptations, he would emerge, with God's grace, with
a deepened faith: for only through confronting temptation could spiritual *growth*
take place.[95]

Moreover, the acquisition of wealth was deemed eminently desirable, provided
it was subsequently put to 'good' uses and not coveted for its own sake or squan-
dered in luxury. The pursuit of wealth was not offensive in the eyes of God so
long as its practitioners observed certain moral principles, not least the setting
aside of a tenth of their income for religious and philanthropic purposes.[96] In short,
there were spiritual rewards, as well as snares, awaiting the businessman whose
soul had been strengthened by faith—rewards not just for the individual businessman but for society as a whole: 'The great problem we have now on hand,
viz., the christianizing of the money power of the world, depends for its principal
hope on the trading class in society', declared another cleric.[97]

Nevertheless, at the end of the day Christian apologists for capitalism were treading a very narrow plank, and those who tried to live by their precepts often found
themselves being put under almost unendurable psychological strain. 'I think there
is a great deal of sound political economy in the New Testament', Chalmers had

---

[92] For further examples, see Ch. 8.

[93] Malthus, in particular, warned against the 'shewiness of commerce and manufacturing' and
extolled the merits of agriculture (Winch, *Riches and Poverty*, 272).

[94] H. Bushnell, 'How to be a Christian in Trade', in id., *Sermons on Living Subjects* (London, 1872),
244, 256–7.   [95] Ibid., 261.

[96] On 'systematic beneficence', see Garnett, 'Gold and the Gospel', 347–58. Joseph Sturge, not a
typical businessman maybe, gave *at least one-third, perhaps over one-half* of all his income to charitable
purposes (A. Tyrrell, *Joseph Sturge and the Moral Radical Party in Early Victorian Britain* (London,
1987), 181).   [97] Bushnell, *Sermons on Living Subjects*, 264.

told the Select Committee on the Irish poor in 1830.[98] Yet the economic laws, supposedly ordained by God, which enjoined the individual to pursue his enlightened self-interest, tended in practice to lead to 'Mammon-worship', and might even find expression in acts of dishonesty and fraud. In short, was 'self-interest' *really* compatible with love of God and with Christian obedience?

In later chapters we will examine more closely the ways in which 'business evangelists' responded to some of the specific dilemmas thrown up by commercial life. But first we must turn to the more secular approach embodied in utilitarianism and 'classical' political economy,[99] and ask whether these creeds were any more successful in 'moralizing' the theory and practice of capitalism.

[98] Cited in P. Hollis, 'Anti-Slavery and British Working-Class Radicalism', in C. Bolt and S. Drescher (eds.), *Anti-Slavery, Religion and Reform: Essays in Memory of Roger Anstey* (Folkestone, 1980), 304.

[99] Of course, 'Christian economics' was not a tightly definable entity totally set apart from the more secular versions of political economy. It is anachronistic, Waterman rightly argues, to distinguish between 'professional economists' and Christian or Evangelical economists when dealing with the opening decades of the 19th c. (Waterman, *Revolution, Economics and Religion*, 229).

3

Political Economy and Morality

The rules of that science [i.e. political economy] had reference to the production of wealth in a nation, but he must inquire what effect the application
of them, in a given case, was likely to have on the morals of a country. Now,
if it were shown to him that the application of those rules added to the stock
of wealth, but tended at the same time, to the destruction of morals amongst
the people, he certainly, to preserve those morals pure, would overlook and
throw aside the principles of political economy.

(Peel, 1828)[1]

UTILITARIANISM AND 'CLASSICAL' POLITICAL ECONOMY

Utilitarianism and political economy were often treated as though they were
branches of the same ideology, but in many respects they differed. The utilitarians
aimed to create an artificial identity of interests through a centrally imposed system of incentives and deterrents which would ensure that individuals, in pursuing their own interests, would not damage the interests of others, an approach
which might lead to a quite far-reaching role for government. One thinks of the
contributions to sanitary reform made by Edwin Chadwick, formerly Bentham's
secretary, whose career demonstrates how the principle of the 'greatest happiness
of the greatest number' could lead to a legitimation of social engineering at the
behest of the expert bureaucrat—the very thing against which twentieth-century
free marketeers, self-appointed disciples of Adam Smith, so bitterly rail.

Political economy, by contrast, tended to assume the existence of a natural harmony of interests created by the free operation of the market. In the vulgar version of Adam Smith handed down to the mid-Victorian generation, an 'invisible
hand' guided human behaviour to beneficent purposes of which individuals were
severally unaware—or imperfectly aware.[2] Government intervention did more harm
than good, since the market responded far more quickly and sensitively to social
needs than any human agency could consciously do. The mid-Victorian doctrine of

---

[1] Cited in B. Gordon, *Economic Doctrine and Tory Liberalism 1824–1830* (London, 1979), 118.
[2] But this could also be presented as a supreme example of divine contrivance. See R. Whately,
Introductory Lectures on Political Economy: Delivered at Oxford, 1831 (London, 1847), 85: e.g. in the
feeding of the metropolis, even the despised corn dealers played a socially valuable role (85–9).

laissez-faire, expounded, for example, by *The Economist*,[3] thus owed much to Adam Smith, even if *laissez-faire* was not an expression used by Smith himself.

Nevertheless, the two ideologies arguably derived from a somewhat similar view of human nature. Bentham's premise was that individuals were driven by a desire to maximize their own happiness. The political economists broadly concurred. For example, read in isolation and divorced from its historical context, the *Wealth of Nations* suggested that man was by nature a striker of bargains, someone who exchanged goods and services of which he stood in little need for the goods and services with which others could provide him: in Smith's own words, humans had a 'propensity to truck, barter and exchange'. The sum total of all these transactions was the market, and it was through the market that human beings related to one another in a complex web of obligations and services, freely undertaken.[4]

Moreover, despite their belief in the existence of a *natural* identity of interests, all the political economists took it for granted that market competition would take place within a framework of law, ensuring that certain kinds of anti-social conduct would be discouraged and punished; indeed, some were even prepared to accept 'unorthodox' policies like factory reform.[5] As Book 5 of the *Wealth of Nations* shows, Adam Smith himself recognized that government had important responsibilities to discharge which it was not expedient to leave to the market: among them the administration of justice and provision for defence. Elementary education, too, Smith thought, should be provided and largely paid for out of public funds.

Conversely, the early utilitarians assumed that existing states were corrupt and inefficient and that the 'greatest happiness of the greatest number' was therefore most likely to be achieved by the free play of market forces. Indeed, Jeremy Bentham, in his early unpublished plan of poor-law reform, actually recommended the handing-over of the indigent to the management of a joint-stock company.[6]

So, despite some important differences, there was a very real congruence between utilitarianism and political economy. As the critics complained, the political economists reduced value to monetary terms, while the utilitarians translated all qualitative factors into quantitative ones—which perhaps made them comparable activities. Nor, of course, was the connection merely a congruence of *ideas*: James Mill, the disciple of Bentham, became a convert to the economic theories

[3] S. Gordon, 'The London *Economist* and the High Tide of Laissez Faire', *The Journal of Political Economy*, 63 (1955), 461–88.

[4] In fact, the final edition of *The Theory of Moral Sentiments* saw Adam Smith using a quite different line of argument (J. Evensky, 'The evolution of Adam Smith's views on political economy', *History of Political Economy*, 21 (1989), 123–45).

[5] L. Robbins, *The Theory of Economic Policy in English Classical Political Economy* (London, 1952), 100–3. Senior, for example, said in his Oxford lectures of 1847–8 that 'the only rational foundation of government . . . is, expediency' (ibid., 45). See M. Blaug, 'The Classical Economists and the Factory Acts—A Re-examination', in A. W. Coats (ed.), *The Classical Economists and Economic Policy* (London, 1971), 104–22.

[6] J. R. Poynter, *Society and Pauperism: English Ideas on Poor Relief, 1795–1834* (London, 1969), 108–9.

of David Ricardo, to propagate whose ideas he helped found the Political Economy Club. The younger Mill also provides a link between the two circles.

In addition, for all its 'statist' potentialities, utilitarianism in the early and middle years of the nineteenth century made a number of important contributions to what might be called the ideology of capitalism. For a start, it obviously strengthened the prevailing individualism of the age. In addition, the commitment of the utilitarians to ideas of bureaucratic rationality—their strong preference for general rules rather than particular local customs, for example—may indirectly have helped shape a social environment within which capitalism could flourish.

Also, more relevant to the theme of this book, utilitarianism also saddled the new social order with an embarrassing legacy. For the tone (rather than the actual content) of the utilitarian creed suggested that the end of life was happiness, to be defined in terms of pleasure and the satisfaction of quantifiable material needs. The initial premise was of man as a calculating hedonist, who, in all his actions, weighed up their likely consequences: would they result in greater happiness, or, to put it another way, would they produce a surplus of pain over pleasure, or vice versa? Such an approach laid the utilitarians wide open to the accusation that they were denying the value of imagination, religion, sentiment, and human altruism. In fact, from the very start, Bentham stood arraigned as a coarse philistine, a reputation confirmed by his oft-quoted aphorism that 'pushpin was as good as poetry'. Typical was the protest of Coleridge, who wrote: 'Men, I still think, ought to be weighed not counted. Their *worth* ought to be the final estimate of their value.'[7]

John Stuart Mill was sufficiently embarrassed by this aspect of utilitarianism to introduce qualifications into the system which, some think, ended up by undermining it. 'It really is of importance, not only what men do, but also what manner of men they are that do it', he wrote in *On Liberty*.[8] In this way, Mill reintroduced the concept of character, together with all those 'mystifying' distinctions between the lower and the higher pleasures which Bentham had been anxious to eliminate. This may have made his arguments more acceptable, but it also represented a crucial loss of nerve.[9]

Moreover, utilitarianism reinforced the disposition (perhaps already present in the writings of most of the economists) to define goodness and badness by the *consequences* of particular actions, so threatening to bring the creed into collision with established religion and with the benevolent impulses. No human activity, it seemed, was good or bad in itself, but only in so far as it led to the enlargement

---

[7] 'Blessed are ye that sow beside all Waters!' (1817), in R. J. White (ed.), *The Collected Works of Samuel Taylor Coleridge, vi, Lay Sermons* (London, 1972), 211. Coleridge claimed that 'the inspired poets, historians and sententiaries of the Jews [were] the clearest teachers of political economy' (ibid., 128–9). [8] J. S. Mill, *On Liberty*, Everyman edn. (1910; first pub. 1859), 117.

[9] S. Collini, *Public Moralists: Political Thought and Intellectual Life in Britain 1850–1930* (Oxford, 1991), 184. Mill's agonized twisting and turning has made it possible for posterity to categorize him as a 'critic of capitalism': see the anthology in which he appears alongside John Francis Bray, Carlyle, Engels and Marx, Ruskin, Matthew Arnold, T. H. Green, Frederick Morris, and George Bernard Shaw (E. Jay and R. Jay (eds.), *Critics of Capitalism: Victorian Reactions to 'Political Economy'* (Cambridge, 1986)).

of pleasure or the diminution of pain. Pleasure thus became synonymous with goodness. And though in penal reform (Bentham's principal field of interest) the application of the utility principle led to policies which harmonized with human-itarian aspirations (the reduction of the number of offences which carried the death penalty, for example), in matters of social policy it had the very opposite effect, as we shall see in Chapter 8. True morality, according to the utilitarians, often obliged one to be cruel to be kind, a precept for which there was little biblical authority.

Political economy could more easily be fitted into a Christian view of the world than utilitarianism. Nevertheless, in the crude versions which Dickens would have encountered in mid-century, this infant 'science', too, possessed many morally offens-ive features. For, by its very nature, political economy was an attempt to make sense of complex social processes by constructing an economic model, within which factors like labour, capital, and rent, could be scientifically analysed. And this model presupposed that adult human beings were motivated by self-interest (Smith's word is 'self-love'[10]), in the sense that they would seek, by all rational means, to max-imize their material advantages. In McCulloch's words, 'the wish to augment our fortunes and to rise in the world—a wish that comes with us from the womb, and never leaves us till we go into the grave—is the cause of wealth being saved and accumulated'.[11] The 'economic man' of the political economists thus had much in common with Bentham's pleasure-maximizer.

Admittedly, Adam Smith cannot with any accuracy be categorized in these terms, something which would have been apparent to some of his mid-Victorian readers. But David Ricardo, whom most historians of economic thought see as the real founder of the discipline, can be. Indeed, the traditional view is that 'a change of paradigms' occurred in early nineteenth-century political economy, as Smith's his-torical empiricism became superseded by Ricardo's predilection for abstract model-making. Scholars have recently challenged this view.[12] But even if they are correct in questioning the extent to which political economy underwent a radical transformation in these years, a shift of emphasis and of tone surely did take place— as the 'Cambridge School' of anti-Ricardians, led by William Whewell and Richard Jones, vigorously complained.[13]

[10] Winch denies that Smith followed a narrow, mechanical, and rationalistic version of the self-interest principle: 'Although by the second half of the eighteenth century the concept of "interest" increasingly connoted in large measure *economic* interest, this was compatible with Smith's employ-ment of the term to cover men's aspirations or ambitions in general; he certainly made no attempt to distinguish narrow and broad interpretations of the term' (D. Winch, *Adam Smith's Politics: An Essay in Historiographic Revision* (Cambridge, 1978), 167–8).

[11] J. R. McCulloch, *The Principles of Political Economy* (Edinburgh, 1825), 53.

[12] For the traditional view, see J. K. Galbraith, *A History of Economics: The Past as the Present* (1989; first pub. 1987), 81. For the revisionist interpretation, see B. Fontana, *Rethinking the Politics of Com-mercial Society: The* Edinburgh Review, *1802–1832* (Cambridge, 1985), 79–81.

[13] L. Goldman, 'The Origins of British "Social Science": Political Economy, Natural Science and Statistics, 1830–1835', *Historical Journal*, 26 (1983), 594, 599–600; S. G. Checkland, 'The Advent of Academic Economics in England', *Manchester School of Economic and Social Studies*, 19 (1951), 59–65; S. Rashid, 'Dugald Stewart, "Baconian" Method and Political Economy', *Journal of History of Ideas*, 46 (1985), 245–57.

In any case, it was the deductive, a priori methodology of Ricardo which won the day. As a result, few would have dissented from John Stuart Mill's later definition of political economy (itself partly derived from Ricardo): a science which 'considers mankind as occupied solely in acquiring and consuming wealth; and aims at showing what is the course of action into which mankind, living in a state of society, would be impelled, if that motive . . . were absolute ruler of all their actions'.[14]

What most concerns us here is that this particular way of understanding society had the effect of reducing *human beings themselves* to abstractions. A functional analysis of society encouraged a habit of mind in which people were subsumed within their economic role. Abstractions, like land, capital, and labour, became endowed with such human qualities as volition and purpose.[15] The *converse* of this was the dehumanization of individual people. Thus labourers were reduced to 'labour' or even, in a common metonym, referred to as 'hands'.[16] Meanwhile, the intricate web of social relationships was presented in economic terms—which is what Carlyle meant when he later talked about the 'cash nexus'.

The Christian Socialist clergyman Wilfrid Richmond felt that this process of simplification profoundly distorted man's understanding of his nature: 'The science becomes a kind of systematic prejudice', he alleged.[17] The intricacies of human conduct, it seemed, were being reduced to a mechanical pursuit of self-interest which denied the full richness of social life and limited human potentiality.[18] How did admirers of political economy respond to such criticisms?

James Fitzjames Stephen simply accused the critics of a misreading:

The world at large rather unjustly view political economists as an iron-hearted race, believing in nothing except statistics, and a set of iron-hearted calculations founded upon them; a charge founded on the fact that they are addicted to what many people consider the bad and even wicked habit of thinking and speaking about one thing at a time, and so arriving at definite results.[19]

---

[14] Cited in E. F. Paul, *Moral Revolution and Economic Science: The Demise of Laissez-Faire in Nineteenth-Century British Political Economy* (Westport, Conn., 1979), 129). This did not mean that that was how Mill thought all human beings really behaved in practice. See S. Hollander, *The Economics of John Stuart Mill, ii, Political Economy* (Oxford, 1985), 959: J. S. Mill, *Collected Works*, ed. J. M. Robson (Toronto, 1965), iii. 460; S. Collini, D. Winch, and J. Burrow, *That Noble Science of Politics: A Study in Nineteenth-Century Intellectual History* (Cambridge, 1983), 137.

[15] 'Men are themselves capital;—they are the product of anterior labour, just as much as the tools or engines with which they perform their tasks' (McCulloch, *Political Economy*, 320).

[16] On Smith's stoical acceptance of the disintegration of the undivided personality as the price that had to be paid to secure the advantages of a commercial society, see I. Hont and M. Ignatieff, 'Needs and Justice in the *Wealth of Nations*: An Introductory Essay', in I. Hont and M. Ignatieff (eds.), *Wealth and Virtue: the Shaping of Political Economy in the Scottish Enlightenment* (Cambridge, 1983), 8.

[17] W. Richmond, *Economic Morals: Four Lectures* (London, 1890), 98.

[18] Ryan argues that this 'romantic' critique came close in places to the Marxian conception of 'alienation' (C. C. Ryan, 'The Fiends of Commerce: Romantic and Marxist Criticisms of Classical Political Economy', *History of Political Economy*, 13 (1981), 80–94).

[19] [J. F. Stephen], 'Money and Money's Worth', *Cornhill Magazine*, 9 (1864), 106. This was a constant theme of Henry Fawcett's: see his 'Address on Economy and Trade', *Transactions of the National Association for the Promotion of Social Science, 1868*, 114. See also Ch. 1.

In 1865 the *Westminster Review*, realizing how important it was to overcome this sort of antipathy to political economy, published a long and sophisticated article in its defence. The article starts with a triumphalist account of the 'beneficial influence' which political economy had allegedly had in the removal of countless monopolies and restrictions: 'at length a state of things has been reached in this country such as Adam Smith in his wildest dreams of unfettered trade could scarcely have conceived'. The anonymous author then sadly acknowledges that 'popular prejudice' was hostile to political economy and that its practitioners had often been accused of 'selfishness, hardness of heart, a preference of material good to moral goodness, and a desire that man should be absorbed in getting rich as the one great object of his existence'. But was this fair?

'The political economist . . . considers human beings in the mass as desirous of selling dear and buying cheap', concedes the *Westminster Review* contributor: 'All his reasonings are based upon that axiom.' On the other hand, he continues, political economists did also find a place in their system for 'force of habit, the love of ease, or the carelessness which so often attends the expenditure of the rich'. More importantly, political economy laid down 'no doctrine whatever with regard to the moral propriety of devoting our energies to "money-making"', still less did it confuse 'self-interest' with 'selfishness'. The former was perfectly compatible with concern for others: for example, men often aspired after money because they wanted to provide for the happiness and comfort of their wife and for the education of their children.

This reflection leads the writer on to a discussion of 'the responsibility of riches' and to the reflection that moral qualities were less evinced in the process of making money than in that of spending it. 'Men may easily become more engrossed in [money-making] than is desirable either for the good of their own characters or for that of the state', he admits. On the other hand, benevolence by itself would not make the world go round: indeed, it was the political economist who often turned out to be the best philanthropist.[20]

CAPITALISM AND HISTORY

However, there is one particular line of criticism of political economy which this *Westminster Review* article evades. The 'science' often caused offence by implying that human nature was everywhere the same and that little notice need be taken of regional traditions and idiosyncrasies. Economic laws (and the principle of utility, too) supposedly had a universal validity. Thus Ricardo's disciple,

---

[20] 'Political Economy', *Westminster Review*, 84 (1865), 106–33. The article is ostensibly a review of Mill's *Principles*, but it omits Mill's careful qualifications, doubts, and hesitations. For further discussion of the political economist as philanthropist, see Ch. 8.

J. R. McCulloch, could write: 'the laws which regulate the production and distribution of wealth are the same in every country and stage of society'.[21] Hence the
complaint of opponents that the new mechanistic ideologies tended to produce a
monotonous or tyrannical uniformity, with quite variegated types of people being
made to conform to a single pattern of behaviour.

John Stuart Mill sought to distance himself from this methodology, which he
knew to be at odds with the newly fashionable historical approach to the study of
social problems: 'political economy in my eyes is a science by means of which we
are enabled to form a judgment as to what each particular case requires', he wrote,
'but it does not supply us with a ready-made judgment upon any case'.[22] Mill
might have taken this line of reasoning considerably further had he known more
about the sociological writings of the eighteenth-century 'Scottish School', including Adam Smith's 'theory of four stages', which traces the origins and development of modern civil society.[23] Alas, the historical approach of the 'Scottish
School' is an interesting intellectual cul-de-sac, and Ricardian model-making soon
displaced it.

Yet political economy did later acquire its own rather crude historical dimen-
sion. This involved a conception of 'progress' according to which society evolved
from a military stage, grounded in compulsion, to an industrial stage, in which
competition between humans was peaceful and commercial. Much of this had been
assumed by Radicals like Cobden and even by Mill, but it was Herbert Spencer
who elevated it into an all-embracing philosophical and sociological system.[24]
There were, Spencer claimed,

two opposed types of social organization, broadly distinguishable as the militant and the
industrial—types which are characterized, the one by the regime of status, almost universal in ancient days, and the other by the regime of contract, which has become general in
modern days, chiefly among the Western nations, and especially among ourselves and the
Americans. . . . The typical structure of the one we see in an army formed of conscripts,
in which the units in their several grades have to fulfil commands under pain of death, and
receive food and clothing and pay, arbitrarily apportioned; while the typical structure of
the other we see in a body of producers or distributors, who severally agree to specified
payments in return for specified services, and may at will, after due notice, leave the organization if they do not like it.[25]

---

[21] McCulloch, *Political Economy*, 57. However, a much more 'historical' approach is adopted by
McCulloch in his *Discourse on the Rise, Progress, Peculiar Objects and Importance of Political Economy*
(Edinburgh, 1824). See the discussion in Fontana, *Commercial Society*, 105–11.

[22] Hollander, *Economics of John Stuart Mill*, ii. 925.

[23] See Winch, *Adam Smith's Politics*, 56–64. But the most lengthy discussion of such a theory appears
in Smith's *Lectures on Jurisprudence*, based on students' lecture notes and not published until the end
of the 19th c.

[24] Spencer's ideas have a long genealogy. It has been suggested that he may well have picked them
up in his youth from the writings of Harriet Martineau (J. D. Y. Peel, *Herbert Spencer: The Evolution
of a Sociologist* (London, 1971), 194, 214), who herself drew upon earlier thinkers like Priestley and
Paine.   [25] H. Spencer, *The Man Versus the State*, ed. D. Macrae (1969; first pub. 1884), 63.

According to Spencer, 'conduct gains ethical sanction in proportion as the activities, becoming less and less militant and more and more industrial, are such as do not necessitate mutual injury or hindrance, but consist with, and are furthered by, cooperation and mutual aid'.[26]

This extended passage comes from a late work, *The Man Versus the State* (1884), where the dichotomy between industrial and militant societies has, to some extent, been assimilated to a slightly different idea, namely, that the all-important transition in human societies is one from 'status to contract'. This, of course, was the central insight of the pioneering anthropologist, Henry Maine, whose book *Ancient Law* (1861), made a powerful impact on the Victorian educated classes.

Intellectual historians have explored the complexities of the relationship between the ideas of Spencer and those of Maine, drawing attention to the differences between the two theorists.[27] Yet Spencer in old age had no compunction in borrowing heavily from Maine,[28] and it is easy to see how popularizers could effortlessly identify 'militant' societies with a regime of 'status' and 'industrial' societies with a regime of 'contract'.

But, as Collini shows, Maine's most original contribution to the debate about morality and the market was to point out that 'the distinctive merits of advanced societies rest[ed] upon what Durkheim was later to call "the non-contractual elements in contract"'. Maine's 'discussion of the assumptions expressed in modern legal arrangements about contract', writes Collini, 'turns out to be littered with references to the advance in "good faith and trust in our fellows", "scrupulous honesty", the respect accorded to "the mere unilateral reposal of confidence", and so on'.[29] In other words, Maine sought to show that 'civil society' depended upon a prior achievement of high standards of probity, reliability, and mutual trust— an important argument with which to refute the enemies of political economy.

However, this elaborate scheme of justification of capitalist relationships was open to attack on two fronts, one being on its historical *accuracy*. But many critics also denied that the allegedly 'progressive' process depicted by the likes of Spencer represented moral progress at all. This was a common ploy with those seeking, in the new industrialized society of Victorian Britain, to revive older 'paternalistic' notions of duty, honour, and reciprocal obligation—notions which, they insisted, could not be integrated into the language or theory of contract. Service was superior to money-making, and the calling of the soldier possessed greater

---

[26] Cited in J. N. Gray, 'Spencer on the Ethics of Liberty and the Limits of State Interference', *History of Political Thought*, 3 (1982), 466–7.

[27] For example, recent scholarship has made clear that Maine had a far more static conception of early society than did Spencer, who stressed social evolution as a *constant* factor (G. Feaver, *From Status to Contract: A Biography of Sir Henry Maine 1822–1888* (London, 1969), 145–6). J. W. Burrow has drawn attention to other features of Maine's work which set it apart from that of most of his contemporaries ('Henry Maine and mid-Victorian ideas of progress', in A. Diamond (ed.), *The Victorian Achievement of Sir Henry Maine: A Centennial Re-appraisal* (Cambridge, 1991), 63).

[28] J. D. Y. Peel, 'Maine as an ancestor of the social sciences', in Diamond (ed.), *Maine*, 183.

[29] Collini, *Public Moralists*, 273.

moral worth than the activities of the merchant or the tradesman. The importance of the reformed public schools of Victorian England was that they transmuted these values into a cult of 'gentlemanliness', according to which high social position depended upon a generous dispensation of money rather than success in its accumulation.

FINANCIAL REWARD AND MERIT

But was this denigration of money-making fair? In his *Outline of the Science of Political Economy*, published in 1836, Nassau Senior argued that the produce of industry belonged entirely to the capitalist whose 'abstinence' had set the whole productive process in motion.[30] Those exercising self-control and prudence would thus, it seemed, reap their just reward, so vindicating the moral code.

However, many of the classical economists also cheerfully admitted that wage and salary determination had little to do with intrinsic merit. For example, Adam Smith, followed by Senior, argued that it was the *lottery principle* which often affected both the level of remuneration and people's willingness to enter particular careers and professions.[31] According to Senior, society actually benefited from this arrangement because

nothing sells so dearly as what is disposed of by a well-constructed lottery, and if we wish to sell salaries dearly, that is, to obtain as much work and knowledge as possible for as little pay as possible, the best means is to dazzle the imagination with a few splendid prizes, and, by magnificently overpaying one or two, to induce thousands to sell their services at half price.

This was exactly what was happening in the Church of England, thought Senior.[32] A similar system, some contended, should be established in the British Army, if only to assist the taxpayer.[33]

Smith and Senior also argued that the remuneration for different occupational groups often depended upon the agreeableness or otherwise of that occupation, which in turn often entailed public perceptions of it as being honourable or dishonourable. 'Honour makes a great part of the reward of all honourable professions', writes Smith: 'in point of pecuniary gain', the higher the social esteem, the lower the pay. Conversely, public executioners, who had a very mean reputation,

---

[30] N. W. Senior, *An Outline of the Science of Political Economy* (New York, 1965; first pub. 1836), 57–60. See the discussion in M. Berg, *The Machinery Question and the Making of Political Economy, 1815–48* (Cambridge, 1980), 120–3; D. P. O'Brien, *The Classical Economists* (Oxford, 1975), 119–20.

[31] A. Smith, *An Inquiry into the Nature and Causes of The Wealth of Nations* ed. E. Cannan (Chicago, 1976; first pub. 1776), bk. 1, ch. 10, pp. 120–1; Senior, *Science of Political Economy*, 210–15.

[32] Senior, *Science of Political Economy*, 214. He thought that the law was better paid than the church because it was less of a lottery.

[33] T. E. Cliffe Leslie, *The Military System of Europe Economically Considered* (Belfast, 1856), 21.

needed to be relatively well paid, compared with other common trades, if anyone was to take on this job at all.[34] In short, far from virtue being rewarded, the opposite was often the case.

But these were not sentiments that could expediently be broadcast by those early Victorian propagandists who were seeking to win a wider audience for the science of political economy. If 'converts' to the creed were to be made, they needed to be convinced that the market was a mechanism which distributed rewards amongst the citizenry in a way that conformed to elementary notions of justice, with the good ending up happily and the bad unhappily—as in all the best-loved fables and fairy stories. But how was this conviction to be disseminated?

POPULARIZATIONS OF POLITICAL ECONOMY

As we have already seen, Chalmers believed that the moral instruction of the poor could safely be left to their *spiritual* leaders, an inculcation of Christian truth being the most effective way of shaping their social behaviour to rational ends. Writing in the 1820s, McCulloch advocated teaching the poor the skills of reading and writing, but he, too, attached even greater importance to their being given a grounding in *morals*: 'the poor ought . . . to be made acquainted with the duties enjoined by religion and morality, and with the circumstances which occasion that gradation of ranks and inequality of fortunes that usually exist'.[35] In other words, the early nineteenth-century view held that it was neither feasible nor desirable to teach political economy directly to 'the poor', since a selection of traditional moral adages would prepare them well enough for the market society from which they would later draw their living.[36] Let government remove 'artificial' obstructions to the operation of the free market, and then individuals could be left free to pursue their own interests.

But did individuals really understand where their own best interests lay? In the 1840s Cobden grudgingly admitted that most landowners and farmers were adhering to agricultural protection because they could not distinguish their real long-term interests from short-term sectional advantage. In his disillusioned old age he even conceded that the class he himself was trying to represent, that of the northern manufacturers, was often woefully deficient in enlightened self-interest.

---

[34] Smith, *Wealth of Nations*, bk. 1, ch. 10, pp. 112–13; also bk. 5, ch. 1, pp. 337–8. For similar reflections, see Senior, *Science of Political Economy*, 202.

[35] McCulloch, *Political Economy*, 359–60. He also saw factory employment as providing a training for the young in 'regular, orderly, and industrious habits', while the streets would simply teach them vice (*Edinburgh Review*, 61 (1835), 464).

[36] In fairness it should be conceded that this was not the view of Malthus, who wanted political economy included in the curriculum of a publicly funded education system (D. Winch, *Riches and Poverty: An Intellectual History of Political Economy in Britain, 1750–1834* (Cambridge, 1996), 278).

More worrying still to orthodox defenders of political economy was the attitude of working men, many of whom, it soon became apparent, remained sunk in moral and intellectual darkness, clinging to antiquated notions like 'a fair day's pay for a fair day's work', in defiance of the economic 'law' which demonstrated that wage levels could only be determined by the free play of market forces. Was it wise, or even kind, to leave these poor benighted souls in a state of superstition which would only bring them suffering? If, as most Radicals believed, happiness meant adjusting oneself to the logic of the market, then the one thing needful was to tell people these basic truths—to impress upon them, while their minds were still open to impressions, that economic laws were as inexorable as physical laws and that it was futile to defy or ignore them.[37]

In any case, by the 1840s few middle-class Victorians thought it safe to leave instruction of the poor in the hands of clergymen, if only because in the big cities it was the very groups particularly in need of 'enlightenment' who tended to be the most detached from all formal religious organizations. The shift in position can be studied in the successive editions of Mrs Marcet's *Conversations on Political Economy* (1816), the most successful of the early ventures in popularization. In the first version, its fictional governess, 'Mrs B', denies that she wishes to teach political economy to the labouring classes. Yet a decade later Mrs Marcet was trying to scatter her pearls of wisdom among the populace at large.[38]

It has been suggested that one reason for the change, which can be traced back to the late 1820s and early 1830s, is that articulate and politically active working men had already made contact with political economy but had been attracted by the heretical versions of it propagated by Ricardian socialists like Thomas Hodgskin, in whose hands the labour theory of value was being put to politically radical ends.[39] To counter this threat, orthodox tracts were written by George Poulett Scrope and by Charles Knight, author of *The Rights of Labour*.[40] Harriet Martineau's didactic *Illustrations of Political Economy* also date from approximately the same period.[41]

The anxieties underlying such propaganda clearly emerge from the 1826 report of the Committee of the Haddington School of Arts:

[37] See S. Rashid, 'Richard Whately and Christian Political Economy at Oxford and Dublin', *Journal of History of Ideas*, 38 (1977), 155 fn. 39. T. H. Green was later to justify compulsory education with the argument that children must first become rational free agents ('Lecture on Liberal Legislation and Freedom of Contract', in R. L. Nettleship (ed.), *Works of Thomas Hill Green* (London, 1888), iii. 374).

[38] R. L. Meek, *Economics and Ideology and Other Essays* (London, 1967), 69.

[39] Smith's (and Locke's) legacy, the labour theory of value, encouraged the recognition of the centrality of labour in the generation of wealth (G. Claeys, 'The Origins of the Rights of Labor: Republicanism, Commerce, and the Constitution of Modern Social Theory in Britain, 1796–1805', *Journal of Modern History*, 66 (1994), 290). [40] Meek, *Economics and Ideology*, 69–72.

[41] In his *Introductory Lectures* of 1831 Whately opined that there were 'some very simple but important truths belonging to the science' of political economy 'which might with the utmost facility be brought down to the capacity of a child, and which . . . the Lower Orders cannot even safely be left ignorant of' (p. 186).

Our mechanics do not sufficiently know the limits of their own, nor the extent of their masters' just rights. . . . Only let the working classes be trained to discrimination, either by that
general science which sharpens the faculties of all who are conversant with it; or let them
be made acquainted with that particular science, part of whose object it is to elucidate the
nature of the relation in which capitalists and labourers stand to each other; and we shall
be as little disturbed by the spirit of combination, as by a revival of the spirit of witchcraft.

True political economy, according to this Report, was 'calculated in a great degree, to remove the jealousies and prejudices entertained by the various ranks of
society towards each other—reconciling the lower to their circumstances, and
promoting the peace and welfare of the community at large'.[42]

In time, even Whately conceded that the task of 'saving' the people from revolution could not be accomplished by 'religions or novels': 'A man, even of the
purest mind and most exalted feelings, without a knowledge of Political Economy,
could not be secured from being made instrumental in forwarding most destructive and disastrous revolutions.'[43]

And so political economy would have to be drilled into the heads of everyone,
especially into the heads of the poor, whose need was greatest—in which case,
the younger one caught them the better. Thus, what had begun as a genuine
attempt to promote happiness had, by a logic of its own, ended up with Mr
McChoakumchild ramming 'the dismal science' down the throats of little children
—not entirely without success, it would seem.[44]

Yet if the diffusion of political economy owed something to social anxieties, it
was also stimulated by the new technologies. In 1827, long before the advent of
Chartism, Henry Brougham and Charles Knight had founded the Society for the
Diffusion of Useful Knowledge (SDUK).[45] Knight's publishing ventures in part
reflect a growing confidence among 'reformers' that their message could be conveyed to the population at large.

But this process of popularization was bound to involve modifications to political economy. For a start, it meant the down-playing, or even the concealment, of
the very real differences dividing the political economists—a group of men, as
Poynter has shown, who were always quarrelling among themselves, although they
usually presented a united face to the outside world.[46] These disagreements, along

---

[42] Cited in A. Tyrrell, 'Class Consciousness in Early Victorian Britain: Samuel Smiles, Leeds Politics,
and the Self-Help Creed', *Journal of British Studies*, 9 (1970), 110–11.

[43] T. A. Boylan and T. P. Foley, *Political Economy and Colonial Ireland* (London, 1992), 130.

[44] E. F. Biagini argues that, in modified form, political economy became taken up by trade unionists, who saw ways in which it could be made useful to their struggles and interests (Biagini, 'British
Trade Unions and Popular Political Economy, 1860–1880', *Historical Journal*, 30 (1987), esp. 811,
837–40).

[45] R. K. Webb, *The British Working Class Reader: 1790–1848* (London, 1955); R. D. Altick, *The
English Common Reader* (Chicago, 1957), 269–83; S. Bennett, 'Revolutions in Thought: Serial
Publications and the Mass Market for Reading', in J. Shattock and M. Wolff (eds.), *The Victorian
Periodical Press: Samplings and Soundings* (Leicester, 1982), 225–57.

[46] Poynter, *Society and Pauperism*, 237.

with famous retractions such as Ricardo's admission that the introduction of machinery might increase unemployment, or Mill's belated repudiation of the wages fund, had no place in this didactic literature, which positively exuded an air of infallibility.[47]

Mill himself disliked this process of simplification. 'The founders of Political Economy have left two sorts of disciples', he complained: 'those who have inherited their methods, and those who have stopped short at their phrases'.[48] Martineau found herself accused by Mill of reducing the system of political economy to an absurdity.[49] Later Mill also took umbrage at Robert Lowe's pedantry: 'Political economy has a great many enemies; but its worst enemies are some of its friends.'[50]

During the mid-Victorian period some political economists also objected that it was futile to try to make their 'science' *popular*. 'A very rapid diffusion of popular knowledge necessarily brings with it a certain dislike and distrust of that abstract reasoning which never can be popular, and which people are only too glad to think unnecessary', concluded Walter Bagehot.[51] Indeed, throughout the whole Victorian period, some proponents of political economy took a gloomy pride in the unpopularity which they had acquired: seeing this as a confirmation that their views must undoubtedly be *true*. Lowe, for example, was not impressed by the objection 'that political economy is generally unpopular, and especially that it finds no favour with the working class': 'The object of science is not to please or to conciliate. It has no policy. It knows no compromise. If false, no popularity can redeem it; if true, no unpopularity can hurt it.'[52]

On the other hand, there were quite as many *optimistic* political economists: men and women who believed that, given a little effort, even difficult and repellent truths could be made acceptable to the general public. But how? As Simon Dentith has argued, the early 'classical economists' had tended to justify their statements 'by reference to an area of discourse which [had] its own independent logic, the logic of the economic, which [cut] across, or [rendered] irrelevant, the usual reference to the moral-political'. However, and here was the nub of the problem, these abstract 'truths' often seemed at variance with appearances and sometimes flew in the face of 'commonsense'.[53]

[47] However, Mill's 'recantation' eventually became incorporated into trade union ideology (Biagini, 'British Trade Unions', 840).

[48] Hollander, *Economics of Mill*, ii. 922; J. S. Mill, 'Leslie on the Land Question', in id., *Collected Works*, ed. J. M. Robson (Toronto, 1967), v. 671.

[49] V. K. Pichanick, *Harriet Martineau: The Woman and Her Work 1802–76* (Ann Arbor, 1980), 49.

[50] Hollander, *Economics of Mill*, ii. 924.

[51] In a survey of Senior's Journals, *Fortnightly Review*, 10 (1871), in N. St. J. Stevas (ed.), *Collected Works of Walter Bagehot* (London, 1965), ii. 378.

[52] R. Lowe, 'Recent Attacks on Political Economy', *Nineteenth Century*, 4 (1878), 862. Herbert Spencer and Henry Fawcett usually took a similar line (H. Spencer, *The Study of Sociology* (1873), 153; Fawcett, 'Address on Economy and Trade', 113–14).

[53] S. Dentith, 'Political Economy, Fiction and the Language of Practical Ideology in Nineteenth-Century England', *Social History*, 8 (1983), 184–8.

It was in the hope of overcoming this difficulty that Harriet Martineau hit upon the bright idea of dressing up the 'lessons' of political economy as didactic fiction, an enterprise the commercial success of which suggests that a real need was being met.[54] It was probably Martineau whom Dickens had in mind when he made his mocking remark in *Hard Times* about 'leaden little books . . . , showing how the good grown-up baby invariably got to the Savings-bank, and the bad grown-up baby invariably got transported'.[55] Fortunately Dickens died before he could encounter Millicent Fawcett's preposterous *Tales in Political Economy* (1874), whose author expressed in her Preface her apologies 'for my plagiarism of the idea, which [Miss Martineau] made so popular thirty years ago, of hiding the powder, Political Economy, in the raspberry jam of a story'.[56]

But to win Doubting Thomases over to the merits of political economy, more was required than merely simplifying it and brightening up its presentation. The main problem, as the pioneering Mrs Marcet realized, was to remove her readers' *moral* distaste for the subject as a whole. Her 'conversations' accordingly open with the intelligent, sensitive, but ignorant young lady, 'Caroline', confessing to her governess, 'Mrs B', that she felt 'a sort of antipathy to political economy'. The governess replies that young ladies would be utterly incapable of entering 'on most subjects of general conversation' whilst they remained 'in total ignorance of it'.[57] But 'Caroline' only makes intellectual progress once she has become convinced that the laws of political economy are both rational and, viewed in a broad perspective, humane; thereafter, she develops into a precocious and enthusiastic student.[58]

Mrs Marcet set about her educational task by stressing the importance of rendering the youth of all classes 'not only moral and religious, but industrious, frugal, and provident'. Unlike infants and savages, she claimed, human beings progress mentally through an ability to calculate the consequences of their actions.[59] Harriet Martineau pursued a similar line of argument. 'Unless the people will take pains to learn what it is that goes wrong, and how it can be rectified', she wrote, 'they

[54] Perhaps she was acting on a hint dropped by Whately, who in his Oxford lectures in 1831 had suggested that political economy could perhaps be made available 'in compilations of history, or of travels, and in works of fiction, which would afford amusement as well as instruction' (*Introductory Lectures*, 188). Some think, however, that Mrs Marcet, with her economic stories and fairy tales of 1833 and 1851, aimed at the lower classes, was the real trail-blazer (G. Routh, *The Origin of Economic Ideas* (New York, 1975), 182–4). See the discussion in Dentith, 'Political Economy', 191–3.
[55] C. Dickens, *Hard Times*, Chapman & Hall edn. (n.d.; first pub. 1854), bk. 1, ch. 8, p. 301. Martineau had been a regular contributor to Dickens's *Household Words* before the two quarrelled over the question of factory legislation.
[56] M. G. Fawcett, *Tales in Political Economy* (1874). For a good example of Mrs Fawcett's naïve optimism, see her encomium on the blessings of free trade (ibid., 102–3).
[57] Mrs Marcet, *Conversations on Political Economy: In Which The Elements of That Science Are Familiarly Explained* (London, 1839; first pub. 1816), 4, 7.
[58] Marcet says that the questions raised by Caroline were 'such as would be likely to arise in the mind of an intelligent young person, fluctuating between the impulse of her heart and the progress of her reason, and naturally imbued with all the prejudices and popular feelings of uninformed benevolence' (ibid., p. vi).   [59] Ibid., 146.

cannot petition intelligently or effectually.'[60] Dealing as it did with the sources and acquisition of wealth, political economy offered a solution to the many social problems which were rooted in poverty: for example, crime and licentiousness. It also taught 'the laws of social duty and social happiness'.[61] Finally, *personal* gratification would be achieved by a study of political economy, since the knowledge gained thereby would stop well-meaning but ignorant people vainly rebelling against the laws of Nature.

This was precisely the spirit in which William Ellis, the founder of the Birkbeck Schools, propagated 'social economy', a popularized version of political economy reformulated so as to be intelligible to small children.[62] Without a knowledge of this subject, claimed Ellis, the working man was lost: 'the causes of the privation and suffering by which he is surrounded and to which he is exposed, must ever remain a mystery to him; and he will never be able to discriminate between what he ought to bear with resignation, and what he may successfully struggle and secure himself against'.[63] Ellis was not only a utilitarian but also an advocate of secular education, which perhaps explains why he thought children too young to understand the Bible (though not, apparently, the principles of economics!).[64]

In his numerous publications, Ellis set out to praise the virtues of prudence and forethought, but he combined these homilies with a highly simplified distillation of the 'science' of political economy, dressed up for a popular readership by employing fictional characters like 'Lord Mereacres', a spendthrift peer, 'John Save-all', a miser, 'Robert Steer-well', an enlightened retired manufacturer, and so on, following a literary genre which had already become well established.[65]

What makes Ellis particularly interesting is the lengths to which he was prepared to go to remove the 'moral' objections so often raised against the 'dismal science'. Undoubtedly this was an assignment to which he was deeply, and disinterestedly, committed: 'A question of political economy is a question of morals', he wrote to a friend in a private letter. 'The conclusions of political economy (rightly understood) are conclusions in morals or no conclusions at all. Political economy, being subordinate, can never be in antagonism to morals.'[66] Religion and 'social economy', as Ellis understood them, had a common purpose in that they both taught people to be thrifty, sober, honest, and industrious. The right use of money and credit was another issue on which the two forces could combine. 'To single

[60] Pichanick, *Martineau*, 52.

[61] H. Martineau, 'On the Duty of Studying Political Economy', in id., *Miscellanies*, 2 vols. (Boston, 1836), i. 276, 278.

[62] See W. D. Sockwell, *Popularizing Classical Economics: Henry Brougham and William Ellis* (New York, 1994), chs. 5–7, and 12. R. Gilmour, 'The Gradgrind School: Political Economy in the Classroom', *Victorian Studies*, 11 (1967), 207–24.

[63] [W. Ellis], *Outlines of Social Economy* (London, 1846), 76–7; and see id., *A Layman's Contribution to the Knowledge and Practice of Religion in Common Life* (London, 1857), 148.

[64] Sockwell, *Popularizing Classical Economics*, 174.

[65] W. Ellis, *Education as a means of Preventing Destitution* (London, 1851).

[66] Ellis to Dr Hodgson, 5 Sept. 1847 (E. K. Blyth, *Life of William Ellis* (London, 1889), 158).

out the most important of the qualities shown to be indispensable to the perfect development of the resources of division of labour and co-operation', Ellis wrote, 'we want truthfulness, trustworthiness, honesty'.[67]

But Ellis took his moralism much further than this. 'Industry and economy, admirable as they are', he once argued, 'do not comprise the whole duty of man.'[68] Only the 'prejudiced', he believed, clung to the fallacious view that political economy was merely a philosophy of the market:

We would not countenance the notion that man is to be considered solely as a competing animal. Let him compete by all means; but he should, besides, be so gifted with sensibilities, sympathies, and aspirations, that if his competitive efforts are crowned with success, the noblest use in his estimation to which the fruits of his competition can be applied, will be in cheering the unsuccessful—in enlightening their ignorance, propping their weakness, correcting their errors, reforming their bad habits, and encouraging their efforts to attain self-reliance and self-respect.[69]

It was left to Benjamin Templar, the headmaster responsible for introducing 'social economy' into the school curriculum, to make the ultimate identification between economics and religion. Social economy, he claimed, taught *reverence*, because it showed

that every man, while working out his plans for his own advancement, is at the same time—though quite unintentionally, and often unconsciously—contributing to the advancement of others—to the public good; that God has so interwoven men's interests, that no man liveth, or can live, to himself alone. It proves that the interests of all classes, even the most opposite . . . are concurrent instead of antagonistic; else civilization, with all its attendant blessings, would be impossible. It shows, too, that the tendency of all legitimate social arrangement is to bring about universal peace, prosperity, friendship, and happiness.

By teaching children social economy, said Templar, he was helping to make them 'devout, grateful, and in the truest, least disputed, sense of the word, religious men'.[70]

Harriet Martineau would not have dissented from Templar's remarks. In her *Autobiography* she claims that all her writings were designed to show that 'eternal and irreversible laws [were at work] in every department of the universe, without any interference from any random will, human or divine'.[71] As Catherine Gallagher shows, this created problems of characterization when Martineau came to compose her didactic fables, based as they were on 'a popular but peculiar blend of optimistic, providential beliefs and pessimistic, mechanical doctrines'.[72] Unwittingly, in her attempts at resolving one moral dilemma, she had merely helped set up another.

---

[67] Ellis, *Layman's Contribution*, 101.
[68] Ellis, *Education as a means of Preventing Destitution*, 79.   [69] Ibid., 113.
[70] B. Templar, 'On the Importance of Teaching Social Economy in Elementary Schools', *Transactions of the National Association for the Promotion of Social Science, 1858*, esp. 323.
[71] Cited in C. Gallagher, *The Industrial Reformation of English Fiction 1832–1867* (Chicago, 1985), 51.
[72] Ibid., 54–5, 61.

COMPETITION AND CO-OPERATION

The attempt on the part of the defenders of the new capitalist order to re-concile economics and morality met with a certain degree of success. But in two areas of public life even the zealots betrayed some embarrassment. One was the desirability of building up an ethical system around the *consequences* of actions, without reference to the *impulses* from which they originated—an issue which will later be explored in Chapter 8. The other concerned the implications of encouraging a view of the world in which competition took centre stage.

John Stuart Mill's twisting and turning on the desirability and the drawbacks of competition are instructive. Of course, Mill never abandoned the concept of competition altogether. The socialists, he famously pointed out, 'forget that wherever competition is not, monopoly is; and that monopoly, in all its forms, is the taxation of the industrious for the support of indolence, if not of plunder'. Without competition there would be the danger of stagnation. 'To be protected against competition', Mill warned, 'is to be protected in idleness, in mental dulness; to be saved the necessity of being as active and as intelligent as other people.'[73]

Mill also reminded socialists 'that competition [was] a cause of high prices and values as well as of low; that the buyers of labour and of commodities compete[d] with one another as well as the sellers; and that if it [was] competition which [kept] the prices of labour and commodities as low as they [were], it [was] competition which prevent[ed] them from falling still lower'.[74] In addition, Mill expressed dismay at the way in which many manual workers resisted piece-work, calling this 'one of the most discreditable indications of a low moral condition' in which parts of that class were still sunk. 'Piece-work', Mill contended, was the perfection of contract;

and contract, in all work, and in the most minute detail—the principle of so much pay for so much service, carried out to the utmost extremity—is the system, of all others, in the present state of society and degree of civilization, most favourable to the worker; though most unfavourable to the non-worker who wishes to be paid for being idle.[75]

On the other hand, in his discussion of the 'stationary state', Mill confessed that he was

not charmed with the ideal of life held out by those who think that the normal state of human beings is that of struggling to get on; that the trampling, crushing, elbowing, and treading on each other's heels, which form the existing type of social life, are the most desirable lot of human kind, or anything but the disagreeable symptoms of one of the phases of industrial progress.

[73] J. S. Mill, *Principles of Political Economy*, in id., *Collected Works*, iii. 794–5.
[74] Hollander, *Economics of Mill*, ii. 784: J. S. Mill, 'Chapters on Socialism' (1879), in id., *Collected Works*, v. 729.
[75] Hollander, *Economics of Mill*, ii. 778–9: Mill, *Principles of Political Economy*, in id., *Collected Works*, iii. 783.

'While minds are coarse they require[d] coarse stimuli', Mill conceded.[76] But he and his wife[77] wanted the competitive struggle made 'fairer' and at the same time gradually raised to a higher moral plane.

The first of these objectives, Mill thought, could be achieved by adjustments to the inequitable income distribution which governed the workings of the contemporary market. He also thought it legitimate to strengthen the weaker of the two bargaining sides—hence his eventual acceptance of the desirability of trade unions and of the need for certain reforms to the laws of property.[78]

Raising the competitive struggle to a higher moral plane presented greater difficulties. In fact, the conclusion is irresistible that Mill basically wanted all the benefits of competition without the unpleasantness and suffering involved in a process which inevitably produced losers as well as winners. However, to this difficulty there was a possible solution: co-operation.

What Mill specifically wanted to see was the establishment of co-operatives which could compete against one another but within which there would be class-collaboration, based perhaps on profit-sharing.[79] Through his disciple, Fawcett, he helped propagate a vision of social harmony based upon conciliation and arbitration—ideas that were later taken up both by 'progressive' liberal employers like A. J. Mundella and also by many moderate trade unionists.[80] Mill also worried that, though competition might be the best security for cheapness, it was 'by no means a security for quality'.[81] Unfortunately, Mill's discussion of these issues lacks clarity, giving substance to the charge that he had partly 'exonerated classical political economy from the charges of narrowness and internal incoherence at the cost of reducing the significance and practical bearing of its conclusions'.[82] (Mill's changes of opinion certainly exasperated Harriet Martineau.[83])

[76] Mill, *Principles of Political Economy*, in id., *Collected Works*, iii. 754.

[77] Harriet Taylor hoped that 'the division of mankind into capitalists and hired labourers, and the regulation of the reward of labourers mainly by demand and supply' would not for much longer be 'the rule of the world' (H. T. Mill, 'Enfranchisement of Women', in A. S. Rossi (ed.), *John Stuart Mill and Harriet Taylor Mill: Essays on Sex Equality* (Chicago, 1970), 105).

[78] Hollander, *Economics of Mill*, ii. 782: Mill, 'Thornton on Labour and Its Claims' (1879), in id., *Collected Works*, v. 658.

[79] Hollander, *Economics of Mill*, ii. 814–15: Mill, *Principles of Political Economy*, in id., *Collected Works*, iii. 795. On Mill's ambiguous views on competitive capitalism and his belief that 'improvement' will propel workers to co-operation, see O. Kurer, 'John Stuart Mill on Government Intervention', *History of Political Thought*, 10 (1989), 479–80.

[80] Biagini, 'British Trade Unions', 839. Trade unionists also noted many of the favourable things said about them by Adam Smith (ibid., 829). See Smith, *Wealth of Nations*, bk. 1, ch. 8, where Smith shows how the masters possess an unfair legal advantage over labourers—for example, in forming 'combinations'.

[81] Hollander, *Economics of Mill*, ii. 785: Mill, 'Chapters on Socialism', in id., *Collected Works*, v. 731.

[82] Collini et al., *That Noble Science*, 140.

[83] She privately declared him 'an enormously overrated man': 'A strong man might change his opinions to the extent that he has; but there must be some weakness *in a thinker* whose compound change,— of kind and degree together,—is so great as John Stuart Mill's' (Martineau to H. Reeve, 21 Feb. 1859, in V. Sanders (ed.), *Harriet Martineau: Selected Letters* (Oxford, 1990), 172). She modified this harsh judgement somewhat when *On Liberty* appeared later that year (Martineau to R. P. Graves, Apr./May 1859, ibid., 179).

However, Mill's ambivalence about competition was shared by other proponents of capitalism. W. R. Greg, it is true, doubted whether co-operation ever could 'or ought to, supersede the principle of competition'; but at least he wanted the experiment to 'have a fair field'.[84] And Martineau was positively enthusiastic about the co-operative movement, at least about the activities of *retail* co-operatives (she had reservations about organizing manufacturing or even wholesaling on this basis).[85] She particularly praised the way in which co-operation developed the 'character' of working men and their wives, in particular, their steadiness, industry, and intelligence, adding, significantly: 'As to the moral superiority of the brotherly principle to that of rivalry, there can, we suppose, be no question.'[86]

Fawcett was similarly struck by the thought that co-operation could not succeed without 'calling forth many of the highest qualities of man's intellectual and moral nature': 'It demands a just appreciation of the characters of others; it calls for an intelligent confidence associated with a judicious watchfulness; and it requires prudence on the part of those who have not been accustomed to foresight.'[87] Fawcett here implies what Martineau had openly conceded: that these admirable human and social qualities were not usually elicited by unbridled market competition.[88]

Co-operation assumed many forms. Charles Kingsley subscribed to a highly personal conception of Christian Socialism which incorporated Robert Owen's view that co-operation might be made to function as a radical *alternative* to capitalism.[89] By contrast, in the hands of the Rochdale pioneers, co-operation later dwindled into a 'mere palliative' for the easing of the lives of labouring families within a largely unchanged capitalist system.[90] Between these two extremes stand Mill and Fawcett, both of whom present co-operation as a progressive development which would hopefully evolve *within* a mature capitalist economy but which, in doing so, would purge market competition of some of its morally obnoxious features.

It is testimony to the power of such assumptions that even Smiles can be found at one point stressing the *co-operative aspects of capitalism itself* through an argument, derived from Adam Smith, which purports to show how the division of labour involved individuals co-operating 'with each other for the mutual

[84] W. R. Greg, *Essays on Political and Social Science, Contributed Chiefly to the Edinburgh Review* (1853), i. 455. He clearly distinguished between forms of co-operation in which the workmen advanced the necessary capital, to which he was sympathetic, and socialism, which he hated (ibid., 458–504).

[85] [H. Martineau], 'Co-operative Societies in 1864', *Edinburgh Review*, 120 (1864), 407–36, esp. 416.

[86] Ibid., 431. She also observed that 'in a co-operative establishment, where the profits belong to everybody, there can be no struggle on behalf of wages at the expense of profits: there can be no despotic determination of the rate of wages by a man or a clique: there can be no intimidation of the workers, nor compulsion put upon them to starve' (ibid., 421).

[87] H. Fawcett, 'Co-operative Societies; Their Social and Economical Aspects', *Macmillan's Magazine*, 2 (1860), 440.

[88] Despite his well-known contempt for factory legislation, Fawcett was, in many ways, one of the trade unionists' favourite political economists (Biagini, 'British Trade Unions', 815–16).

[89] H. Perkin, *The Origin of Modern English Society 1780–1880* (London, 1969), 363.

[90] Ibid., 364, 384, 386–7.

sustenance of all'.[91] The joint-stock company, too, could be depicted as embodying the 'principle of association', a principle which Smiles thought desirable provided that it was not employed for antisocial ends.[92]

THE TRIUMPH OF ALTRUISM?

But Smiles went further than merely underwriting the co-operative principle. Never quite able to convince himself that true merit would necessarily lead to economic success, he constantly emphasized that it was better to be a failure and to preserve one's sense of honour than to achieve material prosperity at any cost. 'Self-culture', as he constantly reiterates in *Self-Help*, mattered much more than 'mere money-making': 'He who recognizes no higher logic than that of the shilling may become a very rich man, and yet remain all the while an exceedingly poor creature. For riches are no proof whatever of moral worth.'[93] This was the central element in what Collini has called the Victorian cult of altruism.

Its most extreme formulation came from the pen of Herbert Spencer, who attempted to resolve the moral dilemmas of capitalism by positing some future utopia. As Professor Bellamy notes, Spencer assumed that social evolution would in time lead to the increasing displacement of 'egoism' by 'altruism'; not only that, but he 'even hinted at a third stage, "aesthetic" society, in which work was subordinated to "higher activities" of a spiritual and intellectual kind'.[94] To quote Spencer's own words, the goal of history was the establishment of social conditions 'under which alone associated activities can be so carried on, that the complete living of each consists with, and conduces to, the complete living of all'. 'The highest life', argued Spencer, would only be reached 'when, besides helping to complete one another's lives by specified reciprocities of aid, men otherwise help to complete one another's lives'.[95] Ironically, then, many who began by providing an apologia for capitalism came close, in the end, to throwing it over completely.

However, so far as businessmen were concerned, Spencerian prophecy was no substitute for practical guidance. The dilemma remained: could they really take

---

[91] S. Smiles, *Thrift* (London, 1886), 5.

[92] Ibid., 98, and id., *Lives of the Engineers* (1862), iii. 289–90. According to another of Mill's admirers, co-operation was 'an application of the joint stock principle', and that principle, embodied in the early railways, was a form of co-operation ('The Opinions of John Stuart Mill: Part II: Co-operation', *English Woman's Journal*, 6 (November 1860), 195–7).

[93] S. Smiles, *Self-Help: With Illustrations of Conduct and Perseverance* (1910: first pub. 1859), 364. For further discussion of Smiles's conception of 'duty' and 'character' see Collini, *Public Moralists*, 100–1.

[94] R. Bellamy, 'Introduction', in id. (ed.), *Victorian Liberalism: Nineteenth-Century Political Thought and Practice* (London, 1990), 9.

[95] H. Spencer, *The Data of Ethics* (London, 1894; first pub. 1879), 149. See T. Gray, 'Herbert Spencer's Liberalism—From Social Statics to Social Dynamics', in Bellamy (ed.), *Victorian Liberalism*, 110–30, and Peel, *Herbert Spencer*, 215–16.

with them into the marketplace the ethical code which they might sincerely profess as private citizens? For, as Chalmers had admitted, commerce, which usefully
tested 'virtue', was also full of pitfalls and moral dangers. A consideration of the
steps which needed to be taken if these pitfalls were to be avoided will be examined in Chapter 5.

But the mere inculcation of a personal code of morality was not enough. Of
more fundamental importance was the establishment of criteria which would distinguish between legitimate and illegitimate commercial transactions—an issue which
was dramatized by the protracted and passionate debate about the meaning and
significance of *slavery*.

4

Selling People is Wrong: Slavery and Political Economy

The connexion is so constant and so clear between industry and freedom, and consequently between increased exertions of voluntary labour, and the milder treatment which approaches the slaves to the condition of liberty, that we may reasonably expect to see the temporary derangement [produced by emancipation] last for a very trifling period.

(*Edinburgh Review*)[1]

Our cause is great, we only seek to second or to remove impediments out of the way of the free operation of the Laws which the Creator has fixed in the nature of things.

(James Cropper, 1822)[2]

Free and slave labour are equally owned by the capitalist.

Where the labourer is not held as capital, the capitalist pays for labour only.

Where the labourer is held as capital, the capitalist not only pays a much higher price for an equal quantity of labour, but also for waste, negligence and theft, on the part of the labourer.

Capital is thus sunk, which ought to be reproduced.

As the supply of slave-labour does not rise and fall with the wants of the capitalist, like that of free labour, he employs his occasional surplus on works which could be better done by brute labour or machinery.

By rejecting brute labour, he refuses facilities for convertible husbandry, and for improving the labour of his slaves by giving them animal food.

By rejecting machinery, he declines the most direct and complete method of saving labour.

Thus, again, capital is sunk that ought to be reproduced.

(Harriet Martineau, 1832)[3]

Adam Smith had defined human beings as creatures which had a 'propensity to truck, barter and exchange'. But could human beings barter and exchange *one another*—in other words, treat their fellows as if they were commodities? Long usage suggested that such behaviour was acceptable, but from the late eighteenth

---

[1] *Edinburgh Review*, 6 (1805), 348–9.
[2] Cropper to Macaulay, 1822, cited in D. B. Davis, *Slavery and Human Progress* (New York, 1984), 180–1.   [3] H. Martineau, *Demarara: A Tale* (London, 1832), 142.

century, attitudes began to change. In 1807 the British Parliament ended the Atlantic slave-trade and in 1833 the negro slaves in the West Indies were emancipated.[4] The second of these steps was the more radical since there were many precedents for the state regulation of commerce, but none for the British state depriving some of its most distinguished citizens of their property.[5] That the West Indian planters had a strong legal case was evident in the handsome compensation which they received by way of settlement—compensation which annoyed the abolitionists but against which few protested on principle.[6] In what ways, then, was the ownership of human beings wrong?

In the eyes of most of the early metropolitan abolitionists, slavery was quite simply an abomination and a sin, to expiate which the nation was called to repentance. This was particularly so with William Wilberforce and other evangelical reformers, who stressed the divinity latent in every human being and asserted the sovereignty of conscience.[7] Slavery, fumed Wilberforce, was 'a system of the grossest injustice, of the most heathenish irreligion and immorality, of the most unprecedented degradation, and unrelenting cruelty'.[8] He went on to argue that so long as the British people could plead ignorance of what was taking place in the West Indian islands, God had spared them, but they could make that excuse no longer: the urgent need was therefore to 'rescue our country from this guilt and this reproach'.[9]

In Wilberforce's view, slavery was inconsistent with the Christian Faith, and this explained why most negroes were 'practically strangers to the multiplied blessings of the Christian Revelation', it being in the interest of the planters to place obstruction in the path of the missionaries.[10] Indeed, a leading Christian abolitionist like Thomas Fowell Buxton was still trying in 1831 to tie the emancipation of the slaves to sabbatarianism: slavery was wicked, not least because it involved the denial to the slaves of the blessings of the Lord's Day.[11]

[4] New, in his biography of Brougham, emphasizes the distinction between abolition of the slave trade, the emancipation of the slaves, and the end of the apprenticeship system (C. W. New, *The Life of Henry Brougham to 1830* (Oxford, 1961), 21). This seems particularly pertinent in the case of Brougham, since his early writings, particularly *An Inquiry into the Colonial Policy of the European Powers* (Edinburgh, 1803), are given over to a demonstration of the immorality of the slave trade, but seem in places (e.g. sect. I, bk. iv) to be furnishing arguments in favour of the retention of slavery itself.

[5] E. F. Hurwitz, *Politics and the Public Conscience: Slave Emancipation and the Abolitionist Movement in Britain* (London, 1973), 18–19.

[6] A series of court rulings in the late 18th c. had established the right of a slave to his freedom once he had set foot on the soil of mainland Britain (J. Walvin, *Black Ivory: A History of British Slavery* (London, 1992), 11–16, 20–1; S. Drescher, *Capitalism and Antislavery: British Mobilization in Comparative Perspective* (London, 1986), 35–7). But these rulings in no way affected the property laws of the West Indian islands.

[7] B. Harrison, 'A Genealogy of Reform in Modern Britain', in C. Bolt and S. Drescher (eds.), *Anti-Slavery, Religion and Reform: Essays in Memory of Roger Anstey* (Folkestone, 1980), 134.

[8] S. Wilberforce, *An Appeal to the Religion, Justice, and Humanity of the Inhabitants of the British Empire on Behalf of the Negro Slaves in the West Indies* (London, 1823), 1.

[9] Ibid., 74–5.   [10] Ibid., 24–5.

[11] P. Hollis, 'Anti-Slavery and British Working-Class Radicalism', in Bolt and Drescher (eds.), *Anti-Slavery, Religion and Reform*, 305.

The abolitionists sought to make their audience empathize with the sufferings of the wretched slaves. One aspect of this suffering came in for particular attention. Slavery was said to subvert family life. Heart-rending scenes were painted of wives being separated from husbands, and parents from children.[12] This was a most worrying state of affairs to those like Wilbeforce who saw the family as 'the source of all domestic comfort and social improvement,—the moral cement of civilized society'.[13]

The abolitionists also believed that the family was being assaulted in an even more serious sense. Addressing the ladies of Glasgow in 1833, the orator George Thompson invited them to put themselves in the position of mothers 'whose daughters [were] liable to the assaults of wicked and evil-disposed men; who [were] prevented frequently from marrying, by the dislike which the negroes have to see their wives indecently exposed and cruelly flogged at the command of a merciless master'.[14] This hinting at the sexual misconduct that arose when temptations were placed before the masters and the overseers who held an unnatural dominion over defenceless females became a commonplace of abolitionist rhetoric.[15]

But the buying and selling of human beings stood condemned on principle, not just for its social and moral consequences. Thomas Clarkson addressed the issue directly in his 1785 essay on *The Slavery and Commerce of the Human Species*. He started off from the premise that 'all were originally free' and that no human being could be assigned to slavery 'without his own *consent*'. From this he deduced that slavery was a violation of the doctrine of 'natural religion' and contrary to 'the dictates of *reason*' and 'the admonitions of *conscience*'.[16] 'It is necessary that all *property* should be inferior to its *possessor*', reasoned Clarkson; but the slave differed from his master only by chance; unlike animals and other creatures, he was in no way naturally inferior to the fellow human being who had lordship over him.[17]

However, the heart of Clarkson's case was a specifically Christian one, as the following passage shows:

No man whatever can be bought or reduced to the situation of a slave, *but he must instantly become a brute, he must instantly be reduced to the value of those things, which were made for his own use and convenience; he must instantly cease to be accountable for his actions, and his authority as a parent, and his duty as a son, must be instantly no more.*

Mankind, warned Clarkson, was 'to exist in a future state, and to give an account of those actions, which they have severally done in the flesh'. This consideration, he said, struck 'at the very root of slavery'.[18] Granville Sharpe took a broadly

---

[12] T. Clarkson, *An Essay on the Slavery and Commerce of the Human Species . . .* (London, 1785), 132; Wilberforce, *Appeal*, 17, 21–2; Hurwitz, *Politics and Public Conscience*, 90.

[13] Wilberforce, *Appeal*, 17.   [14] Hurwitz, *Politics and Public Conscience*, 142.

[15] There were similar accusations made against the sailors who manned the slave ships, before the Atlantic trade was abolished. For the misdemeanours of Captain Kimber, see C. Midgley, *Women against Slavery: The British Campaigns, 1780–1870* (London, 1992), 20–1.

[16] Clarkson, *Slavery and Commerce*, 69–70, 115.   [17] Ibid., 69.

[18] Ibid., 243–4, 248; also, 70.

similar line, arguing that men could not own their fellow men since a life 'peculiarly belongs to God by an inestimable purchase'.[19]

Abolitionists working within these assumptions were as unconcerned with the
question of whether or not slavery paid as they were with the question of whether
theft paid: both were sins and crimes.[20] But alongside this Christian critique there
ran a line of argument which asserted that slavery was not only wicked and impious but also stupid. In the words of Josiah Conder, 'holding men in slavery, is
worse than a crime; it is a blunder; not merely a wrong, but the most disgraceful
of mistakes, a blunder in arithmetic'.[21]

Conder was here invoking a tradition of political economy which can be dated
back to Adam Smith's *Wealth of Nations*. Smith had denounced slavery as backward and inefficient, urging its replacement by free labour—that is, by a market
economy within which labour-power could be bought and sold. 'The work done
by freemen comes cheaper in the end than that performed by slaves', claimed Smith,
because the master had to bear the entire cost of the 'wear and tear of a slave',
while a free labourer, who had a motive to practise frugality, would not cost his
employer as much.[22] Moreover, Smith argued, 'a person who can acquire no property, can have no other interest but to eat as much, and to labour as little as possible'.[23] This meant that slaves were 'very seldom inventive', and so were little
suited to manufacturing industry.[24] Even in agricultural work, Smith asserted, the
employment of free labour had proved its superiority, which was why, all over
Western Europe, bondage had ceased: it simply was not profitable.[25] The agricultural economist, James Anderson, writing in 1789, repeated these points, arguing
that 'labour performed by the slave costs considerably higher, than if the same
labour were performed by free men'.[26]

If this were the case, then how could the widespread use of slave labour in the
contemporary world be explained? Smith's answer fell into two parts. 'The pride
of man', he asserted, made him 'love to domineer', and it was this pride which
often led him to prefer the service of slaves to the service of freemen. Secondly,
Smith explained the continuing use of slave labour in the sugar plantations of the
West Indies and, to a lesser extent, in tobacco production by the fact that these

---

[19] Hurwitz, *Politics and Public Conscience*, 23.

[20] The fact that Wilberforce and his friends were aware of the need to proceed, step by step, in
their campaign against slavery, in no way detracted from their abhorrence of the system and their
determination to abolish it ultimately.

[21] J. Conder, *Wages or the Whip: An Essay On the Comparative Cost and Productiveness of Free and
Slave Labour* (London, 1833), 2.

[22] A. Smith, *An Inquiry into the Nature and Causes of The Wealth of Nations*, ed. E. Cannan (Chicago,
1976; first pub. 1776), bk. 1, ch. 8, p. 90; bk. 4, ch. 9, p. 205). See also J. Salter, 'Adam Smith on
Feudalism, Commerce and Slavery', *History of Political Thought*, 13 (1992), 219–41.

[23] Smith, *Wealth of Nations*, bk. 3, ch. 2, p. 411.   [24] Ibid., bk. 4, ch. 9, p. 205.

[25] Ibid., bk. 3, ch. 2, pp. 412–14.

[26] J. Anderson, *Observations on Slavery Particularly With a View to Its Effects on the British Colonies,
in the West-Indies* (Manchester, 1789), 10. See D. Turley, *The Culture of English Antislavery 1780–1860*
(London, 1991), 26.

two industries were exceptionally profitable and could thus afford the expense.²⁷ In other words, the use of slaves was economically irrational but, where affordable, was sometimes retained for non-economic motives.

In the opening decades of the nineteenth century several contributors to the *Edinburgh Review* linked Smith's economic critique of slavery to an indictment of the 'colonial system'. There was no incentive, they argued, for the West Indian planters to move over to a more 'modern' and productive system of cultivation whilst colonial preferences gave their products an artificial advantage in the British market. British consumers, Smith had earlier observed, suffered a double disadvantage under the colonial system: as taxpayers, they were involved in the heavy expenses of acquiring, defending, and administering the colonies, while, in addition, they were forced to purchase sugar at above-market prices.²⁸ McCulloch elaborated on this point: 'while the people of England will gain by the reduction of the duties, they will also gain by the reduced expenditure that will henceforth be required for the protection and government of the islands', he argued.²⁹ The justification of free labour here merges with a celebration of the benefits of free trade.

Obviously these economic arguments against slavery differed from the theological ones. For example, if slavery were a 'sin', no circumstances could justify it, whereas the political economists were merely arguing that the *consequences* of slavery were socially and economically deleterious—at least in modern societies, though not necessarily in less 'advanced' ones. This historical relativism—found, for example, in a political economist like John Stuart Mill³⁰—in no way weakened abolitionism, so long as the claim that slavery was economically ruinous could be empirically verified. As we shall see, problems arose as soon as evidence accumulated to the effect that slave production *could*, in certain conditions, be highly profitable, even in the modern world.

Moreover, the two approaches differed in other ways. Wilberforce abhorred slavery because he thought it threatened the divine plan for the world by depriving a large section of the human race of that moral freedom through which alone it could achieve redemption. The political economists, by contrast, detested slavery

---

²⁷ Smith, *Wealth of Nations*, bk. 3, ch. 2, p. 412. See the discussion in D. B. Davis, *The Problem of Slavery in Western Culture* (1970; first pub. 1966), 469.
²⁸ Smith's own views on colonialism are to be found in *Wealth of Nations*, bk. 4, ch. 8. Brougham, however, differed sharply from Smith in arguing that, although monopoly and protection were wrong, colonies themselves brought gains to the mother country; see Brougham's *Colonial Policy, passim*. The issue is well handled in W. D. Sockwell, *Popularizing Classical Economics: Henry Brougham and William Ellis* (New York, 1994), 15–21.   ²⁹ *Edinburgh Review*, 54 (1831), 351.
³⁰ In his *Considerations of Representative Government*, Everyman edn. (1910; first pub. 1861) Mill argues that in backward societies slavery actually had its uses: e.g. in teaching people the necessity of obedience so that they could be ready for progress to a higher state. Moreover, despite his detestation of slavery, even in the 1840s Mill was still arguing that if slaves could not be cheaply replenished from without but had to be bred, the slave-owners would have an interest in treating them more humanely (J. S. Mill, *Principles of Political Economy*, in id., *Collected Works*, ed. J. M. Robson (Toronto, 1965), ii. 246–7).

because it violated a fundamental principle upon which their entire system rested: freedom of contract.

Nevertheless, these two lines of argument were in some ways compatible, and many abolitionists made use of both. Thus Brougham, the political economist, often raged passionately against the iniquity of slavery in language just as moralistic as that used by any member of the Clapham Sect. 'There is a law above all the enactments of human codes, the same throughout the world, the same in all times', he told Parliament on 13 July 1830:

It is the law written by the finger of God on the heart of man. And by that law, unchangeable and eternal, while men despise fraud, and loathe rapine and abhor blood, they will reject with indignation the wild and guilty phantasy that man can hold property in man.[31]

And in an article in the *Edinburgh Review*, almost certainly written by Brougham himself, the words, 'Father, forgive them—they know not what they do!', are used about the West Indian planters who had brutally suppressed the Demarara rising.[32]

Conversely, by the 1820s the Evangelicals and Quakers can increasingly be found appealing to the testimony of political economy. Thus, in his 1823 pamphlet, Wilberforce argued that the expense of protecting the sugar colonies probably outweighed any gain these colonies brought the country (Smith's point). While conceding that there might indeed be 'individual instances of great fortunes amassed by every species of wrong doing', he felt sure that 'it would have been a strange exception to all those established principles which Divine Providence has ordained for the moral benefit of the world, if national and personal prosperity were generally and permanently to be found to arise from injustice and oppression'. Honesty was thus the best policy, Wilberforce declared. Some of these thoughts were traditional enough, but the influence of Adam Smith is more evident in Wilberforce's declaration that 'every nation is, in fact, benefited by the growing affluence of others, and . . . all are thus interested in the well-being and improvement of all'.[33]

In the last analysis, however, such arguments were incidental to Wilberforce's case. Yet they central to the more militant phase of abolitionism which gained momentum in many provincial cities during the 1820s. Abolitionism was, of course, a complex, multifaceted movement, which succeeded in mobilizing support from a wide range of social groups the length and breadth of the country; this gave the movement its strength but at the same time has frustrated attempts by historians to characterize it.

However, detailed research has confirmed that by the early 1830s the activists campaigning for the end of slavery were disproportionately concentrated in those populous 'new' boroughs enfranchised for the first time by the Great Reform Act, most of which were also centres of expanding commerce and industry. Thus in April 1827 the Chambers of Commerce of Manchester and of Birmingham, along

---

[31] New, *Brougham*, 406.   [32] *Edinburgh Review*, 40 (1824), 270.
[33] Wilberforce, *Appeal*, 69–70. This speech is partly reproduced in Hurwitz, *Politics and Public Conscience*, 110.

with the merchants and manufacturers of Leeds, demanded free trade and an end to the sugar duties in a gesture clearly directed against the West Indian planter interest.[34] (Most of the older cities, like Bristol, which had a stake in the West Indian economy, predictably came out on the opposite side.[35]) In these thriving communities Adam Smith's analysis of slavery was likely to make more of an impact than unadulterated appeals to the conscience.

We can examine this revamped version of the economic case against slavery in its full, confident flowering from the 1820s onwards through three influential tracts: James Cropper's Address of 1823 to the Liverpool Society of Abolitionists on *The Injurious Effects of High Prices of Produce, and the Beneficial Effects of Low Prices*; Harriet Martineau's 'Tale', *Demarara*, part of her *Illustrations of Political Economy*, published in 1832 (commissioned by Brougham for the Society for the Diffusion of Useful Knowledge); and Josiah Conder's *Wages or the Whip* of 1833.

Cropper's importance lay in the way that he reconciled the economic critique of slavery with the earlier, religiously inspired abolition movement. James Cropper was an East Indian trader (and, as such, had a vested interest in the destruction of the West Indian monopoly). Brion Davis characterizes him as 'a prototype of the self-made entrepreneurs who were transforming the British economy'.[36] Cropper, a zealous Quaker, had once agonized over whether profits were compatible with Christianity, until, in Davis's words, his doubts were 'largely resolved by his discovery of *The Wealth of Nations*', which 'became for him a second bible, whose laws were to be no more questioned than the Ten Commandments'.[37]

Cropper was not the only 'economist' to have strong moral objections to slavery stemming from his religious convictions. Martineau, who came from a family of Unitarians, hurled anathemas against 'the tremendous *sin* [my italics] of holding man as property'; and her use, in this context, of words like penitence and atonement testifies to the intensity of her religious feelings on the subject.[38] As for Josiah Conder, he was an author who wrote countless books which were imbued by his Dissenting faith.[39]

Yet Cropper, Martineau, and Conder all started off from the proposition that slavery was an anachronism and an economic absurdity. 'The cultivation by slaves', contended Cropper, was 'no less strongly marked by folly than by wickedness, and therefore [could] only exist when aided by monopolies and bounties, and must cease in a competition with free labour.' Slavery indeed stood condemned by the

---

[34] J. Walvin, 'The Rise of British Popular Sentiment for Abolition 1787–1832', in Bolt and Drescher (eds.), *Anti-Slavery, Religion and Reform*, 156.

[35] I. Gross has shown that in the 'new' boroughs, 80 per cent of MPs opposed generous terms for the slave holders, as against 51 per cent of the MPs from the 'old' boroughs. Support for abolition ran at much lower levels in the counties ('The Abolition of Negro Slavery and British Parliamentary Politics 1832–3', *Historical Journal*, 23 (1980), 80–4).

[36] See discussion in Davis, *Slavery and Human Progress*, 180–3.   [37] Ibid., 180.

[38] H. Martineau, *The Moral of Many Fables* (London, 1834), 27–30.

[39] Conder, a Congregationalist, served as editor of the *Patriot*, the organ of evangelical nonconformity. He was also a preacher and author of many devotional works (see entry in *DNB*).

principles of Christianity; but, he argued, these principles alone would not be sufficient to persuade men to follow righteousness, whereas they might be expected to advance their own self-interest by observing the laws of political economy. 'Is it not reasonable', Cropper asked, 'to suppose that these are the means appointed by the supreme Governor of the universe, for the extinction of slavery, where higher motives have failed to effect it?'[40]

Conder agreed. The pressure of self-interest, he argued, would prove irresistible now that it was 'all but universally admitted' that free labour cost less than slave labour. (Harriet Martineau reached the conclusion that it was at least 25 per cent cheaper.[41]) As a result, Conder felt confident that 'the produce of free labour would soon drive that of slave labour out of the market, were it not for the bounties and protecting duties which [had] hitherto enabled the West India planter to maintain, not a fair competition, but an odious and pernicious monopoly'.[42] The merit of free labour, he claimed, was that it harnessed the powerful force of self-interest by holding out the prospect of personal gain.[43] However, it is significant that Conder was not entirely sure that the wage system would by itself replace the whip as an efficient spur to hard work once the West Indian slaves were emancipated; the 'safety and beneficial results of any plan of emancipation', he observed, 'would very greatly depend upon the facilities that should be afforded to the self-denying and persevering labours of the Missionaries, who exert so powerful an influence over the slave population' and whose help would be needed to inculcate 'steady industry, sobriety, and fidelity to their employers'.[44]

No such doubts restrained Martineau, who contrasted the situation in the West Indies, where the slaves were constantly protesting about their work and trying to shirk it, with England, where 'lazy people [were] punished by having their work taken from them; there being plenty of industrious labourers who [were] glad to get it'.[45]

But the economic liberals did not rest their case on the claim that freedom would stimulate the labourer to work harder. Conder, for example, also thought that emancipation would provide

a security to the employer, to whom it gives a certain hold upon the party contracting to perform it. If that voluntary contract is not fulfilled, a substantial ground of reasonable complaint is afforded, of which the law would take cognizance. The labourer might justly be punished in such case by suitable penalties.[46]

[40] J. Cropper, *A Letter Addressed to the Liverpool Society for Promoting the Abolition of Slavery On the Injurious Effects of High Prices of Produce, and the Beneficial Effects of Low Prices, On The Condition of Slaves* (Liverpool, 1823), 4, 6, 23.   [41] Martineau, *Demarara*, 74.

[42] Conder, *Wages or the Whip*, 2, 38–9.   [43] Ibid., 80–1.

[44] Ibid., 90. A similar line of argument had earlier been used by J. Anderson in his *Observations on Slavery*, 25.

[45] Martineau, *Demarara*, 11. A clear allusion is here being made to Poor Law reform. See below.

[46] Conder, *Wages Or The Whip*, 81. Archbishop Whately, a committed abolitionist, added an argument of his own: that slavery was dangerous because the slave could not be expected to understand the moral claims of private property (E. J. Whately, *Life and Correspondence of Richard Whately* (1875), 329–30).

In addition, the employer of free labour enjoyed the advantage of being able to discharge his employees when the market had no need of them. Martineau made the point with her customary tactlessness: 'As the supply of slave-labour does not rise and fall with the wants of the capitalist, like that of free labour, he employs his occasional surplus on works which could be better done by brute labour or machinery.'[47]

However, if the employment of free labour was so much more profitable than that of slave labour, what justification was there for compensating the planters for emancipation? On this issue Cropper took a pragmatic line, admitting that 'the change from a bad system to a better may be attended with temporary loss'. It was anyhow cheaper for the country to pay an indemnity to the slave-owners rather than continuing to support the current 'system of crime and oppression'.[48]

However, a few years later the free-trade abolitionists were less willing to be conciliatory. Conder called for immediate and unconditional emancipation, arguing that this would 'carry compensation with it' by rescuing the planter 'from the effect of the standing economical blunder in which he [had] so long and so fatally persisted'.[49] These views were eagerly cited by free-trade Radical MPs hostile to 'wasting' taxpayers' money in 'buying out' the West Indian planters. James Silk Buckingham, for example, denied the legality of 'property in the persons of the slaves to be liberated' and asserted that 'it had been proved, by evidence the most unimpeachable, that free labour was in the end more profitable than slave labour; and, therefore, the proprietors of estates would be rather gainers than losers by the transition from one to the other'.[50] (As John Stuart Mill later argued, this was to confuse the comparative effectiveness of free and slave labour *to the community*, an issue which he thought had been decisively resolved in favour of free labour, with the more open question of whether or not slave-owners would *personally* lose by the emancipation of their slaves.[51])

The advocates of free labour lost their fight against compensation. But five years later, during a parliamentary debate on ending the apprenticeship system, Brougham, a veteran abolitionist, tried to reopen the campaign, going so far as to argue that the £20 million of compensation which the employers had earlier received for the liberation of their slaves had been quite unjustified. The aim had been to offset the loss which the slave-owners were thought likely to incur. But, said Brougham, the sugar plantations were flourishing under a system of free labour, as people like himself had always predicted. The money had thus been 'paid under a mistake in fact', and should in some form or another be repaid, as it would undoubtedly have been 'if such a transaction had happened between private parties'.[52]

---

[47] Martineau, *Demarara*, 142.   [48] Cropper, *Letter*, 26–7.
[49] Conder, *Wages or the Whip*, 91.
[50] Hansard, ix, 1068: 22 July 1833; ibid., 1268: 25 July 1833. On Buckingham, see B. Harrison, 'Two Roads to Social Reform: Francis Place and the "Drunken Committee" of 1834', *Historical Journal*, 11 (1968), 273–4.
[51] The latter, Mill argued, would depend on the numbers of the labouring population, compared with the capital and the land, a ratio which varied over time and space (Mill, *Principles of Political Economy*, in id., *Collected Works*, ii. 249).   [52] Hansard, xl, 1301: 20 Feb. 1838.

Arguments concerning the impropriety of owning slaves had aroused relat- ively few objections (except, of course, from the West Indian interest) so long as it was widely accepted that slavery was unprofitable as well as immoral: the dictates of morality and the prompting of self-interest seemed to go hand in hand. Even those abolitionists whose quarrel with slavery stemmed from their religious con- victions were prepared to accept the reasoning of the economic liberals.

But Brougham's 1838 picture of a thriving West Indian sugar industry was already beginning to look implausible, even before the end of apprenticeship in that year led to a further alarming decline in sugar exports: in Jamaica it had almost halved by 1840. Similarly, whereas Harriet Martineau had predicted that the freeing of the slaves would cause the population to increase,[53] in fact many negro women refused to work and sent their children to school, thereby creating a labour short- age which pushed up wage levels.[54] As the planters had feared would happen, pro- ductivity on their estates declined, prices rose, and exports inevitably suffered. On the eve of emancipation West Indian produce still constituted about 80 per cent of imported British sugar, but by the mid-1840s (even before the tariff changes) it amounted to little more than 50 per cent, by which time it was costing British consumers double what they would have paid in the world markets.[55]

In effect, the British Parliament, by abolishing first the slave trade and then slavery, had displaced the problem but not resolved it. For slavery continued to thrive in other parts of America, and indeed was actually stimulated by abolition in the British colonies. As the price of West Indian sugar rose, Britain turned increasingly to Brazil and Cuba, causing those countries to increase their imports of slaves from Africa.[56] The terrible truth began to dawn on some abolitionists: free-grown produce was not necessarily the cheapest available.[57]

What to do? Giving a preferential advantage to West Indian over foreign slave- grown sugar provided one obvious solution. But it meant an abandonment of free trade, the pillar of the ideology of market liberalism. Prior to emancipation in 1833, radical abolitionists, including Cropper, had called for an equalization of the sugar duties in the hope of shifting home consumption away from the products of the West Indian slave plantations to free produce grown in the East Indies.[58] But after 1833 many abolitionists wanted to *retain* colonial preference in order to help the struggling West Indian islands fend off the 'unfair' competition of Cuba and Brazil.

[53] Martineau, *Demarara*, 99.

[54] C. Bolt, *The Anti-Slavery Movement and Reconstruction* (London, 1969), 18. James Stephen, in his book *Crisis of the Sugar Colonies* (London, 1802), had already clearly explained why voluntary labour could not drive out slave labour in the West Indies purely on economic grounds (S. Drescher, *Econocide: British Slavery in the Era of Abolition* (Pittsburgh, 1977), 156).

[55] Turley, *Antislavery*, 14; H. Temperley, 'Capitalism, Slavery and Ideology', *Past & Present*, 75 (1977), 101.

[56] H. Temperley, 'Capitalism, Slavery and Ideology', *Past & Present*, 75 (1977), 104.

[57] Bolt, *Anti-Slavery Movement*, 19.

[58] Turley, *Antislavery*, 36. The *Slave* promoted the free produce movement, especially via the Quaker Richardson family in Newcastle, and similar propaganda was also carried by Brougham in the *Edinburgh Review* and by Perronet Thompson in the *Westminster* (ibid., 48–9).

Yet, in the event, Parliament chose to do the exact opposite: in 1846 it voted for the equalization of the sugar duties, which had the consequence of removing the protection given to the colonial producers and helping the economies of the slave societies. Four years later, over one-third of the sugar consumed in Britain was foreign, mainly slave-grown.[59]

The dispute over the sugar duties split the abolitionist movement into two contending factions.[60] To many anti-slavery campaigners, goods produced under the auspices of slavery were stolen property which no honest man or government should handle.[61] That was why Joseph Sturge, an active member of the Anti-Corn Law League, was prepared to provide fiscal encouragement for the producers of 'free' sugar.[62] Abolitionists of this school argued that they, too, supported the general principle of free trade but that trafficking in human beings was wrong, as was any activity which encouraged that trafficking.[63] The Quakers in Sturge's circle believed that 'Cobden and Co', by abandoning this position, had sold their souls for free trade.[64] The Irish leader Daniel O'Connell agreed: 'I would not consent to give the people of England, or of Ireland either, cheap sugar at the expense of robbery and stealing', he declared, 'and I will not consent to give it to them by the murder of the Negro.'[65] A similar line was taken by Brougham; commenting retrospectively on equalization, he told Parliament that 'by a gross perversion of the doctrines of free trade, we resolved to obtain cheap sugar at the heavier cost of piracy, and torture, and blood'.[66]

But many abolitionists were not abashed by these admonitions, citing Adam Smith in their support. Cropper, for example, continued to argue that slave labour was so inefficient in comparison with wage labour that the foreign slave-owners would before long be driven by financial necessity to see the merits of emancipation.[67] Despite mounting evidence to the contrary, they obstinately blamed the crisis in the West Indian islands upon temporary factors and accidents.[68] 'To put down slavery', argued the anti-Sturgeite, James Ritchie, 'we have only to let free labour have fair play. It is not the continuance of monopoly, but emigration, that is wanted . . . To put down slavery . . . we must under-sell the slave dealer.'[69]

---

[59] Bolt, *Anti-Slavery Movement*, 20. The 1846 measure phased in the equalization of the sugar duties over five years.

[60] On the splits within the British and Foreign Anti-Slavery Society, see Turley, *Antislavery*, 103.

[61] A. Tyrrell, *Joseph Sturge and the Moral Radical Party in Early Victorian Britain* (London, 1987), 141.

[62] Turley, however, suggests that Sturge was not abandoning his free trade convictions, merely appealing for 'a temporary maintenance of fiscal intervention by the liberal state to bring about the circumstances for the equal competition which would permit the cessation of that intervention' (*Antislavery*, 149).   [63] H. Temperley, *British Antislavery 1833–1870* (London, 1972), 154–5.

[64] Tyrrell, *Sturge*, 141.

[65] C. D. Rice, '"Humanity Sold For Sugar!": The British Abolitionist Response to Free Trade in Slave-Grown Sugar', *Historical Journal*, 13 (1970), 414. O'Connell was himself a committed free trader.

[66] Hansard, cxxxix, 116: 26 June 1855.   [67] Tyrrell, *Sturge*, 48.

[68] Temperley, 'Capitalism, Slavery and Ideology', 111.

[69] J. E. Ritchie, *Thoughts on Slavery and Cheap Sugar: A Letter to the Members and Friends of the British and Foreign Anti-Slavery Society* (c.1844), 24, 26.

The free traders possessed yet another 'moral' argument: the well-being of the West Indian freedmen, they contended, had to be balanced against the suffering of the labouring population at home.[70] Free trade, boasted Ritchie, would benefit 'the over-taxed and under-fed hard-working men and women of Great Britain' who wanted cheap sugar.[71]

Not content with defending their convictions, the free traders moved onto the offensive. John Bright, for one, lambasted Sturge for following a policy that aligned him with the supporters of monopoly, a system which had wrought nothing but mischief and evil.[72] And Cobden opposed Sturge's London Committee's views on sugar duties as 'utterly impractical': 'commerce cannot be bound and cramped in the way you propose', he complained.[73] Ill-judged attempts to excommunicate slave-based products from the international economy would only do more harm than good. (Free traders like Cobden also pointed out the illogicality of this sort of fiscal discrimination, when the Lancashire cotton industry depended so heavily on slave-grown cotton: another 'abuse', but one which no one seriously suggested should be countered by a manipulation of the tariff.[74])

Running parallel with the sugar duties dispute was the disagreement over whether the British should continue to employ the Africa Squadron in an attempt to apprehend foreign slave-trading ships. In his determination to extirpate slavery, Sturge was prepared to suspend his Quaker pacifist principles, believing that force was morally justifiable if it succeeded in putting down a monstrous evil—a position he held in common with the author of the anonymous pamphlet, *Free Trade in Negroes* (1849), which called for the armed suppression of the slave trade involving Spain and Brazil. Some abolitionists wanted to put slave-trading on to the same footing as piracy.[75] Brougham sympathized with this approach.[76] So too, as it happened, did Lord John Russell and Lord Palmerston, and as a result the Africa Squadron was kept in being until 1867–8.[77]

But in the eyes of many doctrinaire free traders there were no advantages, only political dangers, in trying to impede commercial dealings in slave-grown produce. Ritchie, for example, claimed that naval blockades did not work and were anyhow expensive.[78] W. R. Greg agreed: Wilberforce, he declared, had been entirely misguided when, after wisely persuading the legislature to prohibit the traffic in slaves to British subjects, he had then induced the Government to attempt the *armed repression* of the trade—a short cut which, looking to consequences rather than

---

[70] Turley, *Antislavery*, 146–8.

[71] Ritchie, *Slavery and Cheap Sugar*, 28–9. See also Turley, *Antislavery*, 148.

[72] Tyrrell, *Sturge*, 141.   [73] Temperley, *British Antislavery*, 154.

[74] No less a person than Cropper had been an importer of American slave-grown cotton, as John Gladstone had delightedly pointed out (Davis, *Slavery and Human Progress*, 184–5).

[75] Hansard, ci, 365: 22 Aug. 1848 (Lord Denman).

[76] Ibid., 372–4: 22 Aug. 1848. Brougham referred to 'a most trumpery and most ignorant misapplication of the principles of free frade', principles which had no connection whatever with 'crimes—with robbery, piracy, and murder'.

[77] C. Lloyd, *The Navy and the Slave Trade: The Suppression of the African Slave Trade in the 19th Century* (London, 1949), 182.   [78] Ritchie, *Slavery and Cheap Sugar*, 18–19.

causes, had unwittingly worsened the negro's sufferings.[79] There was much truth in Greg's complaint since, as Christine Bolt explains, the provision of various anti-slave treaties simply made the foreign slave traders more callous: they now packed their human cargoes more tightly together and threw slaves overboard if sighted and pursued by British vessels.[80]

Greg's critique of the Africa Squadron went further. 'The supply of slaves, as of everything else', he contended, was 'created by the demand for them. Annihilate that demand, and the supply will cease.' But demand would continue until it had at last been conclusively demonstrated to the entire world, by experiments, that 'slavery [was] an expensive and unwise system'.[81] Meanwhile, as Greg and others protested, the Africa Squadron was wreaking considerable mischief by interfering with the development of normal commerce on both sides of the Atlantic. Greg was particularly impatient with Buxton's attempt to establish 'legitimate trade' with Africa: 'Commerce cannot be *established*', argued this dedicated free trader: 'It must grow up out of natural causes. Commerce is not to be *encouraged*,—it is to be let alone. It never yet throve under *encouragement*.'[82]

Many abolitionists, the Quakers in particular, therefore stuck by their belief that slavery must be combated 'by the employment of those means which are of a moral, religious, and pacific character'.[83] Gladstone concurred with these conclusions, denying the accuracy of the parallel between slave-trading and piracy:

although [slave-trading] is morally a far greater crime than piracy, by the law of nations it is not regarded as so great a crime; and it differs from piracy in this, that hideous as is its moral character, yet it has, if you look to its exterior merely, all the conditions of a great branch of commerce.[84]

Cobden, too, pressed for the disbandment of the Africa Squadron. 'If the armed cruisers can be justified to put down the slave trade', he reasoned with Sturge, 'they may be defended for any purpose'—besides which, their maintenance was a wicked waste of money.[85]

There was only one weakness in this approach: it was based on wishful thinking. Even the British and Foreign Anti-Slavery Society (BFASS) reluctantly came round to admitting that the evidence no longer supported the older view

---

[79] By forcing the slave traders to adopt more inhumane methods in their quest to avoid the vigilance of British cruisers (W. R. Greg, 'Prostitution', *Westminster Review*, 53 (1850), 489–90). Greg had earlier argued the same case in his pamphlet *Past and Present Efforts for the Extinction of the African Slave Trade* (London, 1840), in which he had accused the Evangelical party of having committed a 'crime' as a result of their 'want of severe and scientific thought' (44).

[80] Bolt, *Anti-Slavery Movement*, 21.   [81] Greg, *Extinction of African Slave Trade*, 53, 59.

[82] Ibid., 23.   [83] Bolt, *Anti-Slavery Movement*, 22.   [84] Hansard, cix, 1167: 19 Mar. 1850.

[85] Cobden to Sturge, 31 Dec. 1850, *Cobden Papers* (British Library, Add Mss 43, 656, fos. 174–6). Bright and Gladstone also joined in the campaign for the disbandment of the Africa Squadron, a campaign spearheaded by the Radical free trader, William Hutt, MP for Gateshead (W. L. Mathieson, *Great Britain and the Slave Trade, 1839–65* (New York, 1967), 94–7, 104–11; Lloyd, *Suppression of African Slave Trade*, 107–8); Hansard, civ, 782–7, 803–4: 24 Apr. 1849).

that slavery was doomed to disappear.[86] On the other hand, fiscal discrimination and attempts at the forcible suppression of slave trading merely succeeded in splitting the abolitionist movement.

However, there remained a third strategy behind which all parties could rally, and that was the consumer boycott. Such methods had first been tried in the 1790s, and later in the 1820s (greatly stimulated by Elizabeth Heyrick's famous 1824 pamphlet, *Immediate, not Gradual Abolition*). Then the target had, of course, been West Indian sugar, but after emancipation, efforts switched to attempts at reducing the consumption of slave-grown sugar from countries like Cuba and Brazil.

Later in the century the free-produce movement broadened out to cover *all* goods in which slaves had been employed. No such produce found its way into Sturge's own household.[87] Moreover, in the late 1840s and early 1850s special free-produce stores were set up in London and Manchester.[88] In the middle years of the century these activities became increasingly important as attention shifted to the plight of the slaves in the American South. Sturge committed the BFASS to support of free-labour cotton and sought to enlist the support of 'hundreds of philanthropic capitalists' in a plan to establish a network of 'factories and shops for the manufacture & sale of Free Labor Cotton',[89] while Bright, himself a cotton spinner, took an active part in trying to persuade the Government to support cotton-growing in India, to limit Lancashire's embarrassing dependence on the American South.[90]

Some cotton masters, it is true, continued to rehearse the old free-trade arguments right into mid-century, partly, no doubt, because they had an obvious material interest in maintaining a regular supply of cheap American plantation-grown cotton and were by no means sure that a satisfactory substitute existed.[91] Even after the American Civil War had broken out, there were those who still wrote, with apparent sincerity, in favour of leaving slavery to collapse under the weight of its own contradictions.

Notable here is J. E. Cairnes's well-publicized book, *The Slave Power* (1863). Using arguments that had changed little since the days of Adam Smith, Cairnes summed up the case against slave labour under three headings: it was, he claimed, given reluctantly, it was unskilful, and it lacked versatility. Free labour's superiority could be seen in the prosperity enjoyed by the northern states of America, contrasting, as this did, with the sad state of the backward plantation economy.[92]

---

[86] Greg himself conceded that the sugar duties could not be equalized immediately, while urging the West Indian planters not to expect permanent, or protracted, protection (*Extinction of African Slave Trade*, 92–7). [87] Tyrrell, *Sturge*, 141.

[88] Temperley, *British Antislavery*, 165–6.   [89] Tyrrell, *Sturge*, 164.

[90] G. R. Searle, *Entrepreneurial Politics in Mid-Victorian Britain* (Oxford, 1993), 316–17.

[91] Turley, *Antislavery*, 14–15, 127.

[92] J. E. Cairnes, *The Slave Power: Its Character, Career and Probable Designs*, 2nd edn. (London, 1863), 44, 146. See the interesting analysis in Davis, *Slavery and Human Progress*, 244–54. A similar argument can be found in the paper delivered by the Irish political economist, James Houghton (T. A. Boylan and T. P. Foley, *Political Economy and Colonial Ireland* (London, 1992), 143).

According to one historian, Cairnes's book 'presents an almost wholly fictional account of the South' but is nevertheless 'a very accurate description of what, according to the precepts of the classical school, the South *ought* to have been like'.[93] Little wonder if some prominent economic liberals showed reluctance to give whole-hearted backing to Lincoln's attempts to suppress slavery in the southern states by *force*.[94]

In general, though, slavery proved to be one of those issues on which the devotees of the free market never really succeeded in morally outfacing their opponents. Significantly, in 1844 the ultra free traders, led by George Thompson, failed to win over the BFASS to their way of thinking on the sugar duties issue, the first of many such failures.[95] How is this to be explained? The weakness of the free marketeers' position was twofold. First, slavery seemed to many of their countrymen to be an abuse so grave—a 'sin' in the eyes of God—that the normal 'laws' of social life would have to be suspended in its presence. Second, the Cobdenite case about the economic irrationality of slavery (and so their optimism about its inevitable disappearance) eventually lost much of its credibility.

Hence, the emergence of the consumer boycott movement, which was significant in several ways. For a start, it involved an attempt to moralize the market, not by transforming workshop relationships, but by mobilizing the energies of consumers. Once it was accepted that the *buyer* of slave-grown sugar or cotton had as much moral responsibility as the producer, shopping and consumption became an arena where important moral dramas were played out, important decisions made.[96] The amoral world of commercial transactions, it seemed, might need to be cleansed by the moral conscience of the consumer.

Second, this view of economic life, especially when it took the form of a boycott of slave-grown sugar, assigned a central place to women because it was they who usually took responsibility for the management of the household budget.[97] Indeed, from an early stage in the agitation, female abolitionists came to see the consumer boycott as an activity which very much fell within their own sphere: and this, as Clare Midgley puts it, helped reinforce the idea of a separation between 'women as controllers of household consumption, [and] men as managers of commercial and industrial enterprises'.[98] Abolitionism thus made an important contribution to the prevalent Victorian notion that women were in many ways the superiors

---

[93] Temperley, 'Capitalism, Slavery and Ideology', 111–13. But for a powerful critique of the view that slavery was incapable of generating capitalist growth, see J. Ashworth, *Slavery, Capitalism and Politics in the Antebellum Republic*, i, *Commerce and Compromise, 1820–1850* (Cambridge, 1995), chs. 2, 4.

[94] See Ch. 9.   [95] Rice, 'Humanity Sold for Sugar!', 414–15.

[96] Midgley, *Women Against Slavery*, 201–2. This formed part of what she calls 'bringing home' the issue of slavery.

[97] Turley, *Antislavery*, 79; Midgley, *Women against Slavery*, 138–9. Mrs Bessie Inglis opened a 'free-labour depot' in London in May 1853, and this depot had links, via the Ladies' Olive Leaf Circles, with the League of Universal Brotherhood, which contained many Quaker ladies.

[98] Midgley, *Women against Slavery*, 201–2. Midgley also notes that many women placed the emphasis on *not eating*, rather than *not buying*—thereby foreshadowing the later temperance movement (ibid., 35–6). See also C. Midgley, 'Anti-Slavery and Feminism in Nineteenth-Century Britain', *Gender and History*, 5 (1993), 357.

of men in that their sympathies were more highly developed, their moral antennae more finely tuned. As such, they were often assigned a vital role in the 'policing' of economic life, in order to detect and warn against activities that were morally obnoxious.[99]

To conclude: in the early years of abolitionism the moral and the economic arguments against slavery had been developed, to some extent, in isolation from one another. By the mid-1820s they had drawn together: abolitionists could take comfort from the thought that self-interest and the dictates of conscience pointed to the same outcome. Slavery was evil, but it was also economically irrational, and if this was emphasized often enough and clearly enough, even the planters could be made to see that they would benefit from the suppression of their way of life.

But by the 1850s the wheel had turned full circle, as the moral and economic arguments about slavery began to diverge. What, then, ought to be done about an evil system which showed few signs of disintegrating? On this practical issue the abolitionist movement was divided. But by the 1850s it was generally agreed, over the objections of a few obstinate free marketeers, that boundaries would have to be drawn, so as to demarcate legitimate trade, which could safely be regulated by the operation of the laws of political economy, from a nefarious 'traffic', which was offensive in God's eyes.[100] Slave-owners, declared George Thompson, were 'mammon worshippers', the holders of 'polluted, blood-stained money'.[101] As Brian Harrison observes, 'real' businessmen had to be differentiated from these barbaric criminals if the middle classes were to establish their claim to provide a 'moral leadership for society as a whole'.[102]

But here was a distinction which, once established, was capable of being applied to spheres of social life other than slavery. For example, it later became a commonplace that the Christian must not trade in *any* articles that were themselves illicit or immoral.[103]

Meanwhile, almost everyone could agree on the evils of slavery. Christians insisted on the necessity of human beings having freedom of moral choice. Political economists, however, approached the problem from a different angle. No longer able to argue with confidence that slavery 'did not pay', they now made more of the argument that a market economy presupposed human beings who could 'freely' enter into contracts—a situation which slavery precluded. Moreover, political economy, from Adam Smith's time onwards, had treated as axiomatic the *separation* between capital and labour. But, as Harriet Martineau complained in *Demarara*, the slave-owner was perversely mixing up the two categories by *converting his capital into labour*.[104]

---

[99] See Ch. 7.
[100] The *Morning Post*, denouncing what it called 'free trade in human blood', opined that, as far as most British citizens were concerned, 'the experiment of free trade' applied 'to matters only of legitimate commerce' (Mathieson, *Great Britain and Slave Trade*, 111).
[101] Hurwitz, *Politics and Public Conscience*, 141.   [102] Harrison, 'Genealogy of Reform', 131–2.
[103] H. Bushnell, 'How to be a Christian in Trade', in *Sermons on Living Subjects* (London, 1872), 254.
[104] Martineau, *Demarara*, 142.

Writing a half century after Martineau, T. H. Green repeated her denial that human beings could rightly become the property of other men: 'A contract by which any one agreed for a certain consideration to become the slave of another we should reckon a void contract', he declared.[105] Because human beings were the *authors* of market transactions, they must never be treated as their *objects*.

WAGE SLAVERY?

One of the weaknesses in the arguments of the abolitionists was that they over-looked both the element of co-operation inherent in most slave societies and the element of coercion associated with many kinds of wage labour.[106] The second of these considerations aroused particular anxiety. Was the selling of human beings, on a moral level, that much more offensive than the selling of *wage* labour, given that in practice labourers enjoyed little freedom in accepting or rejecting their employers' terms?

During the famous Preston Lock-Out of 1853–4, one Lancastrian manufacturer told his 'hands' that he wished 'to [buy] their labour, fairly to pay for it, and to be as independent and uncontrolled in the purchase as he [was] in the purchase of hats, clothes, or shoes—free to buy where he likes, and where he can do so cheapest'. Writing seven years later, another Lancastrian businessman, Edmund Potter, agreed: 'Labour must be considered as a mere purchaseable article, like all other commodities, and ought to be bought and sold, and weighed and measured accordingly.'[107] How, then, did the operation of the labour market differ from the transactions of the slave trade, if indeed it differed at all?

Some critics of the early factory system of the industrial north, like Richard Oastler, thought the difference very slight. In his famous letter to the *Leeds Mercury* in 1830 on 'Yorkshire Slavery' he declared: 'The blacks may be fairly compared to beasts of burden, *kept for their master's use*, the whites, to those *which others keep and let for hire*.' At least the slave-owner had an interest in taking rudimentary care of the human beings whom he owned, whereas the children who worked in the Yorkshire woollen mills (who were anyhow, as minors, incapable of making meaningful contracts) were 'doomed to labour from morning to night for one who cares not how soon your weak and tender frames are stretched to breaking!' That was why, in Oastler's view, 'the miserable inhabitants of a *Yorkshire town*' were living 'in a state of slavery, *more horrid* than [were] the victims of that hellish system, "*colonial slavery*"'.[108] In his heated defence of the London tailors,

---

[105] T. H. Green, 'Lecture on Liberal Legislation and Freedom of Contract', in R. L. Nettleship (ed.), *Works of Thomas Hill Green* (1880), iii. 372–3. Perhaps, by analogy, it was almost as invalid for a woman to make a contractual agreement to sell her own body: see Ch. 10.

[106] Davis, *Slavery and Human Progress*, 254.

[107] Cited in Searle, *Entrepreneurial Politics*, 271–3.

[108] C. Driver, *Tory Radical: The Life of Richard Oastler* (New York, 1946), 42–4.

victims of the notorious sweated system, Charles Kingsley, writing twenty years later, similarly asked why, having emancipated the black slaves, we should not now set about emancipating the white ones.[109]

Naturally the slave-owners complained about 'double standards', and these complaints were echoed, in his earlier writings, by William Cobbett.[110] The standard complaint raised by such critics of abolitionism (subsequently echoed by many left-wing historians) was that the attacks on slavery were mounted either to distract attention from appalling working conditions at home or else to make the conditions of wage labourers seem better than they were by comparison with a highly coloured depiction of the barbarities being practised on the slave plantations.[111] 'The great emancipators of negro slaves were the great drivers of white slaves', one of them declared.[112] Indeed, Cobbett's contempt for Wilberforce's 'humbug' spilled over into sneering references to the easy lives being led by the 'fat and lazy negro that laughs from morning to night'.[113] So exasperated were some Chartists by what they saw as the self-serving hypocrisy of the abolitionists, that they even took to breaking up anti-slavery meetings.[114]

But the working-class Radicals took their critique of slavery much further than a mere denunciation of double standards. Unlike Cobbett and Oastler who, in their different ways, were advocating a revived paternalism, the Chartists propagated a concept of 'emancipation' which embraced universal male suffrage, because they believed, as older Radicals had also done, that those denied political rights were themselves submerged in a kind of slavery.[115]

Working-class Radicals also had more fundamental criticisms to make concerning the economic dimensions of wage labour. Bronterre O'Brien, for example, argued that, though slavery was deplorable, 'to emancipate the Negro in a capitalist society was to pass him from chattel slavery to the "more servile and more profitable"

[109] C. Kingsley, 'Cheap Clothes and Nasty', by 'Parson Lot', in *Alton Locke: Tailor and Poet* (London, 1895; first pub. 1850), pp. lxxiii–lxxiv. For Kingsley's invocation of the superior morality of his idealized version of 'feudalism', see ibid., 19.

[110] This marks Cobbett off from Oastler, who professed an antipathy to slavery in *all* its manifestations, declaring that he was proud to have been hit on the temple by a stone aimed at Wilberforce (C. Gallagher, *The Industrial Reformation of English Fiction 1832–1867* (Chicago, 1985), 22–3).

[111] No attempt can be made here to assess the validity of this charge, which has generated an enormous literature. But it is worth remembering Howard Temperley's wise words: 'it [was] no more unusual to find humanitarians using economic arguments than to find their opponents using humanitarian ones' ('Capitalism, Slavery and Ideology', 97).

[112] Hollis, 'Anti-Slavery and British Working-Class Radicalism', in Bolt and Drescher (eds.), *Anti-Slavery, Religion and Reform*, 298.   [113] Ibid., 296–7; Bolt, *Anti-Slavery Movement*, 3.

[114] Hollis, 'Anti-Slavery', in Bolt and Drescher (eds.), *Anti-Slavery*, 309–11. However, it has been pointed out that by no means all working-class radicals took this view and that, on the contrary, many of them saw the struggle against slavery as part of a wider battle for the emancipation of mankind (J. Walvin, 'Rise of British Popular Sentiment', in Bolt and Drescher (eds.), *Anti-Slavery*, 155; B. Fladeland, '"Our Cause Being One and the Same": Abolitionists and Chartism', in J. Walvin (ed.), *Slavery and British Society 1776–1846* (London, 1982), 69–99; B. Fladeland, *Abolitionists and Working-Class Politics in the Age of Industrialization* (Baton Rouge, La., 1984)). Additional support for this view can be found in Midgley, *Women against Slavery*, 151–2.

[115] Gallagher, *Industrial Reformation*, 29–31.

state of wage slavery, where he would be worse off'; better, thought O'Brien, that the Negro remained 'unfree'.[116] This line of argument was developed further by the socialists. Not for nothing has Engels's *The Condition of the Working Class in England* been called 'one of the greatest of antislavery tracts'.[117]

The socialists had good grounds for their suspicions. After all, to quote Brion Davis, Adam Smith had argued that 'where[as] the rich planter was inattentive to high costs of maintenance, the manager of free labour, being frugal, parsimonious and efficient, kept wages as low as possible', a position which implied that 'wage-earners received less return for their labour than did slaves'.[118] We have already seen Harriet Martineau later making this point in the bluntest possible way.

Nor, as Davis had suggested, can it have been a coincidence that 1834, which saw the nominal emancipation of West Indian slaves, was also the year of the Poor Law Amendment Act which 'liberated the English workers from public welfare and offered the unemployed a choice between starvation and the humiliating work-house'.[119] After all, the economic radicals, Martineau to the fore, explicitly linked their attacks on slavery to an advocacy of a free and untrammelled labour market.

From the 1820s onwards the links between anti-slavery and the ideology of free trade became even more conspicuous.[120] Significantly, a majority of anti-slavery MPs either supported the New Poor Law or abstained, just as abolition-ists, though initially split on how best to regulate the labour market, increasingly came out against any legislative interference except for the protection of children.[121] Advocates of *laissez-faire* made similar connections: for example, the youthful Cobden claimed that to escape the operation of legislation which 'regulated or interfered with the labour of the working classes' signified 'the transition from a state of slavery to that of freedom',[122] while a half-century later, Herbert Spencer was declaring that 'all socialism involve[d] slavery' because it obliged the individual to labour 'under coercion to satisfy another's desires'—in his view, slavery's defining characteristic.[123]

However, the legacy of abolitionism was ambiguous. If, on the one hand, its most immediate consequence was to accelerate the move towards the freeing-up of the labour market, it also gave the critics of doctrinaire economic liberalism considerable ammunition. For many anti-slavery crusaders felt deep sympathy for the victims of *all* kinds of exploitation, and these emotions led some of them, Wilberforce included, into tracing a parallel between factory children at home and

---

[116] O'Brien's views are summarized by Hollis, 'Anti-Slavery', in Bolt and Drescher (eds.), *Anti-Slavery*, 299. See also Bronterre O'Brien's *Rise, Progress, and Phases of Human Slavery: How It Came into the World, and How It Shall Be Made To Go Out*, published in *Reynolds's Political Instructor*, from 17 Nov. 1849, cited in M. C. Finn, *After Chartism: Class and Nation in English Radical Politics, 1848–1874* (Cambridge, 1993), 116.

[117] D. B. Davis, *The Problem of Slavery in the Age of Revolution, 1770–1823* (Ithaca, NY, 1975), 467–8.

[118] Davis, *Slavery in Western Culture*, 469.   [119] Davis, *Age of Revolution*, 357.

[120] Turley, *Antislavery*, 147.   [121] Ibid., 147–8.

[122] Cobden to W. C. Hunt, 21 Oct. 1836, in J. Morley, *The Life of Richard Cobden* (London, 1896; first pub. 1881), i. 465.

[123] H. Spencer, *The Man Versus the State*, ed. D. Macrae (1969; first pub. 1884), 100–1.

West Indian slaves.[124] Later humanitarian agitations also drew heavily upon the traditions of abolitionism: for example, Josephine Butler's advocacy of the rights of prostitutes owed much to her memories of the anti-slavery activities in which her family had played a prominent role.[125]

The outright enemies of capitalism also found it easy to turn the arguments of middle-class abolitionists against them, often citing the latter's own words in their assaults on the cruelties of wage labour. As far as the relationship between employers and employees were concerned, there were thus many 'lessons', not just one, to be drawn from the experiences of the anti-slavery struggle. The real significance of abolitionism was that it provided all sides to the argument with a compelling rhetoric and framework of reference.

WOMEN THE SLAVES OF MEN?

If it was wrong for any human being to sell himself into slavery, could a woman sell her own body, as though it were a commodity which had a market value? The issue of prostitution will be explored in Chapter 10. But the practice of wife-selling, isolated episodes of which took place throughout the nineteenth century, suggests that the taboo surrounding the commodification of people had a central place in Victorian middle-class ideology.

In *The Mayor of Casterbridge* Thomas Hardy makes the drunken Michael Henchard say: 'I don't see why men who have got wives and don't want 'em, shouldn't get rid of 'em as these gipsy fellows do their old horses . . . Why shouldn't they put 'em up and sell 'em by auction to men who are in need of such articles?'[126] Hardy's readers, however, treated the possibility of such depraved behaviour with incredulity.

Wife-sales customarily took the form of the woman being led by the halter to a marketplace and then 'knocked down' by the original husband to the highest bidder. Such events, which the press reported in sensationalist terms, were obviously illegal and could lead to both vendor and purchaser being prosecuted for conspiracy to corrupt public morals. However, as Samuel Menefee shows, wife-sales (rare enough occurrences in any case) took place in order to secure divorce and remarriage for those who could obtain this in no other way. Thus the 'purchaser' was often the lover of the wife being sold, the wife freely assenting to the change in her status, and most participants and onlookers apparently saw the ritual by

---

[124] Turley, *Antislavery*, 141.

[125] Midgley, *Women Against Slavery*, 173–4. As she wrote in a letter to M. Aimé Humbert in 1875, 'The cry of women crushed under the yoke of legalised vice is not the cry of a statistician or a medical expert; it is simply a cry of pain, a cry for justice and for a return to God's laws . . . the slave now speaks' (J. Butler, *Personal Reminiscences of a Great Crusade*, 2nd edn. (London, 1898), 188).

[126] T. Hardy, *The Life and Death of the Mayor of Casterbridge*, New Wessex edn. (London, 1975; first pub. 1886), 31–2.

which the transaction was surrounded, drawn from cattle fairs, as a means of regularizing and legitimizing the end of a marriage and the start of a new liaison.

Moreover, as Menefee shows, the wife was not being treated as a mere commodity since the 'selling price' was often derisorily small, clearly in no way proportionate to the services which a woman might render her new 'husband'.[127] This was in sharp contrast to the sale of slaves, which, so long as the law had allowed it, really had operated on straightforward commercial principles. Thus whereas in the late eighteenth century wives were being sold for as little as 10s. 6d., domestic slaves fetched £50 or more.[128] Some contemporaries anyhow thought that wife-sales were innocuous, compared with the 'Negro trade', since the wife 'was happy to think that she was going to have another Husband, for she well knew who would be the Purchaser'.[129] The crucial consideration was that of whether consent had been freely given. But, once again, it all depended upon what was meant by 'consent', there being so many intermediate stages in real life between total, unconditional, joyous approval and forced subjection.

Herbert Spencer was well aware of these complications. He categorized wife-and-husband-purchases as a feature of 'semi-civilized societies', rightly rejecting the idea that they were a significant contemporary phenomenon. But Spencer threw in an interesting afterthought. Whereas in their 'gross forms', such transactions had died out, he said, in more 'disguised forms' they could still be encountered in the modern world, where, despite intense popular disapproval, many people continued to 'marry for money or position'.[130] In other words, Spencer was well aware that *informal* arrangements continued whereby the choice of a marriage partner was partly determined by financial considerations.

Socialists often carried this argument a stage further, alleging that, under prevailing property arrangements, marriage was in essence little more than a form of prostitution. In bourgeois society, claimed Engels, 'the wife . . . differs from the ordinary courtesan only in that she does not hire out her body, like a wage-worker, on piecework, but sells it into slavery once for all',[131] a viewpoint also expressed, more coarsely, by the anonymous author of the pornographic *My Secret Life*.[132]

The orthodox defenders of capitalist society would have hotly denied all such claims. But many shared Spencer's disquiet over the existence of what amounted to an unofficial 'marriage market' in the higher reaches of society. The

[127] S. P. Menefee, *Wives for Sale: An Ethnographic Study of British Popular Divorce* (Oxford, 1981).
[128] Ibid., 157–60.
[129] Drescher, *Capitalism and Antislavery*, 175 fn. 36. The case being commented upon took place in York in 1787.
[130] H. Spencer, *The Principles of Sociology*, in id., *Synthetic Philosophy of Herbert Spencer*, Westminster edn. (New York, 1892–96), i–ii. 765.
[131] F. Engels, *Origin of Family, Private Property and State*, in Karl Marx and Frederick Engels, *Selected Works*, 2 vols. (Moscow, 1958), ii. 230.
[132] See the passage quoted in S. Marcus, *The Other Victorians: A Study of Sexuality and Pornography in Mid-Nineteenth Century England* (London, 1969; first pub. 1966), 159–60. It ends: 'Women are all bought in the market—from the whore to the Princess. The price alone is different, and the highest price, in money or rank, obtains the woman.'

moral dilemmas and personal miseries thus created were dramatized by many of the major Victorian novelists. For example, they constitute an important strand in Dickens's *Dombey and Son*, as well as featuring in several of Thackeray's novels, especially *The Newcomes*. 'We are as much sold as Turkish women', Thackeray makes Ethel Newcome say: 'There is no freedom for us. I wear my green ticket, and wait till my master comes. But every day as I think of our slavery, I revolt against it more.'[133] Trollope had similarly mordant observations to make about *marriage à la mode*.

Later in the century, unions between impecunious British aristocrats and wealthy American heiresses attracted the disapproving phrase 'gilded prostitution',[134] and by Edwardian times the eugenics movement was familiarizing people with the notion that marrying for money might be, not only morally wrong, but also biologically unwise.

Admittedly, few female abolitionists drew a direct connection between their own situation and the slaves they were trying to liberate. Thus, when Priscilla Buxton, who married on Emancipation Day (1 August 1834), was toasted with the wish 'that she might long rejoice in the fetters' she had just assumed 'as well as over those which she had assisted to break', no irony was intended. Precisely because they enjoyed the advantage of male protection conferred on them by the Christian institution of marriage, white middle-class females generally took the view that they had a duty to speak out on behalf of helpless black women.[135]

On the other hand, the commodification of women, through the commercialization of marriage, had implications which some bourgeois feminists were quick to exploit. For example, Mrs Marion Reid's 1843 tract, *A Plea for Woman*, bore the heading: 'Can man be free, if woman be a slave?'.[136] Mrs Reid was here drawing on an older radical tradition, Mary Woolstonecraft, in her *Vindication* (1792), having earlier drawn parallels between British women and slaves—though by slavery Woolstonecraft seems to have had in mind the Oriental harem, rather than the West Indian plantation.[137] In fact, the harem, in the eyes of many abolitionists, stood as an appropriate symbol of slavery, standing, as it did, not only as the antithesis of the monogamous Christian family, but also as an emblem of

[133] W. M. Thackeray, *The Newcomes* (London, 1855), in *The Works of William Makepeace Thackeray*, viii (London, 1898), 338; Ethel is playing with the idea that women are for sale like pictures at an exhibition, which carry a little green ticket when they have been sold (ibid., 288–9). One critic rightly notes that the marriage market is 'a central image in the novel, and the repetition of the mercenary marriage and its outcome between various couples is a unifying structural principle' (J. McMaster, *Thackeray: The Major Novels* (Manchester, 1971), 157).

[134] Also M. E. Montgomery, '*Gilded Prostitution': Status, Money, and Transatlantic Marriages, 1870–1914* (1989). However, significantly, as José Harris puts it: 'Middle-class marriages rarely involved the hard-nosed haggling over property characteristic of marriages among the aristocracy' (*Private Lives, Public Spirit: A Social History of Britain 1870–1914* (Oxford, 1993), 69 and fn.). Harris notes that such aristocratic 'arrangements' ('commodity marriages') had always evoked a good deal of middle-class derision and contempt. [35] Midgley, *Women Against Slavery*, 102.

[136] Ibid., 164.

[137] Ibid., 27. Disliking the cult of feminine emotion, she also argued that women should develop a 'rational humanity'.

sensuality, cruelty, and sloth—all human traits held to be incompatible with a progressive commercial society.

Harriet Martineau, too, drew a specific analogy between the subordinate position of women and the lot of slaves.[138] So did the young Herbert Spencer in a section of his *Social Statics* given over to a denunciation of the 'barbarism' of the desire to command: ' "You must not do as you will, but as I will", is the basis of every mandate, whether used by a planter to his negro, or by a husband to his wife.'[139] The most famous formulation of this theme, of course, is to be found in John Stuart Mill's *Subjection of Women*.[140]

Mill's lead was followed by middle-class feminists like Barbara Bodichon. True, Bodichon conceded that slavery was a greater injustice than an unequal marriage, but she felt the two institutions were so alike in many respects that she could not 'see one without thinking of the other and feeling how soon slavery would be destroyed if right opinions were entertained upon the other question'.[141] By the end of the century, feminist parallels between the plight of women and slavery had become commonplace.[142] For example, in their battle to reform the law which regulated married women's property, women's rights campaigners noted how in some southern American States, where the marriage laws remained archaic, emancipated female slaves were reluctant to take a husband at all, not wanting to enter a new kind of slavery.[143]

Another recurring theme in the case for female emancipation was the contention that men, by 'enslaving' women, were also enslaving themselves. But, interestingly, such arguments had also featured in earlier discussions about the relationship between the employer and his 'wage slaves',[144] as well as in the assault on slavery proper. Indeed, abolitionists, from Oastler to Harriet Martineau, tended to hover between a moralism which pinned the blame for slavery onto the slave-owner, and a half-acknowledged determinism which saw the slave-owner, along with the slave, as being imprisoned within a system from which only outside intervention could bring about an escape.

However, whether or not Victorian patriarchy really did represent a kind of slavery divided contemporaries—and not just on gender lines. To many intelligent and articulate middle-class women, the institution of marriage in a modern,

[138] In H. Martinean, *Society in America* (London, 1837), i. 148–54. See the extract from this book and the editorial discussion in G. G. Yates, *Harriet Martineau On Women* (New Brunswick, NJ, c.1985), 18, 134–9.

[139] H. Spencer, *Social Statics, or The Conditions Essential to Human Happiness Specified* (London, 1868; first pub. 1855), 181.   [140] See Ch. 7.

[141] L. Billington and R. Billington, ' "A Burning Zeal for Righteousness": Women in the British Anti-Slavery Movement, 1820–1860', in J. Rendall (ed.), *Equal or Different: Women's Politics 1800–1914* (Oxford, 1987), 106.

[142] P. Levine, *Victorian Feminism 1850–1900* (London, 1987), 62.

[143] L. Holcombe, *Wives and Property: Reform of the Married Women's Property Law in Nineteenth-Century England* (Oxford, 1983), 158.

[144] See Gallagher, *Industrial Reformation*, 26–7, on the way in which Oastler confronted the evils of the factory system.

'enlightened' society like Britain guaranteed the female half of the population not only security and comfort but also dignity and freedom. But if the conventional approach was to *contrast* Christian matrimony and slavery, some feminists *drew parallels* between them. What abolitionism had therefore done was to help set the parameters for a debate over the kind of relationship which men and women should form with one another. All sides agreed that this relationship should never rest on violence and coercion; but there agreement ended.[145]

FREE TRADE IN CORPSES

> If reform be to bring us laws [the Anatomy Act] like this; if it be to bring us rulers who think it a good thing to make the trade in human bodies free; if this be the 'free trade' they mean to give us; if this be a specimen of their political economy; if 'cheap' human bodies be their sign of national prosperity, in short, if measures like this be the result of Parliamentary reform, better, far better, remain as we were, poor and oppressed, but not put upon a level with the beasts that perish.
>
> (William Cobbett, 1832)[146]

The propriety of selling human beings also became a bone of contention as a result of a number of early nineteenth-century scandals involving body snatching and corpse trading. Drescher rightly sees slavery as arousing horror because it entailed the breaking of many taboos, not least the taboo that human beings must never be reduced to the position of animals or things.[147] But equally deeply rooted in the culture of Western societies are feelings about the sacred status of the corpse and an accompanying horror over the prospect of corpses being put to practical 'uses'.

Yet this taboo, too, as Ruth Richardson has shown, was being violated in the late eighteenth and early nineteenth centuries. For, as medical science developed, the hospitals and anatomy schools needed more corpses for dissection than naturally came their way from their traditional source, the hangman. Since the seventeenth century, the shortfall had been made good by the practice of grave-robbing.[148]

By the late eighteenth century, most anatomists, fearful of punishment and of being held up to popular obloquy, preferred to *buy* their corpses from professional grave-robbers, the 'resurrection men' who had become their main suppliers.

---

[145] See Ch. 7.

[146] Cobbett, *Weekly Political Register*, 1832, cited in R. Richardson, *Death, Dissection and the Destitute* (London, 1989), 100. [147] Drescher, *Capitalism and Antislavery*, 163.

[148] For details of how this 'trade' was conducted, see B. Bailey, *The Resurrection Men: A History of the Trade in Corpses* (London, 1991); M. Fido, *Bodysnatchers. A History of the Resurrectionists, 1742–1832* (London, 1988); H. Cole, *Things for the Surgeon: A History of the Resurrection Men* (London, 1964).

During the 1790s this gruesome, though flourishing, trade was being plied by groups like the Southwark gang, which sold adult corpses for 'two guineas and a crown' and children for 'six shillings for the first foot and nine pence per inch for all it measures more in length'. Unusual, freakish corpses would cost more.[149]

The legal status of unauthorized exhumations was unclear. Whereas stealing a shroud or a coffin was a felony, before 1788 the law decreed that a dead body belonged to no one, and even after 1788 corpse-stealing was merely a misdemeanour. Hence experienced bodysnatchers always stripped a body before removing it, and magistrates could sometimes do little but convict offenders on minor charges, such as trespassing or causing a disturbance.[150] These puny legal obstacles did nothing to deter the grave-robbers. On the contrary, as the eminent physician, Sir Astley Cooper, told the Select Committee of 1828, 'the law only enhances the price, and does not prevent the exhumation'.[151]

By the 1820s, when the market price of a dead adult had risen to the tempting sum of four guineas, a regular trade had become established; allegations were rife that some teachers in the anatomy schools were even selling bodily parts on to their pupils at a considerable profit.[152] In Richardson's perhaps over-coloured account: 'Corpses were bought and sold, they were touted, priced, haggled over, negotiated for, discussed in terms of supply and demand, delivered, imported, exported, transported. . . . Human bodies were dismembered and sold in pieces, or measured and sold by the inch.'[153]

Even greater horrors were shortly to unfold. The Select Committee of 1828 had heard from another expert witness: 'when there is a difficulty in obtaining bodies, and their value is so great, you absolutely throw a temptation in the way of these men to commit murder for the purpose of selling the bodies of their victims'. And this is precisely what happened with the notorious crimes of Burke and Hare, who murdered their victims and then sold the bodies to an Edinburgh anatomy school for between £8 and £10.[154] This sensational affair was shortly followed by the scandal of the 'London Burkers', John Bishop and Thomas Williams, whose crimes were in some ways even more worrying, in that, unlike Burke and Hare, they really had 'graduated' from their earlier career as bodysnatchers.[155] As far as corpses were concerned, the logical end-product of free trade, it seemed, was murder.

The Home Secretary, Robert Peel, was so startled by these developments that he privately gave instructions to Customs House officers 'to permit the import of dead bodies from France without minute inquiry, or at least without exposure', a

---

[149] Richardson, *Dissection*, 52–7; Bailey, *Resurrection Men*, 56–60.
[150] Bailey, *Resurrection Men*, 21–2, 67.   [151] Richardson, *Dissection*, 63.
[152] Ibid., 329 fn. 10. One witness told the 1828 Select Committee that adults cost four guineas, while small corpses were sold at so much an inch (Bailey, *Resurrection Men*, 96). Wakley, in the *Lancet*, accused the London surgeons of regulating 'their scale of charges to the plundered and impoverished student, by the demands of the resurrectionist and murderer, as does the cattle butcher by the demands of farmer and grazier' (Cole, *Things for the Surgeon*, 130).   [153] Richardson, *Dissection*, 72.
[154] Ibid., 132–5; Bailey, *Resurrection Men*, ch. 5.
[155] Richardson, *Dissection*, 195–7; Bailey, *Resurrection Men*, 142–8.

proceeding which he knew to be 'a statutable offence'; but, argued Peel, 'what can be done, if repeated murder is the consequence of an obstruction to the supply of bodies by other means?'[156] Thus did Peel surreptitiously institute a policy of 'free trade in corpses' eighteen years before he sanctioned free trade in corn.

However, Peel well knew that a public outcry would greet the disclosure of the actions at which he was conniving. In correspondence with Bentham he became convinced that there was a better way out of the difficulty, and that was the passage of legislation making the unclaimed bodies of paupers available for dissection —an idea earlier publicized by Southwood Smith in his 1824 *Westminster Review* article, 'The Uses of the Dead to the Living'.[157] This proposal was scrutinized by the Select Committee which Peel had set up in 1828, but the Bill which enshrined the Committee's recommendations had to be withdrawn because it aroused controversy by making no provision for Christian burial. This omission was made good in a new Bill introduced by the Radical MP, Henry Warburton, which eventually, much amended, became the Anatomy Act of 1832.[158]

The Anatomy Act was intensely controversial. Many free marketeers and utilitarians defended it as a necessary aid to modern medical practice. But it was denounced by a mixture of working-class Radicals, Tory paternalists, and humanitarian doctors as a deplorable piece of 'class legislation': why, they asked, should the law discriminate against people whose sole 'crime' was to be poor and helpless?

Once it had been passed, the Anatomy Act acquired an even more evil reputation. According to a contemporary trade unionist from Salford, the 'Dead Body Bill', as he called it, had paved the way for the adoption of the New Poor Law[159]— a charge repeated by Ruth Richardson, who shows how popular opposition to the New Poor Law was closely bound up with hatred and fear of the earlier measure.[160] In fact, however, the two measures served quite different purposes. After all, as John Knott argues: 'the Anatomy Act sought to increase the number of corpses available for anatomical study, and most of these corpses were to be obtained from amongst recipients of poor relief. The New Poor Law's intention, on the other hand, was to reduce the number of paupers.' Nor was the Anatomy Act likely to make poor people any more apprehensive of the workhouse than they already were.[161]

---

[156] Peel to Goulburn, 6 Dec. 1828, in C. S. Parker (ed.), *Sir Robert Peel from his Private Papers*, 3 vols. (London, 1899), ii. 44–5. Corpses were imported not only from France, but there was also a flourishing trade in Irish corpses that were supplied for the Scottish medical schools, Glasgow being an important entrepôt. According to Bailey, 'shippers hoped to escape detection by labelling their crates or casks "fish" or "apples" or "glue"' (*Resurrection Men*, 38).

[157] T. S. Smith, 'The Uses of the Dead to the Living', *Westminster Review*, 2 (1824), 59–97. The correspondence between Bentham and Peel is reproduced at length in Richardson, *Dissection*, 110–14.

[158] J. Knott, *Popular Opposition to the 1834 Poor Law* (London, 1986), 261.   [159] Ibid., 263.

[160] Richardson, *Dissection*, 266–71. See also the discussion in T. Marshall, *Murdering to Dissect: Grave-Robbing, Frankenstein and the Anatomy Literature* (Manchester, 1995).

[161] Knott, *Opposition to Poor Law*, 265.

Possibly much of the criticism which the Anatomy Act attracted verged on the hysterical. The Act itself makes no specific reference to poor inmates of public institutions. The all-important Clause 7 does no more than provide that 'any Executor or other Party having Lawful Possession of the Body of any Deceased Person' can make it available for anatomical dissection, while the following clause lays down the terms under which people can formally bequeath their bodies for dissection after death; and in both clauses there are safeguards against abuse, notably a requirement that close relatives must give their assent.[162] On the other hand, poor people would have been less likely than the well-to-do to know about their 'rights' and how to enforce them; and many of those who died in workhouses or hospitals would have lost contact with the relatives charged with the protection of their interests.[163] The recent reissue of Southwood Smith's article, in pamphlet form, had also reminded everyone that it was the unclaimed bodies of inmates of hospitals and workhouses on which the surgeons and their friends particularly had designs.

But the Anatomy Act aroused disquiet for other reasons than this. For, as Thomas Wakley, the editor of *Lancet*, pertinently noted, the Act was silent on the subject of whether corpses could be *sold*, either during an individual's lifetime or upon death. Referring to this 'startling omission', Wakley complained: 'not one clause is framed with a view to prevent the *buying* and *selling* of dead human bodies,— indeed there is not one word on that subject'.[164] It was around this issue—strangely neglected by modern historians—that the House of Commons largely conducted its heated, but confused, debates.

A handful of MPs clearly disapproved of anatomical dissection on principle, but most members of the House accepted its medical value. Yet how could the necessary corpses be best found without endangering public order and public safety? Many of the Bill's supporters, on both sides of the House (for example, Joseph Hume and Peel), were friends of political economy. Significantly, *their* 'solution' involved reducing the price of corpses by legalizing the 'trade'.[165] This, it was hoped, would effectively stop the crime of 'Burking'. The Attorney-General, a strong supporter of the Bill, took the same line: 'by making the corpse, in future, easily procurable, all temptation to murder would be removed', he declared.[166]

The implication behind such remarks was that, since neither government nor parliament could ban the traffic in human bodies, the most that could be hoped for was that society's interests would be safeguarded by an intervention which depressed the monetary value of this particular commodity. As Peel had argued

---

[162] Clause 7 stipulates that no body can be dissected if the person concerned had earlier objected to this being done or if his nearest relative withheld consent. Under the terms of Clause 8 even the voluntary donation of a body could be vetoed by his nearest kin. Moreover, the Act made human anatomy subject to a system of licensing and inspection.

[163] Knott gives examples of how, in practice, paupers were at risk in the 1830s (*Opposition to Poor Law*, 264).   [164] *Lancet*, 31 Dec. 1831, 486.

[165] See Hume's observations on the subject in Hansard, ix, 580: 17 Jan. 1832.

[166] Ibid., 583–4.

all along, given the fact that sales *were* taking place, the wisest course of action was to legalize the supply.[167] The Attorney-General permitted himself an even greater frankness: 'whatever might be the mischief likely to arise from the legalized sale of dead bodies, the prejudice against it must be removed by reflecting on the still greater mischief of not endeavouring, at least, to put a stop to the frightful practices which had lately prevailed in London'.[168]

The Bill's opponents, however, were not convinced. 'Legalize the sale of dead bodies', warned Wakley, 'and you increase in a tenfold nature the gangs of resurrectionists.' What Wakley wanted was the total suppression of what he saw as an evil practice by making it an offence punishable by transportation for life.[169] Some MPs went even further. By legalizing the traffic in corpses, they alleged, the Anatomy Bill would actually *encourage* 'Burking'.[170]

What alternatives did the Bill's opponents put forward? Thomas Sadler declared his readiness to accept importations from France as a *pis aller*: 'If our neighbours were so entirely free from these prejudices, he would beg to ask, why might not the principles of free trade, which were so liberally applied to other matters, be applied to this?'[171] Others said that they did not object to the dissection of the bodies of murderers and suicidees (in fact the measure under discussion specifically forebade the handing over of executed criminals for this purpose, as had earlier happened under the terms of the 1752 'Murder Act'). In jocular mood, MPs put forward the names of their particular bugbears as possible candidates. The reactionary Tory squire, Colonel Sibthorp, thought dissection an appropriate fate for convicted horse-dealers![172] More to the point, Hunt suggested that surgeons who wanted to pursue their anatomical studies should give up their *own* bodies for dissection—(though 'he had no objection that those surgeons should be exempted who did not receive fees'); and at one stage Hunt also threatened to make available for dissection the bodies of all MPs voting for the Bill before the House, along with the bodies of sinecurists.[173]

But underlying the critics' case was the gut feeling expressed by another MP, who declared that 'he objected to any open sale—to any market of human flesh'.[174] Members of Parliament vied with one another in imagining the horrors that might unfold once this 'natural' feeling was discarded. There were grisly predictions that a husband might sell the body of his wife, for 'there would be found persons to urge him to such an unnatural action for the sake of profit'.[175] Another reminded the House that 'there were those in great cities who did not scruple to barter the chastity of their daughters; and why, therefore, should it be supposed that there were none brutal enough to sell the bodies of their own children to the surgeon?'[176]

[167] Ibid., xii, 320: 11 Apr. 1832.   [168] Ibid., ix, 584: 17 Jan. 1832.
[169] *Lancet*, 24 Dec. 1831, 454; ibid., 8 Dec. 1832, 341.
[170] e.g. Hansard, ix, 304: 15 Dec. 1831 (Sadler); ibid., x, 836: 27 Feb. 1832 (F. Trench).
[171] Ibid., 304: 15 Dec. 1831.   [172] Ibid., x, 837: 27 Feb. 1832.
[173] Ibid., ix, 704: 20 Jan. 1832; x, 839–41: 27 Feb. 1832; xii, 316: 11 Apr. 1832.
[174] Ibid., x, 833: 27 Feb. 1832 (R. Inglis).   [175] Ibid., xii, 665: 18 Apr. 1832 (Robinson).
[176] Ibid., 895: 11 May 1832 (Fane).

Later from the House of Lords came warnings that poor and desperate men, in a moment of thoughtlessness or dissipation, might enter into 'a horrible contract', whereby they sold 'their bodies to Jews, who would exact the pound of flesh, or extravagant compensation for it'.[177] In their calmer moments the critics declared that the anatomy schools would soon be getting all the corpses they needed anyway from the truly voluntary bequests of public-spirited citizens. But Hunt clearly spoke for all the critics when he flatly declared that 'the system of selling dead bodies was inconsistent with English feeling, with the Christian religion'.[178]

In the event, after many delays, Parliament did place the Anatomy Bill on the statute book. Cobbett raged against the authors of this legislation, whom he accused of sanctioning 'free trade in bodies'.[179] Yet the Anatomy Act did not, in fact, represent an unequivocal triumph for the cause of untrammelled free trade. For, as Ruth Richardson herself acknowledges, the Bill's sponsors, though 'stout advocates of non-interference in trade, and of cuts in government expenditure', paradoxically found themselves championing a 'collectivist' piece of legislation, which required the establishment of a 'centrally based and funded bureaucracy'.[180]

It is arguable that the Anatomy Act did not, in the long run, produce the social and moral mischief which the critics had predicted (though its immediate effect was to bring about a decline in the voluntary bequest of bodies[181]). The true significance of the whole story was perhaps that nothing but trouble and resistance would come from the *depersonalization* of human beings, be they alive or dead. The opponents of political economy were not alone in finding this totally abhorrent. For it was coming to be accepted that 'commerce' needed to be morally cleansed and that 'legitimate trade' was incompatible with transactions that in any way resulted, directly or even indirectly, in the buying and selling of bodies, alive or dead, black or white, male or female. Even free traders realized that their beloved principle would have to be modified in the light of this moral axiom. On one thing there was thus near universal agreement: selling people was wrong.

---

[177] Ibid., xiii, 827: 19 June 1832 (Lord Wynford).   [178] Ibid., xii, 904: 11 May 1832.
[179] See opening quotation.   [180] Richardson, *Dissection*, 210.
[181] Fido, *Bodysnatchers*, 172.

5

'Criminal Capitalism'

[The railway speculation mania] penetrated every class; it permeated every household; and all yielded to the temptation. Men who went to church as devoutly as to their counting-houses—men whose word had ever been as good as their bond—joined the pursuit. They entered the whirlpool, and were carried away by the vortex.

(J. Francis, 1851)[1]

The retail merchant, in whose branch of business it is customary to adulterate goods, or sell them in short measure—where, for instance, it is or was the usage of trade to mix chicory with coffee, whiting with flour and barley, sloe-leaves with tea, clay with sugar—finds it no easy question of conscience to resolve whether he should or should not do as others do. . . . Moral inconsistencies and moral difficulties teem thus around us on every side.

(J. D. Milne, 1857)[2]

The advocates of the new society had believed that freeing the market would end 'Old Corruption' and inaugurate greater purity, not only in official, but also in private commercial transactions, where abuses were usually caused by monopolies and by the vested interests which monopolies attracted. After the symbolically important Repeal of the Corn Laws in 1846, a number of 'emancipatory' measures were duly passed: for example, the Usury Laws were finally abolished in 1854,[3] followed by legalization of limited liability in 1855 and 1856. But, contrary to the expectations of the economic liberals, new abuses sprang into life as soon as the older ones disappeared. The result was an outpouring of disquiet at the low standards of commercial morality.

---

[1] J. Francis, *A History of the English Railway: Its Social Relations and Revelations, 1820–1845* (Newton Abbot, 1967; first pub. 1851), ii. 145.

[2] J. D. Milne, *Industrial Employment of Women in the Middle and Lower Ranks*, 2nd edn (1870; first pub. 1857), 44–5.

[3] The Usury Laws fixed maximum interest rates, usually at 5 per cent, though certain transactions were exempted from their provision. A loan which violated the Usury Law could not be enforced by the lender. Adam Smith had argued that such restrictions were justifiable, but Bentham, in his *Defence of Usury* (1787), had called for their repeal (W. R. Cornish and G. de N. Clark, *Law and Society in England 1750–1950* (London, 1989), 227).

FRAUD AND SPECULATION

The origins of this disquiet can be traced back to a series of scandals. First, there were the insurance swindles of the 1830s and 1840s, memorably satirized by Thackeray in *The Great Hoggarty Diamond* (1841) ('the West Diddlesex Assurance Company') and by Dickens in *Martin Chuzzlewit* (1844) ('the Anglo-Bengalee Disinterested Loan and Life Assurance Company'). A further set of scandals was precipitated by the railway boom of the 1840s. Many of the companies which emerged in these years presented false balance sheets, and attracted investors by distributing high dividends paid out of capital, rather than out of income. Such malpractices contributed to the commercial crisis of 1847–8, resulting in what a contemporary financial journalist called 'a train of mercantile disasters that involved losses which could not be brought within the bounds of reasonable calculation'.[4]

These happenings were followed during the 1850s by several banking collapses affecting apparently 'respectable' financial houses like the Strahan, Paul & Bates and the Royal British Banks.[5] Nor, it seemed, were these merely isolated events. The financial journalist, David Morier Evans, felt that the close succession in which the disasters occurred and the similarity of their underlying motives showed that they did 'not represent the simple perverseness of individual natures' but were 'so many indices of a depreciated, and apparently bad, moral atmosphere' enveloping the whole of the commercial world.[6] Some businessmen repeated the indictment, publicly musing whether the country's 'mercantile prosperity', the source of national greatness, could survive for much longer unless the British people disowned 'the fraud and dishonesty with which our commercial honour is so deeply stained'.[7]

Reviewing Samuel Smiles's recently published *Self-Help* in 1860, Dickens mordantly observed that it would be a good thing to be given case studies, not just of entrepreneurial heroes, but also of people like the forger Walter Watts, who were 'the purest examples of "men who have helped themselves"':

The task which Mr Smiles has performed for virtue, ought to be performed for vice. The rising generation gains nothing by being admitted to view human nature only on its brightest side. . . . If in addition to teaching wisdom and caution to ignorant holders of

---

[4] D. M. Evans, *The Commercial Crisis, 1847–1848* (Newton Abbott, 1969; first pub. 1849), 107. There had been an earlier 'panic' in 1825–6. On the railway scandals, see J. Foreman-Peck and R. Millward, *Private and Public Ownership of British Industry in Britain 1820–1990* (Oxford, 1994), 17–18.

[5] J. Foreman-Peck, 'Sleaze and the Victorian Businessman', *History Today*, 45 (1995), 5–8, for further examples of business malpractice.

[6] D. M. Evans, *Facts, Failure and Frauds: Revelations Financial Mercantile Criminal* (New York, 1968; first pub. 1859), 5.

[7] W. Callender, *The Commercial Crisis of 1857: Its Causes and Results* (London, 1858), cited in J. Garnett and A. C. Howe, 'Churchmen and Cotton-Masters in Victorian England', in D. J. Jeremy (ed.), *Business and Religion in Britain* (Aldershot, 1988), 74.

property, it should teach crime to a few budding criminals, it would work out a beneficial mission, notwithstanding.[8]

Dickens was moved to write these lines by news of the spectacular defalcations of a clerk. Here was a problem which we can see, in retrospect, was partly structural. The commercial expansion of preceding decades had led to a huge increase in paper transactions, creating new possibilities of manipulation and fraud.[9] Accountancy was still in its infancy, and Dickens may well have had a point when he blamed short-sighted shareholders for 'cheese-paring' in their auditing arrangements.[10] To some extent, though, the mid-Victorians were experiencing the problems that always occur when commercial and technological progress outstrips the control-mechanisms which ideally should accompany them—a modern equivalent would be computer fraud.

Contemporaries understandably worried that banks and commercial concerns should be so vulnerable to the depredations of their usually low-paid staff. Just as factories, into which millions of pounds of capital had been sunk, lay open to any revolutionary with a firebrand,[11] so nothing, in Dickens's words, was easier than fraud: 'A "pass-book" costs only a few shillings at any City stationer's, or less than the price of a coarse and vulgar crowbar.'[12] Businessmen needed to place total trust in the subordinates whom they employed—but was such an expectation reasonable?

The law courts tended to come down very hard on fraudulent clerks once they had been caught, perhaps because the latter had compounded their offence by insubordination: for those of a higher social class, remorse and social disgrace were usually deemed adequate punishment![13] But dishonest clerks may well have learnt their bad habits from their employers, and, if only for that reason, it seemed essential to stamp out misconduct by the people who actually ran large commercial establishments, whether as owners or as directors.[14] For in these circles, too, it seemed that misconduct was rife.

One reason for financial impropriety in high places may have been the 'entrepreneurial culture' of the age, which magnified the fear of failure and led some merchants and bankers to try to conceal their problems for as long as they possibly could: a desperate stratagem which, in the long run, usually made a bad

---

[8] 'Criminal Capitalists', *All The Year Round*, 3 (9 June 1860), 201–2. But as shown below, Smiles was by no means blind to the existence of 'criminal capitalism'.

[9] G. Robb, *White-Collar Crime in Modern England: Financial Fraud and Business Morality, 1845–1929* (Cambridge, 1992), 23–4.

[10] C. Dickens, 'Very Singular Things in the City', *All The Year Round*, 3 (14 July 1860), 326. Similarly the *Saturday Review* urged shareholders to 'think more of the permanent welfare of their undertakings, and less of the mere market price of their shares' ('Morality of Railway Management', *Saturday Review*, 15 Dec. 1855, 109). Accountancy procedures improved significantly after 1870 (Robb, *White-Collar Crime*, 43, 72).   [11] *The Economist* (3 Dec. 1853), 1353.

[12] Dickens, 'Very Singular Things', 325.   [13] Robb, *White-Collar Crime*, 164.

[14] Ibid., 136.

situation even worse.[15] But perhaps the most important single reason for the cata-
logue of business scandals in the 1850s was the growing size of business firms,
accompanied by the separation of management from ownership and the impossibility of thousands of small investors exercising any real control over the way in
which their capital was being used.

Herbert Spencer thought that 'the corporate conscience [was] ever inferior to
the individual conscience' and that 'a body of men [would] commit a joint act'
which each individual 'would shrink from did he feel personally responsible'; the
'indirectness and remoteness of the evils produced', he reflected, greatly weakened
the restraints on wrongdoing.[16] A clerical moralist, the Revd Robert Bickersteth,
agreed: 'Men will often sanction, in their corporate capacity, a procedure which
in their private capacity they would utterly repudiate and condemn.'[17] Small acts
of wrongdoing would then accumulate, giving rise over time to commercial evils
which no one had really intended.

Such arguments, however, could hardly be used to exonerate the activities
of the company promoters who proliferated in the 1850s and 1860s, some of
whom were total rogues—among them Albert Grant, the probable prototype of
Trollope's 'Augustus Melmotte' in *The Way We Live Now*.[18] Indeed, it has been
estimated that some 17 per cent of all company promotions during the period
1856–83 were fraudulent.[19] But many of their perpetrators escaped justice because,
given the complexity of large-scale commercial transactions, it was not always easy,
especially for shareholders, to determine where incompetence or gross negligence
shaded off into downright dishonesty.[20] Thus, after the collapse of the London,
Chatham and Dover Railway in 1866, *The Economist* observed of its chief engineer and director, Samuel Morton Peto: 'Perhaps he did not himself know, at least
not in full and exactly, how his name was being used, though he was bound to
know.'[21] The same had been true of the financial dealings of 'the Railway King',
George Hudson, during the earlier railway boom in the 1840s.[22] How could outsiders easily ascertain the rights and wrongs of such matters?

The Times, with some justification, blamed Britain's 'reckless system of banking' for having brought about 'periodical crises of danger to the lowest merchant,

---

[15] Ibid., 27.

[16] H. Spencer, 'Railway Morals and Railway Policy', *Edinburgh Review*, 100 (1854), 426–7. In *The
Study of Sociology* (London, 1873), 289, he adds that the 'corporate intelligence' is also lower. It has
been claimed, however, that in his later effusions in praise of market competition, Spencer tends to
forget the significance of the split between ownership and control to which he had earlier drawn attention (D. Wiltshire, *The Social and Political Thought of Herbert Spencer* (Oxford, 1978), 44).

[17] Introd. by R. Bickersteth to Revd H. A. Boardman, *The Bible in the Counting-House: A Course
of Lectures to Merchants* (London, 1854), p. v.   [18] Robb, *White-Collar Crime*, 99–102.

[19] H. A. Shannon, 'The Limited Companies of 1866–1883', *Economic History Review*, 4 (1933), 295.

[20] Robb, *White-Collar Crime*, 23.

[21] *The Economist*, 13 Oct. 1866, cited in P. L. Cottrell, 'Sir Samuel Morton Peto', in
D. J. Jeremy (ed.), *Dictionary of Business Biography* (1985), iv. 650.

[22] Robb, *White-Collar Crime*, 49–50. Historians still cannot agreed on the extent of Hudson's personal 'guilt'.

and misery and ruin to thousands'.[23] There were also well-attested cases of attornies and solicitors speculating with the property assigned to their charge.[24] Yet it was impossible to view all investors who had been dishonestly deprived of their capital at a time of speculative excitement merely as *passive victims*. Dealing with the later commercial scandals of 1858–9, Morier Evans pinned responsibility on the evil of 'over trading' produced by human carelessness and greed.[25] And this greed emanated quite as much from the investing public as it did from company promoters and directors. This was a topic dear to the heart of many Victorian novelists.[26]

The complicity of defrauded investors in their own ruin also provides the theme of Carlyle's famous essay, 'Hudson's Statue': Hudson had

been 'elected by the people' so as almost none other is or was. Hudson solicited no vote; his votes were silent voluntary ones, not liable to be false: he *did* a thing which men found, in their inarticulate hearts, to be worthy of paying money for; and they paid it. What the desire of every heart was, Hudson had or seemed to have produced: Scrip out of which profit could be made.[27]

Samuel Smiles treated Hudson similarly. He drew parallels between the recent veneration of the 'railway king' and the ancient Israelites' worshipping of the golden calf, showing how in both cases idolatry quickly gave way to anger and remorse.[28]

'Mammon-worship' was the phrase often on the moralists' lips. For example, the journalist John Francis thought Hudson had been cast as 'a scape-goat for the sins of the many' but that the real 'sin' resided in the way in which the 'iron road' had become 'the object of public worship'.[29] The *Capel Court Share-Buyer*, noted Trollope sardonically, now served the investor as both Bible and Prayer-book, 'as well as a Compendium of the Whole Duty of Man'.[30]

With the advent of the limited liability company, investors had anyhow ceased to be entrepreneurs of the old kind, but more closely resembled a social group to which severe moral opprobrium still attached, *gamblers*.[31] For how else could the speculative frenzies of 1825–6, the mid-1840s, and the late 1850s be characterized? Bagehot, writing of the first of these episodes, observed that 'the delirium of ancient gambling co-operated with the milder madness of modern overtrading'.[32] The problem, as John Lalor wrote, was that though commerce and gambling were fundamentally antithetical, it was difficult to define quite where

[23] *The Times*, 1 Dec. 1857.   [24] See Ch. 6, p. 116.
[25] D. M. Evans, *A History of the Commercial Crisis 1857–1858 and the Stock Exchange Panic of 1859* (London, 1859), 47.
[26] See N. Russell, '*Nicholas Nickleby* and the Commercial Crisis of 1825', *The Dickensian*, 77 (1981), 144–50.
[27] T. Carlyle, 'Hudson's Statue', in *Latter-Day Pamphlets* (London, 1858; first pub. 1850), 228.
[28] S. Smiles, *Lives of the Engineers* (London, 1862), iii. 386.
[29] Francis, *English Railway*, ii. 144, 241.
[30] A. Trollope, *The Three Clerks* (Oxford, 1989; first pub. 1857), 404.
[31] Robb, *White-Collar Crime*, 25.
[32] W. Bagehot, *Lombard Street*, 12th edn. (London, 1906; first pub. 1873), 159.

one ended and the other began.[33] If this were true in 1852 when Lalor was writing, it was even truer after limited liability had been legalized. Here was a dilemma made all the more acute by the fact that the extension of the practice of commercial speculation coincided with moves to discourage, and even close down, many forms of gambling and gaming.[34]

The National Anti-Gambling League, set up in 1890, prudently steered clear of launching a campaign against 'commercial gambling', just as members of the later Royal Commission on Gambling did not press their investigations into the activities of the Stock Exchange.[35] But neither did the anti-gambling lobby bother to conceal its contempt for high-risk speculation, which seemed to possess many of the same morally obnoxious features as gambling proper, while humorists frequently belaboured the comparison.[36] (Amusingly, many members of the City frequented gaming houses, and the Stock Exchange was known by some as 'Little Tattersall's'.[37]) What, then, did the advocates of a market economy have to say by way of reply?

Some put a brave face on things, arguing that Stock Exchange involvement at least displaced activities that were even more objectionable. Thus one anonymous contributor to the *Westminster Review* chose to present investment in limited liability companies as providing 'better employment' for people's money than 'such as betting-lists, public-house lotteries, and petty usury'. 'If for the demoralizing excitement of gambling the wholesome excitement of trade were substituted', he argued, the lower orders might soon develop those habits of thrift in which they were currently deficient.[38]

A second stratagem was pursued in an article appearing in the same journal seven years later. Its author drew a distinction between gaming, which he thought

---

[33] J. Lalor, *Money and Morals: A Book for The Times* (London, 1852), 81, 83. A number of witnesses to the 1844 Select Committee on Gaming wrestled with this same dilemma (M. Clapson, *A Bit of a Flutter: Popular Gambling and English Society, c.1823–1961* (Manchester, 1992), 20–1).

[34] See Ch. 10.

[35] D. Dixon, *From Prohibition to Regulation: Bookmaking, Anti-Gambling, and the Law* (Oxford, 1991), 85–6. R. Munting, *An Economic and Social History of Gambling in Britain and the USA* (Manchester, 1996), discusses whether speculation really is a form of gambling. He concludes that they are similar in that both activities require losers as well as winners: 'Those who gain can only do so at the expense of those who lose. There must be a transfer of value.' But they differ in that 'gambling itself does not determine or influence the result of the contest' (p. 2). He concedes, however, that trading on the contemporary derivatives markets does closely resemble gambling proper.

[36] The parallel was later drawn by several contributors to B. S. Rowntree's collection of essays, *Betting and Gambling: A National Evil* (London, 1905), esp. 19, 50, 121–2, 147–8. See, too, John Ashton's strictures (*The History of Gambling in England* (New York, 1968; first pub. 1899), 274). In 1890 the Bishop of Manchester, James Moorhouse, warned of the gambling propensity in share dealing (Garnett and Howe, 'Churchmen and Cotton-Masters', 74). For a popular expression of the same viewpoint, see the illustration in Clapson, *A Bit of a Flutter*, 21–2.

[37] *Third Report from Select Committee of the House of Lords into Laws Respecting Gaming, 1844*, vol. vi, pars. 447–8.

[38] 'The Limited Liability Act of 1855', *Westminster Review*, 65 (1856), 47–8. This anonymous author also tries to draw a distinction between commercial speculation, which promoted probity and energy, and gambling, which sapped these qualities (ibid., 48).

anti-social and wasteful, and gambling (financial speculation included) which sometimes served a useful social purpose:

While the objects of the gambler on the turf, and the Stock Exchange, and of the gamester at cards and dice, are identical, experience has proved that the former may succeed, and that the latter must fail in attaining their objects; that the gambler may acquire wealth, but that the gamester must be ruined if he persevere in gaming. By speculating in shares, capital is circulated and commerce increased; thus, whether the speculator be enriched or impoverished, his fellow men are vastly benefited in consequence of his transactions.[39]

But a third article in the *Westminster Review* struck a more conventional note of disapproval and caution:

He who risks his all and more, in lottery tickets or in hops, is not a whit the less a fool because he may gain a fortune. . . . All trade is risk, just as sowing corn is risk; but experience shows that the risk—the legitimate risk—admits of as correct a graduation as that of life insurance. He who buys and sells according to the habit of his own individual trade, and of the trade in general that he belongs to, is no more likely to become insolvent, than he, who being well, eats and drinks as he has been accustomed to do, and as they do who live in the same country with him, is likely to lose his health.

'By toil, and by toil alone, should men be encouraged to gain wealth', argued this writer. (Adam Smith had earlier written something not dissimilar.[40]) Speculation disturbed the market:

Whatever may be the gain is more than compensated for by the depravity, the insecurity to property, the habits of irregular occupation, the secrecy, the violation of the laws of God and man, and by the ruin, or at least injury, brought on the fair trader by disturbance of profits and wages, and by the competition forced upon an honest man, which he cannot meet, from the very fact of his being an honest man.[41]

Speculation made contemporary observers uneasy for a variety of reasons. First, alleged the critics, the share-buying mentality fostered a belief that fortunes could be made *quickly* without the need for the self-denial involved in saving. George Eliot, in *The Mill on the Floss*, writes of how 'this inalienable habit of saving, as an end in itself, belonged to the industrious men of business of a former generation, who made their fortunes slowly, almost as the tracking of the fox belongs to the harrier': a habit which had been 'nearly lost in these days of rapid money-getting,

---

[39] 'Gamesters and Gaming-Houses', ibid., 80 (1863), 86.
[40] 'It seldom happens . . . that great fortunes are made even in great towns by any one regular, established, and well-known branch of business, but in consequence of a long life of industry, frugality, and attention. Sudden fortunes, indeed, are sometimes made in such place by what is called the trade of speculation. . . . A bold adventurer may sometimes acquire a considerable fortune by two or three successful speculations; but is just as likely to lose one by two or three unsuccessful ones' (A. Smith, *An Inquiry into the Nature and Causes of The Wealth of Nations*, ed. E. Cannan (Chicago, 1976; first pub. 1776), bk. 1, ch. 10, p. 127).
[41] 'The Law of Bankruptcy', *Westminster Review*, 52 (1850), 430–2.

when lavishness comes close on the back of want'.[42] She illustrates the generation gap by showing how Mr Tulliver senior, though desperate to retrieve the family fortunes, 'would not consent to put the money out at interest lest he should lose it',[43] while Tom, his son, who scorns the process of slow accumulation, borrows money from a relative and puts it into a speculative venture—which succeeds triumphantly, on the financial level, though the speculation contributes to the coarsening of his character.

Second, there were anxieties over the extent of the credulity displayed by people of *all* social classes when it came to share-dealing. The *Annual Register* in 1824 set the tone for much later writing on the subject:

All the gambling propensities of human nature were brought into action . . . princes, nobles, politicians, placemen, patriots, lawyers, physicians, divines, philosophers, poets —intermingled with women of all ranks and degrees, spinsters, wives and widows, to venture some portion of their property in schemes of which scarcely anything was known except the name.[44]

The commercial crisis of 1847–8 was similarly described. 'Men without houses or homes, clerks at small salaries in banks and merchants' establishments, have as openly proclaimed themselves buyers and sellers of the favourite shares, as if they represented their employers', wrote Morier Evans. 'Speculation . . . waxed more hot and fiery every day; it pervaded every class, high and low, rich and poor, young and old, and I am sorry to be obliged to say that it exerted its influence upon one sex as much as upon another.'[45] Describing the railway 'mania' of the 1840s, John Francis was appalled that mere clerks had left their offices to become jobbers and that domestic servants were reading railway journals.[46] Similarly, in his novel, *Hard Cash*, Charles Reade has gentlemen and their footmen jostling one another on the Exchange, surrounded by 'a motley crew of peers and printers, vicars and admirals, professors, cooks, costermongers, cotton-spinners, waiters, coachmen, priests, potboys, bankers, braziers, dairymen, mail-guards, barristers, spinsters, butchers, beggars, duchesses, rag-merchants'.[47]

Social promiscuity, then, was one source of anxiety. The country's social leaders were excoriated for not setting a better example to their inferiors,[48] while surprise and disgust were expressed over the way in which the socially humble were 'getting out of their depth'.[49] Thackeray exploits the comic possibilities of

[42] G. Eliot, *The Mill on the Floss*, Blackwood edn. (Edinburgh, 1878; first pub. 1860), vol. 1, bk. 1, ch. 12, pp. 187–8. [43] Ibid., vol. 2, bk. 5, ch. 2, pp. 68–9.
[44] Russell, '*Nicholas Nickleby* and Commercial Crisis of 1825', 144.
[45] Evans, *Commercial Crisis of 1847–1848*, 7, 9, 16, 27, 41. [46] Francis, *English Railway*, ii. 144.
[47] C. Reade, *Hard Cash: A Matter-of-Fact Romance* (New York, n.d.; first pub. 1863), 90.
[48] Morier Evans graphically describes the involvement of High Society: 'Earls and Marquises struggled with London capitalists and rustic landowners to add attractiveness by the sanction of their names', while 'MPs, with a few Aldermen, made a traffic on their presumed responsibility' (*Commercial Crisis*, 5).
[49] Disapproval of state lotteries increased when the division into small shares later in the 18th c. for the first time enabled a large number of people in humble circumstances to join in (J. Raven, 'The Abolition of the English State Lotteries', *Historical Journal*, 34 (1991), 375–6). So there had long been

the resulting role reversal in his story of a footman who makes a fortune out of railway speculation, climbs into the best society, and even 'discovers' a remote ancestor who had supposedly come over with William the Conqueror.[50]

Another source of anxiety was the resultant confusion of family roles: 'Brothers speculated with the money of sisters; sons gambled with the money of their widowed mothers; children risked their patrimony', according to one horrified commentator on the 'railway mania'.[51] Moralists took an even stronger aversion to *women* who strayed from the family hearth in order to dabble in shares.[52]

Finally, speculation was allegedly threatening the integrity of public life. Shady financiers were being attracted into Parliament by the prospect of using their influence to 'rig' the share market for their own enrichment—as Undy Scott does in Trollope's early novel, *The Three Clerks* (1857).[53] But Trollope also makes it clear that share-buying could totally take possession of a man's soul: Undy Scott and the civil servant whom he has 'seduced', Tudor Alaric, are shown talking over 'their unholy trade' 'from morning to morning, and from night to night' 'till the prices of shares and the sounds of sums of money entered into Alaric's soul'.[54]

It was common to liken speculation (and the bankruptcy and ruin in which it frequently culminated) to a raging fever, to a collective outburst of insanity ('mania'), or to an atmospheric disturbance.[55] 'The pulse of the people, fierce and excited, grew by what it fed on', wrote Francis.[56] Normal judgement became suspended when the illness struck: John Lalor, in 1852, noted how 'the quiet maiden annuitant, the hard-worked country surgeon, the plodding clerk who has cut pens over the same desk for a quarter of a century, nay, the parson himself, when there is nothing to be done with a little hoard of savings, the product of much self-denial, but to buy consols at 100, feels his blood begin to mount, and the fever to set in' once 'the El Dorado of Capel Court and its neighbourhood' had been

---

a 'double standard' in these matters. See also P. Langford, *A Polite and Commercial People: England 1727–1783* (Oxford, 1989), 572–4, and the discussion in Ch. 10. The view of Adam Smith and Nassau Senior (see Ch. 3), that the lottery principle had its social uses, became lost in the moral indignation.

[50] W. M. Thackeray, *Diary of C. Jeames De La Pluche* (London, 1845–6), in *The Works of William Makepeace Thackeray*, iii (London, 1898). Eventually share prices collapse, and James Plush (a.k.a. C. Jeames De La Pluche) serves a short prison sentence, before settling down happily in his new life as a publican.   [51] Francis, *English Railway*, ii. 154.

[52] See Ch. 7.

[53] Trollope, *Three Clerks*, esp. ch. 24. Everything, including a parliamentary seat, is seen by Undy Scott in terms of its market value.

[54] Ibid., 352–3. Public corruption and private degradation are dealt with even more fully in his later *The Way We Live Now* (London, 1874–5).

[55] e.g. Coleridge, writing in 1817, referred to 'times when Bankruptcies spread, like a fever, at once contagious and epidemic' ('Blessed are ye that sow beside all Waters!' (1817), in R. J. White (ed.), *The Collected Works of Samuel Taylor Coleridge, vi, Lay Sermons* (1972), 207). Sometimes the metaphors became jumbled: the Revd J. B. Owen, for example, writes about 'crises of epidemic speculative mania' (*Business Without Christianity* (London, 1855), 22).

[56] 'Let it be remembered that nations have their fevers as individuals', he added (Francis, *English Railway*, ii. 180).

opened to his imagination.[57] Not even the well-being of a man's family dependants was respected.[58]

Walter Bagehot mused about *why* so many of his contemporaries behaved in this economically irrational way. It had something to do, he felt, with the prevalent 'disposition to excessive action':

Part of every mania is caused by the impossibility to get people to confine themselves to the amount of business for which their capital is sufficient, and in which they can engage safely. In some degree, of course, this is caused by the wish to get rich; but in a considerable degree, too, by the mere love of activity. There is a greater propensity to action in such men than they have the means of gratifying. Operations with their own capital will only occupy four hours of the day, and they wish to be active and to be industrious for eight hours, and so they are ruined. If they could only have sat idle the other four hours, they would have been rich men.[59]

Dickens, on the other hand, took a more conventional line on the subject of speculation, treating it as a contagious fever and attributing outbreaks to a despicable kind of credulity. In *Little Dorrit* (1855–7), for example, the financial swindler, Mr Merdle, is not so much an active agent of evil as a creature produced by the ambition and greed of those who place their faith in him—and entrust him with their money.[60] Dickens, in fact, thought speculative activity had now grown to such a scale that he was able to conceive of it as a metaphor for society as a whole.

So intense was the power of the speculative impulse, declared the moralists, that those affected by it often behaved like drunkards, abandoning all caution and 'giving their signature to everything that was offered'.[61] (That modern capitalism itself perhaps throve on irrationality was not something, of course, which its apologists were prepared to admit.[62]) Like other kinds of 'addiction',[63] speculative gambling was also thought to promote crime, as its 'victims', all sense of morality lost, did not scruple to resort to dishonest behaviour, even to theft and fraud, out of a desperate desire to feed their 'habit'. These descents into the depths provided rich material for melodramatic novels, such as Charles Reade's *Hard Cash*.[64]

---

[57] Lalor, *Money and Morals*, 84. Capel Court was the location of the London Stock Exchange.
[58] See Trollope, *Three Clerks*, 594.
[59] W. Bagehot, *Physics and Politics* (Boston, Mass., 1956; first pub. 1872), 138.
[60] The ubiquity in the Victorian novel of financial collapse, caused by unwise investment/speculation, can be partly explained by the fact that so many major writers personally suffered this painful experience (J. R. Reed, 'A friend to Mammon: speculation in Victorian literature', *Victorian Studies*, 27 (1983–4), 182–3).   [61] Francis, *English Railway*, ii. 145.
[62] 'The capitalist does not grow rich by being orderly, rational, modest', A. J. P. Taylor has argued; 'he does it by flair, by backing a hunch. . . . There is no scheme too wild, no rumour too absurd, to be without repercussions on the Stock Exchange. The public house is the home of common sense' (*The Trouble Makers: Dissent Over Foreign Policy 1792–1939* (London, 1957), 54–5).
[63] See Ch. 10.
[64] The story of the disgrace and downfall of its 'hero', Richard Hardie, is conveniently summarized in B. Hilton, *The Age of Atonement: The Influence of Evangelicalism on Social and Economic Thought 1795–1865* (Oxford, 1988), 140–1.

'LIABILITY'

Little Dorrit is a study of human gullibility. But it also centres on the idea of 'liability'—in all senses of that word, theological, moral, and economic. In particular, the novel draws upon the heated debate which had preceded and accompanied the legalization of limited liability in the Acts of 1855 and 1856. Obviously, many of the arguments employed for and against limited liability were technical. Often, too, they concealed the differing conceptions of material self-interest entertained by those directly affected. But deeper moral principles were also involved. William Brown, the wealthy Liverpool shipowner, spoke for many businessmen when he expressed the fear that ending unlimited liability would mean a fatal lowering of that high standard of commercial morality upon which Britain's prosperity as a trading nation ultimately depended: the country's 'credit', in both senses of that word, was thus at stake. The impersonality of the joint-stock company, operating on the basis of limited liability, was contrasted with the partnership, where the crucial relationship was one of unreserved trust, grounded in mutual personal knowledge.[65]

Limited liability divided the political economists. For example, John Stuart Mill favoured its adoption, but McCulloch was fiercely hostile. Indeed, the latter was reminded of the old lotteries, when a few large prizes had drawn crowds of subscribers until in 1826 the legislature, 'struck with a just sense of the pernicious consequences of the speculative and gambling spirit which was thus diffused throughout the country, wisely suppressed' them.[66] McCulloch thought limited liability was likely to encourage the same sort of recklessness. He particularly disliked its animating principle, the notion 'that profit and risk shall be divorced from each other, and that speculators may undertake adventures, having, on the one hand, the chance of making unlimited profits if they turn out well, and of escaping, though they may ruin others, with a comparatively trifling loss if they turn out ill'.[67]

One eminent lawyer, D. C. Heron, differentiated between economic enterprises to which limited liability was well suited and those where it spelled danger. Adam Smith was right, Heron thought, to argue that joint-stock companies worked well when their operations could be reduced to a routine—but not otherwise. Unfortunately, added Heron, the extraordinary success of the joint-stock principle in recent years had resulted in 'numbers of persons of humble origin, and of

[65] Hence Arthur Clennam's anguished cry when he realizes that his ill-fated speculation has dissipated the assets of which he and his partner are joint custodians: 'But Doyce, Doyce, Doyce; my injured partner!' (*Little Dorrit*, Chapman & Hall edn. (n.d.; first pub. 1857), bk. 2, ch. 26, p. 350). See N. N. Feltes, 'Community and the Limits of Liability in Two Mid-Victorian novels', *Victorian Studies*, 17 (1973–4), 355–69.
[66] J. R. McCulloch, *Considerations on Partnerships with Limited Liability* (London, 1856), 12. On the lotteries, see Raven, 'The Abolition of Lotteries', 371–89.
[67] McCulloch, *Limited Liability*, 25. He anyhow thought that limited liability was not *needed*, since adequate capital could still be raised by family partnerships (ibid., 11–12).

indifferent moral principles' being 'brought into contact with enormous sums of money, the appropriation of which ha[d] been extremely easy'.[68]

To some robust free traders the existence of such abuses in no way invalidated the principle of limited liability itself. The *Saturday Review*, for example, praised the author of the limited liability legislation, Robert Lowe, for recognizing that 'full and untrammelled freedom of association' was, in truth, 'the complement of the freedom of trade'.[69] 'All freedom', it later conceded, implied 'the possibility of license', something which absolute governments were happy to invoke as an excuse for 'restriction and tyranny'; but that was not 'the English way of looking at these matters'. The *Saturday Review* argued that it made no sense to 'shackle freedom to restrain its excesses', since all that was needed was to impose tougher penalties on those convicted of fraud so as to deter potential offenders 'by the wholesome dread of punishment'.[70]

Limited liability did, at least, provide practical help for small investors by giving them a modicum of protection against the depredations of the financially unscrupulous. But, viewed from another angle, limited liability could be presented as little more than 'freedom not to pay one's debts'. This was a highly charged issue, given the conventional view that a merchant or trader forfeited his 'manhood' if he became a bankrupt. In fact, as Barbara Weiss shows, bankruptcy constituted one of the major themes in the novels of many important Victorian novelists, who were fascinated by the way in which financial disaster could both undermine personal identity and create confusion in social and sexual roles, leaving in its wake feelings of deep humiliation and disgrace.[71]

Meanwhile, moralists wrung their hands at the ease with which discharged bankrupts later set themselves up in business—behaviour which perhaps indicated that the British people were losing their sense of *shame* over getting into debt and eluding their creditors. All the more shocking was the class bias inherent in the system: small (mainly working-class) debtors often received harsh treatment, while bankrupts from a higher social position were handled far more leniently.[72]

It was widely felt that one of the greatest failures of mid-Victorian parliaments lay in their inability to formulate bankruptcy laws which satisfied the business

---

[68] D. C. Heron, 'Joint-Stock Frauds: Should the Accounts of Joint Stock Companies be Audited by a Public Officer?', *Transactions of the National Association for the Promotion of Social Science, 1861*, 185. He suggested, as a remedy, regular inspection and audit by a public officer, perhaps appointed by the Board of Trade (ibid., 190).

[69] 'The Law of Partnership', *Saturday Review*, 16 Feb. 1856, p. 293.

[70] 'The Treatment of Fraud', ibid., 1 Mar. 1856, pp. 340–1.

[71] B. Weiss, *The Hell of the English: Bankruptcy and the Victorian Novel* (Lewisburg, 1986). The misery and disgrace of 'failing' and of having a bailiff in the house are graphically depicted in George Eliot's *The Mill on the Floss*. See, too, Thackeray's depiction, in *The Newcomes*, of the consequences of the collapse of the fraudulent Bundelcund Bank.

[72] 'In the year of grace 1868, it seems not to be a crime to owe money, provided you owe enough . . . In England there are very different laws for rich and poor bankrupts' ('Rich and Poor Bankrupts', *All The Year Round*, 19 (16 May 1868), 545).

community, on the one hand, while upholding conventional moral standards, on the other,[73] a failure which Herbert Spencer blamed on the state's propensity to meddle with matters that did not concern it instead of concentrating on its 'negatively-regulatory function'.[74]

Perhaps the most ambitious attempt to square this particular circle was the 1849 Bankruptcy Act, which stipulated that bankrupts be given certificates of discharge, categorized by reference to the degree of blame attaching to their conduct, so that the fraudulent, the improvident, and the merely unfortunate would receive, respectively, a third-class, second-class, and first-class certificate.[75]

But the ingenious device of certification did not work, partly because the courts failed to apply the law consistently, but also because, as a lawyer experienced in bankruptcy work told the Walpole Commission in 1854:

A court of law cannot be converted into a school of morality, except so far as its punishments are substantial. The bankrupt is either a knave or he is not. If he is a knave, he cares for nothing but his 'white-washing'. If he is an honest man, he merits no punishment.[76]

Acts of 1861 and 1869 accordingly repealed these provisions, leaving responsibility for winding up a bankrupt's estate to the creditors. But this seemed to be going too far in the *opposite* direction, and it needed further legislation in 1883 to put an end to this 'creditor-managed system' under which ingenious debtors had, in practice, found it easy to evade their obligations.[77]

The problem of bankruptcy law reform was exacerbated by the changing Victorian attitudes to debt. According to the older view, businessmen must, if at all possible, show caution and individuals avoid debt. Successive Acts of Parliament which sought to reduce the incidence of imprisonment for debt may have pleased humanitarian reformers, but they worried those who felt that a deterrent to irresponsible behaviour had been removed.[78] However, by the middle of the century such moralistic preoccupations co-existed with the perception that in the bewilderingly complex world of modern commerce many debtors were either

[73] G. R. Searle, *Entrepreneurial Politics in Mid-Victorian Britain* (Oxford, 1993), 176–81, on the exasperation of Chambers of Commerce and other business pressure groups at the inability of landlord and lawyer-dominated parliaments to devise the legislation they wanted. For the definitive study of bankruptcy legislation, V. M. Lester, *Victorian Insolvency: Bankruptcy, Imprisonment for Debt, and Company Winding-up in Nineteenth-Century England* (Oxford, 1995).

[74] H. Spencer, 'Specialized Administration', *Fortnightly Review* (1871), in id., *The Man Versus the State*, ed. D. Macrae (London, 1969; first pub. 1884), 307.

[75] Weiss, *Hell of the English*, 43–4; Lester, *Victorian Insolvency*, 67–70.

[76] Weiss, *Hell of the English*, 45.

[77] The two main abuses were the misuse of liquidation procedures and the improper use of proxies (Lester, *Victorian Insolvency*, 178–82). Moreover, the creditor-managed system did not adequately meet the needs of *small* creditors (ibid., 208–9).

[78] On the complex question of when, in fact, imprisonment for debt was finally abolished, ibid., ch. 3.

victims to be pitied or else people who had been simply unfortunate. Moreover, in many branches of business, successful enterprise could not be undertaken without large capital, and capital usually had to be raised on credit. From here it was but a short step to the belief that living on credit (being creditworthy) was a test of character—was 'creditable', in a moral sense.[79]

The case of William Ellis illustrates the confusion into which many advocates of the market economy had stumbled. Ellis hovered between two quite different explanations of bankruptcies and insolvencies. One of them emphasized individual guilt and linked such 'dreadful calamities' to 'panics and convulsions', which, in turn, were 'consequences of ignorance, inexperience, and recklessness'. Yet, almost in the same breath, Ellis could liken bankruptcies to famines and epidemics, which, when they occurred, society had 'no alternative but to endure . . . as best it [might]'.[80]

Underlying this confusion was a grudging recognition that the freeing of the money markets, following the repeal of the usury acts, had not only made it easier to obtain credit, but was also exposing people to greater risks because the opening up of new fields of investment encouraged gamblers' habits among investors and led many of them to ignore traditional Christian teaching. All that apologists for free-market capitalism like Ellis could suggest by way of a remedy was a renewed *educational* effort. The extension of credit, he argued, 'while dangerous to the ignorant and unconscientious', was 'a great industrial power if wielded with intelligence and circumspection'.[81] Robert Lowe concurred with this view: the solution to indebtedness, he thought, lay in the development of 'habits of providence and forethought'.[82] Interestingly, Lowe also thought it folly to try to keep people honest by fear of punishment, and took the utilitarian view that it was 'better that debts should be paid unequally than that . . . property should be destroyed in the effort to ascertain an equality which yields a purely metaphysical and imaginary satisfaction to the thirsty creditor'.[83]

We will return at the end of the chapter to a more detailed exploration of how the mid-Victorians sought to extricate themselves from these perplexing moral dilemmas. But first we will examine another issue which reinforced anxieties about the country's reputation for probity: the commercial adulteration of the country's food and drink, one of the most blatant manifestations of 'criminal capitalism'.

---

[79] Hilton, *Age of Atonement*, ch. 4. S. Collini makes a similar point: mid-19th c. Britain was 'an economic world in which reputation played a powerful part: to be known as a man of character was to possess the moral collateral which would reassure potential business associates or employers' (*Public Moralists: Political Thought and Intellectual Life in Britain, 1850–1930* (Oxford, 1991), 106).

[80] W. Ellis, *A Layman's Contribution to the Knowledge and Practice of Religion in Common Life* (London, 1857), 418. Twisting yet again, Ellis added that society might, however, 'extract instruction and improvement for the future out of its present suffering'.   [81] Ibid., 322.

[82] R. Lowe, 'Have We Abolished Imprisonment for Debt?', *Fortnightly Review*, 21 (1877), 313.

[83] Viscount Sherbrooke [Lowe], 'What Shall We Do With Our Bankrupts?', *Nineteenth Century*, 10 (1881), 315–16. Compare this with the *Westminster Review*'s earlier presentation of the law as 'schoolmaster' ('The Law of Bankruptcy', 422).

FOOD ADULTERATION

'Of the many social problems which this country presents for the philanthropist and the political-economist to unravel', declared a participant at the 1870 Social Science Association, 'that of adulteration of food and drink is one of the most important.'[84] As with financial fraud, it was a problem which, though discussed almost exclusively in moral terms, had an economic origin. With urbanization proceeding apace, the geographical gap between consumers and producers of food was bound to widen, and the increasingly impersonal nature of food retailing created loopholes for various kinds of fraud, both at the level of manufacturing and of retailing. Consumers found it very difficult to detect such deception.

Nevertheless, a sensation was caused when, from 1851 onwards, the *Lancet* began publishing Arthur Hill Hassall's scientific analyses of food and drink, based upon the most advanced microscopical and chemical techniques then known.[85] By use of these modern methods Hassall was able to prove that scarcely a single item of common consumption was not widely adulterated, sometimes in ways highly damaging to health. Stung by these exposures, Parliament set up a Select Committee of Enquiry in 1855, and its report, which broadly substantiated Hassall's findings, put powerful ammunition in the hands of MPs seeking legislative redress.

Dickens threw *Household Words* behind the reformers and gave voice to the widespread feeling of shock and dismay. 'Every warm-blooded animal expresses indignation if its food be meddled with', Dickens's collaborator, Henry Morley, declared: 'the food of the British consumer is meddled with, and he is warm-blooded; he is, therefore, irritable and suspicious on the subject of provisions'.[86] The journal later carried a whimsical little story, again by Morley, about a starving alderman who, having studied Dr Hassall's book, could find nothing that he and his family could safely eat.[87]

The 1856 Select Committee succinctly laid out the reasons for the public disquiet on the subject of food adulteration: 'Not only is the public health . . . exposed to danger, and pecuniary fraud committed on the whole community', it declared, 'but the public morality is tainted, the higher commercial character of the country seriously lowered both at home and in the eyes of foreign countries.'[88] These charges will be examined later. But, first of all, it is worth asking why, faced by such a seemingly intolerable evil, Parliament and government took so long to intervene: for it was not until 1875 that effective legislation, providing an appropriate mechanism for enforcement, reached the statute book.[89]

[84] P. Bevan, 'What Legislative Measures Ought to be Taken to Prevent the Adulteration of Food, Drink, and Drugs', *Transactions of the National Association for the Promotion of Social Science, 1870*, 390.
[85] The earlier work of Frederick Accum had been discredited (J. Burnett, *Plenty and Want: A Social History of Diet in England from 1815 to the Present Day* (London, 1966), 190–2).
[86] *Household Words*, 5 (17 July 1852), 423.   [87] Ibid., 11 (31 Mar. 1855), 213–16.
[88] *Report from Select Committee on Adulteration of Food, &tc* (1856), p. iii.
[89] By the Sale of Food and Drugs Act. On this and the earlier largely ineffectual legislation, Burnett, *Plenty and Want*, 202–7.

Obviously there were vested interests exerting political influence to preserve the *status quo*. Their spokesmen made the most of the practical problems involved in reform: for example, one MP, Peek, a merchant, sneered at the ignorance of analysts, the so-called experts, and insisted that regulation could only be conducted by those with practical experience of the trade.[90] Others worried lest legislation should give rise to an 'objectionable system of informing and spying',[91] and pointed out the dangers of entrusting adjudication to local magistrates, some of whom would themselves be retailers anxious to 'do down' their rivals. In vain did reformers argue that this was a bogey, since the question of whether or not food had been adulterated would be decided on expert advice. The sceptics countered this argument by asking: 'Who would analyse the analyst?'[92]

In addition, many Radical MPs felt a gut dislike of any proposal which might extend the powers of either local or central government. John Arthur Roebuck, one of the most vociferous members of this group, raged against all such 'interference': 'there was a peddling legislation that was more mischievous than leaving things in their original mischief'.[93] Roebuck also feared the creation of precedents. Why should food and drink be treated differently from 'the sale of calico, cutlery, and similar articles?', he asked: 'the State ought not to pretend to protect the buyer by a warranty in the one case more than in the other'.[94] As for John Bright, he clearly saw parallels between the attempts to regulate the sale of food and drink and the earlier agitation by the factory reformers, and he used exactly the same arguments and rhetoric against the former which he had once deployed against the latter: the whole campaign, Bright felt, was a slur on the reputation of tradesmen, many of whom would emigrate, since if they were to be harassed and 'tracked by Government officers and inspectors every hour of the day, life would not be worth having'.[95]

If Bright used more extreme language than was prudent in a government minister (he made the above utterance while President of the Board of Trade), this was almost certainly because the adulteration issue had become entangled with the merits and demerits of free trade, about which Bright, of course, entertained very strong feelings. Bright spoke after several Tory MPs had linked their observations about the protection of the poor to sneering references to 'the free breakfast table'.[96] This infuriated the Radicals, who were at pains to point out that it was actually the most heavily taxed foods that were usually the most heavily adulterated.[97] The need for troublesome adulteration legislation could be avoided entirely, they intimated, by the simple expedient of lightening the indirect tax burden![98]

---

[90] Hansard, ccxxii, 606: 19 Feb. 1875.   [91] Ibid., xliv, 846–7: 7 July 1859.

[92] Ibid., clvii, 546: 14 Mar. 1860.   [93] Ibid., clvi, 2033: 29 Feb. 1860.   [94] Ibid., 2035.

[95] Ibid., cxciv, 731, 734: 5 Mar. 1869.

[96] e.g. Lord E. Cecil, who called for 'a breakfast table free from all impurities' (ibid., 721–2).

[97] Ibid., 727 (Pollard-Urquart).

[98] 'The heavy taxes imposed upon [tea, sugar and coffee] are incentives to their sophistication': let there be 'A Free and Pure Breakfast-table' ('The Adulteration of Food and Drugs', *Westminster Review*, 91 (1869), 203).

The strength of economic liberalism in the 1850s and 1860s can also be seen in the success enjoyed by opponents of reform when they invoked the principle of 'caveat emptor'.[99] The early (ineffectual) adulteration measures only became law at all because they interfered as little as possible with freedom of trade.[100] As a result, the pioneering Bill of 1860, to use Hassall's own words, was 'weak, diluted, and itself adulterated'.[101] Even these modest measures proved too much for some ardent free marketeers. Roebuck, for example, declared his belief that 'the buyer was the best person to protect himself, and so soon as a man was found to be selling impure and bad articles he lost his customers'.[102] Bright, who anyhow thought the problem grossly exaggerated, attributed adulteration in part to 'the very great, and, perhaps, inevitable competition in business', but also to 'the ignorance of customers', which, he optimistically declared, was gradually diminishing.[103]

But the weakness of the principle of 'caveat emptor' was its inapplicability to the everyday lives of the urban poor who were most at risk. As one MP put it, 'the poor man . . . had enough to do to earn his bread without spending time in analysing it'.[104] Another made the point that the poor could not easily change their retailer, still less find 10s. 6d. to pay an analyst's fee.[105] *Household Words* might regale its readers with what amounted to a DIY guide to food and drink analysis,[106] but although one can readily imagine 'the Irrepressible' performing these elaborate tests before he sat down to his evening meal, Dickens himself was the last person to suppose that herein lay the long-term answer to an acute social problem. In any case, as the *National Review* later observed, no one seriously expected the principle of 'caveat emptor' to be applied to the stamping of coins or to the employment of false weights and measures![107] Yet, in the words of another journalist, 'if it be no moral offence to exchange a pound of counterfeit coffee for a good shilling, how can it be a moral offence to exchange a counterfeit shilling for a pound of good coffee?'[108]

---

[99] Even in the 1880s the obdurate Herbert Spencer was still likening adulteration laws to the statutes of Edward III's reign 'under which innkeepers at seaports were sworn to search their guests to prevent the exportation of money or plate' (*Man Versus the State*, 71).

[100] e.g. Ayrton only supported the 1860 Bill because, while it prohibited a tradesman from guaranteeing as pure food which was actually adulterated, it still allowed goods to be sold without a guarantee: 'That provision . . . left it to a tradesman to carry on his business as he pleased' (Hansard, clvi, 2031: 29 Feb. 1860).

[101] [A. H. Hassall], 'Adulteration, and Its Remedy', *Cornhill Magazine*, 2 (1860), 96.

[102] 'The simple thing the Committee had to consider was, whether it was wise to spend their time in useless legislation', he concluded (Hansard, clvii, 544: 14 Mar. 1860).

[103] Ibid., cxciv, 733: 5 Mar. 1869.   [104] Ibid., clvi, 2026: 29 Feb. 1860 (Wise).

[105] Ibid., ccxxii, 611: 19 Feb. 1875. (Salt). Theoretically an aggrieved citizen could secure redress by a civil action or instigate a criminal indictment, neither a practical proposition.

[106] *Household Words*, 5 (17 July 1852), 423–6.

[107] Robb, *White-Collar Crime*, 153; Hansard, clvi, 2026: 29 Feb. 1860 (Wise); ibid., cliv, 849: 7 July 1859 (Walter). But Bright denied that the latter was a valid parallel, the ascertainment of correct weights and measures being a so much simpler process (ibid., cxciv, 734: 5 Mar. 1869).

[108] 'Adulteration of Food', *Westminster Review*, 201.

Yet the more robust defenders of market freedom were unabashed by these objections, and some even claimed that most adulteration was both harmless (for example, chicory in coffee, and alum in bread) and beneficial in that it brought certain commodities for the first time within the reach of poor consumers. Others reasoned, with greater plausibility, that poor people often preferred adulterated foodstuffs like glazed China teas. But this, though true enough, may simply have been because poor consumers knew no better: 'It is heartless sophistry to say that they like these mixtures', protested *Household Words*: quite simply, the poor had 'never tasted anything better'.[109]

Perhaps presenting food adulteration in this way as 'essentially a poor man's question', to cite Hassall's own phrase,[110] was not an entirely wise proceeding. It did, of course, exploit a middle-class audience's sense of pity at the plight of the weak and vulnerable, but, particularly when used by a paternalist Tory like Robert Cecil,[111] it also laid reformers open to the accusation that they were treating 'the people of this country like children'. In many ways that precisely describes what the interventionists were doing: the operation of the free market required participants to be informed and responsible adults, and reformers were implying that the poor, through no fault of their own, had not yet achieved such a status.

But the case for legislative restriction remained a weighty one, and even if the morally dubious paternalistic rhetoric were abandoned, three very strong arguments in its favour could still be deployed. First, as Hassall conclusively showed, many adulterations *did* directly threaten the public's health. 'Trade is one thing, poisoning our food another', protested Hassall. 'Surely there is no necessary connection between the two; and if connected, the sooner the connection is severed the better.'[112] These arguments even doctrinaire Radicals found difficulty in resisting —hence, the priority given to the criminalization of *dangerous* adulteration.[113]

Yet even if additives were not harmful in themselves, they could *indirectly* injure consumers through the replacement of highly nutritious substances by relatively useless ones—something which happened, for example, when milk was watered.[114] Second, to a lesser or greater extent, nearly all adulterations involved deception. A notable victim was the Exchequer, which suffered considerable financial loss.[115] The other victim was obviously the consumer. Indeed, Mill thought the sale of adulterated foodstuffs far more objectionable than the unregulated sale of poisons: for whereas the latter could be justified by reference to the principle of individual

---

[109] *Household Words*, 3 (12 Apr. 1851), 52.

[110] A. H. Hassall, *Adulterations Detected: Or, Plain Instructions For the Discovery of Frauds in Food and Medicine* (London, 1857), 38. There are many parliamentary expressions of this viewpoint: e.g. Hansard, clvi, 2026: 29 Feb. 1860 (Wise).

[111] 'The poor man being unable to protect himself, he contended that it was the duty of this House to step in and protect him' (Hansard, cliv, 847–8: 7 July 1859).

[112] Hassall, *Adulterations Detected*, 39; see also Bevan, 'Adulteration', 391.

[113] Thus a supporter of the 1872 Act (Muntz) observed that 'if anyone chose to mix beans with coffee, or water with milk, no one under this Act could say anything' (Hansard, ccix, 1507: 6 Mar. 1872).

[114] Hassall, *Adulterations Detected*, 6.   [115] Ibid., 18.

liberty, no one could reasonably object to public controls for the prevention of fraud.[116]

And it was the very scale of this fraud, when exposed, which caused amazement. For example, Hassall's investigations showed that chicory, with which most coffee was heavily adulterated, was itself often made of roasted corn, acorns, and such like substances,[117] causing one journalist to observe: 'to such a pitch of refinement has the art of falsifying of alimentary substances reached, that the very articles used to adulterate are adulterated; and, while one tradesman is picking the pockets of his customers, a still more cunning rogue is, unknown to himself, deep in his own'.[118]

But this leads on to the third of the reformers' arguments: the deleterious long-term impact of adulteration on the moral character of its perpetrators and on the trading community's reputation for probity. Hassall laid particular emphasis on these two points: 'It is impossible for a man to be guilty of adulteration, and yet be an honest and a moral man, although doubtless there are many adulterators who flatter themselves with the belief that they are so; it is, however, but an attempt at self-deception.' Adulteration, wrote Hassall, also engendered

the greatest mistrust on the part of the buyer, who loses confidence in those with whom he deals, and in this way sometimes the honest trader comes to be looked upon with the same suspicion as the adulterating merchant, manufacturer, or tradesman. Another consequence is, that the status of that portion of the trading community which sells articles of consumption is lowered, and is looked upon with misgiving in all its transactions. Lastly, the character of the whole nation suffers in consequence of the prevalence of adulteration.[119]

Stamping out unfair practices would thus be in the interests of the majority of honest tradesmen and merchants. Wakley, the *Lancet*'s editor, argued that such people would positively benefit from his paper's revelations.[120] Hassall sang the same song: the honest trader had 'much to gain, for while he will be able to secure fair prices for a genuine commodity, his name, also, will be made known to the public, and he will be upheld in his true light and character, as an upright and honourable tradesman'.[121] This was also to become a favourite argument with those who deprecated unregulated *laissez-faire* on more general grounds: 'An honest silver-smith', Robert Williams later observed, 'looks upon the Hall-mark as a benefit and a security to the seller as well as to the buyer.'[122]

The problem of food adulteration came to a climax in mid-century, but significantly abated thereafter. This owed much to more stringent regulatory

---

[116] J. S. Mill, *On Liberty*, Everyman edn. (London, 1910; first pub. 1859), 151–2.

[117] Cited in S. S. Sprigge, *The Life and Times of Thomas Wakley* (London, 1897), 464–8.

[118] *Quarterly Review* (Mar. 1855).

[119] A. H. Hassall, *Food and Its Adulterations* (London, 1855), p. xxxv.

[120] Sprigge, *Wakley*, 462–3.   [121] Hassall, *Food and Its Adulterations*, 2.

[122] R. Williams, 'Laissez-Faire', *Fraser's Magazine*, 1 (1870), 76–7. Hassall suggested that the answer to adulteration might be for the public to insist on buying goods that were expressly warranted ('Adulteration', *Cornhill Magazine*, 2 (1860), 95).

legislation, the need for which Parliament slowly and reluctantly came round to accepting. But the economic liberals had not been entirely wrong when they predicted that market forces would eventually contribute to a solution of what was really a temporary problem. For commercial developments, in particular the rise of the multiple retail shop, meant that by the 1890s adulteration had become, in most cases, a financially unattractive stratagem: the new branded foods were purchased in large quantities because those who advertised them stressed their 'purity', and the manufacturers, wholesalers, and retailers dared not forfeit consumer confidence by engaging in any impropriety.[123] Perhaps, too, the palates and taste buds of working-class consumers gradually improved, as brightly coloured, pungently flavoured foods and drinks lost some of their former popularity.

Unfortunately the adulteration of food and drink was only one aspect of a much larger problem. As one Christian moralist wrote in 1854:

The production of spurious and counterfeit goods forms an extensive branch of manufacture. And to such a pitch has this species of fraud been carried in some departments, that only a few years ago, I was assured by a Christian tradesman that in the line of business in which he was engaged, there were not more than three or four firms with whom he was acquainted, who did not adulterate the article by which he gained his living, so that he found it most difficult to stand his ground against such fraudulent competition. In all this a two-fold guilt is incurred—the guilt of dishonesty, and the guilt of deceit.[124]

Smiles broadly agreed: 'There are tradesmen who adulterate, contractors who "scamp", manufacturers who give us shoddy instead of wool, "dressing" instead of cotton, cast-iron tools instead of steel, needles without eyes, razors made only "to sell", and swindled fabrics in many shapes.'[125]

Trollope broadened the indictment: 'Do we recognize the dishonesty of our tradesmen with their advertisements, their pretended credit, their adulterations, and fake cheapness?', he asked:

Do not such of us as are tradesmen ourselves fall into the same courses, without the slightest conscience stricken sense of dishonesty? Have we the slightest feeling of a sin against truth or honesty when we hear some learned lawyer use all his wit to protect a criminal by legal chicanery?[126]

---

[123] The Co-operative Movement also played an important part in improving food standards (Burnett, *Plenty and Want*, 201–2).

[124] H. Stowell, *A Model for Men of Business: Or, Lectures on the Character of Nehemiah* (London, 1854), 146–7. Stowell wrote of the violation of the 8th and 9th Commandments.

[125] S. Smiles, *Self-Help: With Illustrations of Conduct and Perseverance* (London, 1910; first pub. 1859), 337.

[126] Anthony Trollope, *The New Zealander*, ed. N. J. Hall (Oxford, 1965; written 1855–6), 211. One of Trollope's biographers links his concern with commercial dishonesty to the sad history of his father-in-law, Edward Heseltine, who, after retiring in 1852 as the manager of the Rotherham Bank, was found to have been responsible for 'large deficiencies', amounting to several thousand pounds, in the bank's accounts, for which he was unable or unwilling to provide an explanation (V. Glendinning, *Trollope* (London, 1992), 223–5).

Protectionist Tory journals, like *Blackwood's Magazine*, were also understandably keen to draw attention to such contemporary abuses. Adulteration, from this viewpoint, symbolized the more general deterioration in the character of commercial life which free trade had brought in its wake: 'Trade honesty used to be the pride of England. Where is it gone?', lamented one essayist.[127] *Blackwood's Magazine* evoked the value system still cherished by 'some of us yet living' who preferred, whether in trade or in politics, to deal with those whom they could trust, people who would 'neither adulterate principles nor commodities'.[128]

The *Blackwoods'* articles raised the larger issue of whether blame for malpractice could be pinned solely on manufacturers and traders. For as Hassall had admitted when discussing food adulteration, it was the ferocity of *competition* which drove some businessmen, against their better judgement, into unethical behaviour.[129] Perhaps, in that case, part of the fault lay with consumers who were pursuing cheapness too zealously, regardless of all other considerations. In 1858 *Household Words* carried a sad little tale about a piano-dealer who had been driven into bankruptcy by a ruthless bargain hunter, only to be rebuked by a Commissioner for 'reckless trading and making away with stock'.[130]

But this, in turn, suggested the further reflection, that 'buying in the cheapest market' might also have been responsible for the bad working conditions and low pay found in many trades and industries. 'It is we, the consumers, who cause low prices, and consequently low wages', wrote an Anglican clergyman who was later involved in the campaign to 'moralize' the consumer through a 'Consumers' League'.[131] Yet Charles Kingsley suspected nothing would happen to help his sweated tailors since 'all classes, both manufacturers and the consuming public, profited by the system which kept the tailors down'.[132]

Yet if all, or most, citizens were 'guilty', where was salvation to be found?

THE MORALIZATION OF THE MARKET?

The simplest resolution of this dilemma was to evade it by insisting that, a few unfortunate abuses notwithstanding, the extension of the market had in fact promoted *higher* ethical standards. This was the line adopted by *The Economist* in an

---

[127] 'Civilisation—The Census', *Blackwood's Magazine*, 77 (1855), 24.

[128] 'Hints for Legislators', ibid., 73 (1853), 505. The adulteration issue also offered Protectionist Tories an issue on which they could loudly and angrily proclaim their commitment to protecting the helpless poor against their unscrupulous exploiters ('Blue Laws', ibid., 107 (1870), 488).

[129] Hassall, *Adulteration Detected*, 8–9. The same might be said of the adulteration practised by the keepers of beerhouses.

[130] 'Buying in the Cheapest Market', *Household Words*, 18 (28 Aug. 1858), 256–8.

[131] W. Richmond, *Economic Morals: Four Lectures* (London, 1890), 56–8.

[132] C. Kingsley, 'Cheap Clothes and Nasty', by 'Parson Lot', in *Alton Locke: Tailor and Poet* (1895; first pub. 1850), pp. lxxiii–lxxiv.

article, published in February 1851, entitled 'Scientific, Educational, and Moral Progress of the Last Fifty Years',[133] which was essentially a little homily on what Adam Smith had earlier said: namely, that 'whenever commerce is introduced into any country, probity and punctuality always accompany it'.[134]

Did scandals like the collapse of Strahan, Paul and Co. later cause *The Economist* to change its mind? Not a bit of it. In a new article, 'The Morality of Trade and of Law', it repeated its earlier panegyric, this time even more robustly:

Trade carries with it a rigid morality . . . It may be contaminated by rogues, as religion is contaminated by hypocrites, and as statesmanship is brought into discredit by vulgar, meddling, restrictive plodders, but it naturally inculcates punctual and rigid honesty, and dishonest traders are false to their calling. . . . To rigidly keep engagements, to be punctual in the performance of contracts to pay debts the very day they are due, to live frugally and within their means, to accumulate capital, and gather increasing influence in society, are the virtues of the middle and lower classes rather than of the higher, and of the commercial rather than the landed interest. In fact, almost all improvements in business habits have originated in towns amongst the middle and mercantile classes.[135]

Why, then, were business malpractices occurring at all? According to *The Economist*, they had been much exaggerated by members of the pre-industrial social classes, who were jealous and resentful of the emerging new order: 'Hence all [its] proceedings are closely watched, and every blot on the commercial escutcheon is pelted with all the missiles that the classes they are trespassing on, or which envy them, can hurl against it.' But, if blame was to be allotted to anyone, it should mainly go to the solicitors and attorneys who had given the businessmen bad advice! Men from the legal professions, the paper argued, were ruled by codes of conduct 'made in an age of less moral enlightenment than the present' and this led them continually 'to defend what [was] morally and commercially wrong'. *The Economist*'s conclusion was that 'mercantile men, after this exposition, will be careful how they place their consciences in the hands of lawyers'.

Henry Maine gave a new twist to this sort of argument by propounding the following paradox:

The spectacle of frauds, unheard of before the period at which they were observed, . . . shows clearly that, before they became possible, the moral obligations of which they are the breach must have been more than proportionately developed. It is the confidence reposed and deserved by the many which affords facilities for the bad faith of the few, so that, if

---

[133] *The Economist*, 1 Feb. 1851, pp. 110–11.

[134] Smith argued that commerce developed not only 'business habits' but, by making a man's fortune rest on his *reputation*, raised moral standards. It also rescued citizens from the demoralizing influence of 'dependency', which had been so prevalent under 'feudalism'. *The Economist* writer cannot have known all these passages, some of which appear in the then unpublished *Lectures on Jurisprudence* (N. Rosenberg, 'Adam Smith and the stock of moral capital', *History of Political Economy*, 22 (1990), 8–11).

[135] *The Economist*, 23 June 1855, pp. 671–2. The order of sentences has been slightly altered.

colossal examples of dishonesty occur, there is no surer conclusion than that scrupulous honesty is displayed in the average of the transactions which, in the particular case, have supplied the delinquent with his opportunity.[136]

In other words, frauds only occurred in societies where the general standard of honesty, rooted in custom rather than enforced by 'Imperative Law', inspired widespread trust.[137]

Walter Bagehot (a later editor of *The Economist*) also took a philosophical view of the periodic commercial breakdowns and scandals, though on somewhat different grounds. Bagehot was ready to concede that it was the desire for quick profits which underlay most business dishonesty. In an intensely competitive world, small traders, trying to make their fortune, wanted instant success and produced an inferior article in order to get it: '[the] constant levelling of our commercial houses is . . . unfavourable to commercial morality'.[138] Bagehot felt that old-established mercantile houses, on the other hand, lived 'by a *continuity* of trade, which detected fraud would spoil'.

Yet while there were those, like Gladstone, who hoped that Britain would throw up venerable commercial dynasties with just such a high sense of 'honour' on the model of Renaissance Italy (did he have his own family in mind?), Bagehot himself did not take this line at all:

No country of great hereditary trade, no European country at least, was ever so little 'sleepy', to use the only fit word, as England; no other was ever so prompt at once to seize new advantages. . . . The rough and vulgar structure of English commerce is the secret of its life; for it contains 'the propensity to variation', which, in the social as in the animal kingdom, is the principle of progress.[139]

The 'Darwinian' language of this passage is significant, representing as it does the brutal 'you can't make omelettes without breaking eggs' sort of approach encouraged in the later nineteenth century by a misapplication of Darwin's evolutionary theories. 'The survival of the fittest', a phrase coined by Herbert Spencer rather than Darwin himself, could be invoked in support of the view that 'success' denoted 'fitness', which in turn was an expression of 'worth'. In 1860 a bemused Darwin wrote to a friend: 'I have received, in a Manchester newspaper, rather a good squib, showing that I have proved "might is right"; and therefore that Napoleon is right, and every cheating tradesman is also right.'[140]

The view that capitalist enterprise necessarily involved a merciless winnowing of failure and a rewarding of success and that it was thus pointless for anyone to

---

[136] H. S. Maine, *Ancient Law* (London, 1861), 306–7.   [137] Ibid., 305.

[138] Bagehot, *Lombard Street*, 10.

[139] Ibid., 10–11. But Bagehot, too, emphasized the importance of 'trust' in commercial life (ibid., 160–1).

[140] E. Richards, 'Darwin and the Descent of Woman', in D. Oldroyd and I. Langham (eds.), *The Wider Domain of Evolutionary Thought* (Dordrecht, 1983), 89–90, 108 fn. 122.

try to stop the operation of the 'law of nature' soon became widespread in the United States. However, it is much less frequently encountered in Britain.[141] On the contrary, as we have already seen, even apologists for capitalism were determined to find ways in which the market could be 'tamed' and moralized.[142] What role did Christianity have to play in this operation?

We have already seen how great a stress many clergymen laid on the necessity of business integrity. Unfortunately, when it came to *practical* remedies against fraud and malpractice, the Christian evangelists had little to offer. Boardman argued that since speculation was 'not only a violation of the Scripture code of morals, but a huge fountain of social corruption', trading in stocks should be regulated by the same general rules which governed other branches of commerce.[143] But how, in practice, speculation (a species of gambling) was to be distinguished from 'legitimate commerce', he had no clearer idea than those who had earlier broached the proposal.[144] As for the Revd W. H. Lyttelton, he could only suggest 'some kind of *combination* of master manufacturers with the inferior members of the world of commerce, and of customers with tradesmen' aimed at delivering 'individual men from many overpowering temptations to which they are now exposed in almost every kind of industry'.[145] Finally, a few Anglican clergymen, later active in the Christian Social Union, planned a 'white list' of good employers, in the hope that consumer pressure might contribute to the moralization of the market—an idea that can be traced back to Kingsley's earlier attempt to organize a consumer boycott of clothes made in 'sweat shops'.[146]

Meanwhile, secular writers also struggled to find practical ways of stamping out commercial misconduct. Some, like Trollope, got no further than reiterating banalities such as that men went astray when they abandoned honesty for expediency and that, in the long run, they would suffer for their immorality.[147] But

---

[141] e.g. Collini notes how Fawcett links the concept of self-help to the idea of competition and struggle, but *not* as part of a 'Social Darwinian' contest to secure the elimination of the 'unfit', but rather to denote the citizen's struggle with himself, which Fawcett, like so many other Victorian moralists, saw as a necessary step in the strengthening of 'character' (*Public Moralists*, 192–3).

[142] There was also an interesting *plebeian* concept of the 'moralization of the market', which partly overlaps with, partly diverges from, mainstream 'bourgeois' versions (P. Joyce, *Visions of the People: Industrial England and the Question of Class, 1848–1914* (Cambridge, 1991), chs. 4–5; E. F. Biagini, *Liberty, Retrenchment and Reform: Popular Liberalism in the Age of Gladstone, 1860–1880* (Cambridge, 1992), ch. 2).   [143] Boardman, *Bible in the Counting-House*, 114–15.

[144] Nor have later commentators enjoyed greater success. See the attempt at drawing boundaries in E. B. Perkins, *Gambling in English Life* (London, 1950), 3–4.

[145] Revd W. H. Lyttelton, *Sins of Trade and Business* (London, 1874), p. vi.

[146] Kingsley, 'Cheap Clothes and Nasty', esp. p. lxxxi. Kingsley added the warning that well-to-do consumers who bought cheap clothes sometimes picked up the infections of the poverty-stricken tailors (ibid., p. lxxvii). On the ideas animating the CSU, see J. Garnett, 'Hastings Rashdall and the Renewal of Christian Social Ethics, c.1890–1920', in J. Garnett and C. Matthew (eds.), *Revival and Religion Since 1700: Essays for John Walsh* (1993), 297–316: also, E. J. Garnett, 'Aspects of the Relationship Between Protestant Ethics and Economic Activity in Mid-Victorian England', D.Phil. thesis (Oxford, 1986).   [147] Trollope, *Three Clerks*, 346, 352–3.

clearly something *practical* needed to be done, if only because, as Mill argued, 'short-sighted frauds' committed by a few unscrupulous exporters could close down a trade to other fellow-countrymen for many decades to come.[148] Mill's solution, like Ellis's, was a strengthening of the laws against commercial fraud and, even more, improvements to the machinery of enforcement, with a public prosecutor initiating proceedings in the case of the more serious and conspicuous offences. But Mill recognized that the only other resource 'which the present constitution of society' afforded against acts of commercial misconduct was 'a sterner reprobation by opinion'.[149] Thus, Mill, like so many of his contemporaries, pinned his main hopes upon the prospect of *moral progress*.[150]

Herbert Spencer dramatized the urgent need for such progress in his essay, 'The Morals of Trade', which describes how the 'pressure of competition' drove weak-willed and wicked men into adulteration, fraud, dishonest salesmanship, and so on. 'Trade is essentially corrupt', Spencer conceded. 'It has been said that the law of the animal creation is "Eat and be eaten"; and of our trading community it may be similarly said that the law is—cheat and be cheated.' Spencer grimly concluded that 'a system of keen competition carried on . . . without adequate moral restraint, [was] very much a system of commercial cannibalism'.[151]

In fact, America presented Spencer, as it had earlier presented Dickens, with an awful example of the lengths to which unbridled commercialism could be taken. Angered by American acts of literary piracy (the disregard, in other words, of the sanctity of 'intellectual property'), Spencer warned an American friend that unless the citizens of that country displayed more respect for other people's claims, its institutions faced collapse.[152] The behaviour of unscrupulous New York

---

[148] 'There are nations whose commodities are looked shily upon by merchants, because they cannot depend on finding the quality of the article conformable to that of the sample . . . ; and among other instances given by Mr Babbage, is one in which a branch of export trade was for a long time actually stopped by the forgeries and frauds which had occurred in it' (J. S. Mill, *Principles of Political Economy*, in id., *Collected Works*, ed. J. M. Robson (Toronto, 1965), ii. 110–11).

[149] Cited in S. Hollander, *The Economics of John Stuart Mill, ii, Political Economy* (Oxford, 1985), 821–2: Mill, *Principles of Political Economy*, in *Collected Works*, v. 733.

[150] Spencer did have one practical suggestion to make: that the activities of an incorporated body should be confined to the fulfilment of the purpose for which it was incorporated ('Railway Morals', 447–8).

[151] H. Spencer, 'The Morals of Trade' (1859), in H. Spencer, *Essays, Scientific, Political, and Speculative* (1893), 134. For further lamentations of this kind, see 'Representative Government—What Is It Good For?', *Westminster Review*, Oct. 1857 (reprinted in Spencer, *Man Versus the State*, 244) and 'From Freedom to Bondage', 1891 (ibid., 315). Martineau, too, sometimes took up a similar position: see V. K. Pichanick, *Harriet Martineau: The Woman and Her Work 1802–76* (Ann Arbor, 1980), 71.

[152] Spencer to E. L. Youmans, 10 Jan. 1882, in D. Duncan, *The Life and Letters of Herbert Spencer* (London, 1908), 210. Dickens had been provoked into including some tart observations in his *American Notes* on the American predilection for 'smart dealing', which, he said, had caused many a swindle, public and private, and had 'done more in a few years to impair the public credit, and to cripple the public resources, than dull honesty, however rash, could have effected in a century' (*American Notes for General Circulation*, Chapman & Hall edn. (n.d.; first pub. 1842), ch. 8, p. 287). See B. Harding, 'Transatlantic Views of Speculation and Value, 1820–1860', *Historical Research* 66 (1993), 209–21.

businessmen particularly offended Spencer: 'Competitive warfare carried on in this style, might not unfitly be called commercial murder', he wrote.[153]

In his more ambitious theoretical works Spencer tried to establish the exact parameters of commercial virtue. 'General acceptance of the maxim that honesty is the best policy', he argues in *The Data of Ethics*, 'implies general experience that gratification of the self-regarding feelings is eventually furthered by such checking of them as maintains equitable dealings.' By this Spencer meant that shop-keepers' bills should be instantly paid and that it was desirable to avoid shoddy workmanship and adulteration and the hypothecating of other people's property in speculation. Spencer found the latter practice particularly deplorable since it aggravated 'those commercial panics which bring disasters on multitudes and injuriously affect all'.[154] Sharp practice, the product of an undeveloped ethical consciousness, would also be damaging, Spencer thought, if it resulted in the elimination of competition.[155]

But was it realistic to ask businessmen to refrain from exploiting any competitive advantage that came to hand? The principle of 'justice' certainly sanctioned the enforcement of the 'market' price, whatever that might be. On the other hand, Spencer's principle of 'negative benevolence' forbade 'unduly pressing against another an advantage which circumstances gave'.[156] Spencer illustrated the practical predicaments to which this could give rise through a discussion of employers' responsibility for wage determination. Employers, he argued, should not abuse their position to force down pay to the lowest possible level. On the other hand, he added, 'a seemingly-generous employer, who looks only at direct results, may, by his generosity, intensify the miseries of the most miserable, that he may mitigate the miseries of the less miserable'. Furthermore, an unwillingness to economize on wages could easily lead to bankruptcy, which would hit everyone dependent on him.[157]

Spencer obviously did not believe that competition in itself was wrong. But he drew the moral that economic growth needed to be (and in the fullness of time would be) accompanied by ethical improvement—encouraging signs of which he already affected to see in the form of a 'new and better chivalry', from which would arise 'a higher standard of honour'.[158] Putting an end to what he called the 'idolatry' of the worship of wealth for its own sake would be a step in the right direction.[159] Spencer also thought it desirable to end the uncritical association of wealth with respectability,[160] a viewpoint which he shared with Smiles.

---

[153] Spencer, *The Principle of Ethics*, in id., *The Synthetic Philosophy of Herbert Spencer*, Westminster edn. (New York, 1892–6), ii. 282.

[154] Spencer, *The Data of Ethics* (1894; first pub. 1879), 207–8.

[155] Spencer, *Principle of Ethics*, in id., *Synthetic Philosophy*, Westminster edn., ii. 282.

[156] Ibid., 296.   [157] Ibid., 291–2.

[158] Spencer, 'Morals of Trade', 148. See also Spencer's letter to Huxley, 6 Feb. 1888, in Duncan, *Spencer*, 281.   [159] Spencer, 'Morals of Trade', 141–3.

[160] Spencer, 'Railway Morals', 422.

As for dishonesty, all could agreed that this was economically irrational, while 'trust' was the glue which held most commercial transactions together. Capitalism, then, though it rested upon a creed of selfishness, required in its practitioners a certain disinterestedness if it were to function effectively. Unfortunately, what was desirable for the commercial community as a whole might not coincide with the short-term interests of a particular businessman. A whole generation of Victorian moralists wrestled with this thorny conundrum.

Proselytizing Christians emphasized the ways in which misconduct brought about its own nemesis, but so did others with a more secular outlook on life. Thus the financial journalist, David Morier Evans, took consolation from the reflection that the 1858 commercial crisis—a crisis partly brought about, he believed, by human gullibility and greed—would end up by throwing 'the people more completely on their moral resources' and teaching them 'that they must be more faithful to principle'.[161]

Similarly, Samuel Smiles treated the rise and fall of the railway 'mania' as a kind of moral parable, in which 'folly and knavery', rapacity and credulity, produced their own inevitable reaction.[162] But one also detects an ambivalence in Smiles's writing on the issue of whether there really was a self-correcting principle at work in commercial life. 'Honesty is the best policy', he stoutly maintains in *Self-Help*.[163] This virtue, he continues, was 'still happily in the ascendant amongst common people, and the general business community of England [was] still sound at heart, putting their honest character into their respective callings'. But there were 'exceptional cases, of low-minded and grasping men', who carried out all manner of knavery. Fortunately, 'the Sadleirs, Dean Pauls and Redpaths, for the most part, come to a sad end even in this world'.

But Smiles was too honest himself not to concede that 'the successful swindles of others [might] not be "found out"' at all. However, he felt that financial gains so obtained would remain with their acquirers 'as a curse and not as a blessing'. Smiles thus ended up by arguing, in quasi-religious language, that wealth ultimately counted for nothing compared with the possession of 'a heart at peace'. Contrary to popular belief, Smiles emphatically did not glorify success as such. 'Better lose all and save character. For character is itself a fortune', he preached.[164] Conventional pieties about living within one's means, avoiding the sin of avarice, and so on, followed naturally from this diagnosis.[165]

William Ellis likewise combined his popular explanations of the workings of the market with moralistic warnings against various forms of deception and sharp practice—behaviour which he castigated as sinning against law and morality. Like Smiles, Ellis hoped that misconduct would lead to worldly failure: 'Dealers who allow themselves to be seduced into such practices deserve to be abandoned by their customers; and by their consequent ruin to be held up as a warning to all

[161] Evans, *The Commercial Crisis, 1857–1858*, 106.   [162] Smiles, *Engineers*, iii. 374–5, 386.
[163] Smiles, *Self-Help*, 334.   [164] Ibid., 337–8. Also see Ch. 3.   [165] Ibid., 349, 362–3.

who would introduce distrust and double-dealing into trade.' Moreover, fraud should be treated as a crime, on a par with murder, violence, burglary, and theft, Ellis urged.[166]

But these were 'solutions' to the problem of commercial malpractice which rested on appeals to the individual conscience. What else could be done to raise the tone of business life?

ENTREPRENEURIALISM AND 'FINANCE'

Thomas Carlyle came up with one of the most ingenious attempts to purge capitalism of its morally obnoxious features. Carlyle's originality was that he combined a contempt for political economy in all its utilitarian and Ricardian manifestations with an often grudging admiration for the organizational skills and speculative daring of the major capitalists. Even in 'Plugson of Undershot', with his despicable preoccupation with 'buying in the cheapest and selling in the dearest market', Carlyle detected a heroic potential:

Not without man's faculty, insight, courage, hard energy, is this rugged figure. His words are none of the wisest; but his actings cannot be altogether foolish. Think, how were it, stoodst thou suddenly in his shoes! He has to command a thousand men. And not imaginary commanding; no, it is real, incessantly practical. . . . For these his thousand men he has to provide raw-material, machinery, arrangement, house-room; and ever at the week's end, wages by due sale.[167]

The Carlylean vision of such a heroic 'captain of industry'[168] left its imprint on Victorian fiction, helping to disseminate the notion that manufacturers resembled, or could be converted into behaving like, the virile, all-conquering warrior chieftains of old.[169] Some successful Victorian businessmen, like W. E. Forster, tried to adapt their lives to such a model.[170]

What Carlyle was in fact doing was splitting off the entrepreneurial aspects of capitalism from its financial base—divorcing the profit-maximizing and speculative elements from the creative and organizational ones. Mid-Victorian writers commonly employed this strategy. For example, Smiles, in his *Lives of the Engineers* (1863), portrays his heroes—mechanical geniuses like the Stephensons, Watt, Telford, and Brunel—as creative workmen, indifferent, even hostile, to the pecuniary implications of their activities.

---

[166] Ellis, *Layman's Contribution*, 117–18, 277–8.
[167] T. Carlyle, *Past and Present*, Ward, Lock & Co. edn. (London, 1910; first pub. 1843), 283–4.
[168] Carried on in the writings of John Ruskin: e.g. *Unto This Last* (London, 1862).
[169] e.g. Mr Thornton in Mrs Gaskell's *North and South* (London, 1854–5).
[170] See the very revealing [anonymous] article by Forster, '"Strikes" and "Lock-Outs"', *Westminster Review*, 61 (1854), 119–45.

Thus, according to Smiles, Thomas Telford 'died in comparatively moderate circumstances' and 'although he could not be said to have an indifference to money, he yet estimated it as a thing worth infinitely less than character' since his 'wants were few, and his household expenses small'. What Telford did have was

the highest idea of the dignity of his profession; not, however, because of the money it would produce but of the great things it was calculated to accomplish. In his most confidential letters we find him often expatiating on the noble works he was engaged in designing or constructing, and the national good likely to flow from then, but never on the pecuniary advantages he himself was to reap.[171]

Writing of the expansion of the railway system, Smiles was thus able to dissociate himself entirely from the speculative mania which enveloped it in the 1840s, a development which he assailed in uncompromisingly moralistic language.[172]

The *Westminster Review* agreed: the recent railway boom, it said, had really been 'a mania for stock jobbing. Railways had no more to do with the object of the speculators in them, than bulbs with the tulip mania of 1635'.[173] One is reminded of George Eliot's character, Caleb Garth, to whom ' "business" never meant money transactions, but the skilful application of labour'.[174]

Dickens's famous 'ambivalence' about capitalist enterprise can be explained by the fact that he, too, tended to set off the 'creative' side of business life against its financial agents: the Chereeble brothers against the usurer, Ralph Nickleby, in *Nicholas Nickleby*, Rouncewell the Ironmaster against the Smallweeds in *Bleak House*, and Daniel Doyce against Mr Merdle in *Little Dorrit*.

But in his later novels Dickens was realistic enough to concede that it was the despicable 'financiers' who held the whip hand. Doyce, the ingenious mechanic, commands our admiration in *Little Dorrit*; but we are made aware that the world from which he comes, that of the small-scale partnership, is doomed to disappear before the advance of Mr Merdle, the speculator, with his roots in decadent 'high society', a type that will surely inherit the earth. In fact, it has been noted that one of Dickens's favourite ploys is to confront the contemporary economic scene with the heroic entrepreneurial ideals which had once animated it but from which

---

[171] Smiles, *Engineers*, ii. 487–8. He made similar observations about Stephenson (ibid., iii. 375–6).

[172] Ibid., iii. 373–4.

[173] 'Railway Management', *Westminster Review*, 53 (1850), 413. Sturge, himself a railway director, deplored 'the gambling turn which the share market had taken' and urged his fellow directors to show a greater sense of social responsibility, e.g. by not using 'inside information' for the purpose of personal enrichment (A. Tyrrell, *Joseph Sturge and the Moral Radical Party in Early Victorian Britain* (London, 1987), 32).

[174] G. Eliot, *Middlemarch*, Penguin edn. (London, 1965; first pub. 1871–2), ch. 56, p. 596: 'He knew values well, but he had no keenness of imagination for monetary results in the shape of profit and loss; and having ascertained this to his cost, he determined to give up all forms of his beloved "business" which required that talent. He gave himself up entirely to the many kinds of work which he could do without handling capital' (ibid., ch. 24, p. 284).

it had recently diverged.[175] However, in his final completed novel, *Our Mutual Friend*, Dickens shows power being monopolized by an unholy combination of louche financiers, greedy lawyers, and heartless 'men about town': 'shares' are all. There could be no prospect of 'moralizing' these parasites.

This brings us, in conclusion, to the central paradox of Victorian attitudes towards business. Martin Wiener and others have rightly pointed out that in Victorian Britain manufacturing enjoyed less social prestige than banking or stockbroking: members of landed families who would not have dreamt of dirtying their hands in industry increasingly rubbed shoulders with wealthy members of the City, and some even pursued a career in finance.

Yet, morally, the positions were reversed. As George Robb puts it: 'The banker was the stereotypical villain of melodrama—the forecloser of mortgages, the despoiler of widows and orphans.'[176] Industrialists often received a more favourable press. Thus in Miss Muloch's novel, *John Halifax, Gentleman* (1877), the self-made John Halifax, a woollen manufacturer of massive integrity, refrains from investing in the shaky local bank (he 'took a patriarchal pleasure in investing [surplus money] in land, cheaply for the benefit of his mills, and those concerned therein'), but later plays the role of the Good Samaritan by depositing £5,000 of his own money in a brave move which succeeds in stopping panic withdrawals.[177]

Is there not something highly revealing in the way that the Victorians tended to attach social value to what they morally despised and vice versa? It perhaps suggests that, despite all the brave talk about 'moralizing' modern commerce (a commercial system which increasingly rested on the investments of shareholders who had no personal responsibility for the day-to-day utilization of their capital), the best that could be achieved was to find havens of moral probity and respectability from which, hopefully, the spirit of profit-making could be exorcized. The attempt to do this forms the subject-matter of the next two chapters.

[175] Following Lukacs, J. M. Brown writes of the way in which the values associated with the heroic epoch of bourgeois development were used by Dickens 'as a means of criticising the contemporary social situation and behaviour of the mid-Victorian middle class itself' (*Dickens: Novelist in the Market-Place* (London, 1982), 41).   [176] Robb, *White-Collar Crime*, 57.

[177] Halifax's ambition was to emulate Chevalier Bayard and his motto, *Sans peur et sans reproche* (Miss D. M. Muloch, *John Halifax, Gentleman* (London, 1877).

6

Professionalization and 'Etiquette'

The mid-Victorian years witnessed the freeing of many forms of trade (through the repeal of the Navigation Acts, for example), but this was also a time when professionalization was proceeding apace: between 1860 and 1873 six new professional associations became established in engineering alone.[1] By definition a profession enjoys a degree of autonomy, often with the blessing of the state which allows its members to control entry and registration.[2] But this, of course, is a deliberate attempt to protect certain select occupations from the pressures of market competition.

The rationale behind such 'privileges' is that professional men and women do not practise a trade from which they expect to profit but offer the community a service, a claim which most professional organizations make good by formulating a code of conduct for their members, infractions of which can lead to disciplinary action. But these procedures, as Professor Perkin has shown, represent a deliberate defiance of the 'entrepreneurial ideal'.[3] Little wonder, then, that as the professional middle class developed its own specific interests and aspirations during the course of the nineteenth century, it began increasingly to separate itself off from the commercial world. Two of the professions affected by this development will now be examined: law and medicine.

THE LEGAL PROFESSION: SURVIVAL OF A 'GUILD'?

With the exception of the Church, the law was the oldest of the professions. It differed from most modern professions because it was built up around practices and privileges many of which dated back to medieval times, and also because it acted as the custodian of an esoteric body of knowledge which uninitiated laymen found at least partially incomprehensible.[4]

[1] T. R. Gourvish, 'The Rise of the Professions', in T. R. Gourvish and A. O'Day (eds.), *Later Victorian Britain, 1867–1900* (London, 1988), 30.

[2] For a good survey of the subject, see P. J. Corfield, *Power and the Professions in Britain 1700–1850* (London, 1995), who notes that it became a 'British tradition' for the state to devolve controls to professional bodies (p. 209).

[3] H. Perkin, *The Origin of Modern English Society 1780–1880* (London, 1969).

[4] D. Duman, 'Pathway to Professionalism: The English Bar in the Eighteenth and Nineteenth Centuries', *Journal of Social History*, 13 (1980), 616–18.

For both these reasons, to many political economists and members of the commercial community alike, the law embodied all that was wrong with Britain's *ancien régime*, associated, as it was, with Old Corruption and with what Cobden was wont to call feudal 'hocus-pocus'. The main purpose of Bentham's long life of arduous study, never fulfilled, had been to create a modern, codified law which would be clear, logical, and intelligible, so doing away with the dilatoriness and expense of the current system. This continued to be one of the most cherished objectives of the utilitarians: their house organ, the *Westminster Review*, argued that codification would bring innumerable advantages to the country and that 'in a merely pecuniary point of view a good code would pay its expenses in the shape of labour saved twenty times over'.[5]

Those seeking institutional modernization, with a view to facilitating commercial progress, were bound to look on lawyers with an unfavourable eye. Older gibes—that lawyers thrived on dishonesty and the fomentation of discord—were revived and placed into a somewhat new context. For example, writers in the 1850s and 1860s worried over whether barristers should decline certain kinds of brief on moral grounds and whether they too often engaged in cross-questioning techniques that were 'eminently un-English and unfair'.[6] John Stuart Mill broadened the indictment. Lawyers, he complained, lived by a one-sided advocacy: at least part of their business consisted of 'deception, and avowedly so'.[7] By comparison, Mill was able to present commerce in a flattering light. Business transactions, he claimed, depended upon the merchant's reputation for trustworthiness, whereas dishonesty provided much of the work for 'the exorbitantly paid profession of lawyers, so far as their work [was] not created by defects in the law'.[8] Herbert Spencer went further, denying that lawyers really formed a proper professional group at all since, though not drawing a state salary, they were practically 'members of the executive organization'.[9]

The other common charge levied against the legal profession by the advocates of the market economy was that heavy reliance upon precedent and tradition made its members insufficiently responsive to the wishes and needs of their business clients. Hence, exasperation over the provision of legal remedies for commercial disputes prompted many Chambers of Commerce to advocate 'tribunals of

---

[5] 'The State of English Law: Codification', *Westminster Review*, 83 (1865), 467. The writer observed that this, however, would be the 'smallest part of the gain'.

[6] See Macaulay's famous strictures in his 'Francis Bacon' (July 1837), in T. B. Macaulay, *Critical and Historical Essays*, Everyman edn. (London, 1907), ii. 317). See, too, [F. Parker], 'The Profession of Advocacy', *Cornhill Magazine*, 12 (1865), 105–15. James Fitzjames Stephen defended advocacy as a profession, arguing that its practice was essentially moral, though he admitted that professional standards were being 'evaded by a noisy and conspicuous section of its members' ('The Morality of Advocacy', ibid., 3 (1861), 458–9).

[7] J. S. Mill, *Collected Works of John Stuart Mill*, ed. J. M. Robson (Toronto, 1965–91), xxvi. 389.

[8] J. S. Mill, *Principles of Political Economy*, in id., *Collected Works*, ed. J. M. Robson (Toronto, 1965), ii. 110–11.

[9] H. Spencer, 'Representative Government—What Is It Good For?', *Westminster Review*, Oct. 1857, reprinted in id., *The Man Versus the State*, ed. D. Macrae (1969; first pub. 1884), 247.

commerce' from which lawyers would either be excluded entirely or where they would have to consult a layman knowledgeable about the practicalities of business life.[10]

But underlying such complaints was a far more deep-seated quarrel with the very foundations of the British legal system, portrayed by many political economists as an archaic survival from an earlier era of guilds and monopolies. Jeremy Bentham, himself a lawyer, had earlier alleged that the 'mystery' of the law served 'as a fence to keep out interlopers'.[11] Another lawyer, A. V. Dicey, developed this line of criticism in an article published in 1867:

When the rules of the Bar came into existence, all professions, almost all trades, were protected. At the present day, when free trade is the all but universal rule in all careers, it is incumbent on any profession, such as that of law or medicine, to show cause why it should enjoy the special advantages of protection.

It was therefore 'singularly unfortunate that the professional tone of the Bar, however exalted in other respects', rather encouraged than discouraged 'the idea that men are not bound to do the work for which they [were] paid', as a result of the way in which its members were shielded from the free play of competition.[12]

The 'protection' of which Dicey disapproved in fact took two forms. Some of the profession's 'monopolistic' practices derived from long-established custom (for example, the rule that only the qualified could plead was merely a custom 'enforced' by the Inns of Courts); others resulted from the social pressure of the circuit messes (for example, the privileged position occupied by 'Silks').[13] Other 'privileges' had been conferred by statute, amongst which the most controversial was the solicitors' monopoly of conveyancing, first established, in peculiar circumstances, in 1804.[14]

Moreover, to the amazement of the free traders, the very decade which saw the repeal of the Corn Law had also seen the passing of the Solicitors and Attorneys Act of 1843, which strengthened the solicitors' monopoly by creating the post of 'registrar of certificates' charged with examining prospective members of the profession and placing their names on the register, a post which was immediately entrusted to the Law Society.[15] Henceforward, no one could be appointed to any Government Board as a solicitor or attorney if he had not been formally enrolled in this way. (A later Act of 1888 gave the Law Society the right to strike off the register the names of solicitors found guilty of misconduct.)

[10] G. R. Searle, *Entrepreneurial Politics in Mid-Victorian Britain* (Oxford, 1993), 178–80.

[11] Cited in Corfield, *Power and the Professions*, 94.

[12] A. V. Dicey, 'Legal Etiquette', *Fortnightly Review*, NS 2 (1867), 178–9.

[13] Duman, 'Pathway to Professionalism', 618–19; D. Duman, *The English and Colonial Bars in the Nineteenth Century* (London, 1983), 44–6.

[14] B. Abel-Smith and R. Stevens, *Lawyers and the Courts: A Sociological Study of the English Legal System 1750–1965* (London, 1967), 23; H. Kirk, *Portrait of a Profession: A History of the Solicitors' Profession, 1100 to the present day* (London, 1976), 130–1.

[15] This Bill emanated from the Law Society itself: see Hansard, lxvi, 414: 13 Feb. 1843; Kirk, *Portrait of a Profession*, 36.

Sheltered in both these ways from true market competition, lawyers had acquired formidable powers of price-fixing. This particularly annoyed one Radical barrister, Andrew Edgar. Addressing the Social Science Association in 1858, Edgar alleged that 'several important rules of our jurisprudence would be greatly modified by the application of sound economical principles'. The remuneration of attorneys, he complained, dated back to the days 'when it was thought just and expedient to fix the wages of labour and the price of food'. Yet the 1843 Act had 'extended the system of fixed charges enforced by law to a large class of business—that of conveyancing—which before that time was left to the ordinary principle of demand and supply'—with predictably deplorable consequences. 'Unquestionably a system entirely open, under which everything would find its proper level, and every service its proper price', he argued, 'would ultimately prove the most complete remedy for the evils of which the public had long complained, and under which the profession has deeply suffered.'[16]

Free traders were equally annoyed by the existence of what amounted in practice to a network of restrictive practices within the legal system, or 'legal etiquette', the name by which it was euphemistically known. *The Times* persistently asked why clients had to employ a barrister only through the good offices of a solicitor, and what were the origins and basis of that rule.[17] Such a division of work hardly seemed to be making a contribution to the efficiency of the legal system, and *The Times* was not alone in suspecting that clients were simply being exploited by being put to the expense of hiring two lawyers when one would have sufficed. 'The rule which prevents a barrister from either being an attorney or being partner with an attorney', Dicey agreed, 'is as distinct a rule against the freedom of trade as would be a regulation to prevent a bootmaker from selling shoes or a publisher from being also a bookseller.'[18]

One Radical MP, James Barclay, an Aberdeen merchant, openly criticized all such 'restraints of trade': 'To his mind, it was a question whether the public would not be better served if the Legal Profession were entirely thrown open, and the close corporations called Inns entirely abolished.' If working-class trade unionists behaved as barristers did, added Barclay, 'there would be no end of reprobation passed upon them', and he defied his fellow MPs 'to point out the case of a single trades' union in which working men conducted themselves so utterly in

---

[16] A. Edgar, 'Professional Remuneration', *Transactions of the National Association for the Promotion of Social Science, 1858*, 127–31. In the mid-19th c. the method of charging for conveyancing was by items of service, a system which led to the sort of abuse being criticized by Edgar in this paper. *Ad valorem* charging did not become general until the passing of the Solicitors Remuneration Act of 1881 (Abel-Smith and Stevens, *Lawyers and the Courts*, 197–8). In 1864 the Lord Chancellor himself stated that the remuneration of attorneys and solicitors currently bore 'no reference to the skill, ability, or judgement which each individual [employed] in his work' (Hansard, clxxvi, 176, 5: 21 June 1864).

[17] Kirk, *Solicitors' Profession*, 135, 173–6. There was even desultory talk about fusing the two branches of the legal profession, but nothing came of this.   [18] Dicey, 'Legal Etiquette', 172.

defiance of all the principles of political economy as did certain members of standing at the Bar'.[19]

Understandably, some trade unionists, under attack for their 'unscientific'
approach to the economy, drew the same analogy. For example, a 'Journeyman
Engineer' (Thomas Wright) wrote to the *Pall Mall Gazette* in May 1867 challenging the legal profession to explain why its members were committing the self-
same 'errors' of which they were happy to accuse the organized working class. A
lively debate ensued, as barristers wrote in indignantly to claim that the Bar was
'a perfectly free and open trade'.[20] But Wright himself remained unimpressed by
what he called the 'special pleading' of barristers who denied the charge of price-
fixing: 'No man with the slightest knowledge of the world', he observed, 'requires
to be told that a barrister who defended prisoners at the Old Bailey at 6d apiece
would be treated as a social and professional outcast, even if he were not formally
disbarred.'[21] What was essentially at stake here was whether or not the 'social code
of the Bar' really did possess coercive power, analogous to that which trade unions
exercised over their own members: in other words, when did social disapproval
shade over into compulsion?[22]

Reviewing this dispute in a properly judicious spirit, Dicey declared that there
was something to be said on behalf of both sides. The Bar resembled a trade union
in three senses, he argued. It acted 'in restraint of trade'; it used the social opinion of the profession in order to limit the freedom of action of its members; and
it aimed, by limiting freedom of competition, to achieve a higher status for the
profession as a whole. On the other hand, unlike a trade union, the Bar did not
have severe sanctions at its disposal; it did not try to equalize the gains of its different members, though attempts were sometimes made to set minimum fees; and
it enjoyed a public position from which it derived certain privileges but also certain
legal disabilities. The last point led Dicey to conclude that the rules of the Bar
were 'in theory at least, not only rules for the benefit of the members of the guild,
but also rules established to protect the interest of the general public'.[23] As we
will see, this was in some respects the crucial argument employed by the defenders
of professional privilege—though it proved to be a highly controversial one.

[19] Bar Education and Discipline Bill: Hansard, ccxxxviii, 129–30: 21 Feb. 1878. He repeated his
analogy between trade unions and corporations of members of the Bar (ibid., 137). Barclay's specific
complaint concerned the retention of barristers in order to prevent their being engaged on the other side.

[20] See Dicey, 'Legal Etiquette', 169–71; Kirk, *Solicitors' Profession*, 46. Wright repeats these stric-
tures about 'double standards' in ['The Journeyman Engineer'], *Some Habits and Customs of the Working
Classes* (London, 1867), 58–9 and, at greater length, in *The Great Unwashed* (London, 1868), 113–16.
See A. Reid, 'Intelligent Artisans and Aristocrats of Labour: The Essays of Thomas Wright', in
J. Winter (ed.), *The Working Class in Modern British History* (Cambridge, 1983), 171–86.

[21] However, Wright felt that the most flagrant examples of monopolistic abuses were being committed, not at the Bar, but by solicitors (*Great Unwashed*, 113–15).

[22] A modern legal historian declares that barristers who 'undercharged' risked expulsion from the
circuit mess, a serious sanction (A. M. Manchester, *A Modern Legal History of England and Wales,
1750–1950* (1980), 69).

[23] Dicey, 'Legal Etiquette', 176. For the background, see Duman, *English and Colonial Bars*, 48.

But there was yet one more quarrel which the political economists had with the Bar, and that concerned the *form* of remuneration enjoyed by its members. Barristers did not draw a salary or a fee but an 'honorarium' (conventionally fixed at one guinea).[24] This meant that they could not sue their clients for non-payment and that their clients could not pursue *them* for professional negligence.[25] Nor could barristers engage in a partnership with another barrister or solicitor or hold a permanent post while practising as an advocate.[26] From the vantage point of the orthodox political economists, all these provisions signified an irrational departure from the market model governing other modern commercial transactions. One Conservative Member, Charles Lewis (significantly a solicitor), asked Parliament in 1876: 'What was there in the origin, the history, or the nature of the service rendered by a person called a barrister-at-law which exempted him from the operation of the ordinary principles of morality and fair dealing?'[27]

The replies which Lewis received give a very revealing insight into the attitudes of the legal profession and show how remote were these attitudes from entrepreneurial values. 'It was scarcely possible for any gentleman in commercial life, however eminent, to appreciate correctly what would or would not injure that Profession', one legal Member scathingly observed.[28]

A few of his colleagues did their best to enlighten the uninitiated. Thus, according to Henry Jackson:

The position of a barrister in relation to his client is well understood, though it is difficult to define. It is one of exceeding delicacy, of the greatest devotion on the one side, and of the utmost trust on the other. It is the position of advocate as distinct from that of agent or servant, and this distinction depends upon the absence of that very right to recover the promised honorarium which it is the object of this Bill to confer. Once establish the right to recover the fee, the relation of advocate ceases, and that of principal and agent takes its place.

Jackson warned that altering 'the *status* of the most liberal Profession in the world' would 'not only lower the character and position of its members, but be a great disadvantage to the public at large'.[29] A similar line was taken by Gathorne-Hardy, who asked: 'Was Parliament all of a sudden to interfere with them and make them traders and bargainers in every case they undertook?'[30]

This legislative attempt to do away with the barristers' immunity from suits for negligence was defeated by 130 votes to 237, but it left Bagehot contemptuous of the whole line of rationalization propounded by the profession's defenders: 'the fact is that, through their clerks, the lawyers in good practice strike as sharp

---

[24] Duman, *English and Colonial Bars*, 42–3.   [25] Duman, 'Pathway to professionalism', 622.
[26] Duman, *English and Colonial Bars*, 41–2.
[27] Hansard, ccxxix, 340, 343: 10 May 1876. These remarks were made on the second reading of the Bar and Advocates Fees Bill.
[28] Ibid., 326, 327: this was a dig at the Bill's sponsors, most of them eminent businessmen, e.g. C. M. Norwood and Sampson Lloyd, both leading lights in the Chambers of Commerce movement.
[29] Ibid., 322–3.   [30] Ibid., 335.

bargains as any tradesman in the country', he told the readers of *The Economist*, and he refused to believe that the practical grievance which Parliament had just debated could forever 'remain unredressed in deference to the sentimentalities of professional alarm'.[31]

Was Bagehot right to be so sceptical? Giving evidence to a Select Committee in 1850, Sir J. Jervis had observed that it was 'contrary not only to the etiquette, but, I am happy to say, to the universal practice at the Bar, ever to notice or talk of fees'.[32] By contrast, James Fitzjames Stephen, himself a distinguished legal figure as well as a prolific journalist, frankly conceded that the rule that the services of the barrister (and the physician) were gratuitous lay at the root of a great deal of hypocrisy and falsehood. Nevertheless, Stephen still thought that the rule enshrined a valuable principle, namely

that the skills of both the lawyer and the physician ought to be regarded to some extent as an advantage, not to its possessor merely, but to all who stand in need of it, and that the rewards to be earned by those who acquire it are not to be measured exclusively by commercial principles. This rule, like many others, is an attempt . . . to give form to the sentiment that men have a common interest in the administration of justice and in the cure of disease, and that those who specially devote their attention to such subjects should, in doing so, be actuated not merely by the ordinary selfish motives of interest and ambition, but also by the nobler wish to promote the common good.[33]

How, in practice, did lawyers justify such claims? First, they argued that they laboured under a moral obligation of protecting the general public against incompetence. This avowal would have been difficult to substantiate earlier in the nineteenth century when professional accreditation, in both branches of the profession, was still so haphazard and amateurish.[34] But it made more sense later: in 1851 the four Inns of Court set up their own Council of Legal Education, whose written examination (originating in 1862) became compulsory for barristers after 1872.[35]

The importance of thus excluding the unqualified was something on which several speakers laid stress during the second reading the Legal Practitioners Bill of 1874. The MP for Salford, W. T. Charley, put the case as follows:

---

[31] 'Barristers' Fees and Duties', *The Economist*, 34 (13 May 1876), 563–4, cited in N. St J. Stevas (ed.), *Collected Works of Walter Bagehot* (1965–85), vii. 281–2. Another critic of legal privilege was H. Spencer; see his attack on the system whereby barristers were prepaid for services which they might or might not render (H. Spencer, *The Principles of Ethics*, in id., *The Synthetic Philosophy of Herbert Spencer*, Westminster edn. (New York, 1892–6), ii. 283, and in 'Representative Government', reprinted in *Man Versus the State*, 248).   [32] Manchester, *Modern Legal History*, 73.

[33] [J. F. Stephen], 'Professional Etiquette', *Cornhill Magazine*, 8 (1863), 103.

[34] An Act of 1729 empowered judges and masters of rolls, or two masters in Chancery, to inquire into the fitness of prospective solicitors and attorneys, but adequate examinations were only instituted in 1836, aided by the Incorporated Law Society. See Hansard, lxvi, 412: 13 Feb. 1843; Manchester, *Modern Legal History*, 52–3; Abel-Smith and Stevens, *Lawyers and the Courts*, 53–4.

[35] Corfield, *Professions*, 92. Duman notes that the bar was the last of the professions to introduce a mandatory examination system for candidates (D. Duman, *The Judicial Bench in England 1727–1875* (London, 1982), 174).

It may be said—'Why not have free trade in law?' Well, if the State chooses to say that there shall be free trade in law, be it so, and I wish the State joy of the result; but so long as there is a body of men who are required to undergo a severe course of training and very great expense to qualify themselves for their profession, and who are subjected to very severe discipline in consideration of certain privileges being conceded to them, I say it is the duty of the State to protect those persons from being preyed upon by adventurers and mountebanks, and that if the State were to act otherwise, instead of sanctioning free trade, it would be sanctioning piracy.[36]

Charley also drew an analogy between the demands enshrined in his Bill and the recent legislative curbs on the activities of medical 'quacks'. On what principle, he asked, was 'the medical quack restrained from preying upon the public and upon the medical profession, while the legal quack [was] allowed without any restraint at all to prey upon the public and the legal profession'?[37] To illustrate the need for such restrictions, Charley gave instances of 'sham attorneys' who had frightened debtors into payment of their debts, and other similar abuses.[38] Thus one strong argument in favour of the lawyer's special privileges was that, at bottom, the interests of the profession and the interests of the public were identical: Charley's Bill, claimed its backers, 'was one in the interest of the public . . . for if it were merely in the interest of the legal profession, it would not be acceptable to the House'.[39]

The second justification was more nebulous, and concerned the 'dignity of the profession'. This aspiration to enhance the *status* of lawyers led to 'reforms' like the Solicitors Act of 1860, which established a preliminary examination in general knowledge in order to exclude from the profession all those who were not 'gentlemen'.[40] Indeed, as Dicey himself perceived, many aspects of 'etiquette' were there in order to raise the social character of the Bar and to produce a higher professional *tone*.[41] Even the setting of minimum levels of remuneration was sometimes defended by such 'moral' arguments: 'fairness' and honesty, some suggested, might be easier to keep up if professional men were not constantly faced with the immediate problem of making ends meet![42]

However, all such talk ran counter to the market ideal, which stipulated that remuneration should depend upon individual effort and the principle of competition. In short, the legal world formed an enclave which harboured older values and traditions that were generally in retreat in other parts of 'civil society'.

---

[36] Hansard, ccxx, 1278–9: 8 July 1874.

[37] Ibid., 1271. On the campaign against medical 'quacks', see below.

[38] Ibid., 1272–4. Note that Lewis, so keen to undermine the privileges of barristers, was equally zealous in the protection of his own profession, that of solicitor.

[39] Ibid., 1281 (Charles Lewis). Admittedly, formal legal procedures were expensive, but, according to one barrister, 'cheap law' risked encouraging litigation and would anyhow seldom be 'first-rate' (Montague Cookson, 'The New Judicature', *Nineteenth Century*, NS 19 (1876), 289).

[40] Manchester, *Modern Legal History*, 72.   [41] Dicey, 'Legal Etiquette', 178.

[42] Kirk, *Solicitors' Profession*, 204.

Not, of course, that ancient professional traditions were entirely immune to change; on the contrary, both branches of the law underwent considerable transformation during the course of the nineteenth century. The impetus to reform, as Daniel Duman shows, came from two groups. First, there were some younger 'modernizers' within the profession in the 1860s and 1870s who saw the desirability of removing blatant anachronisms and abuses. It was from such quarters that there arose the demand for the creation of a central legal authority and for the abolition of the honorarium.[43]

These 'moderates' enjoyed some success. For example, they secured the formation of the Bar Committee in 1883 (reconstituted as the Bar Council in 1894) in their quest to stamp out certain 'unethical' practices and to improve professional training. As a result of such changes, lawyers (solicitors, particularly) enjoyed much more social esteem at the end of the century than they had done at its beginning. Significantly, among the 'unprofessional' practices which the reformist *Law Times* sought to eradicate was 'touting for business', in other words, advertising.[44]

Very different, however, was the perspective of a second group of reformers, radical critics of the legal profession (including a handful of lawyers like Andrew Edgar) who wanted to go much further and use parliamentary statute to break the profession's monopoly powers—powers which the first group of 'reformers' were indirectly trying to defend.[45] These 'radicals' included political economists who followed in the footsteps of Adam Smith. And Smith, remember, had once called for a form of 'payment by results' in order to expedite the conduct of judicial business.[46]

However, the radical campaign to open up the law to free market competition achieved little. This was probably not because the free-market case lacked cogency. Still less does it seem that the defensive arguments used by legal spokesmen, namely, that their members were a high-minded set of men animated by a strong sense of duty and concern for the common weal, were all swallowed uncritically by the wider public.

In fact, the portrayal of lawyers in Victorian fiction is predominantly hostile: Mr Tulliver senior was not alone in thinking all lawyers 'raskills'.[47] There is no

---

[43] Duman, 'Pathway to Professionalism', 622–3; Duman, *English and Colonial Bars*, 55.

[44] Manchester, *Modern Legal History*, 66–8. Solicitors also earned more.

[45] Duman, 'Pathway to Professionalism', 622–3.

[46] A. Smith, *An Inquiry into the Nature and Causes of The Wealth of Nations*, ed. E. Cannan (Chicago, 1976; first pub. 1776), bk. 5, ch. 1, pp. 239–43. Judges were to be rewarded on the basis of the number of suits decided and there was to be competition between the various courts. Smith, however, favoured the establishment of a judicial power distinct from the executive. See J. Robertson, 'The Legacy of Adam Smith: Government and Economic Development in the *Wealth of Nations*', in R. Bellamy (ed.), *Victorian Liberalism: Nineteenth-Century Political Thought and Practice* (London, 1990), 25.

[47] G. Eliot, *The Mill on the Floss*, Blackwood edn. (Edinburgh, 1878; first pub. 1860), vol. 1, bk. 1, ch. 2, p. 7.

equivalent in Charles Dickens's fiction of the benevolent doctor, Allan Wood-court:[48] instead, within the covers of the same novel, we meet such predatory figures as Mr Tulkinghorn and Mr Vholes. Dickens's hostility to lawyers was espe-cially intense; but it was not unique. Trollope, for example, complained that the barrister found it consistent with his dignity 'to turn wrong into right, and right into wrong, to abet a lie, nay, to create, disseminate, and, with all the play of his wit, give strength to basest of lies, on behalf of the basest of scoundrels',[49] and his novels are peopled with unattractive lawyers.[50]

Now, one reason why lawyers earned on average considerably more than doc-tors was the fact that, whereas the latter were sometimes inhibited by what Anne Digby calls 'society's assumptions about professional altruism towards the poor', lawyers operated under no such restraints.[51] Well might Samuel Warren, writing in 1848, warn attorneys and solicitors that the public now expected them to acknow-ledge their 'obligation . . . to observe, to cultivate, truth and honour' and to regu-late their conduct by more lofty ethical standards.[52] The clear implication of Warren's book of course is that most lawyers' conduct fell short of this ideal.

Thus one gets the distinct sense that the legal profession by no means won the argument into which it had been drawn by its free-trade critics. Lawyers were able to fend off fundamental attacks on their interests mainly because they were so strongly entrenched in Parliament and in other branches of the State.[53] If we are to examine the ways in which Perkin's 'professional ideal' succeeded in estab-lishing a plausible claim to disinterested public service and in thus tempering the crude market philosophy embedded in the assumptions of political economy, we must look elsewhere.

MEDICINE: THE MAKING OF A MODERN PROFESSION

The process can best be studied through an examination of the medical profes-sion, which assumed a recognizably modern form with the Medical Practitioners Act of 1858. Medicine is especially interesting because, unlike law, the Church,

---

[48] See below, pp. 129–30.

[49] Anthony Trollope, *The New Zealander* ed. N. J. Hall (Oxford, 1965; written 1855–6), 63.

[50] R. D. McMaster, *Trollope and the Law* (Basingstoke, 1986). Trollope's own father was a Chancery lawyer. However, his most famous fictional barrister, Mr Chaffanbrass, is portrayed in a more bal-anced way by the time of *Phineas Redux*.

[51] A. Digby, *Making a Medical Living: Doctors and Patients in the English Market for Medicine, 1720–1911* (Cambridge, 1994), 163.

[52] S. Warren, *The Moral, Social and Professional Duties of Attornies and Solicitors* (London, 1848), esp. 107. Warren specifically warned his legal audience against speculating with their clients' property and putting undue pressure on testators (ibid., 368, 382).

[53] But Duman shows that the barristers, who constituted at most 20 per cent of all MPs in late Victorian Britain, could not by themselves have blocked all reform (*English and Colonial Bars*, 65–6).

and the armed services, it was slow to disentangle itself from trade. Throughout the Victorian period many chemists and druggists practised 'counter-prescribing' with almost complete freedom from any ethical, professional, or legal restrictions.[54] Even the *Lancet* admitted that many operatives in the large towns 'look[ed] upon physic as a trade' and preferred to deal with chemists, whom they saw as their social equals. Some well-to-do people, in their hour of need, also turned to such purveyors of 'fringe medicine'.[55] The late Victorian boom in the production and sale of patent medicines similarly testifies to the continuing spirit of entrepreneurialism within medicine, a line of business which James Morrison, earlier in the century, had successfully pioneered.[56]

Even within the medical profession proper there were historical links with trade. The physicians may always have been a university-educated élite, but surgeons, who until 1745 had been linked with barbers, traditionally served an apprenticeship and enjoyed the status of practitioners of a skilled 'craft', while apothecaries had originally formed a part of the Grocers' Company of the City of London.[57] Moreover, doctors had long depended, as lawyers did not, on patrons who expected deference in return for their fees: in Freidson's terminology, the medical profession was thus 'client-dependent', rather than 'colleague-dependent'.[58] Under the old poor law some parishes had actually remunerated doctors by a kind of 'payment by results'.[59] And during the early years of the New Poor Law, the subordinate status of the doctor had been still further emphasized by the practice whereby parishes grouped together to fill medical appointments by *tender*, a method of recruitment which prioritized cheapness at the expense of professional attainments.[60]

Doctors traditionally had their own examination-based system of formal accreditation, but it did not meet everyone's approval. For example, when Adam Smith was asked to support a proposal for making medical qualification dependent on two years of university study, he had flatly refused. Smith argued that the public interest would be better served by open competition. Nor was he concerned with 'professional reputation', believing that each man should work to achieve his own position in the local community, not rely upon some paper

[54] H. Marland, 'The Medical Activities of Mid-Nineteenth Century Chemists and Druggists, with Special Reference to Wakefield and Huddersfield', *Medical History*, 31 (1987), 439.

[55] Ibid., 428.

[56] Morrison claimed in his advertisements that any number of medical complaints could be cured by swallowing large quantities of 'Morrison's pills' (essentially a vegetable laxative) (R. Porter, *Health for Sale: Quackery in England, 1660–1850* (London, 1989), 228–31). Wakley was one of Morrison's fiercest critics.

[57] Until 1745 surgeons were united with barbers in the Company of Barber-Surgeons, which was reconstituted as the Royal College of Surgeons of London in 1800. Many practitioners combined their work with the sale and dispensing of drugs, some even selling other goods like tea, tobacco, and alcohol (I. Waddington, *The Medical Profession in the Industrial Revolution* (Dublin, 1984), 187–8).

[58] Duman, 'Pathway to professionalism', 616; Waddington, *Medical Profession*, 195.

[59] Digby, *Making a Medical Living*, 228–9.　　　[60] Ibid., 36, 44, 244.

qualification.[61] True, Smith expressed disapproval of what he called 'a most disgraceful trade' in medical degrees, but he pointed out that this trade did at least have one beneficial consequence, in that it multiplied the number of doctors, thereby reducing their fees, or at least stopping these fees from rising:

Had the universities of Oxford and Cambridge been able to maintain themselves in the exclusive privilege of graduating all the doctors who could practise in England, the price of feeling a pulse might by this time have risen from two or three guineas, the price which it has now happily arrived at, to double or treble that sum.[62]

And although in *Wealth of Nations* Smith argued that people would not give their confidence to 'people of a very mean or low condition',[63] which meant that doctors needed to be well remunerated, he rested his case, essentially, on the principle of 'caveat emptor': a doctor who killed his patients or did them no good would soon lose custom, while a skilful doctor would prosper.

In a reference to these remarks in a parliamentary speech of August 1844, the Home Secretary, Sir James Graham, said that Smith had shown in them 'more playfulness than is generally characteristic of that author'.[64] But many (though by no means all) mid-Victorian Radicals sympathized with Smith's sentiments. Suspicious in general of doctors' professional pretensions, they were particularly hostile to the survival of the specialist Royal Colleges, which seemed to embody many of the worst abuses associated with the old guilds. Why not emancipate the long-suffering public by abolishing all this pedantic sectionalism and then establishing 'free trade in medicine', they asked?

This was certainly the solution favoured by the MP for Edinburgh, Adam Black, a bookseller-publisher and an advanced Radical. In 1858 Black called for a repeal of all legislation

which had given a monopoly to the body of physicians in London, and placed restrictions upon the other branches of the profession. If that monopoly and those restrictions were abolished, he believed that the parties who were now engaged in fighting with one another would be perfectly well satisfied at the results. Give them a 'fair field and no favour'. That was the best course which could be adopted.[65]

Echoing Adam Smith, Black argued that no examination system could be guaranteed to exclude the incompetent and that, in any case, 'the best test of a medical man's competency was the opinion of the public'.[66]

---

[61] 'That in every profession the fortune of every individual should depend as much as possible upon his merit and as little as possible upon his privilege is certainly for the interest of the public' (cited in J. Rae, *Life of Adam Smith* (New York, 1965; first pub. 1895), 278–9). The episode is discussed in T. D. Campbell and I. S. Ross, 'The Utilitarianism of Adam Smith's Policy Advice', *Journal of History of Ideas*, 42 (1981), 86–7.   [62] Cited in Waddington, *Medical Profession*, 141.
[63] Smith, *Wealth of Nations*, bk. 1, ch. 10.   [64] Hansard, lxxvi, 1896: 7 Aug. 1844.
[65] Ibid., cl, 1409: 2 June 1858.   [66] Ibid., cxlvi, 717: 1 July 1857.

John Chapman, a doctor by training though currently editor of the *Westminster Review*,[67] was a persistent critic of the claim that the medical profession had the right to a privileged position. In his aptly named article, 'Medical Despotism', Chapman complained that the medical associations were trying to erect a system of protection in the name of a spurious philanthropy. Place all medical institutions on 'a footing of perfect equality', he argued, and then the principle of competition would 'begin to work its miracles'. Chapman championed the sovereignty of the consumer:

The nature of the demand determines that of the supply: until the people at large shall become sufficiently enlightened to distinguish between an ignoramus and a man of science, the majority of medical men will continue to practise with a minimum of knowledge, and charlatans and quacks will continue to prevail.[68]

What was specifically at issue in the 1850s was the attempt by a group of medical 'reformers', who enjoyed strong parliamentary backing, to set up a Medical Council for the accreditation of doctors' qualifications.[69] Black was not the only Radical MP to view this enterprise with suspicion. A colleague, William Coningham, announced his intention of voting against all such measures 'on principles of free trade, because he did not want to establish a great monopoly'.[70] So did Thomas Duncombe, who, while not objecting to accreditation as such, disliked what he saw as a move to establish an official monopoly: 'This country had already got a State religion and a State education; and it was now about to get State physic.'[71]

The suggestion that medical practice should be elevated to the same position as the Christian ministry struck many MPs as bogus, Lord Elcho, for one, observing that there was no 'Apostolic Succession' in the medical world.[72] Meanwhile Chapman warned against 'the gigantic evil of a State Church' being paralleled by 'the establishment of a State medicine, the professors of which are to enjoy all the State medical patronage, to institute a medical creed to which all candidates for examination must subscribe'. Have we learnt nothing from the Corn Laws, Chapman asked?[73]

---

[67] On Chapman, see S. Rosenberg, 'The Financing of Radical Opinion: John Chapman and the *Westminster Review*', in J. Shattock and M. Wolff (eds.), *The Victorian Periodical Press: Samplings and Soundings* (Leicester, 1982), 167–92.

[68] *Westminster Review*, 65 (1856), 559–60. See also J. Chapman, *Medical Institutions of the United Kingdom: A History Exemplifying the Evils of Over-Legislation* (London, 1870), where he calls for the liberation of existing medical institutions 'from the blighting influence of "Protection"' (p. 119).

[69] Here the model was Parliament's decision of 1852, entrusting the Pharmaceutical Society of Great Britain (founded in 1841, incorporated by charter in 1843) with the maintenance of an official register of all chemists across the country (Corfield, *Professions*, 157).

[70] Hansard, cxlvi, 754: 1 July 1857.   [71] Ibid., 721–2: 1 July 1857.   [72] Ibid., 727.

[73] 'Medical Despotism', 540. Nor could Chapman see the need for a state register when this function, he claimed, was already being accomplished 'by the Medical Directories, which are everywhere obtainable for a few shillings' ('Medical Education', *Westminster Review*, 70 (1858), 162).

In similar vein, the youthful Herbert Spencer stoutly denied that there was any cause for regulating the medical profession as some 'reformers' wanted: the latter's case, he argued,

rests upon the assumption that men are not fitted to take care of themselves. It treats them as so many children. It puts the people into leading strings. Poor things! if we do not look after them, they will be going to ignorant quacks for advice, and, perhaps, get poisoned!

Should anyone foolishly choose, 'for the sake of saving a little money, to employ an uneducated empiric in this way', concluded Spencer, 'he must take the consequences, be they what they may'.[74] Consistent to the end, Spencer many years later refused to become an honorary member of St Andrews's Medical Graduate Association because the legislative demands of the medical profession violated the principles he had 'long publicly held respecting the functions of the State and the liberties of the subject'.[75]

In fact, as we shall see, Parliament was not prepared in 1858, or even later, to confer on doctors a *complete* monopoly of medical practice. Nor, to be fair, was this what most doctors wanted.[76] All the same, the very mention of 'free trade in medicine' provoked paroxysms of alarm and indignation from the medical profession. Why?

The doctors' central claim was that unqualified and unregistered medical practitioners endangered the health of their patients. This was the argument which William Cullen, the President of the Royal College of Physicians at Edinburgh, had earlier used to refute Adam Smith:

In the practice of medicine none of [the] reasons for unfettered competition are of any force. . . . The community are scarcely able to judge . . . of the merits of medical men. . . . The life and health of a great portion of mankind are in the hands of ignorant people. . . . The legislature should take especial care that the necessary art should, as far as possible, be rendered both safe and useful to society.[77]

To a leading spokesman of the medical reform movement like Thomas Wakley, the crusading editor of the *Lancet*, this was the all-important consideration:

in order to protect human life, in order to prevent unnecessary human suffering, it was indispensable to protect [patients] from dupes, and to prevent them from becoming the victims of a profligate, mercenary, and extortionate set of men, by maintaining a proper restriction as to medical practitioners.

---

[74] 'The Proper Sphere of Government' (1843), in J. Offer (ed.), *Herbert Spencer: Political Writings* (Cambridge, 1994), 45–7. Spencer, too, drew the analogy between a State Church and state regulation of medical qualifications (ibid., 44–5).

[75] D. Duncan, *The Life and Letters of Herbert Spencer* (London, 1908), 153.

[76] W. L. Burn, *The Age of Equipoise: A Study of the Mid-Victorian Generation* (London, 1968; first pub. 1964), 202 n.

[77] Cited in D. L. Cowen, 'Liberty, Laissez-Faire and Licensure in Nineteenth-Century Britain', *Bulletin of History of Medicine*, 43 (1969), 31. See also Digby, *Making a Medical Living*, 56–7; Corfield, *Professions*, 180.

The House did not allow unqualified people to practise law: was the protection of human life, then, less important than the protection of property?[78] If so, this was perverse, since most legal mistakes were retrievable, but a medical error could have life-threatening consequences. The duty of the Legislature, argued a contributor to the *Lancet*, was thus 'very plain':

If it is right to abolish the lottery, if it is right to extinguish gaming-houses, as subversive of public morals, it is, *a fortiori*, a duty to suppress quackery, inasmuch as in addition to its repugnancy to public morals, it is injurious to the public health.[79]

True, not all MPs were impressed by the claim that medicine was an 'exact science'[80]—and with reason, considering the state of mid-Victorian medical knowledge. The growth in the prestige of doctors during the Victorian period certainly owed little to improvements in medical science, since significant therapeutic advances did not occur until the early twentieth century.[81] Nor, incidentally, did the so-called quacks lack reputable defenders.[82] On the other hand, it was widely accepted that few 'laymen' properly comprehended the body's ailments, lacking, as they did, the requisite training. 'Free trade in medicine' was therefore impractical because patients were incompetent to judge the proficiency and the expertise of doctors, as Cullen had argued.[83]

Now, doctors clearly had an interest in discrediting the notion that 'health' was a commodity which patients could purchase at their own discretion. The attacks on 'quacks', explains Anne Digby, can, at least in part, be understood as a well-organized assault on patients' 'self-help', that is to say, on the notion that patients were free to choose or to reject orthodox medical treatments.[84] For much the same reason, doctors strongly objected to Friendly Society clubs, another manifestation of 'patient-power'—even though it has recently been shown that, at its best, contract practice gave poor 'consumers' very good value for money as well as a modicum of control over the organization of health care.[85] But the medical profession, of course, set its face like stone against all such arguments.

[78] Hansard, lxxvi, 1907: 7 Aug. 1844.   [79] *Lancet*, 9 July 1842, p. 514.
[80] e.g. R. Grosvenor declared: 'certainly the state of medical science in the country would not justify the House, in his opinion, in giving them such large power' (Hansard, cxl, 1013: 20 Feb. 1856).
[81] Waddington, *Medical Profession*, 197–8. This is also one of the main themes of Digby's *Making a Medical Living*.
[82] e.g. the *Quarterly Review* thought that it was 'no more possible to put down quackery in medicine than it [was] to put down quackery in politics or religion' ('Medical Reform', 67 (1840–1), 55–7). The *Saturday Review* went further, expressing some sympathy towards people operating in the fields of homeopathy and hydropathy ('Medical Education', 12 Apr. 1856, p. 471). The so-called quacks, of course, mounted a spirited defence of their craft; see e.g. the tract by the homeopathist J. J. G. Wilkinson, *Unlicensed Medicine* (London, 1855), with its rousing call for 'MEDICAL FREEDOM' and its abuse of the hated Wakley.
[83] J. L. Berlant, *Profession and Monopoly: A Study of Medicine in the United States and Great Britain* (Berkeley, 1975), 151.   [84] Digby, *Making a Medical Living*, 63.
[85] Ibid., 122; D. G. Green, *Working-Class Patients and the Medical Establishment: Self-Help in Britain from the Mid-Nineteenth Century to 1948* (Aldershot, 1985), 88.

Cynics therefore had a point when they affirmed that doctors, in asking for professional recognition and control, were principally seeking to advance their own interests, interests which were partly social—a desire to raise their status—and partly economic, since doctors obviously stood to gain from acquiring legislative protection against the competition of the troublesome interlopers whom they dismissed as 'quacks'. In short, when doctors went on to invoke the 'dignity of their profession' and to profess a disinterested concern for the health and well-being of their patients, they may, to some extent, have been wrapping up their own pecuniary interests in high-sounding phrases.[86]

Perhaps because they were aware of the suspicions that their claims had aroused, most doctors could not quite bring themselves to demand that the state should totally *prohibit* unqualified doctors from practising.[87] But Wakley, in demanding some controls, constantly reminded his audience that Parliament was 'legislating for the poor, and for those who could not judge'.[88] Later commentators picked up this point: 'Free competition between members of the recognized medical corporation and those beyond its pale may or may not have all the advantages attributed to it by political economists', wrote Robert Williams, 'but these advantages must not be allowed in excuse of large profits made by the wholesale murder of the ignorant and the poor.'[89]

This conflation of the 'ignorant' and the 'poor' (and the identification of both groups with children) was a common ploy in the rhetoric of those seeking to turn medicine into a fully fledged profession. Its purpose, as Spencer irritably observed, was to convey the notion that most patients were in a state of such utter *helplessness* that they were unable to act the part of free and informed agents necessary if a market was to function satisfactorily—precisely the argument which had been used by the advocates of legislative curbs on adulteration (whose number included, of course, no less a personage than Wakley himself).

Nor did such denials of the viability of an untrammelled medical market proceed solely from the doctors. In the words of one Liberal MP, Charles Neate: 'Free trade and unrestricted competition were very good in, but very bad out, of their place. Free trade was a very good servant, but a very bad master.' It was to monopoly, Neate audaciously declared, that Britain owed much of its progress in the arts and sciences. Besides, did the House 'wish to see free trade extended to the legal profession or to the Church?' Coming from a Liberal MP who was also a political economist, this 'heretical' observation is interesting, since it testifies to the widespread recognition even in the 1850s that areas of life existed from which market forces should be rigorously excluded.[90]

---

[86] Berlant, *Profession and Monopoly*, 165–6.
[87] See Hansard, lxxvi, 1910: 7 Aug. 1844: Wakley. The *Lancet*, on the other hand, often called for nothing less than the complete exclusion from practice of all who did not possess enough skill to ensure the safety of the public health ('Thoughts on the Real and Imaginary Grievances of the Medical Profession', 27 Aug. 1842, p. 743).   [88] Hansard, lxxvi, 1910: 7 Aug. 1844.
[89] R. Williams, 'Laissez-Faire', *Fraser's Magazine*, 1 (1870), 76.
[90] Hansard, cxlvi, 720: 1 July 1857. On Neate, see below.

The medical politics of mid-Victorian Britain, however, did not take the form of a simple confrontation between 'free traders' and 'reformers' seeking a privileged position for their profession. For the medical world was also internally riven by other bitter disagreements and divisions, the most potent being the quarrel between the specialists of the Royal Colleges and the often poorly paid general practitioners. Wakley of the *Lancet*, the leading 'reformer', thus found himself engaged in a battle on two fronts, since, as well as fighting against the 'quacks', he was also trying to represent those provincial surgeon-apothecaries who chafed at the privileges of that well-connected metropolitan élite, the consultants.[91] As the *Lancet* put it, there were two hostile forces 'working in contravention' of the profession's interests: on the one hand, the 'monopolists' who advocated restrictions which shackled professional life, and, on the other, 'the unlicensed practitioners, who resist[ed] the enforcement upon all who aspire[d] to exercise the healing art, of a uniform test, fitted to act as a safeguard to the general health'.[92]

In some respects, then, the campaign for medical reform, far from being an uncomplicated 'conservative' reaction against the excesses of market liberalism, possessed a militantly 'radical' character. Wakley himself, after all, had first secured election to the Commons in 1835 as Radical MP for Finsbury, a largely working-class constituency. True, he belonged to the 'humanitarian' wing of Radicalism: we have already encountered his assaults on food adulterators who mulcted the ignorant and the poor, and we will later see how violently he opposed the 'cruelties' of the New Poor Law. But Wakley was also a doughty supporter of most mainstream Radical causes (including free trade). So, too, was his parliamentary ally, Henry Warburton. Indeed, it has been argued that both men came out of the same Benthamite tradition[93]—hence their inveterate hostility to hereditary privilege and monopoly.

It was because he so hated irresponsible privilege that Wakley was prepared to attack manifestations of it within his own profession. Indeed, he had first risen to public prominence by exposing the incompetent medical lectures being put on under the auspices of the Royal College of Surgeons, the leaders of which he denounced in colourful language.[94] Under his editorship the *Lancet* then proceeded to wage a fierce campaign aimed at the 'complete breaking up of the restrictions and monopolies by which the members of the different colleges have been plundered of their rights'.[95] Wakley's Radical friend Duncombe joined him in this crusade, calling for 'a medical reform bill with something like a schedule A with Gattons and Old Sarums in the medical world'.[96]

---

[91] R. D. Cassell, 'Lessons in Medical Politics: Thomas Wakley and the Irish Medical Charities, 1827–39', in *Medical History*, 34 (1990), 412.   [92] 'Thoughts on Grievances', *Lancet*, 742.

[93] Cowen, 'Liberty, Laissez-Faire and Licensure', 31.

[94] M. Bostetter, 'The Journalism of Thomas Wakley', in J. H. Wiener (ed.), *Innovators and Preachers: The Role of the Editor in Victorian England* (Westport, Conn., 1985), 281–2; M. J. Peterson, *The Medical Profession in Mid-Victorian London* (Berkeley, 1978), 26.

[95] *Lancet* (1830–1), 598, cited in Waddington, *Medical Profession*, 59.

[96] Hansard, cxlvi, 722: 1 July 1857.

Thus the medical reformers' prime objective was to destroy the old corrupt corporations and guilds, not to free medicine from *all* restraints. They wanted to retain the exclusivity of the profession, but to do so by modernizing the whole process of medical training and registration, in the process abolishing archaic practices and setting up a uniform national system. An article in the *Lancet* brings out the essential ambiguity of their project: 'The mainspring of everything great or useful in medicine and its collateral arts is, and ever has been, private enterprise', it declared, and 'monopoly and exclusiveness in every shape' was the enemy. But, after this orthodox expression of market liberalism, the *Lancet* went on to argue that it was 'a rule founded upon a natural law of political economy' that admission into the medical profession should be restricted to the duly qualified.[97]

Moreover, since the 'medical reformers' aspired to 'democratize' the medical profession by empowering the rank-and-file GPs,[98] the situation did not parallel that of contemporary America, where reformers wanted to replace *laissez-faire* by regulation (largely out of a desire to crack down on abortionists).[99] In Britain the desire was rather to replace a ramshackle system of control exercised by unaccountable, 'privileged' guilds by a uniform, rational system of accreditation that was largely in the hands of a modern, self-regulating profession.

The cross-currents which Wakley and his friends introduced into the debate on the future of the medical profession proved a headache for a succession of governments. Ministers appreciated that there was something ridiculous about a licensing system giving wide-ranging powers to a heterogeneous collection of nineteen different authorities, among them the Royal Colleges, various university faculties, and the Archbishop of Canterbury—authorities which then sought to underbid one another by offering 'soft' degrees in return for low fees.[100] Feeling rationalization of this mess to be long overdue, Peel's friend, Sir James Graham, Home Secretary in the early 1840s, accordingly introduced his own reform proposals.

Graham had initially hoped that the medical profession might be able to sort out its own affairs, but his personal preference was for some system of central control, exercised by a National Council entirely nominated by the Crown.[101] However, this brought down on his head the fury of the *Lancet*: 'Subject the medical government of this country by means of such [a Council] to the control of a minister of the Crown', it fumed, 'and the independence of the profession is gone forever.'[102] Moreover, whether his proposed Council included or excluded members

---

[97] 'Thoughts on Grievances', *Lancet* (1841–2), 606.

[98] Waddington, *Medical Profession*, 87–8.

[99] However, Roy Porter suggests that one reason for the passing of the 1858 Act was fear within the profession that orthodox medicine would lose out to 'sects' in the battle for public favour, as was happening in the USA (*Disease, Medicine and Society in England, 1550–1860* (London, 1987), 50).

[100] Graham, in other respects an orthodox free trader, found this sort of 'competition' quite unacceptable (Hansard, lxxvi, 1897–8: 7 Aug. 1844).   [101] Ibid., lxxvii, 1218: 25 Feb. 1845.

[102] Cited in A. B. Erickson, *The Public Career of Sir James Graham* (Oxford, 1952), 247–8.

of the Royal Colleges, it was certain to offend powerful branches of the medical profession. In 1845 Graham gave up his attempts at reform in disgust.[103]

The impasse was eventually broken by the 1858 Act, which was necessarily a compromise measure, involving as it did a cunningly devised trade-off between competition, state control, and self-regulation.[104] The Chief Medical Officer at the Local Government Board, John Simon, had earlier produced a draft Bill, making provision for a strong Medical Council, but this failed to survive parliamentary scrutiny.[105] Instead, to the displeasure of the *Lancet*, there came into existence a General Medical Council, with, *inter alia*, representatives from the old Royal Colleges, who thus survived into the modern era.[106]

The 1858 Act conferred on this Council responsibility for drawing up a Register from the names of those who had passed the examinations set by approved licensing bodies (no uniform examination system materialized). Roy Porter argues that Parliament had thus achieved 'what the doctors never could; it had, symbolically at least, united the much-divided medical profession, by defining them over and against a common Other, not to say enemy' by excluding 'the unqualified homeopaths, medical botanists, quacks, bone-setters, itinerants and the like'.[107] The Act also made it a criminal offence for unregistered doctors to make false claims about their qualifications.[108] Yet, at the same time, although excluded from *public* office, 'registered' doctors were not given a monopoly of *private* medical practice.[109]

In this way, as Berlant argues, the liberal value system, so dear to the Victorians, was maintained, with the Registry functioning as 'an official consumer guide'.[110] What Cowen calls 'the principle of definitive regulation' had triumphed over a system of 'restrictive regulation'.[111] In short, although the advocates of 'free trade in medicine' had been defeated in 1858, their objections to state-sanctioned professional monopolies had helped to shape the resulting legislation. Meanwhile, in Berlant's words, the 1858 Act provided a regulatory framework within which qualified members of the medical profession could improve their economic standing by 'using

[103] Erickson, *Graham*, 254.

[104] For a description and analysis of the Medical Act of 1858, Digby, *Making a Medical Living*, 31.

[105] R. Lambert, *Sir John Simon 1816–1904 and English Social Administration* (London, 1963), 464–5. See R. G. Smith, *Regulating British Medicine: The General Medical Council* (Chichester, 1992).

[106] The *Lancet* wanted the body of GPs to send their own representatives to the GMC, an objective which they did not achieve until the passing of the Medical Act of 1886. In fact, the Bill was a bitter disappointment to most GPs (I. Loudun, *Medical Care and the General Practitioner, 1750–1850* (Oxford, 1986), 297). [107] Porter, *Disease, Medicine and Society*, 51.

[108] This followed the provisions of Graham's 1844 Bill, which deliberately placed 'no restriction on private practice whatever; it would be open to every man to prescribe and administer medicine without any previous examination or proof of qualification' (Hansard, lxxvi, 1898: 7 Aug. 1844).

[109] Peterson, *Medical Profession*, 36. In other words, they could not, for example, become medical officers to Boards of Guardians or hold posts in the army and navy.

[110] Berlant, *Profession and Monopoly*, 161.

[111] Cowen, 'Liberty, Laissez-Faire and Licensure', 30–40. For the changes to this system effected by the later Act of 1886, Lambert, *Simon*, 580–1, Peterson, *Medical Profession*, 31.

state administrative devices to give [themselves] a number of competitive advantages in the market'.[112]

There are two ways of evaluating the 1858 Act: some see it as having been passed
in the interest of the public, while others think it important for enabling medical
practitioners to achieve 'a degree of monopoly in respect to the provision of particular types of services in the market'.[113] The latter interpretation is supported by
evidence that the exclusion of the unlicensed from state employment gave registered
doctors a distinct advantage. It may also be significant that in the twenty years
after 1861 the growth of the medical profession lagged behind that of the population as a whole, causing medical incomes to rise.[114] In short, claims Waddington,
'the profession derived significant monopolistic advantages from registration'.[115]

As historians have recently pointed out, doctors were certainly conscious of the
economic advantages of restricting entry into what they perceived to be an 'overstocked' profession.[116] An examination of the development of 'medical ethics' bears
out their case. After all, a seminal work like Thomas Percival's *Medical Ethics* (1803)
was less concerned with the protection of the patient than with 'etiquette', that is
to say, the regulation of disputes between doctors, something which became a real
problem as a result of the cutthroat competition of the 1820s and 1830s. Thus
Percival commends '*esprit de corps*' within the profession and warns doctors to
'avoid all contumelious representations of the Faculty at large, all general charges
against their selfishness or improbity; and the indulgence of an affected or jocular
scepticism, concerning the efficacy and utility of the healing art'.[117] The *Lancet*,
too, strove constantly to put an end to undercutting and 'poaching'.[118]

As the nineteenth century unfolded, doctors increasingly took steps to promote
'genteel rather than entrepreneurial behaviour'—for example, through the discouragement of advertising and by making personal recommendation the main line
of communication between GP and patient.[119] But, here again, the primary aim
was the enhancement of the status of the doctor, not the well-being of the patient.

Such concerns over status cannot simply be reduced to economic terms. 'Are
we a profession or a trade, are we gentlemen or are we not?', one doctor asked in
1868. The public, he claimed, accepted medical practitioners as gentlemen only
in so far as they

---

[112] Berlant, *Profession and Monopoly*, 162, 167.

[113] N. Parry and J. Parry, 'Social Closure and Collective Social Mobility', in R. Scace (ed.), *Industrial
Society: Class, Cleavage and Control* (London, 1977), 112. See also Berlant, *Profession and Monopoly*,
167–8.

[114] Waddington, *Medical Profession*, 147–9. The chapter from which this discussion is drawn is
entitled 'Occupational Closure'.   [115] Ibid., 152.

[116] Ibid., 143–6; Digby, *Making a Medical Living*, ch. 5.

[117] T. Percival, *Medical Ethics: Or, a Code of Institutes and Precepts Adapted to the Professional Conduct
of Physicians and Surgeons* (Manchester, 1803), esp. 45–6. To be fair, Percival also stresses the moral
obligations to patients (p. 30). See also I. Waddington, 'The Development of Medical Ethics—
A Sociological Analysis', *Medical History*, 19 (1975), 39.

[118] Waddington, *Medical Profession*, ch. 8; Digby, *Making a Medical Living*, 59–62.

[119] Digby, *Making a Medical Living*, 60–1, 177.

regard our profession as a profession strictly and not as a compound of a profession and a trade; and those of our body are excluded from such a status who accept the compromise and add the business of a trade, the sale of medicines to the practice of their profession. For this is a point of which society is very tenacious; a gentleman must not engage in retail trade.[120]

From the very start this had been what doctors seeking to raise their professional status had hoped to achieve: 'Give us but emancipation from [dependence on the sale of medicines], and we become a new order of men: no longer to be regarded as petty traders, whose profits are elevenpence in the shilling, but men of science, whose proper business consists in supplying the art of medicine at its proper value.'[121] It is significant that George Eliot's finely observed Dr Lydgate obstinately refuses to dispense drugs, even to clients who expect him to do so, believing that 'it must lower the character of practitioners, and be a constant injury to the public, if their only mode of getting paid for their work was by their making out long bills for draughts, boluses, and mixtures'.[122] Hence the determination of doctors to switch over from the sale of commodities to the sale of services, a transition which, in their eyes, represented the transition from a trade to a profession.[123]

In Trollope's *Dr Thorne*, the hero is criticized by his fellow doctors for acting like a tradesman:

A physician should take his fee without letting his left hand know what his right hand was doing; it should be taken without a thought, without a look, without a move of the facial muscles . . . the true physican should hardly be aware that the last friendly grasp of the hand had been made more precious by the touch of gold.[124]

It is also significant that the 1847 Bill of Warburton and Wakley, which would have given physicians the right of recovering charges for attendance and advice, elicited so furious an objection from the Royal Colleges: 'The physician would

---

[120] I. Ashe, *Medical Education and Medical Interests* (Dublin, 1868), 146, cited in N. Parry and J. Parry, *The Rise of the Medical Profession: A Study of Collective Social Mobility* (London, 1976), 131–2.
[121] Published letter from 'A Member of the Provincial Medical and Surgical Association' (1842), cited in Digby, *Making a Medical Living*, 37.
[122] G. Eliot, *Middlemarch*, Penguin edn. (London, 1965; first pub. 1871–2), 483. This stance, observes Eliot shrewdly, offended both the physicians and some patients, who derived satisfaction from 'paying bills with strictly-made items', thinking that this ensured that they were getting value for money. The local surgeon-apothecary drily observes: 'the question is whether the profit on the drugs is paid to the medical man by the druggist or by the patient, and whether there shall be extra pay under the name of attendance' (pp. 484, 487)—which, in strictly *economic* terms, was precisely what was at stake.
[123] Digby, *Making a Medical Living*, 37, 44, 80. 'What is the difference between a druggist and a medical man?', asked one doctor. 'I would have answered one charges for physic and the other for brains' (ibid., 151).
[124] Cited in ibid., 312. Trollope elsewhere expressed anxiety over the fact that medicine was not 'entirely free from that plague of the nineteenth century, the advertising system', but he took a far more favourable view of doctors than he did of lawyers (*The New Zealander*, 67–75).

under those clauses be converted into a tradesman', they declared.[125] This, as we have seen, was precisely the stand which barristers were later to take.

Not that doctors, as a professional group, really did show quite so olympian a disregard for the pecuniary side of their activities. For, as James Fitzjames Stephen slyly points out, though the payment of professional men was often regulated by custom rather than competition ('The doctor's guinea was well known long before modern gold discoveries, and it is difficult to believe that it will ever be much altered'), there were still 'ways and means, as all professional men know, of evading this'.[126]

Digby has described many of the stratagems employed by GPs in their desperate struggle for a prosperous, or even a comfortable, livelihood (doctors, on average, commanded a significantly smaller income than lawyers). Entrepreneurial energy, she shows, had always to be tempered with a concern for professional propriety. It was not considered genteel, for example, to harass middle-class patients to pay their bills.[127] Significantly, too, a higher status attached to doctors who sent out an annual bill, as distinct from those who catered for cash patients.[128]

On the other hand, starting off with a standard fee of one guinea, doctors found that there were many ways of supplementing this meagre income: by charging a double fee for sitting up all night or for an all-day visit, by charging separately for each visit or consultation, by adding in travelling expenses and/or by encouraging patients to visit *them*, and so on.[129] Wealthy doctors, for their part, seem to have heeded the warning which Percival had earlier given in his *Medical Ethics*: not to 'give advice gratis to the affluent, because it is an injury to [their] professional brethren'.[130]

Yet market principles could only be carried so far, a point clearly made in a poor-law medical journal:

Such is the nature of medical practice that there never is and never can be any regular market price for medical services. The peer and the cottager, if they have a broken leg or an inflammation of the lungs, require the same attendance, the same medicines for their cure; yet they cannot by any possibility pay the same amount of remuneration.[131]

Many poor-law doctors, employees working within the public sector, were thus led to develop an ideology of community service and to parade their commitment to altruistic values. But stories also abound of the kindness shown by many

---

[125] Waddington, *Medical Profession*, 101. The College of Physicians reiterated this point in its Memorandum to the 1856 Select Committee. (It is perhaps ironic that it had been the members of the prestigious Colleges, in their capacity as consultants, who had so severely damaged the reputation of the medical profession as a whole by covertly engaging in a trade in the corpses that they needed for their anatomical lessons.) 'Free trade in corpses' is discussed in Ch. 4.

[126] [J. F. Stephen], 'Money and Money's Worth', *Cornhill Magazine*, 9 (1864), 102–3.

[127] Digby, *Making a Medical Living*, 156.   [128] Ibid., 37.   [129] Ibid., 185–6.

[130] Percival, *Medical Ethics*, 47.

[131] *Provincial Medical and Surgical Journal*, 1848, cited in J. T. Hart, 'The *British Medical Journal*, general practitioners and the state 1840–1990', in W. F. Bynum, S. Lock, and R. Porter (eds.), *Medical Journals and Medical Knowledge: Historical Essays* (1992), 228–9.

private GPs in performing errands of mercy for poor people from whom they neither expected nor demanded any payment whatever.[132]

Partly as a consequence of this, doctors, however problematic their social status and however ambiguous their economic practices, were indubitably gaining in
moral prestige in mid-Victorian Britain.[133] The rise of the medical press also helped
to create an enhanced sense of professional solidarity, leading to growing public
respect.[134] This was a development sensitively registered by contemporary novelists. For example, George Eliot, in *Middlemarch*, makes Lydgate the carrier of the
idea of disinterested scientific progress—until, that is, he is destroyed by his selfish
and frivolous wife.[135] And in Mrs Gaskell's *Wives and Daughters* (1864–6) Molly
Gibson is not merely expressing her love for her GP father when she says 'I call
it a very fine thing to think of what he does or tries to do'; for the superiority of
the medical ethic over vulgar commercial considerations is a thread running
through the entire novel.[136]

But it is Dickens, through his portrayal of Allan Woodcourt in *Bleak House*,
who provides the most vivid idealization of what a medical career might signify.
Along with Rouncewell, the Ironmaster, Woodcourt is characterized as a paragon
of the Smilesian virtues, a man notable for his quiet and cheerful 'persistence'.[137]
But whereas Dickens ends his novel showing us Rouncewell in enjoyment of his

---

[132] This meant that affluent patients were effectually cross-subsidizing the poor, a rudimentary kind
of welfare system, suggests Digby. Nursing, too, claimed Florence Nightingale, had nothing to do with
money, but was undertaken 'to satisfy the high idea of what is the *right*, the *best*'. Nightingale also
dubbed competition 'the enemy of health', to which 'combination' was the antidote (cited in M. Poovey,
*Uneven Developments: The Ideological Work of Gender in Mid-Victorian England. Women in Culture and
Society* (Chicago, 1988), 193).

[133] Once again, a cynical interpretation is possible. Some doctors must have realized that a reputation for 'disinterestedness' could be good for business, argues Berlant (*Profession and Monopoly*, 162,
147).

[134] Ironically, however, Ernest Hart, editor of the *British Medical Journal*, which played a large part
in this development, stood accused of murdering his first wife and stealing BMA funds. He and his
successors also showed great entrepreneurial flair in the exploitation of advertising revenue (P. Bartrip,
'The *British Medical Journal*: a retrospect', in Bynum *et al.* (eds.), *Medical Journals and Medical Knowledge*,
126–43).

[135] Eliot, *Middlemarch*. Despite his 'spots of commonness', that is to say, a burning ambition, a certain arrogance and insensitivity to others' feelings, the medical profession itself is celebrated: 'Many
of us looking back through life would say that the kindest man we have ever known has been a medical man, or perhaps that surgeon whose fine tact, deepened by deeply-informed perception, has come to
us in our need with a more sublime beneficence than that of miracle-workers' (p. 720). The author
shares Lydgate's conception of the doctor's role as one that offers 'the most direct alliance between
intellectual conquest and the social good' (p. 174).

[136] E. Gaskell, *Wives and Daughters* (Oxford, 1987; first pub. 1864–6). Molly's stepmother betrays
her utter baseness when she makes the mercenary comment: 'If this Mr Smith is dying, as you say,
what's the use of your father's going off to him in such a hurry? Does he expect any legacy, or anything of that kind?' (p. 179), and when she later uses the information overheard in a discussion between
her husband and another doctor to seek a personal advantage. On other contemporary fictional por-
trayals of doctors, see M. F. Brightfield, 'The Medical Profession in Early Victorian England, as Depicted
in the Novels of the Period (1840–1870)', *Bulletin of History of Medicine*, 35 (1961), 238–56.

[137] Conversely, it is Rick's inability to stick at his medical education which demonstrates his lack of
'character' (C. Dickens, *Bleak House*, Chapman & Hall edn. (n.d.; first pub. 1852–3)).

well-deserved fortune as an enterprising manufacturer, Woodcourt has eschewed all such worldly ambitions by his decision to work among the poor (marriage to the rather prim heroine will be his sole reward).

But what Woodcourt sacrifices in pecuniary terms is more than compensated for by the esteem which he wins through his display of courage, kindliness, and devotion to duty. Woodcourt is a standing reproach to the egotistical and acquisitive characters who dominate *Bleak House*. But, significantly, what he offers the poor is not just practical service and assistance. For Dickens makes his doctor-hero the embodiment of the spirit of true Christianity (in contrast to the bogus manifestations personified in religion's 'official' representatives). This becomes clear in the famous scene in which, his medicines of no further help to the dying Jo, Woodcourt comforts the boy by reciting to him the Lord's Prayer.[138] Dickens, then, is showing the reader ways in which a life of professional service is capable not only of offsetting the coarse materialistic competitiveness of the age, but also of pointing the way back to the original concept of Christianity.

CONCLUSION

It has been argued that the professional middle classes of Victorian Britain succeeded in generating their own specific ideal, an ideal which 'was contradictory in that it embraced both a support for and an attack upon the entrepreneurial ideal of competition and competence, a support for and an attack upon the status of industrial endeavour'.[139]

What both professional men and entrepreneurs had in common was a respect for *achieved* merit, as distinct from success conferred by birth or patronage. However, businessmen relied on the operation of market forces, from which professional men sought to insulate themselves by using examinations as an alternative mechanism of selection and promotion. And, since examination success usually presupposed the prior acquisition of a 'liberal education', the resulting professional ethos could be profoundly hostile both to entrepreneurial values and to the spirit of utilitarianism and political economy.[140]

In *The Choice of a Profession* (1857), Byerley Thomson devotes many interesting pages to comparing commerce and the professions *from a purely worldly point of view*. It was generally accepted, he argues, that business secured 'an earlier means of access to competence, and wealth' but that a profession presented 'a

---

[138] Dickens, *Bleak House*, vol. 2, bk. 2, ch. 16, pp. 246–8.

[139] Gourvish, 'Rise of the Professions', 15, 34.

[140] Frederick Temple, with his contempt for what he saw as the mechanical philistinism of contemporary political economy, clearly exemplifies this point (S. Green, 'Archbishop Frederick Temple on Meritocracy, Liberal Education and the Idea of a Clerisy', in M. Bentley (ed.), *Public and Private Doctrine* (Cambridge, 1993), 165).

readier road to position in society, and to honour'.[141] 'The man who looks upon money, and its acquisition as the sole object of life', concludes Thomson, 'will, of course, declare for business, whereas the man who has been accustomed to additional views of existence will weigh the question more carefully.'[142]

However, such expressions of disdain for money and all its works should not be taken too literally. As Stephen pertinently observed:

The truth about all payments by fees is that they differ from other wages of labour only in form. They are contrivances by which men of such a position in life as to be averse to the details of a bargain are enabled to avoid the unpleasantness of abating the price of their services, whenever they are rendered; but in fact they are regulated, like other services, by supply and demand, though in rather a roundabout way, and thus those who live on them are not really more dependent than their neighbours on the price of gold.

Stephen noted that lawyers, for example, were affected by the general state of trade: 'Plenty of money means plenty of buying and selling, plenty of joint-stock companies, plenty of marriages, and, therefore, plenty of contracts, plenty of letters to write, plenty of deeds to draw, and plenty of briefs to deliver, and good fees on their back.'[143]

All of this has a decidedly topical ring to it. For in recent decades it has become fashionable to take a sceptical view of the alleged disinterestedness of the professional middle classes.[144] *The Times* was expressing very similar suspicions way back in the 1860s: all professional men, it observed, behaved as 'a class by themselves':

There is no profession in which this instinct is stronger than it is among medical men. . . . Their science is far from being exact, their art is little more than empirical, there are powerful heresies to combat, and a dangerous spirit of scepticism abroad; they stand together, therefore, like one man. Like the etiquette of the Bar, medical etiquette fosters a kind of honour which is a safeguard against baseness. Still it is often carried much too far, and operates, in the same way as official routine, in crushing individual conscientiousness.[145]

Professional men were well aware of the cynicism with which many members of the laity viewed their practices and did their best to dispel it. 'The object of an authorized medical profession is not to forward the interests of a particular body of men', wrote Charles Cowan defensively, 'but to benefit the community; and legislative efforts to exclude the ignorant empiric are not for the purpose of

---

[141] H. B. Thomson, *The Choice of a Profession* (London, 1857), 11.

[142] Ibid., 17. An 'Ex-Competition Wallah' took a somewhat similar view when reviewing the pros and cons of joining the Indian Civil Service ('The Indian Civil Service as a Profession', *Macmillan's Magazine*, 4 (1861), 267–8). The propriety of discussing the Church in such terms remained problematical: see [J. F. Stephen], 'The Church as a Profession', *Cornhill Magazine*, 9 (1864), 750–60.

[143] [J. F. Stephen], 'Money and Money's Worth', *Cornhill Magazine*, 9 (1864), 102–3. Moreover, from the 18th c. onwards, many attorneys were professionally involved in a variety of market transactions (Corfield, *Professions*, 73).

[144] Illich has presented some kinds of professional activity as 'a new kind of cartel' (cited in Digby, *Making a Medical Living*, 35).   [145] *The Times*, editorial, 'Medical Etiquette', 11 July 1865.

advancing the interests of the medical profession, but, to secure the public from imposition and injury':

We are anxious that this view of the question should be clearly understood, for the whole subject has too often been regarded as nothing more than a scramble for loaves and fishes, an effort on the part of medical men to increase their own gains and to diminish those of their less qualified competitors.

Cowen assured his readers that medical men probably gained nothing in a pecuniary sense from the suppression of 'empirics', before adding that, in any case, only 'a false delicacy and a feeble morality' would deter them from pursuing the public interest simply because members of the profession might incidentally benefit thereby.[146]

At this point the critics might observe that the doctor doth protest too much. And yet, self-serving though their behaviour and rhetoric might sometimes be, members of professions *were* able to make a powerful claim to being animated by a desire for service rather than profit. Their case had been strengthened by the transformation which had taken place in their occupations since the eighteenth century. Once traditional, closed corporations which emphasized the gentlemanly status of their members, the learned professions had all, to a lesser or greater extent, turned themselves into associations committed to the pursuit of knowledge, in which career success owed more to competition than it did to connections.[147]

Of these newly modernized professional groups, some, such as civil servants, functioned as agents of the state; others, most notably doctors, fiercely defended their 'independence', though this often involved a measure of state recognition and supervision.[148] But all affirmed their commitment to a particular code of conduct, of which they were collectively guardians. As Penelope Corfield puts it, 'A profession signalled a public affirmation, as in a "profession" or "confession" of faith . . . Clergymen at their ordination promised to put duty to their faith before personal inclination; physicians endorsed the "Hippocratic Oath"; and attorneys vowed before the courts to act honourably.'[149]

Of course, contemporaries argued over whether the modern professions were merely the old guilds in a new guise or whether they really did promote social betterment. In 1861 Charles Neate, a Fellow of Oriel College and a 'Noetic' as well as briefly a Liberal MP, devoted two interesting lectures to this subject at Oxford University. 'Monopolies of any sort, and at any time, can only be defended on the ground that the work to be done cannot be done so well by open competition', Neate reasoned: 'they are not, they never were, properly intended for the benefit of those who exercised them, but for the benefit of the community to whom

---

[146] C. Cowan, *The Danger, Irrationality, and Evils of Medical Quackery* (London, 1839), 32–3.
[147] See the excellent discussion in Duman, *Judicial Bench*, ch. 7.
[148] 'Independence' of course meant emancipation from dependence on patrons.
[149] Corfield, *Professions*, 19, 204.

at one time they were useful, and still continue to be so in the instances of the learned professions'. Neate felt that some of the rules of the Bar did not satisfy this criterion, but he took a generally benign view of the role of modern professional men:

When we need the assistance of a clergyman, a lawyer, or a physician,—we are resorting to an adviser of whose qualifications for his task we are ourselves no adequate judges, to one at least who knows or ought to know much more of his business than we do ourselves; and therefore it is for the general good that the State, or those bodies to whom the State delegates this duty, should guarantee the fitness and ability of the members of these professions, by restricting admission into them to those whose qualifications have been duly ascertained.[150]

The fact that such protestations did not elicit stronger objections than they did[151] is an indication that, even in the heyday of *laissez faire*, some areas of social life were thought too sensitive to be subjected to the *full* rigours of market competition.[152]

Let us end with Albert Dicey's interesting reflections on what essentially distinguished a profession from a trade. The chief difference, Dicey suggested, was

that in the case of a profession its members sacrifice a certain amount of individual liberty in order to insure certain professional objects. In a trade or business the conduct of each individual is avowedly regulated by the general rules of honesty and regard to his own interest.

Dicey observed that whereas one class of contemporary 'theorists' conceived that all professions should become trades, another class wished to make trades into professions.[153] In the short run, at least, it seemed that Dicey's second group of theorists might be having rather the better of the argument.

[150] C. Neate, *Two Lectures on Trades Unions, delivered in the University of Oxford in the Year 1861* (Oxford, 1862), 13–14.
[151] For satirical attacks on the greed and corruption of lawyers and doctors (Corfield, *Professions*, esp. 47–8, 56–9, 80).
[152] Not, of course, that professional men were ever able to insulate themselves entirely from market forces. As Corfield argues, professions could achieve power for their members only when there was 'a favourable conjunction of consumer demand and some control of supply' (ibid., 246).
[153] Dicey, 'Legal Etiquette', 177 fn. 1.

7
Family and Women

Marriage being instituted for the mutual comfort and support of the parties to it, and also for the propagation of the species and the sustenance and education of the offspring, is an engagement susceptible of all the varieties of form which consent can establish, provided they be not contrary to these ends. It may, indeed, be considered merely as a partnership entered into for certain purposes by two persons of the opposite sexes; and although the stipulations which they may make with each other might properly be enforced by society, it does not appear to us to be so obviously distinguished from every other species of partnership that its terms, whether as to the nature or the duration of the union, should not be chosen and determined by the partners themselves.

(*Westminster Review*, 1864)[1]

Man is the brain, but woman is the heart of humanity; he its judgement, she its feeling; he its strength, she its grace, ornament, and solace.

(S. Smiles, 1871)[2]

'Young ladies don't understand political economy you know', said Mr Brooke.

(George Eliot, 1871–2)[3]

THE MALTHUSIAN DILEMMA

There was another even more important area of life into which it was generally agreed that commercial values should not intrude: the family, which was supposedly based on mutual love. Hence the horror evinced by the practice of wife-selling.[4] Economic considerations, it was further agreed, should ideally play no part in the choice of a spouse. But should financial calculations be a factor in the procreation and rearing of children? This became a very lively issue, as a result of the theories propounded by Thomas Malthus.

As we have seen, Malthus had originally advanced his 'principle of population' in order to refute the doctrine of human perfectibility, but, in doing so, he had

---

[1] 'The Laws of Marriage and Divorce', *Westminster Review*, 82 (1864), 469.
[2] S. Smiles, *Character* (London, 1871), 38.
[3] G. Eliot, *Middlemarch*, Penguin edn. (London, 1965; first pub. 1871–2), ch. 2. Dorothea, we learn, was annoyed 'at being twitted with her ignorance of political economy, that never-explained science which was thrust as an extinguisher over all her lights' (pp. 39–40). [4] Ch. 4.

unwittingly created an association in many of his readers' minds between political economy and misanthropy.[5] Such connotations were reinforced when the 'law
of population' was taken up by David Ricardo and made an element in the 'Iron
Law of Wages', which purported to prove that labourers could not raise their wages
above the level needed to perpetuate themselves in existing numbers. The lot of
the labourer under capitalism, it seemed, would continue to be one of unrelieved
misery.

In the second edition of his *Essay*, Malthus somewhat lightened the gloom by
adding 'moral restraint' to warfare and disease as devices for escaping the population trap, a modification which, as we have seen, allowed Chalmers to practise
his own particular brand of Christian optimism. Yet 'moral restraint' implied either
deferred marriage, which was what Malthus himself had meant, or the artificial
restriction of births within marriage, a dangerously controversial proposal.[6] (The
accusation by some of his detractors that Malthus was hinting at the desirability
of infanticide was, of course, an absurdity.)

One can trace the embarrassment that these issues generated through the writings of one of Malthus's most assiduous popularizers, Harriet Martineau. As a
woman, Martineau had to treat the population question very delicately, but, even
so, her cautiously worded recommendation of late marriage and 'prudence' left
her open to attack from two diametrically opposed quarters: from the Radical
autodidact, Francis Place, who accused her of timidity, and from the Tory
Quarterly Review, which affected to be outraged by her offences against decency.[7]
Martineau was clearly wise to steer clear of all discussion of birth control.
Advocating it aroused such strong prejudices that it led to John Stuart Mill being
arrested as a young man for distributing leaflets on the subject. Never again did
he go beyond population control on *general* grounds: thus the *Principles of Political
Economy* urges on the working classes the desirability of 'provident habits of conduct' which would ensure that population bore 'a gradually diminishing ratio to
capital and employment', but without offering any suggestions about how this might
be achieved.[8]

Francis Place, who believed that political economy could be 'as clearly demonstrated as that the squares of the two sides of a right angle are equal to the square
of the hypotenuse', showed greater boldness, explicitly linking the law of population to the practice of birth control.[9] Ricardo and William Ellis were sympathetic
to this project, but McCulloch took strong exception to it.[10]

---

[5] Ch. 2.   [6] M. Mason, *The Making of Victorian Sexuality* (Oxford, 1994), 258–63.
[7] V. K. Pichanick, *Harriet Martineau: The Woman and Her Work 1802–76* (Ann Arbor, 1980), 64–6.
Martineau treats the question in *Weal and Woe in Garveloch* (London, 1832). See G. G. Yates, *Harriet
Martineau On Women* (New Brunswick, NJ, *c*.1985), 205–6.
[8] J. S. Mill, *Principles of Political Economy* (London, 1848), in id., *Collected Works*, ed.
J. M. Robson (Toronto, 1965), iii. 765.
[9] M. Mason, *The Making of Victorian Sexual Attitudes* (Oxford, 1994), 176; D. Winch, *Riches and
Poverty: An Intellectual History of Political Economy in Britain, 1750–1834* (Cambridge, 1996), 282–3.
[10] Mason, *Victorian Sexual Attitudes*, 176, 180.

Moreover, when in 1877 the Drysdale brothers launched their 'Malthusian League', they encountered considerable hostility; indeed, the Drysdales' linking of birth control to an extremely doctrinaire version of economic individualism probably had the effect of bringing *both* causes into disrepute.[11] George Drysdale, a doctor, was unusual in his insistence that the regular 'exercise' of the sexual organs was conducive to good health, but his provocative book, *The Elements of Social Science* (the first edition of which dates back to 1855), also draws very heavily upon the classic political economists, from whose writings he had made 'copious notes' while a medical student—so much so that later editions read like a popularization of the theories of Mill, for whom he entertained a lifelong admiration.[12] A similar ideological approach characterized other members of the Malthusian League, notably Charles Bradlaugh—like Mill, an advocate of co-operatives, but an outspoken critic of the socialist analysis of class relationships.[13]

However, most Victorian popularizers of 'political economy' prudently kept aloof from the birth control movement, which soon developed along thoroughly commercial lines, with 'literature in chemists' shops, announcements in urinals, lectures by travelling salesmen, fly posters, advertisements in papers, and . . . circulars sent to couples who had announced a birth in the press'.[14] Turning their backs on this 'sordidness', most political economists plumped instead for a strategy which merely held out the hope that wage labourers could escape the most baleful consequences of the 'law of population' by deferment of marriage (supplemented by emigration).

However, even this kind of discreet propaganda split the Christian world. Controlling the sexual appetites obviously fitted in well enough with conventional Christian morality. On the other hand, to many of his detractors, it seemed that Malthus was flying in the face of God's commandment to mankind to multiply and replenish the earth, even that he was casting doubt on God's power and benevolence by denying that all human beings had access to the resources needed to sustain life.[15]

Moreover, as Michael Mason has shown, this issue also continued to sow dissension amongst the political economists, mainly because they could not agree over whether the advance of civilization was spontaneously producing a reduction in the intensity of sexual impulses. Did the evidence really suggest that 'reason' was

---

[11] George Drysdale first began elaborating his theories in 1856–7 in the fifteen issues of his own 8-page journal, *The Political Economist; and Journal of Social Science* (R. Ledbetter, *A History of The Malthusian League 1877–1927* (Columbus, Oh., 1976), 19). The Malthusian League offended both the moral conservatives and the socialists, the latter strongly objecting to the League's view that workers must adopt family limitation if the problem of poverty was to be solved (ibid., 97). See also R. A. Soloway, *Birth Control and the Population Question in England, 1877–1930* (Chapel Hill, NC, 1982), 59.

[12] Mason, *Victorian Sexual Attitudes*, 189–213. The 1859 edn. of the *Elements* incorporates material first appearing in Drysdale's periodical, *The Political Economist*, during 1856–7.

[13] Mason, *Victorian Sexual Attitudes*, 176.   [14] Mason, *Victorian Sexuality*, 63.

[15] Paley had earlier seen population growth as a sign of prosperity and of God's favour.

gradually assuming control over the 'passions'?[16] Malthus himself had initially assumed the *primacy* of the sex drive, though he had later qualified this assumption by suggesting the possibility of 'moral restraint'.[17] A number of his avowed 'disciples', however, took a rather different line—among them, Mill, a 'progressive anti-sensualist' who looked forward hopefully to a time when the 'animal instinct' would gradually lose its 'disproportionate preponderance'.[18] A middle position between these two extremes was adopted by Nassau Senior, who propounded the 'comfort theory', which postulated that, although neither the lure of luxuries nor the goad of necessity would dampen the attractiveness of marriage, a desire for 'comfort' might be expected to affect the marriage rates of all but the very poor and the very wealthy.[19]

Senior's, however, was a very sophisticated line of argument, and it remains the case that political economy, in its popular forms, seemed to be preaching to the poor man the desirability of sacrificing his 'natural' affections in the cause of economic self-advancement, advice which many contemporaries found morally disgusting (it even offended so staunch a political economist as W. R. Greg[20]). Dickens memorably satirized 'vulgar Malthusianism' through the character of 'Bitzer', the prize pupil who had totally internalized the lessons of political economy: '*I* don't want a wife and family', declares Bitzer, so why should the factory hands want them either? 'If they were more provident, and less perverse, . . . what would they do? They would say, . . . "I have only one to feed, and that's the person I most like to feed".'[21]

MARRIAGE AS CONTRACT?

There was another potentially mercenary aspect to marriage, stemming from its very nature. In Christian societies the institution of marriage has always had a twofold character, being both a contract and a sacrament. But what if the contractual aspect of marriage were allowed to *predominate*? After the institution of civil marriage in 1837, such a development seemed a distinct likelihood.

[16] For further discussion, see Ch. 10.

[17] Mason, *Victorian Sexuality*, 260–1, 268. Malthus distinctly disassociated himself from 'any artificial and unnatural modes of checking population, both on account of their immorality and their tendency to remove a necessary stimulus to industry' (cited in Winch, *Riches and Poverty*, 285).

[18] Mill, *Principles of Political Economy*, in id., *Collected Works*, iii. 766. Mill hoped that this would be one of the happy consequences of the emancipation of women, on which see below. Mason outlines his concept of 'progressive anti-sensualism' in *Victorian Sexuality*, ch. 5.

[19] Mason, *Victorian Sexuality*, 280–1.

[20] Greg blamed the high proportion of unmarried adults on 'the growing and morbid LUXURY of the age' and called for the adoption of a more 'simple' life (W. R. Greg, *Why Are Women Redundant?* (London, 1869), first published in *National Review* (Apr. 1862), 19–24).

[21] C. Dickens, *Hard Times*, Chapman & Hall edn. (London, n.d.; first pub. 1854), bk. 2, ch. 1, pp. 375–6.

Now, some middle-class Victorians could see *advantages* in treating marriage as yet one contract among many. In 1864 an anonymous contributor to the *Westminster Review*, who had clearly been reading Henry Maine, contended that 'the whole history of the law of persons disclose[d] the general fact, that one most material element in its development consist[ed] in the gradual evolution of the doctrine of contract from that of status'. Marriage, he argued, would necessarily be affected, and in a beneficial way, once it became placed on the footing of 'voluntary agreement'.[22]

Some of the pioneering feminists of mid-Victorian Britain took such suggestions one stage further by advocating, in effect, the endowment of women, on the French model. Bessie Rayner Parkes, in particular, called on middle-class parents to set up their daughters so that they could later enter marriage as equals. 'English readers will shrink from thus regarding marriage as a commercial firm', she conceded: 'they will say that a husband and wife are one, and that he must not weigh what he gives her against what she gives him; that such a state of feeling is monstrous, and destructive to all the best and holiest interest of married life.' Parkes sympathized with these objections, but pointed out that the *practice* of marriage differed from the *theory*.[23] Most people, she asserted, privately recognized that marriage was 'a judicious mixture' of business relationship and sacred union, a relationship which God intended to be 'partly spiritual, partly natural'.

In a sense, argued Parkes, marriage already constituted a kind of business partnership, with 'woman's power of household management' constituting her 'natural capital'. This assumed a natural division of labour in which 'her husband brings the money and she brings the domestic work'.[24] Unfortunately, Parkes acknowledged, few young men viewed domestic knowledge and practice in quite this way.[25] That being so, women should be free to establish their 'independence' through work, having first received parental help in the form of a proper education.

Her friend and political associate, Barbara Leigh Smith (Bodichon), made the point more forcibly. 'Fathers have no right to cast the burden of the support of their daughters on other men', she declared. 'It lowers the dignity of women; and tends to prostitution, whether legal or in the streets.'[26] Mill and Harriet Taylor broadly agreed. However, Mill's position was a complex one which requires closer attention.

JOHN STUART MILL

The Subjection of Women (1869) seems to prefigure modern ideas about sexual equality in so many ways that it is easy to overlook how period-bound it actually

---

[22] 'Laws of Marriage and Divorce', 468–9.
[23] B. R. Parkes, *Essays on Woman's Work* (London, 1865), 148–9.   [24] Ibid., 149–50.
[25] Ibid., 153.   [26] B. L. Smith, *Women and Work* (London, 1857), 11.

is, and how closely Mill's campaign to win women the parliamentary vote was embedded into a political economist's sense of the need to emancipate society from precapitalist restraints.

The starting-point of the essay is a total rejection of the 'chivalric' attitude to women, most famously expressed by John Ruskin in *Sesame and Lilies*. In Mill's view, chivalry was essentially an attribute of feudalism, in which the 'relation between husband and wife [was] very like that between lord and vassal', except that the wife was held 'to more unlimited obedience than the vassal was'. Mill contrasted this antiquated prejudice with the modern idea 'that, above all, merit, and not birth, [was] the only rightful claim to power and authority'.[27]

Mill's other main argument was that in industrial societies the social roles of men and women were becoming less distinct, a development which meant that marriage would inevitably assume more and more the character of a 'partnership'. Mill, like the *Westminster Review* writer, had in his head the notion of a progression from status to contract. But to Mill the contractual term, 'partnership', also carried a rich variety of meanings and did not simply denote a formal legal or business arrangement. On the contrary, Mill stressed that all true partnerships rested upon *affection* and, in particular, upon *sympathy*.

Moreover, in Mill's eyes, sympathy entailed equality, since contractual relationships could only be formed between equals. The most frequent case of voluntary association, next to marriage, he pointed out, was 'partnership in business, and it is not found or thought necessary to enact that in every partnership one partner shall have entire control over the concern, and the others shall be bound to obey his orders'.[28] Thus Mill conflated sympathy and equality, and then presented both as the foundation of all true contractual relationships.

But Mill was an advocate of a modern market economy in yet another sense. Being what later analysts have called a 'humanist', he emphasized what men and women shared by virtue of their common humanity. 'What is now called the nature of women is an essentially artificial thing', the product of social conditioning, he declared.[29] Mill's central claim, then, was that only through experimentation could one ascertain what women were capable of doing.[30] From this, he drew the logical deduction that

what women by nature cannot do, it is quite superfluous to forbid them from doing. What they do, but not so well as the men who are their competitors, competition suffices to exclude them from; since nobody asks for protective duties and bounties in favour of women; it is only asked that the present bounties and protective duties in favour of men should be recalled . . . Whatever women's services are most wanted for, the free play of competition will hold out the strongest inducements to them to undertake.[31]

---

[27] J. S. Mill, *The Subjection of Women*, ed. S. Mansfield (Arlington Heights, Ill., 1980; first pub. 1869), 81–2. Ironically, a hostile reviewer of the book complained that Mill himself was really treating women chivalrously! ('Mill on the Subjection of Women', *Edinburgh Review*, 130 (1869), 576–7).
[28] Mill, *Subjection*, 39.   [29] Ibid., 21.   [30] Ibid., 23.   [31] Ibid., 26–7.

Thus, by allowing women to compete, one widened the market, thereby boosting efficiency and conferring a benefit on the consumer, since 'any limitation of the field of selection deprive[d] society of some chances of being served by the competent, without ever saving it from the incompetent'.[32]

In *Representative Government*, written a few years before *The Subjection of Women*, Mill had already revealed how much his views on women's emancipation depended upon the premises of political economy. His analysis, he declared, took no account of differences of sex, because he thought this to be 'as entirely irrelevant to political rights as difference in height or in the colour of the hair':

If the principles of modern politics and political economy are good for anything, it is for proving that [questions of what individuals are fit to do] can only be rightly judged of by the individuals themselves: and that, under complete freedom of choice, wherever there are real diversities of aptitude, the great number will apply themselves to the things for which they are on the average fittest, and the exceptional course will only be taken by the exceptions. Either the whole tendency of modern social improvements has been wrong, or it ought to be carried out to the total abolition of all exclusions and disabilities which close any honest employment to a human being.[33]

In *The Subjection of Women* Mill invoked the authority of political economy even more directly:

To ordain that any kind of persons shall not be physicians, or shall not be advocates, or shall not be members of Parliament, is to injure not them only, but all who employ physicians or advocates, or elect members of Parliament, and who are deprived of the stimulating effect of greater competition on the exertion of the competitors, as well as restricted to a narrower range of individual choice.[34]

Modern feminists have complained that Mill's treatment of the position of women is sometimes confused and that in places he concedes too much to the 'enemy' by qualifying his doctrine of contract through the introduction of the notion of *customary expectations*.[35] This notion was a dangerous one for Mill, since it allowed his opponents to argue that husbands might reasonably 'expect' their wives to devote

[32] Ibid., 18. Similarly, in *Principles of Political Economy* Mill criticized the 'disproportionate preponderance' of the 'exclusive function' of motherhood in women's lives and advocated 'the opening of industrial occupations freely to both sexes' (*Principles of Political Economy*, in id., *Collected Works*, iii. 765–6).

[33] J. S. Mill, *Considerations on Representative Government*, Everyman edn. (London, 1910; first pub. 1861), 290.   [34] Mill, *Subjection*, 49–51.

[35] See J. S. Mill, *On Liberty*, Everyman edn. (London, 1910; first pub. 1859), 158–9. Mill's main concern was to dissociate himself from the proposal that marriage should be dissolvable at the wish of either partner—a proposal which, if adopted in Victorian Britain, would almost certainly have worked to women's disadvantage. He also raised the issue of obligations incurred to 'third parties', in this case the children of the marriage. See R. W. Krouse, 'Patriarchal Liberalism and Beyond: From John Stuart Mill to Harriet Taylor', in J. B. Elshtain (ed.), *The Family in Political Thought* (Brighton, 1982), 165–6.

themselves to the production and rearing of children and not to embark upon a career or to take up public service.[36] Mill's confusion when discussing these issues probably reflects his uncertainty over whether married women really would want to work when they were (quite properly) given the freedom to do so, or whether they would voluntarily opt for more traditional feminine roles, including 'the one vocation in which there [was] nobody to compete with them', that is to say, motherhood.[37] Perhaps here is a case of what Parkes meant when she wrote that Mill 'occasionally retreats upon the moral intuitions of the human heart in a way that exposes him to censure from those who are willing to push intellectual conclusions to their farthest limits'.[38]

Despite these hesitations, Mill never wavered in his principled rejection of the idea of the 'sympathetic' woman. As we shall see, it was conventional during the nineteenth century to claim that women, with their capacity for altruism and the finer feelings, exercised a civilizing influence by checking and controlling the brutal and overrational qualities so strongly embodied in the male. These traits, it was often argued, made women peculiarly well suited to philanthropic activities.[39]

But Mill, supported by Harriet Taylor, vigorously took issue with all such assumptions. Not only did he dispute contemporary stereotypes of manliness and womanliness: he also saw women's much-vaunted softness as a product of an inadequate upbringing, which he hoped better education and increased public responsibilities would remove. Women's contribution to public opinion, thought Mill, 'would be modified for the better by that more enlarged instruction, and practical conversancy with the things which their opinions influence, that would necessarily arise from their social and political emancipation'.[40]

In general, then, the thrust of Mill's argument is that men and women should be treated on the same footing because they had essentially similar natures— a 'functionalist' approach to human life that was all of a piece with his writings as a political economist. Such arguments were to play a crucial role in Mill's advocacy of women's suffrage, which he based, not so much on any supposed

[36] Indeed, there is a passage in *The Subjection of Women* (p. 48) where Mill treats this as a possible and tolerable outcome.

[37] Ibid., 41, 47–50. See Krouse, 'Patriarchal Liberalism', 145–72. In fairness to Mill, one should add that many socialists, too, were later to claim that women would not choose to work once the male breadwinner was in receipt of a 'living wage' (S. S. Holton, *Feminism and Democracy: Women's Suffrage and Reform Politics in Britain 1900–1918* (Cambridge, 1986), 16).

[38] Parkes, *Woman's Work*, 160.

[39] In fact, conventional opinion was divided on the extent to which middle-class ladies could with propriety immerse themselves in philanthropic work. Compare F. Prochaska, *Women and Philanthropy in Nineteenth Century England* (Oxford, 1980), 15, with J. Harris, *Private Lives, Public Spirit: A Social History of Britain 1870–1914* (Oxford, 1993), 26.

[40] Mill, *Subjection*, 89. Mill also thought women's 'moral sense' to be both 'negative' and selfish, not really disinterested (ibid., 87), as did Harriet Taylor (H. T. Mill, 'Enfranchisement of Women' (1851), in A. S. Rossi (ed.), *John Stuart Mill and Harriet Taylor Mill: Essays on Sex Equality* (Chicago, 1970), esp. 116).

'natural right', as on more practical grounds. 'Can it be pretended', he asked the Commons in his famous speech of May 1867,

that women who manage an estate or conduct a business—who pay rates and taxes, often to a large amount, and frequently from their own earnings—many of whom are responsible heads of families, and some of whom, in the capacity of schoolmistresses, teach much more than a great number of the male electors have ever learnt—are not capable of a function of which every male householder is capable?[41]

This provoked a tart retort from an MP opposed to votes for women who observed that Mill 'would do well if he imported into this sort of question not so much political economy, and a little more common sense'.[42] The gibe was unfair, but it correctly identified the links between Mill's views on the role of women in public life and his economic theories.

POLITICAL ECONOMY AND THE 'WOMAN QUESTION'

But Mill's was not an isolated case. For there had been close connections between middle-class feminism and political economy, as exemplified in the career of Harriet Martineau, who was prominent in both causes.[43] It is also significant that the famous pioneer of women's education, Barbara Bodichon (née Leigh Smith), should be the daughter of Benjamin Smith, the chairman of the Anti-Corn Law League,[44] who grew up to form a close working relationship with many of the prominent Radical leaders and intellectuals of the age, including William Ellis; in fact, the school which she founded in 1854 at Portman Hall was strongly influenced by the ideas of the famous exponent of 'social economy', as practised in the Birkbeck Schools.[45] Emily Davies and Barbara Bodichon also knew Mill well and lobbied vigorously on behalf of his election to Parliament and his subsequent suffrage reform campaign, and both worked with him in securing a change to the law relating to married women's property.[46] Finally, Bessie Rayner Parkes admired Mill's *Principles* almost as much as she admired his *Subjection of Women*.[47]

---

[41] Hansard, clxxxvii, 818: 20 May 1867.   [42] Ibid., 832.

[43] Yates, *Harriet Martineau On Women*. On Martineau's views about women's work, see below.

[44] The latest biography is by S. R. Herstein, *A Mid-Victorian Feminist, Barbara Leigh Smith Bodichon* (New Haven, 1985).

[45] W. D. Sockwell, *Popularizing Classical Economics: Henry Brougham and William Ellis* (New York, 1994), 162; H. Burton, *Barbara Bodichon 1827–1891* (London, 1949), 50–1; L. Holcombe, *Wives and Property: Reform of the Married Women's Property Law in Nineteenth-Century England* (Oxford, 1983), 57–8, 62–3.   [46] Holcombe, *Wives and Property*, 115–16, 145–7.

[47] J. Rendall, ' "A Moral Engine": Feminism, Liberalism and the *English Woman's Journal*', in J. Rendall (ed.), *Equal or Different: Women's Politics 1800–1914* (Oxford, 1987), 118.

Those who fell under Mill's influence, men as well as women,[48] tended to concentrate on three issues, all of which raised questions about the way in which political economy was related to women's freedom: first, the removal of sexual discrimination against females in respect of the parliamentary vote: second, the amendment of the Women's Property Acts: and, third, the ending of discrimination against women in the workplace.

Mill's most direct impact was obviously on the early women's suffrage movement, to which, in its parliamentary manifestations at least, he gave a character which it retained for several decades. True, Jacob Bright, the leading spokesman for the cause after Mill's defeat in the 1868 general election, was inclined to buttress his claims with 'natural rights' arguments. But this line of reasoning played no part in the expositions of the two MPs mainly responsible for raising women's suffrage in the Commons at annual intervals throughout the 1870s and 1880s: Henry Fawcett and Leonard Courtney, both of whom, significantly, were political economists proud to call themselves Mill's loyal disciples.

Fawcett, in fact, went further than Mill in emphasizing that he was advocating a limited property-based franchise.[49] Likewise his friend Courtney, who combined support of middle-class women with outright opposition to the movement to give farm labourers the vote.[50] The tone of this generation of Radical suffragists is well caught by another friend of the cause, Philip Muntz, who told the Commons that 'he knew a lady worth £70,000 or £80,000 a year, who, in the election of Members of Parliament, had no vote at all, while her gardener, her groom, and other male servants had a vote each'; Muntz said that he 'was not in favour of granting votes to all women, but he thought that in some cases they ought to have them'.[51] Even Barbara Bodichon and her female friends were prepared to echo these sentiments,[52] perhaps because they realized how much more difficult it would be for MPs to oppose women's suffrage if it was presented in these terms.[53]

Mid-Victorian Liberals used a similar rhetoric in the course of the fight to give women control over their own property. Shaw-Lefevre, for example, commended the Married Women's Property Act by declaring: 'Let [women] have as far as

[48] For a very different interpretation, one which emphasizes the 'separatist' strands in late Victorian feminism, see P. Levine, *Feminist Lives in Victorian England: Private Roles and Public Commitment* (Oxford, 1990), 116, 121, and *passim*).

[49] Hansard, ccxv, 1239–48: 30 Apr. 1873.

[50] Ibid., ccxl, 1869: 19 June 1878: ibid., ccxliv, 413: 7 Mar. 1879. Significantly, Courtney specifically dissociated himself from 'natural rights' arguments, saying that he was a pure utilitarian.

[51] Ibid., cci, 236: 4 May 1870.

[52] The petition she helped organize for presentation to Parliament on 7 June 1866 declared that it was 'an evident anomaly that some holders of property are allowed to use [their property rights], while others, forming no less a constituent part of the nation, and equally qualified by law to hold property, are not able to exercise this privilege' (B. L. S. Bodichon, *Objections to the Enfranchisement of Women Considered* (London, 1866), 2).

[53] Bagehot noted that the 1870 Bill merely followed 'the constitutional maxim of giving parliamentary representation to those who are taxed' (W. Bagehot, 'The Suffrage for Women', *The Economist*, 28 (7 May 1870), 565–6, cited in N. St J. Stevas, *Collected Works of Walter Bagehot* (London, 1974), vi. 397–8).

possible fair play, remove unequal legislation, and women would then speedily find their true level, whatever that might be.'[54] Little wonder, perhaps, if a stern political economist like Robert Lowe should have been so strong a supporter of women's property law reform.

Far more troublesome and problematical was the issue of 'women and work'. Was it really wise to allow women to compete directly with men in those trades where they possessed no physical disadvantages? Earlier in his career even Mill had worried lest an influx of women into paid employment might produce an over-stocking of the labour market, and it had required Harriet Taylor to remove his anxieties on this score.[55] In the end, as we have seen, Mill took the view that equal-ity of treatment for women was not only elementary justice, but also made eco-nomic sense, since, as he implied rather than stated, female entrants to the labour market, like immigrants, would *in time* create new jobs, even though they might destroy men's jobs *in the short run*.

W. R. Greg was a stern critic of Mill's views on female suffrage, but the two men could at least agree over the folly of attempting to exclude females from indus-trial careers where they might usurp the employment of men. Greg characterized this as 'an objection to the principle of *competition* in the abstract':

It is clearly a waste of strength, a superfluous extravagance, an economic blunder, to employ a powerful and costly machine to do work which can be as well done by a feebler and a cheaper one. Women and girls are less costly operatives than men: what they can do with equal efficiency, it is therefore wasteful and foolish (*economically considered*) to set a man to do. By employing the cheaper labour, the article is supplied to the public at a smaller cost, and therefore the demand for the article is increased.

But Greg went on to suggest that objections to women's work might reasonably be made on social or moral grounds, implying that such objections would largely fall to the ground if women left employment on marriage.[56]

Harriet Martineau was a feminist committed to women's advancement, as Greg was not. Nevertheless, she, too, believed that 'political economy' taught very clear lessons to those wrestling with the problem of women and work. 'There are arts to which female faculties are particularly appropriate which women cannot prac-tise on account of the monopolizing spirit of the men', she complained,[57] instanc-ing the actions of the 'caste or guild' of Clerkenwell watchmakers who were attempting

---

[54] Holcombe, *Wives and Property*, 151. See the pertinent observations in W. R. Cornish and G. de N. Clark, *Law and Society in England 1750–1950* (London, 1989), 402. On the fears about the likely consequences of reform, see the examples cited in M. Poovey, *Uneven Developments: The Ideological Work of Gender in Mid-Victorian England. Women in Culture and Society* (Chicago, 1988), 74.

[55] H. T. Mill, 'Enfranchisement of Women', 104–5.

[56] Greg (*Why Are Women Redundant?*, 33–4) specifically praised the female workforce for the won-derful development of the country's textile industry. But he also seems to have thought that the threat to male jobs would be reduced if single women were encouraged to emigrate—a key theme in this pamphlet.

[57] [H. Martineau], 'Female Industry', *Edinburgh Review*, 109 (1859), 326. This article aroused con-siderable interest when it appeared (Holcombe, *Victorian Ladies at Work* (Newton Abbot, 1973), 10).

to exclude dextrous female workers. 'We need not explain to our readers that the monopolists punish themselves, as well as the public, and tens of thousands of our countrywomen' when they behave in this way, she added.[58] The fields of employment which really *were* overstocked were the professions of schoolteacher and governess, where uneducated women drove down one another's wages.[59] 'We must improve and extend education to the utmost; and then open a fair field to the powers and energies we have educed', was thus the moral of her story.[60] This train of reasoning led Martineau to attack all factory legislation that avowedly had women's protection at heart.

Mill, too, took this line, as did his disciple, Henry Fawcett. Disliking *all* legislative interference with the working hours of adult operatives,[61] Fawcett particularly set his face against restricting women's labour because he believed that this forced women 'to be crowded into the employments still left open', where they toiled 'for wages insufficient to maintain them in the barest decency'.[62] By the same account, Fawcett deplored trade unionism, not just for the reasons generally given by orthodox political economists, but also because he saw union organization as a crude attempt on the part of male workers to exclude female competitors.[63]

Henry Fawcett tended to express his views with a brutality which was foreign to Mill's nature; indeed, paradoxically enough, as Stefan Collini notes, this bold pioneer of the women's movement was also, in his capacity as a political economist, a gruff disparager of all sentimentality and a subscriber to a cult of 'manliness'. On occasions the group of which he was a leading luminary even went so far as to accuse the revered Mill of possessing 'feminine' qualities![64]

But a similar doctrinaire hardness can be found in Fawcett's wife, Millicent, who later emerged as the leading figure in the mainstream Women's Suffrage Movement. One must remember that Mrs Fawcett was a significant political economist in her own right. As a young woman she had helped her husband write his *Manual*, as well as producing a number of works of popularization such as *Political Economy for Beginners* (1870) and *Tales in Political Economy* (1874).[65] A rigid defender of *laissez-faire* at a time when it was going out of fashion, Mrs Fawcett strongly disapproved of 'professional philanthropists', whom she accused of standing between individuals and the consequences of their actions—a harsh

---

[58] Martineau, 'Female Industry', 326.

[59] Ibid., 330. Greg, too, had urged proper training for governesses and teachers (*Why Are Women Redundant?*, 34–5). [60] Martineau, 'Female Industry', 336.

[61] On Fawcett's implacable opposition to the 9 Hour Day, W. H. G. Armytage, *A. J. Mundella 1825–1897* (London, 1951), 132–4. It is revealing that as late as 1879 Courtney even found words of praise to bestow publicly upon Martineau (Hansard, ccxliv, 421: 7 Mar. 1879).

[62] L. Stephen, *Life of Henry Fawcett* (London, 1885), 177.

[63] Later, as Postmaster-General, Fawcett was proud of his achievement in increasing the number of female clerks at the Post Office—who were recruited, of course, by open competition (ibid., 443–4).

[64] Thus in *The English Utilitarians* Leslie Stephen wrote of Mill's 'feminine qualities', while privately he deplored Mill's lack of 'masculine fibre'. So, predictably, did his brother James Fitzjames Stephen (S. Collini, *Public Moralists: Political Thought and Intellectual Life in Britain, 1850–1930* (Oxford, 1991), 193–4).

[65] L. Goldman (ed.), *The Blind Victorian: Henry Fawcett and British Liberalism* (Cambridge, 1989), 76–7.

restatement of Mill's views on the same subject.[66] But her greatest contempt was reserved for legislative restrictions on women's work, which she portrayed as an expression of male selfishness, seeing in it 'the old Trade Union spirit to drive women out of certain trades where their competition is inconvenient', to quote from her letter to *The Times* of June 1873.[67] There is even evidence that it was Millicent who converted her husband to adopting this hostile view of factory legislation.[68]

Millicent Fawcett's desire to anchor 'women's rights' in the teachings of political economy can also be found among the circle of women who had earlier come together to launch the *English Woman's Journal* in February 1858. In fact, the history of this journal, as related by Jane Rendall, throws a fascinating light on the close interconnection between political economy and 'feminism' in mid-Victorian Britain.

Bessie Rayner Parkes ran the paper as a limited liability company, with moral and financial support from Barbara Leigh Smith.[69] The joint stock principle was adopted because, following Mill, Parkes regarded it as peculiarly appropriate to 'the small means and more delicate physical powers of women' wishing to co-operate with one another.[70] 'If twenty ladies in any town would club together £5 a-piece', she argued, 'they might open a stationery shop, to which, if they gave all their own custom, they might secure a profit after employing a female manageress and if the business increased, female clerks also.'[71]

The *English Woman's Journal* urged the opening up to middle-class women of many professions, along with posts in commerce and trade, though it did not favour women working directly alongside males.[72] It also followed Martineau in its handling of the issue of the 'overstocked' market for governesses.[73] Admittedly Parkes

---

[66] D. Rubinstein, 'Millicent Garrett Fawcett and the Meaning of Women's Emancipation, 1886–99', *Victorian Studies*, 34 (1991), 365–80.

[67] *The Times*, 9 June 1873, cited in Goldman (ed.), *Fawcett*, 79. See also M. G. Fawcett, 'A reply to the letter of Mr Samuel Smith, MP, on women's suffrage' (1892), in J. Lewis (ed.), *Before the Vote Was Won: Arguments For and Against Women's Suffrage* (London, 1987), 439. Josephine Butler, too, opposed the protection of women through factory legislation (B. Harrison, 'State Intervention and Moral Reform in nineteenth-century England', in P. Hollis (ed.), *Pressure From Without in Early Victorian England* (London, 1974), 313).

[68] Goldman (ed.), *Fawcett*, 77–9. For a diametrically opposed view, see Holcombe, *Wives and Property*, 5. P. Levine concedes that many of the pioneering 'feminists' were staunch opponents of the Factory Acts, but points out that a new generation of women involved in employment questions took a very different view (*Victorian Feminism 1850–1900* (London, 1987), 122). But for a later protest against industrial protection for women see H. Blackburn, *Women's Suffrage: A Record of the Women's Suffrage Movement in the British Isles* (London, 1902; repr. New York, 1971), 226.

[69] Rendall, 'Moral Engine', 112–38.   [70] Parkes, *Woman's Work*, 167–8, 180–2.

[71] [B. R. Parkes], 'The Opinions of John Stuart Mill: Part 2: Co-operation', *English Woman's Journal*, 6 (Nov. 1860), 202. The whole passage is italicized in the original.

[72] Rendall, 'Moral Engine', 119–22. Hence Rendall's claim that what the paper represented was the desire of many middle-class women for 'work which offered a new way of extending the sexual division of labour into the capitalist economy' (J. Rendall, *The Origins of Modern Feminism: Women in Britain, France and the United States, 1780–1860* (Basingstoke, 1985), 186).

[73] Rendall, 'Moral Engine', 121.

herself, as we will later see, held a number of quite traditional views about women's employment, but many contributors boldly rested their case on the principles of free trade. Jessie Boucherett, for example, wanted to admit 'women freely into all employments suitable to their strength', leaving the market to decide what occupations women were suited to.[74] The question of whether women would thereby displace men in the labour market she very peremptorily disposed of: competition must run its course, she argued, even if this meant that some men might be driven to emigrate.[75]

On the issue of female labour there was a measure of agreement between supporters and opponents of women's emancipation. Thus the *Saturday Review*, an outspoken opponent of 'votes for women', did at least concur with Martineau's view that it was self-destructive folly for native watchmakers to try to exclude women from their craft:

As soon as the one sex produces substantial claims to any department of the labour field, the market will be glad to avail itself of anything which will bring prices down. If the cost of production can be lowered by the employment of female labour in watchmaking, the Clerkenwell manufacturers will bid for it and secure it, here as well as in Geneva.[76]

Was such an outcome, however, something that men would tolerate, and would it be in the long-term interest of society as a whole? Many male political economists tended to draw back at this point, asserting the existence of a 'proper and natural division of labour' and arguing that uncontrolled competition in the labour market between men and women would tragically weaken the family, on which civilized life depended.[77] What did the female proponents of 'women's work' have to say to this objection?

THE AMBIGUITIES OF FEMINISM

In practice, faced by this conundrum, the female contributors to the *English Woman's Journal* divided. Of course, they nearly all asserted the *right* of women to enter any occupation they chose.[78] Nor would they countenance the traditional

[74] Ibid., 125. Rendall also cites a letter from Emily Faithfull to the same paper, saying that she was asking no favours for women, only that they 'should not be obstructed, and that she should be paid for her labour the same wages that a man would be paid for the same work equally well done' (ibid., 125). Emily Davies, too, was unhappy at contributors who seemed to be 'setting Political Economy at defiance' (ibid., 132).

[75] Ibid., 130–1. Note that her 'solution' to the problems arising from the competition of men and women for the same jobs was the polar opposite of Greg's.

[76] 'The English Woman's Journal', *Saturday Review*, 10 Apr. 1858, pp. 369–70.

[77] This was the response of William Neilson Hancock, the Irish political economist, to another Irish political economist who had argued for a free labour market (T. A. Boylan and T. P. Foley, *Political Economy and Colonial Ireland* (London, 1992), 151).

[78] e.g. Parkes insisted on this, despite her other reservations, on which see below: Parkes, *Woman's Work*, 216–21. See Rendall, 'Moral Engine', 132.

male objections to women entering the labour market. Barbara Leigh Smith, for example, argued that girls made better wives and mothers if they had first been trained for a trade, but she also pointed out that many females would not marry at all, while others would want to go on working after their marriage.[79] She also tackled head-on the objection that it was somehow *unlady-like* to receive financial reward for one's work. On the contrary, Smith declared, this was an irrational and absurd prejudice, since a salary was evidence that women were producing something which others wanted. 'What they produce will go to the right people', she argued, 'and they, the producers, will gain a power; for money is a power'— an interesting revelation of her acceptance of many of the premises of political economy.[80]

On the other hand, Smith was not entirely consistent in her commitment to this creed and she certainly did not press her case to its logical conclusion as Jessie Boucherett did. Men need not fear female competition in the labour market, she argued, because women, in the main, would 'only enter those professions which [were] destined to be perpetual, being consistent with the highest development of humanity'—by which she meant 'the arts, the sciences, commerce, and the education of the young in all its branches'. Smith did not think that many women would be attracted to the waging of war, to politics, or to the law,[81] a viewpoint which asserts women's moral superiority over men but also assumes the existence of 'separate spheres', rooted in the different natures of the two sexes.[82] Not even a commitment to political economy, it seems, could destroy the hold over her mind of these older views about gender roles.

If Barbara Leigh Smith drew back from the full implications of basing the rights of women on the laws of political economy, her friend and colleague, Bessie Parkes, went further, offering a searching critique of some aspects of undiluted market relationships. People should not be encouraged to fall into habits of dependence, she conceded, but at the same time she doubted whether the political economist 'who warns us that charity is often only another name for self-indulgence or feeling, sowing the seeds of greater misery than it professes to alleviate' should be followed in all respects, given the 'limitations to this doctrine imposed by justice and by religion'.[83]

According to Parkes, political economy worked on 'arithmetical', not 'moral' principles, and this had a bearing on the question of women's work:

[79] Smith, *Women and Work*, 10–11. The view that marriage was women's natural destiny was severely criticized in the magazine (Rendall, 'Moral Engine', 124–5).

[80] Smith, *Women and Work*, 48.   [81] Ibid., 51.

[82] On the ideology of separate spheres, S. K. Kent, *Sex and Suffrage in Britain, 1860–1914* (Princeton, 1987), 33–4. Bodichon similarly hedged her bets when arguing the case for female enfranchisement, combining arguments which emphasized the special contribution which women, because of their domestic experiences, would be able to make to public life, but also drawing attention to the mass of intelligence, knowledge, and public spirit left untapped among the female half of the population (Bodichon, *Objections*, 4; B. L. S. Bodichon, *Reasons for the Enfranchisement of Women* (London, 1866)).

[83] Parkes, *Woman's Work*, 100–1.

They are cheaper than men . . . , because the man demands wages equal to the support of a family, therefore it will always be cheaper to use them. But as moral beings, we are bound to consider and to remark that political economy is simply a science, and may be studied with or without reference to practice.[84]

'Not by bread alone do men or nations live; nor for household uses only can any woman live to whom God has granted means or leisure', she argued.[85] On the other hand, 'her house and not the factory is a woman's happy and healthful sphere',[86] and, if women had a mission in life, it was therefore to work for the dissemination of the 'domestic virtues' throughout society as a whole. 'The wife, in our civilization, is the centre of domestic and also of social life', Parkes concluded.[87]

Millicent Fawcett, too, ended up espousing views about gender relationships which sharply diverged from Mill's. In her youth she had been a subtle 'humanist', cleverly side-stepping the issue of what a woman's nature really was by emphasizing, as Mill had done, the crucial role of education:

every woman who had had the advantage of sound mental training, could make the best possible use of her special faculties or talent, simply because education would have discovered what those faculties or talents were, and with this assistance she would have a much greater chance than at present of finding and occupying her proper sphere. For woman's—the same as man's—sphere is precisely that situation in which she is doing the highest and best work of which she is capable.[88]

Nevertheless, in 1868 when this article was published, Mrs Fawcett was still keen to deny that women and men possessed fixed, innate characteristics.

However, after her husband's death Millicent increasingly came to use 'essentialist' arguments in support of women's enfranchisement, a departure from the 'humanist' views of Mill, to whom she continued to pay allegiance. 'If men and women were exactly alike', she mused in 1890, 'the representation of men would represent us, but not being alike, that wherein we differ is unrepresented under the present system.' This led her to the conclusion that women's suffrage was needed 'to strengthen true womanliness in woman' and to ensure that 'the womanly and domestic side of things' weighed more and counted for more 'in all public concerns'.[89] Interestingly enough, Helen Taylor, too, pursued this strategy,

---

[84] Ibid., 222–3.   [85] Ibid., 224.   [86] Ibid., 219.

[87] Ibid., 221. This was also the view of more cautious proponents of women's education; Emily Shirreff, later Mistress of Girton College, opined: 'society will suffer in proportion as women . . . join the noisy throng in the busy markets of the world' (E. Shirreff, *Intellectual Education and Its Influences on the Character and Happiness of Women* (London, 1858), 418).

[88] Like Shirreff, she also argued that educated women made better mothers (M. Fawcett, 'The Education of Women of the Middle and Upper Classes', *Macmillan's Magazine*, 17 (1868), 515).

[89] M. G. Fawcett, 'Home and Politics', *c.*1890, in Lewis (ed.), *Before the Vote Was Won*, 419, 423. She also took part in various puritanical crusades aimed at protecting women from male sexual exploitation, though not the campaign against the CD Acts (Rubinstein, 'Fawcett', 377, 370–2). This distinction between 'humanism' and 'essentialism' is not always easy to apply: a woman could, after all, invoke the experiences of motherhood without being an out-and-out 'essentialist'.

in striking contrast to her mother, Harriet.[90] The developing women's suffrage movement, in other words, now tended to underline the *differences* between men and women; public life, it was argued, needed to be 'feminized', that is to say, imbued with some of those moral qualities that made for 'true womanliness', qualities which Mrs Fawcett defined as 'mercy, pity, peace, purity and love'.[91]

Why did the late Victorian women's suffrage movement tend to drop 'humanist' for 'essentialist' arguments? No doubt, once the movement's centre of gravity had moved outside Parliament, as its activists strove to mobilize their 'sisters' in support of the cause, it made greater tactical sense to lay stress on the distinctive (and perhaps morally superior) qualities which characterized women as a whole. For if men and women were broadly similar in their natures, the apparent differences between them being merely the product of social conditioning, then it could be argued by their opponents that men were effectively representing their female relatives. Moreover, the social and political conservatism typified by Henry Fawcett and Leonard Courtney threatened to open up class divisions among the very people being proselytized by the women's suffrage pioneers. If the suffrage crusade were to progress, women needed to be approached on the basis of what they allegedly had *in common*.[92]

But, more important still, invocations of 'home influences' and 'feminine' forms of philanthropy clearly tapped in to deeply held convictions about the world, to which most middle-class Victorians, male and female, still subscribed.[93] Of course, the danger of using such arguments, even if only tactically, was that this unwittingly reinforced the beliefs of men who totally *opposed* giving women the vote. An anti-suffragist like Gladstone, for example, believed that 'a permanent and vast difference of type ha[d] been impressed upon women and men respectively by the Maker of both': a conviction that led him to reject votes for women as undesirable because likely to bring about the intrusion of the State into the 'sacred' precinct of the family, where it might 'dislocate, or injuriously modify, the relations of domestic life' and 'trespass upon the delicacy, the purity, the refinement, the elevation' of woman's nature.[94] Even such self-confident apologists for capitalism as John Bright and W. E. Forster, or the political economist, W. R. Greg,[95] can be found articulating similar views about the nature of women in the course of denying them the right to vote in parliamentary elections.

---

[90] Holton, *Feminism and Democracy*, 12.

[91] Fawcett, 'Home and Politics', 423. Josephine Butler often made similar claims, though, like many suffragists, she promiscuously used an array of contradictory arguments in pursuit of her case (see J. E. Butler (ed.), *Woman's Work and Woman's Culture* (London, 1869), pp. xiii, xvi, xxxvi–xxxvii).

[92] Holton, *Feminism and Democracy*, 18–21.

[93] As A. Tyrrell argues, the invocation of 'heart', 'home', and 'influence' not only fitted in well with a Ruskinian conception of domesticity, but could also lead to a widening of the conventions of public life, within which women could play a direct role (A. Tyrrell, ' "Woman's Mission" and Pressure Group Politics in Britain (1825–60)', *Bulletin of the John Rylands Library*, 63 (1980), 228–9).

[94] Letter of 1892, cited in Lewis (ed.), *Before the Vote was Won*, 446.

[95] Greg, *Why Are Women Redundant?*, esp. 30–2.

This raises two enormously important issues. First, why did so many friends of political economy wholeheartedly reject Mill's contractual view of marriage as an equal partnership, along with the accompanying case for equality of political rights? And, second, whence came the notion of 'separate spheres' and what role did it play in the development of the ideology of capitalism?

THE CRITIQUE OF CONTRACT

To get to grips with the first of these issues one must first understand that to most Victorian commentators, Radicals and political economists included, there was something unsound, even obnoxious, in treating the marriage relationship as though it paralleled the relationship which prevailed in a business partnership.

For if, as a contributor to the *Edinburgh Review* reasoned, 'marriage be considered a mere civil contract independent of any sacramental obligation which religion may superinduce, it would appear to follow from the essential nature of contracts, that it [was] capable of being dissolved at any time by the will of the contracting parties'.[96] James Fitzjames Stephen in *Liberty, Equality and Fraternity* made the same connection: if marriage was a commercial-style contract in which both 'partners', at least in theory, enjoyed equal freedom and power, then there seemed no logical reason why 'marriage, like other partnerships', could not 'be dissolved at pleasure'.[97] Of course, in both the above cases, a *reductio ad absurdum* argument was being employed, the two writers in question being keen to discredit any view of marriage which might facilitate or legitimize divorce.

A visceral dislike of treating marriage in primarily contractual terms also inspired the opposition to the Married Women's Property Acts. One persistent critic, the Conservative MP, Beresford Hope, alleged that such a reform would transform every household into 'a limited company consisting of two partners, neither of whom could be fixed with liability for the debts of the establishment'. He also inveighed against the greater legal rights enjoyed by women in some northern American States, which he claimed had led to 'free trade in divorce'.[98]

The objections to marriage as contract varied, but they can conveniently be classified under four broad headings. First, there were Christian 'traditionalists' who emphasized its sacramental nature and who repeated the Church's teaching that man and wife became, at marriage, 'one person': from this vantage point, the contractual language used by some 'progressive' theorists completely missed the point, since persons self-evidently could not enter into a contract with themselves.[99]

---

[96] [T. E. Perry], 'Rights and Liabilities of Husband and Wife', *Edinburgh Review*, 105 (1857), 185.

[97] J. F. Stephen, *Liberty, Equality, Fraternity*, ed. R. J. White (Cambridge, 1967; first pub. 1873), 195. At least, says Stephen, this is the deduction that he draws from Mill's book.

[98] Holcombe, *Wives and Property*, 156, 158.   [99] 'Mill on the Subjection of Women', 581.

Second, many secular thinkers who rejected the appeal to Revelation and to Church authority contested the contractual approach to marriage, though for rather different reasons. We have seen that Mill thought that contracts could only be entered into by free and equal partners; but, objected many Victorians, men and women were no more equal in this sense than were parents and children. James Fitzjames Stephen, for example, maintained that the permanence of a marriage contract ultimately depended upon the whim of the stronger party, in other words, on the will of the husband.[100] (In fact, Stephen took his objections even further by denying that contracts required 'equality' at all.[101])

Third, there were those who tempered their enthusiasm for contract as the animating principle of modern commercial society with a recognition that, were it to be applied literally to the family, the human race would swiftly perish, a consideration to which the childless Mills may have attached insufficient weight. In the famous words of Spencer: 'Import into the family the law of the society, and let children from infancy upwards have life-sustaining supplies proportioned to their life-sustaining labours, and the society disappears forthwith by death of all its young.'[102] The family could not be run on the same lines as the business world, it was said, because competitive individualism, the driving force in commerce, stood as the very antithesis of familial affection.

But this leads on into the fourth argument used against the importation of the principle of competition into the realm of the family: the need to create a space which was 'fenced off' from the demoralizing pressures of commerce. Even many devotees of political economy wanted a boundary of this sort to be maintained. Wherein lay the attraction of the latter idea to those who also felt a commitment to the new market-oriented society?

DOMESTICITY AND THE SANCTITY OF THE HOME

We have seen that, in discussing the relationship between family values, on the one hand, and the imperatives of the market, on the other, John Stuart Mill had been inclined, not so much to assimilate the two phenomena, but rather to attempt a demonstration that they were both in the process of being transformed by the

---

[100] 'To treat a contract of marriage as a contract between persons who are upon an equality in regard of strength, and power to protect their interest, is to treat it as being what it notoriously is not' (Stephen, *Liberty, Equality, Fraternity*, 196). See K. J. M. Smith, *James Fitzjames Stephen: Portrait of a Victorian Rationalist* (Cambridge, 1988), 189. The dependent status of children raised further moral dilemmas: should their interests be left in the hands of their 'natural' protectors, their parents, or, as the early factory legislation suggested, did children often need protecting *from* their own parents?

[101] Stephen, *Liberty, Equality, Fraternity*, 206–9. According to Stephen, all that was proved 'by the fact that status . . . tends to be replaced by contract, is that force changes its form' (p. 202).

[102] H. Spencer, *The Principles of Sociology*, in id., *Synthetic Philosophy of Herbert Spencer*, Westminster edn. (New York, 1896), i–ii. 721. See, too, H. Spencer, *The Man Versus the State*, ed. D. Macrae (London, 1969; first pub. 1884), 136–8.

same social forces. Mill had specifically drawn attention to the way in which modern commercial developments were breaking down the old 'feudal' code of chivalry and, by making men and women more equal, reconstituting marriage as a 'partnership', a development which in turn involved a modernization of the relationship between men and women from which both sexes (and society at large) would greatly benefit. From this perspective, capitalism was a force that was slowly 'civilizing' the family, particularly in the case of the more co-operative—some called it the more 'feminine'—versions of that system.[103]

Herbert Spencer agreed, at least in part, with this view. 'A further approach towards equality of function between the sexes' was taking place, he thought, with the decline of 'militancy' and the rise of commercial societies based on the idea of 'voluntary co-operation'. But Spencer differed from Mill in thinking that this process still had some way to go before the 'political *status* of women [could be] raised to something like equality with that of men'. Social dangers would arise if women were enfranchised prematurely, Spencer warned.[104]

However, underlying the theories of both Mill and Spencer was an optimistic assessment of modern commercial life which many, perhaps most, middle-class Victorians (including even Mill and Spencer in certain moods) found it hard to square with what they saw going on around them. Not surprisingly, then, the *dominant* ideology of mid-Victorian Britain stood Mill's theory on its head by presenting family and the home as the social agencies that would 'civilize' the ruthless, competitive, cutthroat world of business, or at least provide a much-needed refuge from commercial pressures.

Davidoff and Hall trace the origins of this 'domestic ideology' back to 'the Puritan belief in the spiritualization of the household' which found expression in the ritual of family prayers, and contend that these beliefs took on a new intensity during the Evangelical Revival.[105] The ideology also drew upon an older view of women as 'dependent' and therefore as in need of a retreat 'away from the dangers of the "world" into the home which they could construct as a moral haven'.[106] The early nineteenth-century revival of Old Testament fundamentalism may also have contributed to such a view of the home and to the patriarchalism that accompanied it.[107]

---

[103] On co-operation as a 'feminine' alternative to 'manly' capitalism, Boylan and Foley, *Political Economy and Colonial Ireland*, 149.

[104] Spencer, *Sociology*, in *Synthetic Philosophy*, Westminster edn., i–ii. 767, 769–70. On Spencer's reasons for wishing to exclude women from the franchise, see J. Meadowcroft, *Conceptualizing the State: Innovation and Dispute in British Political Thought 1880–1914* (Oxford, 1995), 82. However, in his earlier writings, Spencer had used arguments in favour of sexual equality that were much closer to Mill's: see H. Spencer, *Social Statics, or The Conditions Essential to Human Happiness Specified* (1868; first pub. 1855), ch. 16. He also shared Mill's impatience with the conventional tendency to 'over-exalt' women (D. Duncan, *The Life and Letters of Herbert Spencer* (London, 1908), 405).

[105] L. Davidoff and C. Hall, *Family Fortunes: Men and Women of the English Middle Class, 1780–1850* (London, 1987), 108–9; F. Prochaska, *The Voluntary Impulse: Philanthropy in Modern Britain* (London, 1988), 22–3.   [106] Davidoff and Hall, *Family Fortunes*, 114–15.

[107] Harris, *Private Lives*, 74.

But a new inflection to this ideology appeared during the 1830s and the 1840s when, because of changes in the labour market, its advocates were no longer able to assume, as the Evangelicals had earlier done, that the household *combined* the complementary worlds of men and women.[108] Instead the home was increasingly seen as the woman's domain, from which the male breadwinner would be absent for long stretches of time.[109]

Such developments led to an increased emphasis upon the home as a sanctuary, not necessarily in a literal Christian sense, but rather as a shelter from the perils besetting all those who ventured out into the harshly competitive, amoral world of work.[110] Writing in 1847, the Unitarian minister, John James Taylor, could celebrate it as 'the nursery of all kind and pure and humane affections', where children were 'trained to obedience, habituated to respect the law, and prepared by their domestic discipline for the higher obedience of citizens'.[111] Five years later, Henry Mayhew depicted 'the dwelling of the family' in similar terms, calling it 'a kind of social sanctuary—a spot sacred to peace and goodwill, where love alone is to rule, and harmony to prevail'.[112]

The priestess of this new cult was Mrs Sarah Ellis, the author of a succession of best-selling books which furnished her female readership with the ideals by which she wanted them to shape their lives. The home, she insisted, was where religious habits and principles were learned and the 'domestic character of England' formed, under the aegis of its womenfolk—the shrine where lodged the vestals charged with preventing the sacred flame from being extinguished.[113] Running a home, Ellis argued, was a *vocation*, which obliged a wife and mother to abandon self and acquire 'a new nature', dedicated to promoting not only the happiness of her male relatives, but also their spiritual health.[114]

It was not exactly that men were born with coarser natures than women, but, in Mrs Ellis's view, their daily occupations had the effect of rendering them so. Happily for women,

---

[108] Davidoff and Hall, *Family Fortunes*, 181.

[109] C. Hall, 'The early formation of Victorian Domestic Ideology', in S. Burman (ed.), *Fit Work for Women* (London, 1979), 15–32; C. Hall, 'The Butcher, the Baker, the Candlestickmaker: The Shop and the Family in the Industrial Revolution', in E. Whitelegg *et al.* (eds.), *The Changing Experience of Women* (Oxford, 1982), 2–16.

[110] The home, as Walter Houghton well puts it, became 'a place apart, a walled garden, in which certain virtues too easily crushed by modern life could be preserved, and certain desires of the heart too much thwarted be fulfilled' (W. Houghton, *The Victorian Frame of Mind 1830–1870* (New Haven, 1957), 341–8, esp. 343).

[111] H. M. Wach, 'A "Still, Small Voice" from the Pulpit: Religion and the Creation of Social Morality in Manchester, 1820–1850', *Journal of Modern History*, 63 (1991), 435. Christianity itself was widely thought to embody family values (J. Seed, 'Unitarianism, Political Economy and the Antinomies of Liberal Culture in Manchester, 1830–50', *Social History*, 7 (1982), 21).

[112] Cited in L. Nead, *Myths of Sexuality: Representations of Women in Victorian Britain* (Oxford, 1988), 33.

[113] S. S. Ellis, *The Women of England, Their Social Duties and Domestic Habits*, 9th edn. (London, 1839), 10, 25; also 39.   [114] Ibid., 22–7.

such are their early impressions, associations, and general position in the world, that their moral feelings are less liable to be impaired by the pecuniary objects which too often constitute the chief end of men, and which, even under the limitations of better principle, necessarily engage a large portion of his thoughts.[115]

Mrs Ellis represented women as exercising their moral authority most directly via their relationship with their children, over whom they had an influence stemming more from maternal example than from actual instruction. This was to become a platitude of Victorian thought. 'Home is the first and most important school of character', Samuel Smiles was later to say: 'It is there that every human being receives his best moral training, or his worst.' Smiles explained that this placed a great responsibility on women, because it was 'the mother, far more than the father, [who influenced] the actions and conduct of the child' through the good example she set in the home.[116]

Now, maternal example of this kind, as Chalmers had earlier remarked, would be of incalculable benefit to young men when they first embarked on a commercial career, since hideous moral hazards awaited those who had not previously been fortified by an upbringing in an environment where high ethical standards prevailed.[117] However, according to the ideologists of domesticity, women could exercise an equally important influence over their *husbands*.

Before proceeding further, it is important to note that Mrs Ellis was not a Tory lady but a progressive liberal with Quaker connections, sympathetic to anti-slavery,[118] peace, temperance, and the abolition of capital punishment, all Quaker concerns, and that she specifically addressed *The Women of England* to 'that great mass of the population of England which is connected with trade and manufactures, as well as to the wives and daughters of professional men of limited incomes'.[119] Clearly, then, it was an intense anxiety over the moral atmosphere prevailing in the *contemporary business world* which principally inspired all her books.[120]

Could men from such households as these be recalled by their wives to a sense of their higher duty? Mrs Ellis felt optimistic on this score, since she did not believe that England's fathers, husbands, and brothers had 'all gone over to the side of mammon'. However, if some men had 'fallen', she argued, the fault lay in the system:[121]

The great facilities of communication, not only throughout our own country, but with distant parts of the world, are rousing men of every description to tenfold exertion in the

[115] Ibid., 50–1.   [116] Smiles, *Character*, 31, 36.

[117] T. Chalmers, *The Application of Christianity To The Commerce and Ordinary Affairs of Life, In A Series of Discourses* (Glasgow, 1820), 188.

[118] It may, however, be significant that the female abolitionists had, in Clare Midgley's words, often drawn attention to 'women's moral superiority, their stronger adherence to Christian principle and their greater sensitivity' (*Women against Slavery: The British Campaigns, 1780–1870* (London, 1992), 110).   [119] Ellis, *Women of England*, 19.

[120] Davidoff and Hall, *Family Fortunes*, 184.   [121] Ellis, *Women of England*, 56.

field of competition in which they are engaged; so that their whole being is becoming swallowed up in efforts and calculations relating to their pecuniary success.[122]

Absorbed in the quest for 'worldly aggrandizement', businessmen were constantly
tempted to close 'their ears against the voice of conscience'.[123] Worse still, their
desperate straining after success bred 'envy, and hatred, and opposition', with every
man's hand raised against his brother, each 'struggling to exalt himself, not merely
by trampling upon his fallen foe, but by usurping the place of his weaker brother,
who . . . is consequently borne down by numbers, hurried over, and forgotten'.[124]
    According to Mrs Ellis, it was therefore 'the especial duty of women to look
around them, and see in what way they can counteract this evil, by calling back
the attention of man to those sunnier spots in his existence, by which the growth
of his moral feelings have been encouraged, and his heart improved'.[125] Women,
ignorant maybe of the ways of the world, had been endowed by their Creator with
a kind of moral intuition that instinctively told them what was right and wrong:

How often has man returned to his home with a mind confused by the many voices, which
in the mart, the exchange, or the public assembly, have addressed themselves to his inborn
selfishness, or his worldly pride; and while his integrity was shaken, and his resolution gave
way beneath the pressure of apparent necessity, or the insidious pretences of expediency,
he has stood corrected before the clear eye of a woman, as it looked directly to the naked
truth, and detected the lurking evil of the specious act he was about to commit. Nay, so
potent may have become this secret influence, that he may have borne it about with him
like a kind of second conscience, for mental reference, and spiritual counsel, in moments
of trial.[126]

    In such passages Mrs Ellis seems to have been articulating views which were
quite widely held in mid-Victorian Britain, and her moral was picked up by several Christian evangelists. H. A. Boardman, for example, urged husbands experiencing business troubles to confide in their wives, a practice, he said, that would
rescue them from many a foolish and wicked deed:

What is veiled in impenetrable darkness to your eye, is all luminous to hers. She sees, as
by intuition, what you ought to do; and has the mingled courage and kindness to tell you
. . . Inferior to himself she may be, in strength of mind and information; and yet she may
have qualities which will make her a safe Mentor.[127]

    But the spiritual blessings bestowed by a wife presupposed the existence of a
proper domestic environment. Significantly, Dickens in his *American Notes* linked
what he saw as the Americans' excessive 'love of trade', verging on corruption,
with the alleged proclivity of American married couples to live 'in hotels, having
no fireside of their own, and seldom meeting, from early morning until late at

---

[122] Ibid., 55.   [123] Ibid., 51.   [124] Ibid., 52.   [125] Ibid., 56.   [126] Ibid., 53.
[127] Revd H. A. Boardman, *The Bible in the Counting-House: A Course of Lectures to Merchants* (London,
1854), 193–4.

night, but at the hasty public meals'.[128] Family life would only have a civilizing influence if the family itself were formed on the right lines.

What did the cult of domesticity have to say about the apparently divergent characteristics of men and women? We have seen that Mrs Ellis herself tended to refer back to environmental conditioning. But later in the century the division was frequently explained as the outcome of biology. For example, Charles Darwin, in *The Descent of Man* (1871), contended that gender differences were physical and innate, akin in some respects to the differences between the races:

> Woman seems to differ from man in mental disposition, chiefly in her greater tenderness and less selfishness ... Woman, owing to her maternal instincts, displays these qualities towards her infants in an eminent degree; therefore it is likely that she would often extend them towards her fellow-creatures. Man [by contrast] is the rival of other men; he delights in competition, and this leads to ambition which passes too easily into selfishness. These latter qualities seem to be his natural and unfortunate birthright.[129]

The rhetoric has undergone a significant shift, but the conclusion is similar: a *complementary* relationship exists between the sexes, man being naturally adapted to the competitive environment of work, with women possessing softer, in many ways more admirable, moral qualities. A healthy society, it seemed, depended upon these 'male' and 'female' elements being kept in a harmonious balance.

CONTRADICTIONS IN THE IDEOLOGY OF DOMESTICITY

However, the maintenance of such a balance presented problems. What Collini calls 'sentimentalized rhapsodies to the role of feminine influence as an antidote to [male] "selfishness"'[130] were by themselves not enough. For a start, the male breadwinner first needed to be successful in business if he were to protect his womenfolk from injury and thus preserve the sanctuary of the home from violation. Thus, as Barbara Weiss has shrewdly observed, in the popular paintings and the drama of the mid-Victorian period bankruptcy is frequently depicted through images of bailiffs, watched by weeping females, stripping the house of its much-loved furniture and possessions.[131] Business failure, she also notes, sometimes acts in the Victorian novel as a cathartic event leading to a gender role-reversal, as men fall under the domination of the women to whom they are now indebted—a

---

[128] C. Dickens, *American Notes for General Circulation*, Chapman & Hall edn. (London, n.d.; first pub. 1842), ch. 18, p. 288.

[129] C. Darwin, *The Descent of Man*, 2nd edn. (1874, rev. 1899; first pub. 1871), 563–4.

[130] Collini, *Public Moralists*, 87.

[131] B. Weiss, *The Hell of the English: Bankruptcy and the Victorian Novel* (Lewisburg, 1986), 51. As an example in 'high art', Weiss instances the distress of Mrs Tulliver over the loss of her domestic props in George Eliot's *The Mill on the Floss*. But, in the eyes of many conservatives, even more horrific was the image of husbands coming home for dinner only to find that their wives had been hauled off to jail for non-payment of debts, as a result of the Married Women's Property Act (Holcombe, *Wives and Property*, 157).

distressing situation in the eyes of those who accepted the ideology of 'separate spheres'.[132]

At the same time too great a commitment to business success on the man's part could react adversely on his neglected wife and children. That is why bankers are often portrayed in fiction as being so dedicated to their occupation that, even if honest, they risk becoming devotees of Mammon, with dire consequences for their dependants. This provides the theme of Mrs Gore's novel, *The Banker's Wife*.[133] More memorable is Dickens's *Dombey and Son*, in which, before his 'change of heart', the merchant Mr Dombey Senior has difficulty in separating his family feelings from his passion for his firm. So strong is this delusion that Dombey tends to see even his beloved son Paul as a property in which he holds a stake, while, facing the possibility that he might beget a daughter, he reflects that 'in the capital of the House's name and dignity, such a child was merely a piece of base coin that couldn't be invested'.[134] Five years later, in *Hard Times*, Dickens returned to this theme, the corruption of familial relationships by commercial calculation.

There was an associated danger: the danger that too rigid a separation between home and marketplace might mean that the two social worlds did not connect at all in any serious way. As we saw in an earlier chapter, some Victorian moralists felt that, once they had entered the office, they had entirely left behind them all those moral precepts which were taken seriously around the family hearth. Dickens treats this situation comically in *Great Expectations* through the character of Wemmick, who leads a totally split existence: a callous calculating clerk when working in the legal office, but a kind-hearted and sentimental fellow once he has 'drawn up the drawbridge' at his Walworth residence, 'the Castle': 'No; the office is one thing, and private life is another', declares Wemmick: 'When I go into the office, I leave the Castle behind me, and when I come into the Castle, I leave the office behind me. . . . My Walworth sentiments must be taken at Walworth; none but my official sentiments can be taken in this office.'[135]

Note that although Dickens dramatizes in *Great Expectations* the issue of the divided self, there are no women (apart from a servant) at Walworth, though Wemmick does look after his father, the 'Aged P', with almost maternal solicitude. Dickens's concern is with *role*, not gender—the way in which family and work, each with a different principle of cohesion, have become disconnected from one another.[136]

---

[132] However, the two businessmen whom Weiss instances as having experienced this fate, Robert Moore in *Shirley* and Mr Thornton in *North and South*, both feature in novels that were written by women, Charlotte Brontë and Mrs Gaskell. Weiss suggests that a certain feminine wish-fulfilment might be in operation here! (Weiss, *Hell of the English*, 100).

[133] N. Russell, *The Novelist and Mammon: Literary Responses to the World of Commerce in the Nineteenth Century* (Oxford, 1986), 78.   [134] Weiss, *Hell of the English*, 115.

[135] C. Dickens, *Great Expectations*, Chapman & Hall edn. (London, n.d.; first pub. 1861), ch. 25, p. 220; ch. 36, pp. 310–11.

[136] This can perhaps be seen as a manifestation of what J. Tosh calls 'masculine domesticity', i.e. the 'domestication' of *men*, many of whom found in the home and family, not only a welcome release from work, but an arena for the display of tenderness and playfulness. Such behaviour led to anxieties

Was such a 'disconnection' desirable? There certainly existed in mid-Victorian Britain those who actually hoped that domestic values might shape the conduct of commercial life—for example, 'paternalists' like Arthur Helps and Thomas Carlyle.[137] John Duguid Milne, too, deplored 'the loss suffered by society in the want of feminine influence on the hard and materialistic character of our industrial relations on social life in general'—in other words, he hoped that women could be brought to exercise their civilizing influence *in the marketplace*.[138]

Bessie Rayner Parkes extended such arguments by suggesting that 'the more completely society [was] infused with those ideas which modif[ied] the action of purely scientific laws, the easier it [would] be for women to work without being crushed by its machinery'.[139] And a later generation of radicals and socialists sometimes held up the loving family as a model for a radically reconstructed social order in which co-operation would replace competition.[140]

On the other hand, most orthodox defenders of commercial society steered well clear of such 'heresies', which they identified either with old-school Tories or with new-style socialists. Allowing financial calculations into domestic relationships would indeed threaten the integrity of the family,[141] but, conversely, family values had to be confined to their proper place. Harriet Martineau, for example, denounced as false any 'analogy between a state and its members, and a parent and his family';[142] and Herbert Spencer agreed with her in dismissing those who ignored or downplayed the importance of this social frontier as sentimentalists seeking to set the truths of political economy at nought: the importation of the ethics of the family into society at large, Spencer insisted, was the essential fallacy of socialism, a fallacy which, if acted upon, would inevitably lead to disaster.[143] Thus only a minority of the defenders of the capitalist order had any truck with the view that the family offered a model around which the wider society should be reorganized.

that sons might grow up effeminate—hence the growing popularity of a public school education ('Authority and Nurture in Middle-Class Fatherhood: The Case of Early and Mid-Victorian England', *Gender and History*, 8 (1996), 48–64, and 'New Men? The Bourgeois Cult of Home', *History Today*, 46 (1996), 9–15).

[137] Ch. 11.

[138] J. D. Milne, *Industrial Employment of Women in the Middle and Lower Ranks*, 2nd edn. (London, 1870; first pub. 1857), 29. Milne believed that woman's moral superiority should be expressed in the commercial world and in public life, as well as within the confines of the home (ibid., 112–13). Perhaps not surprisingly, many contemporaries thought that this book, which appeared anonymously in its first edition, had been written by a woman (H. Martineau to H. Reeve, 31 Jan. 1859, in V. Sanders (ed.), *Harriet Martineau: Selected Letters* (Oxford, 1990), 168).

[139] [B. R. Parkes], 'The Opinions of John Stuart Mill', *English Woman's Journal*, 6 (Sept. 1860), 7.

[140] Houghton, *Victorian Frame of Mind*, 347.

[141] This theme is handled with some subtlety in *The Mill on the Floss*. We are meant to disapprove strongly of Mrs Glegg, who lends money to her nephew but only on the understanding that she receives interest on her investment: 'I don't approve o'giving; we niver looked for that in my family' (G. Eliot, *The Mill on the Floss*, Blackwood edn. (Edinburgh, 1878; first pub. 1860), vol. 2, bk. 5, ch. 2, pp. 87–8). [142] H. Martineau, *Cousin Marshall* (London, 1832), 131.

[143] Spencer, *Sociology*, in id., *Synthetic Philosophy*, Westminster edn., i–ii. 721. J. D. Y. Peel, *Herbert Spencer: The Evolution of a Sociologist* (London, 1971), 222.

Between the two extremes represented by the 'paternalists', on the one hand, and by Spencer, on the other, Mrs Ellis took up an intermediate position. Unfortunately, like others of her ilk, she was distressingly vague about what precisely she hoped to achieve. She clearly was not advocating any ambitious scheme of social reconstruction such as those favoured by the socialists. She merely wanted to reform the family, so that, through family values, the tone of business life might be raised to a higher plane. However, the existence of a separation between home and market, each with its distinct ethos, she took as axiomatic. In fact, to quote her own famous phrase, home and market occupied a 'distinct and separate sphere',[144] paralleling the division between men and women.

Yet, as Catherine Gallagher notes, this results in a paradox which is always surfacing in Mrs Ellis's writings: society could be made similar to the family only if the family remained rigorously *isolated* from it. Ellis, she claims, was arguing that 'women develop their moral superiority only by their exclusion from the marketplace', which in turn conveyed 'the notion that domestic life should compensate for the unavoidably hardening and unsatisfying struggles of social existence'. The ideology of domesticity, Gallagher concludes, 'was thus . . . a contradictory system, at once associating and disassociating the spheres of private and public life'.[145]

THE PROBLEM OF EDUCATION

The problematic relationship between home and work also intruded into discussions on the nature of the education appropriate for the two sexes. John Stuart Mill's philosophy suggested that little distinction should be made between boys and girls. Even Mrs Marcet had earlier advocated that women should learn political economy, if only so that they did not unwittingly propagate 'errors' to their young charges.[146] As for Harriet Martineau, she thought that it was the duty of all, men and women alike, to understand the teaching of 'natural law', for want of which they would inevitably go astray.

Dickens was therefore making an acute point when, in *Hard Times*, he presents Mr Gradgrind, a devotee of political economy, as almost completely gender-blind—until, that is, his eventual 'conversion'. Gradgrind's children Tom and Louise are put through exactly the same educational mill: both are forced to grapple with all the dreary 'ologies'. Now, of course, Dickens's point is that this 'unnatural' (in his view) upbringing was directly responsible for Louise growing up an emotional cripple, a fate from which she is only 'rescued' by the artless Sissy Jupe, whose

---

[144] S. S. Ellis, *Daughters of England, Their Position in Society, Character and Responsibilities* (London, 1842), 7.
[145] C. Gallagher, *The Industrial Reformation of English Fiction 1832–1867* (Chicago, 1985), 119–20.
[146] Mrs Marcet, *Conversations on Political Economy: In Which The Elements of That Science Are Familiarly Explained* (London, 1839; first pub. 1816), 9; in 1816 edn., pp. 11–13.

simple feminine nature has made her happily impervious to all the efforts of her teachers.[147]

What subjects, then, *were* fit for a girl to study? The 'experts' were divided. One particular difficulty, which has an important bearing on the theme of this book, centred upon the relationship between domestic science and political economy. One might suppose that the advocates of 'separate spheres' would want a total divorce between political economy, which revealed the 'laws' regulating the commercial world, and the theory and practice of running a household. However—and here was the complication—the 'domestic economy' recommended by the likes of Mrs Ellis clearly bore certain resemblances to political economy itself. The perfect housewife, after all, was supposed to be *businesslike*.

Thus in *Daughters of England* Ellis explicitly calls for 'integrity' in the handling of all money matters: 'The habit of keeping strict accounts with regard to the expenditure of money is good in all the circumstances of life', especially when other people's property was entrusted to the housekeeper's care.[148] Another early Victorian exponent of the 'ideology of domesticity', Mrs Taylor, similarly employed the language of commerce to describe the tasks of motherhood and household management: 'That house only is well conducted where there is a strict attention paid to order and regularity. To do everything in its proper time, to keep everything in its right place, and to use everything for its proper use, is the *very essence* of good management.' Hence, Mrs Taylor said, the importance of keeping careful accounts and of regularly meeting servants' and tradesmen's bills.[149] Interestingly, Martineau, a female political economist, rationalized her unusual position by stoutly maintaining in her book, *Household Education* (1848), that the most ignorant women she had known had also been the worst housekeepers.[150]

Later in the century, Samuel Smiles made the connection between the spheres of the home and of commercial life even more explicit:

Habits of business do not relate to trade merely, but apply to all the practical affairs of life—to everything that has to be arranged, to be organized, to be provided for, to be done. And in all these respects the management of a family, and of a household, is as much a matter of business as the management of a shop or of a counting-house. It requires method, accuracy, organization, industry, economy, discipline, tact, knowledge, and capacity for adapting means to ends.[151]

But might not the converse of this apply? In fact, no one seriously claimed that a businesslike housewife was acquiring skills and experience which would enable her to run a mercantile establishment, a bank, or a factory. But Mrs Marcet was not alone in arguing that political economy, viewed from one angle, was essentially the precepts of 'household economy' applied more widely—extended, that

---

[147] However, even in the 1850s when *Hard Times* was written, such attitudes towards elementary education were becoming dated.   [148] Ellis, *Daughters of England*, 367.
[149] Davidoff and Hall, *Family Fortunes*, 176.   [150] Ibid., 186.
[151] Smiles, *Character*, 53–4.

is, from the sphere of the family 'to that of a whole people—of a nation'.[152] Bessie Parkes likewise believed that 'political economy is to the nation what domestic economy is to the family'.[153]

This in turn suggested the intriguing, even unsettling, reflection that perhaps the state itself was but an individual household writ large. The early suffragists eagerly seized upon such notions. According to Mrs Fawcett, 'women who [were] immersed in domestic affairs should be good economists, knowing how to save and how to spend judiciously', a compelling reason, this, she argued, for giving them the parliamentary vote.[154]

Smiles defined the relationship between domestic and political economy in a more conventional way: 'While it is the object of Private Economics to create and promote the well-being of individuals', he wrote, 'it is the object of Political Economy to create and increase the wealth of nations.'[155] All the same, he thought that the two activities were sufficiently similar for boys and girls to receive broadly the same education.[156] Yet the anonymous contributor to the *Saturday Review* in 1858, after conceding that the laws of political economy forbade the exclusion of women from occupations for which they were naturally suited, went on to insist that a woman's 'ultimate function' was 'to manage her home, to bring up children, and to attend to household duties'; most women would *eventually* become wives and mothers, not bookkeepers and accountants, he claimed, and the training they needed for this 'calling' could only be learnt at home, 'not at the desk and counter'.[157]

IDEALS AND REALITIES

Up until now it has been assumed that the ideals of domesticity reflected the realities of contemporary life, but, of course, this was far from being the case.[158] In fact, as Davidoff and Hall argue, Mrs Ellis was proposing a radical departure from what she, and others, felt to be a growing trend in domestic arrangement by breaking with 'the unhappy state of affairs in the middle-class homes of England, where gentility had been winning too many victories over practicality'.[159]

On the economic front, too, reality diverged from the ideal. In the middle years of the century, for example, over 30 per cent of the workforce consisted of females, many of them married women. This created no moral difficulties when husband and wife both contributed to the running of the family enterprise, as had

---

[152] Marcet, *Conversations*, 14.   [153] 'The Opinions of John Stuart Mill', 4.
[154] Fawcett, 'Home and Politics', 421.   [155] S. Smiles, *Thrift* (London, 1886), 1.
[156] Ibid., 57, 145–6.
[157] 'The English Woman's Journal', *Saturday Review*, 10 Apr. 1858, pp. 369–70; factory girls 'make the worst wives', he opined.
[158] How much of a grounding in reality the ideals of domesticity and female spirituality had, it is difficult to say. See J. Rendall, *Women in an Industrializing Society: England 1850–1880* (Oxford, 1990), 49.   [159] Davidoff and Hall, *Family Fortunes*, 182.

happened since time immemorial on most farms and in some branches of the retail trade (though most of *these* women would not appear in the census statistics). Neither, as Davidoff and Hall show, was it uncommon for wives and daughters of small businessmen to act as bookkeepers for their male relatives. Mrs Fawcett was therefore ruffling nobody's feathers when she urged the 'considerable pecuniary advantage' of married women assisting 'their husbands in their business or profession'.[160] For so long as female work was being conducted under the auspices of the male head of household, no affront would be given to delicate sensibilities.

But the largest single group of female workers in late Victorian Britain were, of course, domestic servants, which shows that the commonplace distinction between work and home was in some respects a highly artificial one, since for these employees, home *was* work, and the 'lady of the house', as well as playing the role of guardian of the sacred domestic flame, functioned also as an *employer*. Yet Bessie Parkes insisted that it was 'the bounden duty of every mistress of a family not to beat down those she [came] in contact with below the point where their labor gain[ed] a wholesome maintenance'. She justified this obligation as follows:

In the market we must buy and sell at market price, because our finite natures cannot possibly take in the moral condition and physical necessities of those who have produced the goods we want to acquire; but in the *domestic* relation of employers and employed, a certain margin is cut off from the rule of political economy, and embraced within that of religion.[161]

The more conventional line was simply to regard female domestic servants as surrogate members of the family which they had 'joined', standing in somewhat the same 'natural' relationship to their employer's wife as daughters did to their mother.[162]

What about other kinds of waged work? Mrs Ellis, interestingly, was not averse to the idea of her middle-class female readers earning a living outside the home, provided that they confined themselves to occupations which were 'by no means polluting to the touch, or degrading to the mind'.[163] But there were two kinds of economic activity, at totally opposite ends of the social scale, which, because they

---

[160] Fawcett, 'Education of Women', 515. Women could also help their husbands at a more practical level: indeed, the way in which a man's success or failure in his career could hinge on whether his wife was good, conscientious, and thrifty, or weak, vain, and hedonistic, supplied Victorian novelists with one of their main themes (Weiss draws attention to the contrasting fortunes of Dr Lydgate and Fred Vincey in *Middlemarch*) (Weiss, *Hell of the English*, 73).

[161] 'The Opinions of John Stuart Mill', 7.

[162] H. Martineau's confusions on the matter of domestic servants are instructive. On the one hand, she rejoiced that service was 'becoming a mere contract for wages' and that the 'old aristocratic feeling which made the dependant proud of the trust of his master was dying', and she also insisted that the work of domestic service, like all modern trades, required proper instruction and training. On the other hand, Martineau welcomed the prospect of servants being 'incorporated with the family organisation', where they could receive kindness, comfort, consideration, and so on. Martineau thus seems to want to have it both ways, seeing domestic servants now as trained employees free to bargain in the labour market, now as members of a loving family ([Martineau], 'Modern Domestic Service', *Edinburgh Review*, 115 (1862), esp. 415, 430, 438–9). [163] Ellis, *Women of England*, 346.

seemed to involve transgressing the accepted notions of a woman's role, caused great moral anxiety.

The first of these fields was investment. One consequence of the economic separation of ownership from control was an increase in the numbers of investors and a broadening of the social backgrounds from which the investing public was drawn. Unsurprisingly, many were women, mostly well-to-do widows. No legal or even social barriers prevented such females from playing an important economic role by putting up risk capital and by playing the stock exchange.

As early as 1824 the *Annual Register* had expressed surprise over the prominent role of female investors: women 'of all ranks and degrees, spinsters, wives and widows', were participating in the speculative mania, it noted. Similarly, during the commercial crisis of 1847–8, Morier Evans declared how 'sorry' he was to see the fair sex dabbling in stocks and shares, about which they knew nothing. And Smiles was amused, but dismayed, at the behaviour during the railway boom of 'amiable ladies who had the reputation of "bears" in the share-markets'.[164] (Contemporaries were also unsettled by the spectacle of young girls and women involving themselves in the 'vice' of gambling, and sometimes argued that females, even more than men, needed protection against their own folly.)[165]

One detects in such passages an unease that important economic decisions and the future of male-run enterprises had fallen partly dependent on the whim of ill-informed women, who had deserted their proper domestic role. These anxieties may also have fed unconsciously upon a form of political discourse common in the early eighteenth century when, according to Professor Pocock, capitalism was perceived in terms of speculation rather than calculation and, as such, was thought to inhabit a 'feminine' world of fantasy: 'it was the hysteria, not the cold rationality, of economic man that dismayed the moralists'. The investor, adds Pocock, 'was seen as on the whole a feminized, even an effeminate being, still wrestling with his own passions and hysterias and with interior and exterior forces let loose by his fantasies and appetites, and symbolized by such archetypically female goddesses of disorder as Fortune, Luxury, and most recently Credit herself'.[166] All of this was disturbingly at odds with the nineteenth-century idealization of entrepreneurial man as a 'masculine conquering hero' or 'captain of industry'. The role of female investors may thus have disturbed contemporary commentators by drawing

---

[164] S. Smiles, *Lives of the Engineers* (1862), iii. 373–4. See Ch. 5, and also S. Walsh, 'Bodies of Capital: *Great Expectations* and the Climacteric Economy', *Victorian Studies*, 37 (1993), 73–94, esp. 84–5. Lee Holcombe, too, notes the hostility felt at the possibility of married women dealing in shares and conducting other business transactions (*Wives and Property*, 153).

[165] R. Munting, 'Social Opposition to Gambling in Britain: An Historical Overview', *International Journal of the History of Sport*, 10 (1993), 302. See also Revd F. Close, *The Evil Consequences of Attending the Race Course Exposed: A Sermon Preached in the Parish Church of Cheltenham, 17 June 1827*, 3rd edn. (London, 1827), 10, and for later expressions of incredulity that women were prepared to jeopardize their 'womanliness' by gambling, B. S. Rowntree (ed.), *Betting and Gambling: A National Evil* (1905), viii and 69.

[166] J. G. A. Pocock, *Virtue, Commerce and History* (Cambridge, 1985), 113–14.

attention to the realities of a finance-based capitalism, thereby puncturing the heroic myths of a 'masculine' economic order.

The other branch of female work to cause moral concern was the participation of women in hard manual labour (for example, coal-mining) or in factory-based employment (as in the Lancashire cotton industry), both of which involved large numbers of women mingling with other men away from the protective care of their male relatives. Although cotton manufacturers were prominent in his Manchester chapel, a Unitarian minister like Taylor made clear his detestation of such operations, arguing that they were destructive of the home.[167] Even Smiles felt that society suffered demoralization when men and women competed against one another in the workplace, and explicitly disapproved of women working in factories.[168]

Those implacably opposed to the social values inherent in the new industrial society were the loudest in drawing attention to the moral dangers. 'This system of permitting the unlimited centralization of manufacturing wealth', claimed Richard Oastler, had broken up families which had once worked 'independently in their domestic circles', consigning thousands of human souls to mills and work-shops where they fell under the tyrannical rule of a single man: 'It is, in a great measure, to this source that much of the discontent and demoralization of the country is attributable.'[169] Indeed, such critics sometimes alleged that women had thereby been exposed to the attentions of philandering male supervisors: the most sensational symptom, thought some, of the way in which modern industry was subverting the morals of the British people.

These attacks succeeded in driving many factory owners and their ideological apologists onto the defensive. Thus both Samuel Greg, the cotton owner, and Edward Baines Junior, spokesman for the Yorkshire woollen industry, rushed forward to defend the 'morals' of the factory districts by, for example, attempting to demonstrate that illegitimacy rates in their areas were significantly lower than those prevailing in the rural countryside.[170]

But none of these apologias for the role of women in industrial life succeeded in convincing the sceptics. What, then, was to be done? By 1840 the domestic economy idealized by Oastler was clearly beyond retrieval. Given these circumstances, many middle-class Victorians understandably concluded that the only solid protection against the dangers which Oastler had publicized was, as far as practical, to remove women from the workplace entirely, leaving them as the guardian angels of the home. From the security of this environment they might then exercise a wholesome influence over the predominantly male world of work, though,

---

[167] Wach, 'Still, Small Voice', 436.   [168] Smiles, *Character*, 59–60.

[169] C. Driver, *Tory Radical: The Life of Richard Oastler* (New York, 1946), 427.

[170] S. Greg, *Two Letters to Leonard Horner, Esq., on the Capabilities of the Factory System* (London, 1840), 16–17; E. Baines, *The Social, Educational and Religious State of the Manufacturing Districts* (London, 1843), 54, 58–60. While conceding that country people were healthier, Mrs Marcet, too, was keen to point out that crime levels were higher among the agricultural than among the manufacturing classes, though urban crimes, as she noted, received greater *publicity* (*Conversations*, 67–70).

as we have seen, exactly how this was to be achieved remained a puzzle to which no obvious solution suggested itself.

CONCLUSION

To conclude: political economists and defenders of the new market economy alike conceded that the principle of competition should on no account be applied *directly* to family relationships. Even Mill, a moderate 'contractarian', acknowledged that the family constituted an arena for the cultivation of an ethical life and the development of individuality.

But though broad agreement had been reached on this point, entrepreneurial opinion divided sharply when it came to defining the nature of the bond between husband and wife. To some extent this issue split even the ranks of the women campaigning for their right to work. A minority of Victorians, both men and women, can be found urging full equality between the sexes. But most emphasized the domestic virtues and talked of 'separate spheres'.

There were therefore two strategies for reconciling the realities of modern commerce with the ethical demands of family existence. One attempted to demonstrate the interconnections between the two worlds, the other sought to throw up a barrier between them in order to prevent 'cross-contamination'. Although many individuals oscillated between these two strategies, most supported the notion of 'separate spheres', if only because the alternative required a radical re-evaluation of the nature of the family such as few Victorian middle-class men were prepared to make. But, of equal importance, the outcome shows that, to the Victorian middle classes, capitalism only seemed tolerable if certain areas of human life could be insulated from the materialism and the acquisitive materialism which lay at its heart.

8

The Problem of Poverty and Pauperism

Do you, then, deny, or, have your forgotten, those declarations: 'In the sweat of thy face shalt thou eat bread'; 'Six days shalt thou labour'; 'If any will not work neither let him eat?' The whole system of man's responsibility, and of his future reward or punishment, depending upon his being 'diligent in business, fervent in spirit, serving the Lord', seems completely set aside by your reasoning.

(Herbert Spencer, 1836)[1]

They call us 'political economists' and 'hard-hearted utilitarians': I say the political economists are the most charitable people in this country; the Free-traders are the most liberal to the poor of this land. . . . Let the Government of the country be conducted on such a principle, that men shall be enabled, by the labour of their own hands, to find an independent subsistence by their wages.

(Richard Cobden, 1844)[2]

The last two chapters have focused on the Victorians' attempts to insulate certain areas of life from the operation of market forces. We now turn to the problems involved in the *implementation* of market principles in specific fields of policy where this was bound to generate controversy and misgivings. What to do about the dependent poor was just such an issue, one which politicians and governments could not duck. Yet the difficulty here was that, as we have seen, political economy, with its rhetoric of self-help and independence and its warnings about the pauperizing effect of assistance, seemed to run flat counter to the Parable of the Good Samaritan, with its inculcation of the duty incumbent on all Christians to show charity towards those in need and distress. Nowhere did the moral dilemma of capitalism appear more sharply.

It was of course the New Poor Law of 1834 which dramatized the difficulty.[3] Whether or not this important piece of legislation really did involve a breach with the fundamental principles of Christianity is a debatable point, as we shall see. But the Act certainly brought about a departure from customary expectations, since

---

[1] 1836 newspaper article on the Poor Law by H. Spencer, in J. Offer (ed.), *Herbert Spencer: Political Writings* (Cambridge, 1994), 181.

[2] J. Bright and J. E. Thorold Rogers (eds.), *Speeches on Questions of Public Policy by Richard Cobden, MP* (London, 1908; first pub. 1870), i. 118: Speech in London on 11 Dec. 1844.

[3] Compare A. Brundage, *The Making of the New Poor Law: The Politics of Inquiry, Enactment and Implementation, 1832–39* (London, 1978), 182; W. C. Lubenow, *The Politics of Government Growth: Early Victorian Attitudes Toward State Intervention, 1833–1848* (Newton Abbot, 1971), ch. 2.

many of the poor felt that they had had their immemorial 'rights' taken away from them, a complaint endorsed by many 'outsiders'. For the new creed emphasized individual competition and economic interest, at the expense of what one historian has called the 'rituals of magisterial benevolence' which had once regulated the face-to-face relationships between donor and recipient.[4] How was such a drastic change justified?

MORALITY AND THE NEW POOR LAW

The New Poor Law was the culmination of a debate about rural indigence, poverty, and pauperism which had been raging for the previous half-century.[5] Basically the problems of rural society stemmed from scarcity and distress in the farming districts caused by population pressure and the collapse in agricultural prices following the unnatural expansion of the Napoleonic years.

Hence the specific evil against which the Poor Law Amendment Act attempted to protect society was the 'allowance system', retrospectively associated with Speenhamland (i.e. topping-up grants)—a device used over parts of southern England, but not in the manufacturing north. Believing that such arrangements deterred the farm labourer from seeking an independent living, nearly all the experts called for their abolition. But what could then be done about the 'surplus' of labour in the agricultural market which such a 'reform' would release? Assisted emigration to the colonies had many advocates. By the 1810s there were also those, David Ricardo included, who thought that an escape from the Malthusian trap lay in purchasing foodstuffs from abroad, to be paid for by the export of manufactured goods, the production of which would provide employment in the towns;[6] industrialization might thus offer a solution to the problems of rural society.

However, the Whig landowners, from whose ranks came the Cabinet Ministers who sponsored the 1834 Act, knew little about the manufacturing north.[7] Nor did those 'Liberal Tories', who played a crucial role on the Poor Law Commission. The latter had been heavily influenced by the writings of Malthus, Copleston, Whately, and other 'Christian economists', but they felt no particular sympathy for industrialization.[8] As for the northern capitalists proper, they viewed the New Poor Law ambivalently. For while the Liberal factory owners, in particular, often

---

[4] P. Dunkley, 'Whigs and Paupers: The Reform of the English Poor Laws, 1830–1834', *Journal of British Studies*, 20 (1981), 137–44. For a different interpretation, P. Mandler, 'The Making of the New Poor Law *Redivivus*', *Past & Present*, 117 (1987), 131–57.

[5] See the excellent study by J. R. Poynter, *Society and Pauperism: English Ideas on Poor Relief, 1795–1834* (London, 1969).

[6] Ricardo also stressed that the new taste for luxuries might operate as a check on breeding, foreshadowing Nassau Senior's emphasis on the role of *ambition* in solving the population problem (Poynter, *Society and Pauperism*, 242).

[7] Though they did perhaps favour a new agrarian capitalism (Dunkley, 'Whigs and Paupers', 138, 149).

[8] P. Mandler, 'Tories and Paupers: Christian Political Economy and the Making of the New Poor Law', *Historical Journal*, 33 (1990), 81–103, for a brilliant exposition of this thesis.

expressed general approval of the 'principles of 1834', they did not really want these principles to be applied to their *own* terrain.[9]

The New Poor Law, then, did not originate as a response to the problems of the industrial town. It was, rather, the consequence of a market philosophy which had been shaped by the problems of agriculture in the opening decades of the nineteenth century at a time when 'industrial take-off' had not yet made the big cities and the manufacturing centres the principal object of concern. Many of these earlier axioms and assumptions were subsequently carried through into the 1834 Act.

So much is evident from the famous passage from the 1834 Commissioners' Report, which spells out the philosophical rationale for the legislation which followed:

It appears to the pauper that the Government has undertaken to repeal the ordinary laws of nature: to enact, in short, that the penalty which after all must be paid by someone for idleness and improvidence is to fall, not on the guilty person or on his family, but on the proprietors of lands and houses incumbered by his settlement. Can we wonder if the uneducated are seduced by a system which offers marriage to the young, security to the anxious, ease to the lazy, and impunity to the profligate?[10]

These were sentiments with which the educated classes had been familiar for decades, thanks to the writings of a long line of political economists, stretching from Adam Smith through to Ricardo and Chalmers. 'The remedy against the extension of pauperism does not lie in the liberalities of the rich', Chalmers had earlier declared: 'it lies in the hearts and habits of the poor. Plant in their bosoms a principle of independence—give a high tune of delicacy to their characters—teach them to recoil from pauperism as a degradation.'[11]

But in one important respect the 1834 Poor Law Amendment Act *did* break new ground. In the early 1820s most 'reformers', not content with the phasing out of the allowance system, had called for nothing less than a total abolition of publicly funded poor relief. Adam Smith had favoured such a solution, though he did not think that it could be made in one stride; Malthus later gave countenance to 'abolitionism' of a more doctrinaire kind, as did Ricardo in his *Principles of Political Economy and Taxation*.[12] Some Ultra Tories, wishing to restore a system of *private* paternalism, joined the ranks of the political economists on this issue.[13]

The high water mark of abolitionism is often taken to be the Report of the 1817 Select Committee. However, the idea was still receiving enthusiastic support in the early 1830s from influential figures like Henry Brougham, Lord Chancellor in

[9] e.g. Muntz of Birmingham: Hansard, lvi, 405: 8 Feb. 1841. Edward Baines thought the measure a response to the southern landlords' neglect of their social responsibilities (N. C. Edsall, *The Anti-Poor Law Movement, 1834–44* (Manchester, 1971), 46).

[10] Poor Law Commissioners, *Report of HM Commissioners for Inquiring into the Administration and Practical Operation of the Poor Laws, 1834*, 27, 34, cited in Edsall, *Anti-Poor Law Movement*, 5.

[11] In letter of 7 Feb. 1811, cited in R. M. Young, 'Malthus and the Evolutionists: The Common Context of Biological and Social Theory', *Past & Present*, 43 (1969), 121.

[12] Poynter, *Society and Pauperism*, 239. Winch shows, however, that, whatever impression some of his remarks may have made, Malthus himself did not really think it either practical or desirable to secure the immediate and unconditional abolition of the Poor Laws (D. Winch, *Riches and Poverty: An Intellectual History of Political Economy in Britain, 1750–1834* (Cambridge, 1996), 232, 269–71, 307, 320–2). [13] Mandler, 'Tories and Paupers', 84.

the Whig Government,[14] and from Harriet Martineau. In her story *Cousin Marshall* (1832), the latter makes one of her characters echo Malthus by saying:

The best plan, in my opinion, yet proposed, is this:—to enact that no child born from any marriage taking place within a year from the date of the law, and no illegitimate child within two years from the same date, shall ever be entitled to parish assistance. This regulation should be made known, and its purpose explained universally.[15]

Even *after* the inauguration of the New Poor Law, abolitionist views can still be encountered. For example, in his long essay, 'The Political Economy of the Bible', published in 1844, Chalmers asserted that 'the charity of the churches in the New Testament, made up of the alms of the faithful, was voluntary in its origin'.[16] *Compulsory* beneficence, he always insisted, was both unchristian and absurd:

The force of law and the freeness of love cannot amalgamate the one with the other. Like water and oil they are immiscible. . . . We cannot translate beneficence into the statute book of law, without expunging it from the statute book of the heart.[17]

In his 'Second Letter to Peel', Bishop Copleston took a similar line: to 'be virtuous, be humane, be charitable by *proxy*' was a contradiction in terms, he declared.[18]

Another obstinate adherent to abolitionism, Herbert Spencer, was still, even into the 1870s and 1880s, insisting that publicly funded relief schemes obliterated the connection between cause and effect, so encouraging individuals to abandon responsibility for their own behaviour.[19] He even deprecated public support for the sick and the old, arguing that, when young and hale, people were paid as much as competition proved them to be worth.[20] One had to be cruel to be kind: 'The transition from State-beneficence to a healthy condition of self-help and private beneficence, must be like the transition from an opium-eating life to a normal life—painful but remedial.'[21]

However, despite the strength of abolitionist sentiment, the abolitionist solution fell by the wayside. For this, there are several reasons. Fear of the social consequences of suddenly ending poor relief must obviously have impinged on ministerial minds.[22] In addition, Martineau's alarmism notwithstanding, from the mid-1820s onwards evidence was accumulating which disproved Malthusian

---

[14] Dunkley, 'Whigs and Paupers', 132.

[15] H. Martineau, *Cousin Marshall* (1832), 119. In this extraordinary tale, calamitous social breakdown is predicted unless abolition be adopted.

[16] T. Chalmers, 'The Political Economy of the Bible', *North British Review*, 2 (1844–5), 50.

[17] T. Chalmers, *On the Power, Wisdom and Goodness of God as Manifested in the Adaptation of External Nature to the Moral and Intellectual Constitution of Man* (London, 1853; first pub. 1833), 231.

[18] R. A. Soloway, *Prelates and People: Ecclesiastical Social Thought in England 1783–1852* (London, 1969), 142–3.

[19] H. Spencer, *The Principles of Ethics*, in id., *The Synthetic Philosophy of Herbert Spencer*, Westminster edn. (New York, 1892–6), ii. 381–2.

[20] Ibid., 379. T. Gray thinks this inconsistent with Spencer's theories about the 'ethics of the family' ('Herbert Spencer's liberalism—from social statics to social dynamics', in R. Bellamy (ed.), *Victorian Liberalism: Nineteenth-Century Political Thought and Practice* (1990), 122).

[21] Spencer, *Principles of Ethics*, in id., *Synthetic Philosophy*, ii. 394.

[22] Dunkley, 'Whigs and Paupers', 126.

predictions of a steadily continuing *growth* of dependence. At the same time, the conviction took root that it was possible to remove the abuses of the poor law without abolishing it entirely—a conviction that finally triumphed when Chadwick succeeded in persuading the poor-law commissioners that the solution to population pressure lay in promoting improved labour productivity.[23]

Although this was not an important reason for its rejection, abolitionism also had an ideological flaw which Bentham had earlier identified in his poor-law proposals, partly published in 1797. Bentham had argued that, unless private philanthropy succeeded in entirely filling the gap,[24] simple abolition of all poor relief might well mean that the indigent poor faced the risk of death by starvation, a worse fate than that meted out to most condemned criminals, who, if imprisoned, would at least be housed and fed. As a result, abolitionism would actually provide hungry people with an incentive to commit robbery, since, if undetected, they would directly benefit: if apprehended, their fate would be no worse.

John Stuart Mill later pursued an almost identical line of argument. It was undesirable, he wrote, to leave everything to private philanthropy: 'charity almost always does too much or too little; it lavishes its bounty in one place, and leaves people to starve in another'. And Mill went on to repeat Bentham's main contention, that 'since the state must necessarily provide subsistence for the criminal poor while undergoing punishment, not to do the same for the poor who have not offended is to give a premium on crime'.[25] Like Bentham, Mill also feared that the abolition of the poor law might increase mendicity (i.e. begging).[26] Thus, whereas there was some sort of a case, *on political economy grounds*, for freeing the labour market from the 'distortions' produced by poor relief and its accompanying burden of heavy public expenditure, the principle of *utility* called for a different solution.

What was needed was a mechanism which discouraged indiscriminate relief and maintained a clear distinction between the pauper and the independent labourer, while preserving the principle, enshrined in the Elizabethan poor law, that the destitute poor should not die on the streets. The workhouse test and 'lesser eligibility' seemed a neat way of meeting this need.[27]

The precise manner in which 'lesser eligibility' reached the statute book remains contentious, but there seems little doubt that Bentham was the first person to enunciate clearly the axioms upon which the New Poor Law was based. However, it is important to note that, whereas Bentham anticipated the architects of the New Poor Law in his anxiety to stigmatize pauperism, he did *not* take the view that

---

[23] Ibid., 135.

[24] Bentham was sceptical about this necessarily happening (Poynter, *Society and Pauperism*, 124).

[25] J. S. Mill, *Principles of Political Economy*, in id., *Collected Works*, ed. J. M. Robson (Toronto, 1965), iii. 962.

[26] Later in the century, Mill's disciple, Henry Fawcett, who regarded the Poor Law as resting on a 'socialistic' basis, nevertheless felt that the principle of lesser eligibility would limit the damage that a publicly funded relief system might otherwise have caused (S. Collini, *Public Moralists: Political Thought and Intellectual Life in Britain, 1850–1930* (Oxford, 1991), 183).

[27] Certainly neater and less objectionable than Whately's suggestion that paupers might be tattooed on the foot or some other visible place and that females taking public relief should have their hair cut off (Soloway, *Prelates and People*, 162).

this necessarily involved drawing a distinction between the 'deserving' and the 'undeserving'. The idle and the work-shy, Bentham thought, might indeed comprise the majority of workhouse inmates, but cracking down on such people mattered less than determining the issue of *necessity*: 'A man may be a very worthy good sort of man: but so ought we all to be: and if everyman who is so were to bring in his *bill* for being so, who would there be to pay it?'[28] Mill later took a similar line: 'The state must act by general rules. It cannot undertake to discriminate between the deserving and the undeserving indigent', he wrote.[29]

However, whether through intellectual confusion or out of expediency, most of the sponsors and supporters of the New Poor Law persisted in claiming the very opposite. Joseph Hume, for example, told the Commons that the Act's purpose was 'to make a distinction between poverty undeserved and those who had become poor through their own vice or misconduct'.[30] Lord John Russell, one of the authors of the New Poor Law Amendment Act, echoed these sentiments,[31] as did Sir Robert Peel.

Opponents of the Act found it easy to ridicule such claims. Breaking rank with their own front bench,[32] many Tory Radicals argued that the poor had a *right* to subsistence, a right endorsed both by the Bible and by the English Constitution.[33] In the heated oratory of Busfeild Ferrand, these two sources of authority became conflated:

They would not see much longer the constitutional laws of this country and the laws of the Bible . . . trampled under the feet of this triumvirate [i.e. the three Poor Law Commissioners]. . . . The effect of the law had been to break through the old-established laws of this country, as well as those of the Bible itself, which enjoined men to 'succour the poor and needy'.[34]

William Cobbett argued a similar case.[35] While Richard Oastler denounced the New Poor Law as 'an act of TREASON against the constitution, against Christianity, against the State, and against the King, as well as against the Poor'.[36]

---

[28] Cited in Poynter, *Society and Pauperism*, 127. If Bentham's comments sound callous, one must remember that he (and Chadwick) both mistakenly assumed that reform of the poor laws would be accompanied by the classification and segregation of workhouse inmates, to prevent the old, the young, the sick, and the able-bodied being herded together in the same mixed wards, and also by so-called collateral aids—covering a bewildering variety of welfare and educational services.

[29] Mill, *Principles of Political Economy*, in id., *Collected Works*, iii. 962.

[30] Hansard, lvi, 168: 29 Jan. 1841.   [31] Ibid., 172.

[32] Mandler, 'Tories and Paupers', 96–7.

[33] Henry Drummond, too, claimed that the New Poor Law breached 'the poor man's right to relief' (M. Francis and J. Morrow, *A History of English Political Thought in the 19th Century* (London, 1994), 105–7).   [34] Hansard, lxiv, 146: 17 June 1842.

[35] Edsall, *Anti-Poor Law Movement*, 22. See J. Knott, *Popular Opposition to the 1834 Poor Law* (London, 1986), 31–2. In Knott's words, 'It was this old moral economy notion, that the poor had a *right* to relief, which was to clash head-on with the political economy beliefs embodied in the New Poor Law' (ibid., 34).

[36] From *Damnation, eternal damnation to the fiend-begotten, coarser-food New Poor Law*, cited in C. Driver, *Tory Radical: The Life of Richard Oastler* (New York, 1946), 339. These Tory Radicals occasionally enjoyed the backing of certain 'popular Radicals': e.g. on one memorable occasion, Wakley publicly called upon the Tories and the landowners to act as 'the natural leaders of the poor' (Hansard, lvi, 385: 8 Feb. 1841).

The defence deployed by the authors of the New Poor Law, that it rewarded the deserving and punished the undeserving, made many Tory Radicals particularly angry. Who were mere mortals to draw such distinctions? Did not the Bible say, 'Let he among you who is without fault cast the first stone'? One old-fashioned squire, Colonel Sibthorp, actually blamed the seemingly reprehensible behaviour of some poor people on the circumstances in which they found themselves.[37]

On the other hand, some opponents of the 1834 Act followed a different tack, among them the Radical MP for Birmingham, George Muntz, who protested that the New Poor Law 'made no distinction between the honest, industrious man and the idle, dissolute, and drunken vagabond' and was thus no better than the old discredited allowance system.[38] The critics had strong grounds for such allegations. After all, the mechanical nature of the 'lesser eligibility' principle had been specifically designed to obviate the need for sensitive discrimination between claimants.

It was this well-founded suspicion that, notwithstanding the pious rhetoric of the New Poor Law's defenders, it was the 'deserving' poor who often landed up in the workhouse, which almost certainly underlies the 'horror stories' circulating about the newly constructed 'Bastilles'. Significantly the 'victims' in these anecdotes are invariably depicted as virtuous and helpless people, trapped by a cruel regime. In particular, the practice of separating husband and wife was singled out as proof of the Act's unnatural malignity.[39] It has also been noted how many of the stories of Poor Law brutality which appeared in journals like *The Times* (some of them fabricated) involved the suffering of children or of mothers.[40] How could anyone subscribe to a law, however scientific it purported to be, which led to this sort of immoral attack on the sanctity of the family?

To such allegations of inhumanity there were two stock responses. First, it was said that it was the duty of *private philanthropy*, after careful inquiries into character and circumstances, to reward the deserving poor, leaving the public authorities with their unpleasant but necessary duty of coping with the 'residuum'. Lord John Russell, for example, declared that the New Poor Law still left 'ample scope for the exertions of private charity', but he argued that true charity 'ought to be spontaneous, not defined and rendered obligatory by law, but left . . . to those persons who had ample means of relieving their neighbours, and whose feeling, while it led them to do so, was likely itself to reward them for its exercise'.[41] Mill's

---

[37] Ibid., lvii, 746: 30 Mar. 1841.

[38] Ibid., lvi, 404: 8 Feb. 1841. See also J. Fielden's similar complaint: ibid., lxiv, 645–6: 27 June 1842, and Edsall, *Anti-Poor Law Movement*, 17.

[39] Thus Wakley told MPs how at the Kensington Union 'there was separation with a vengeance', the fathers of families being sent to Kensington, the mothers to Chelsea, the daughters to Fulham, and the sons to the parish of Hampstead (Hansard, lvi, 162: 29 Jan. 1841). See also ibid., 445: 8 Feb. 1841.

[40] D. Roberts, 'How Cruel Was the Victorian Poor Law?', *Historical Journal*, 6 (1963), 97–107. On the alleged cruelties, see Knott, *Popular Opposition to the Poor Law*, 229–31.

[41] Hansard, lvi, 173: 29 Jan. 1841.

reasoning was similar: 'What the state may and should abandon to private charity, is the task of distinguishing between one case of real necessity and another.
Private charity can give more to the more deserving.'[42] This point received additional emphasis later in the century.

Second, the defenders of the New Poor Law urged their opponents to think
more about long-term social consequences and worry less about the justice being
meted out to particular individuals. This was the approach which landed the Whig
Government in hot water over the bastardy clauses of the Poor Law Amendment
Act. For sound administrative reasons, the Act, in its original draft, pinned the
liability for an illegitimate child upon the mother rather than the father.[43] In vain
did the Leader of the House, Lord Althorp, aware of the unpopularity of this provision, plead with Members not to take the 'exceedingly easy and simple' path of
considering bastardy 'as a question of feeling': let them discuss it, he urged, 'in
their legislative capacity, as a question of reason', giving weight to 'the benefit of
the community in general'.[44] The plea went unheeded, and the bastardy clauses
were substantially altered during the passage of the Bill through Parliament, the
only part of the scheme to suffer such a fate.[45]

This episode well illustrates the problems experienced by the defenders of the
New Poor Law. Its rationale was basically a utilitarian one, centred upon an ethic
of *consequences*. In a sentimental age, people were being asked to harden themselves against the influence of kindly feelings. Mistrust of 'sympathy' was almost
universal among the political economists and their sympathizers. For example, Mrs
Marcet made her Governess warn Caroline against 'mistaken principles of benevolence': 'without knowledge to guide and sense to regulate the feelings, the best
intentions will be of little use'.[46] And later in the century James Fitzjames Stephen
denounced the 'kindly philanthropists' who advocated the relaxation of the Poor
Law as 'sentimentalists': men who, out of a misplaced sense of guilt, simply refused
to face up to 'facts'.[47]

Politicians influenced by the new creed, like Russell, Peel, and Sir James
Graham, joined in the refrain. 'If under the guise of improvement', Russell warned
Parliament in 1841,

---

[42] Mill, *Principles of Political Economy*, in id., *Collected Works*, iii. 962.

[43] Edsall, *Anti-Poor Law Movement*, 13.

[44] Hansard, xxiv, 523–4: 18 June 1834. On the wrangle among the bishops on this clause, see Soloway,
Prelates and People, 172–4. Bishop Blofield of London, who had supported the clause, had to make a
tortuous defence of his seemingly 'un-Christian' position. For popular attacks on the bastardy provisions, see Driver, *Oastler*, 346–7; Knott, *Popular Opposition to Poor Law*, 273.

[45] In 1844 bastardy was dissociated entirely from the operation of the Poor Law (T. Mackay, *History
of the English Poor Law* (London, 1904), 315–18).

[46] Mrs Marcet, *Conversations on Political Economy: In Which The Elements of That Science Are Familiarly
Explained* (London, 1839; first pub. 1816), 7–8, also 156.

[47] Collini, *Public Moralists*, 190–6. For the view that expenditure on philanthropy often partook of
the character of 'guilt money', see G. S. Jones, *Outcast London: A Study in the Relationship Between
Classes in Victorian Society* (Oxford, 1971), 250. Jones argues that, given the absence of a measure for
the equalization of the Metropolitan Poor Rate, the West End saw charitable donations as an alternative way of meeting its obligations to the poorer districts.

you again permitted the labourers to live on charity, and reduced them to their former state of dependence, although the proceeding might have an air of popularity at first, and be lauded by many persons as showing great benevolence, you would, in fact, destroy the moral character of the labourer; you would weaken his strength, and undermine his integrity; you would lay the foundation of a great overgrown population, whom your laws could not restrain, whom even the sanctions of religion would be hardly able to curb into obedience, and you would be taking the surest means to ruin the foundation of society.[48]

Faced by the protests of the kind-hearted, the mid-Victorian advocates of a 'scientific' relief policy took a grim satisfaction in their own rectitude, although they knew that their actions would be misunderstood by the ignorant and expose them to mockery and abuse. Thus when Senior called the Whig administration which introduced the Poor Law Amendment Act a government 'willing, in a good cause, to brave unpopularity',[49] he was bestowing upon it the highest praise of which he was capable.

In short, like dutiful parents who had the long-term good of their child at heart, governments had to show sternness in their policy towards the poor. The really 'guilty' people were those who failed to recognize this necessity. Harriet Martineau drove home the point with her customary exaggeration: 'There is no use in pleading our good intentions; the fathers of the Inquisition are ever ready with their plea of good intentions. . . . we have been doing the pleasure of fiends under a persuasion that we were discharging the duty of Christians.'[50]

The acid test was whether the values of self-reliance were being encouraged. 'Any scheme, however well intentioned it may be', reasoned Fawcett, '[would] indefinitely increase every evil it [sought] to alleviate if it lessen[ed] individual responsibility by encouraging the people to rely less upon themselves and more upon the state.'[51] Peel, too, justified the workhouse test with the argument that it 'would have the effect of doing justice to the humble, but industrious ratepayer, whilst it would also improve the moral character, and ultimately, as a consequence, the physical condition of the labourer himself'.[52]

Peel's reference to ratepayers might seem to be giving the game away. But, in fact, the defenders of the New Poor Law repeatedly insisted that their main concern was to elevate the people's morals and some argued that they would support the Act even if it *drove up* public expenditure—an outcome which, its critics complained, was likely to materialize in the short run, anyway. Senior made the point forcefully:

---

[48] Hansard, lvi, 450: 8 Feb. 1841.

[49] [N. Senior], 'Poor Law Reform', *Edinburgh Review*, 74 (Oct. 1841), 26.

[50] H. Martineau, *The Moral of Many Fables* (London, 1834), 63, 64. See also W. Chance, *Our Treatment of the Poor* (London, 1899), 154–6.

[51] H. Fawcett, *Manual*, 310, cited in L. Goldman (ed.), *The Blind Victorian: Henry Fawcett and British Liberalism* (Cambridge, 1989), 102.

[52] Hansard, lvi, 412: 8 Feb. 1841. Those who took this view would have been cheered, as the Poor Law Commissioners certainly were, by evidence that the stringent operation of Poor Law had indeed led in some districts to an increase in the number of friendly societies (G. Finlayson, *Citizen, State, and Social Welfare in Britain 1830–1990* (Oxford, 1994), 82–3).

We attach . . . little comparative importance to the pecuniary results of the Poor Law Amendment Act. If the difference between the rates of 1836 and those of 1840 had still been raised but merely to be thrown away, our prosperity would have been little impaired. Every year of a war costs ten times as much. The real evil of the profusion was the indirect evil—the real benefit of the economy is its indirect benefit.[53]

Even allowing for a certain dash of hypocrisy, it may well be that this concern with character and work incentives was paramount in the minds of the defenders of the 'principles of 1834'.[54]

What view of human nature was being assumed by those who stressed the centrality of 'character'? Among the advocates of the New Poor Law one finds a cacophony of voices. To Senior the able-bodied pauper was 'the result of art': 'He is not the natural offspring of the Saxon race. Unless his pauperism is carefully fostered by those who think it their interest to preserve it, he rapidly reverts to the *normal type*—the independent labourer.'[55] 'The poor', Senior concluded, 'were not the authors of the system which had ruined their freedom, their industry, and their morals. It had been imposed on them by the ignorance and vanity of the higher orders, and the avarice and fraud of the middle classes.'[56]

Such reasoning could produce a strange kind of social determinism which seems at odds with many of the principles of political economy, though perhaps it was a logical extension of utilitarianism. Change the defective system of social stimuli and deterrents, Martineau advised, and beneficial results would quickly follow. 'It is rather hard upon the poor', she declared in *Cousin Marshall*, 'that we should complain of their improvidence when we bribe them to it by promising subsistence at all events. Paupers will spend and marry faster than their betters as long as this system lasts.'[57]

However, such an emphasis is rather at odds with that found in the writings of other 'political economists', like W. R. Greg, an unbeliever whose theories seem nevertheless strongly tinged by the doctrine of Original Sin.[58] Unlike Senior, who apparently viewed men and women as naturally industrious and productive when not corrupted by foolish laws, Greg took a darker view of human nature: 'Selfishness and indolence are natural to uncorrected humanity. Few will exert themselves who can subsist without exertion'—hence the need for 'the goad of

[53] Senior, 'Poor Law Reform', 32. See a similar claim by the Whig MP F. Maule (Hansard, lvi, 422: 8 Feb. 1841).
[54] P. Dunkley argues that whereas small farmers were primarily interested in economy, the large landlords, more insulated from market forces, did not attach so much importance to this factor ('Paternalism, The Magistracy and Poor Relief in England, 1795–1834', *International Review of Social History*, 24 (1979), 392).   [55] Senior, 'Poor Law Reform', 33.
[56] Ibid., 28.   [57] Martineau, *Cousin Marshall*, 52; Martineau, *Moral of Many Fables*, 66.
[58] For Greg's views on Christianity, R. J. Helmstadter, 'W. R. Greg: A Manchester Creed', in R. J. Helmstadter and B. Lightman (eds.), *Victorian Faith in Crisis: Essays on Continuity and Change in Nineteenth-Century Religious Belief* (1990), 187–222.

necessity'.[59] This, unsurprisingly, was also the line adopted by clergymen looking to combine the teachings of Scripture with the lessons of political economy. Thus Herbert Spencer's uncle, the Revd Thomas Spencer, could write: 'The depravity of human nature is constantly represented in the Bible as displaying itself in the universal tendency of man to indolence, and to the neglect of the duties which he owes to himself and to his family.' Hence the need for a severe poor law.[60]

But whether optimistic about human nature, like Senior and Martineau, or pessimistic, like Greg and Thomas Spencer, all those who favoured the principle of 'lesser eligibility' were propounding an ethic which many Christians thought to be at variance with Our Lord's message of forgiveness and compassion.[61] 'Lesser eligibility' also seemed to be encouraging people to display the worst kind of calculating selfishness.

Why did the New Poor Law, which aroused these strong moral objections, nevertheless endure for so long? In part because, as the 'realists' of both parties said at the time, there was no obvious alternative. When in 1838 John Fielden introduced a motion to repeal the 1834 Act, it attracted only seventeen votes.[62] Its opponents were long on rhetoric, short on practical propositions, and the suggestions which they did advance merely showed how eclectic a group they were. Moreover, by the mid-Victorian years critics were inhibited by the appearance of statistics showing a substantial fall in poor law expenditure and consequently in local taxation: 'the money saved since 1834 amounts, I heard, to some 34 million', wrote one Liberal backbencher in July 1860, 'but far more has been saved than can be estimated, for we were drifting before to ruin'.[63]

By the mid-nineteenth century, with the growth of the prestige of political economy, the New Poor Law had to some extent become taken for granted. As José Harris notes, 'there was . . . a widespread sense in the 1850s and 1860s that, at least in the economic sphere, the fundamental principles of public policy had been fixed for all time by an earlier political generation' whose achievement it was to have taken social and economic policy 'out of politics' by a series of historic

---

[59] [W. R. Greg], 'Charity, Noxious and Beneficent', *Westminster Review*, 59 (1853), 70. Greg denounced socialism for 'its failure to take account of man's fallen estate' (W. R. Greg, *Essays on Political and Social Science, Contributed Chiefly to the Edinburgh Review* (London, 1853), i. 494, 488). However, in certain moods Greg could write optimistically of the disappearance of pauperism and 'the ultimate abolition of compulsory poor-rates'—but this would only happen 'as political wisdom improve[d]' (*Enigmas of Life* (London, 1872), 119).

[60] T. Spencer, *Objections to the New Poor Law Answered* (London, 1841), 9. In fact, however, the pamphlet reads more like a diatribe against *any* kind of poor law rather than as a defence of the 1834 measure. Thomas Spencer displayed rather more compassion towards those who had suffered economic failure after he himself had invested half his capital in a railway company which went bankrupt! (D. Wiltshire, *The Social and Political Thought of Herbert Spencer* (Oxford, 1978), 21).

[61] 'Now, was that a Christian Legislature?', asked Wakley heatedly during a debate on the poor law question (Hansard, lvi, 392: 8 Feb. 1841).　　　　　　[62] Edsall, *Anti-Poor Law Movement*, 127.

[63] Trelawny diary, 24 July 1860, T. A. Jenkins (ed.), *The Parliamentary Diaries of Sir John Trelawny, 1858–1865*, Camden fourth series (London, 1990), xl. 142.

measures, of which the 1834 Poor Law was one.[64] The adoption of a deterrent approach to poor relief could now be treated as the hallmark of a progressive society, a society which had successfully effected the transition from status to contract.[65]

Finally, the violent criticism of the New Poor Law abated somewhat now that it was being operated more 'flexibly': in the manufacturing districts, for example, outdoor relief largely survived—to the chagrin of the 'purists'. In fact, the most effective deterrent may have been, not so much the workhouse test, as the 'settlement' provisions which made it possible for the authorities to send the urban unemployed back to the villages where they had grown up—ironically so, since the settlement laws, an unwelcome survival from the pre-1834 regime, had been attacked by the political economists, from Adam Smith onwards, for impeding labour mobility.[66]

But anything that had the appearance of a concession or a retreat worried former *admirers* of the New Poor Law. *The Economist* asked whether 'lesser eligibility' was being implemented as seriously as it should be,[67] while Greg feared that sound policy was being sacrificed for reasons of expediency.[68] In 1869 the *Saturday Review* launched a campaign on this issue, complaining that weak administration in the metropolis was encouraging 'mendicity, and . . . those habits which lead to mendicity—recklessness, unthrift, and a disposition to rely on others'. Reliance on outdoor relief could not but lead to 'communism': 'Why should people save their own property, when they can have their bite at the savings of other persons *ad libitum*? Why should they practise economy, when they can dip their hands into the pockets of others?'[69] Other contributors to the journals lambasted the negligence of the guardians and even called for the total abolition of the whole poor-law system if affairs did not speedily improve.[70]

But 'abolitionism' had fallen outside practical politics in the 1830s, and there was never a serious possibility of it being adopted thirty years later. What instead happened was an attempt to return to the full rigours of the principles of 1834. A key figure in this development was the President of the Poor Law Board, George Joachim Goschen, himself a dedicated student of political economy. Because there were not enough workhouses, complained Goschen, abuses were creeping back into the administration of relief.[71] Out of such anxieties arose his famous Minute

---

[64] J. Harris, *Private Lives, Public Spirit: A Social History of Britain 1870–1914* (Oxford, 1993), 197. The other two measures she cites are the Repeal of the Corn Laws and the 1844 Bank Charter Act.

[65] Mackay, *Poor Law*, 18–19.

[66] M. Rose, 'Settlement, Removal and the New Poor Law', in D. Fraser (ed.), *The New Poor Law in the Nineteenth Century* (London, 1976), 25–44.

[67] *The Economist*, 25 Jan. 1851, p. 82.   [68] Greg, 'Charity', 62–88.

[69] 'Charity and Mendicity', *Saturday Review*, 30 Oct. 1869, p. 567; 'Pauperism, Charity, and the Poor-Law', ibid., 25 Dec. 1869, p. 812.

[70] 'Thoughts and Experiences of a Guardian of the Poor', *Macmillan's Magazine*, 22 (1870), 103–5. Another contributor to the same journal, C. B. Clarke, wrote urging a return to Malthus's principles ('The Existing Poor Law of England', ibid., 23 (1870), 51).

[71] Hansard, cc, 1786: 25 Apr. 1870.

of 1869, which urged Boards of Guardians to 'test' their applicants with greater stringency.[72]

But would the newly enlarged electorate have the maturity to acknowledge its responsibilities? Even Parliament, Goschen feared, could no longer be trusted to do its duty:

> It might be an unpopular thing to say . . . , but Political Economy had been dethroned in that House and Philanthropy had been allowed to take its place. Political Economy was the bugbear of the working classes, and philanthropy, he was sorry to say, was their idol. In all legislative assemblies wherever numbers and numbers alone had prevailed, the doctrines of political economy had never taken root.[73]

Note that Goschen is here redefining 'philanthropy' to signify a frame of mind, which he then identifies with legislative interference.

What, then, of philanthropy proper? The Goschen Minute had tried to disarm the critics by pointing out that, despite the apparent harshness of its proposed treatment of those on public relief, the tender-hearted still had a large and useful sphere of activity before them in the work of private charity. Did this mean that philanthropy constituted a sort of 'no-go' area, from which political economy could be excluded, or did the work of philanthropists need to be subjected to the same disciplines that the New Poor Law had attempted to bring to bear on the public sector?

PRIVATE PHILANTHROPY

> Why should people give away their money plentifully to those who had not taken care of their own money? Tom saw some justice in severity; and all the more, because he had confidence in himself that he should never deserve that just severity.
>
> (George Eliot, 1860)[74]

> No one ever [seriously] claimed for political economy, . . . that it ha[d] any right to encroach on the domain of charity or mercy.
>
> (R. Lowe, 1878)[75]

Historians have viewed private philanthropy in one of two different ways. Some, like Olive Checkland, argue that because charity is 'a one-sided action, expecting no quid pro quo, it is a misfit in the economic structure of modern society, which

---

[72] On the changes made to the Poor Law system at about this time, B. Rodgers, *The Battle Against Poverty, i, From Pauperism to Human Rights* (London, 1968), 39.

[73] Goschen in Commons, June 1877 (A. D. Elliot, *Life of Lord Goschen 1831–1907* (London, 1911), 163–4).

[74] Tom Tulliver's observations, in G. Eliot's *The Mill on the Floss*, Blackwood edn. (Edinburgh, 1878; first pub. 1860), vol. i, bk. 3, ch. 5, p. 353.

[75] R. Lowe, 'Recent Attacks on Political Economy', *Nineteenth Century*, 4 (1878), 868.

rests on the principle of exchange'.[76] Others, like Geoffrey Finlayson, emphasize the *complementary* relationship between the poor law and 'organized' charity in nineteenth-century Britain by showing how, underlying them both, ran the same social and moral values: thrift, self-control, and 'independence' (what Finlayson calls 'help from within', as distinct from 'help from without').[77]

In support of Olive Checkland, one could show how the voluntary societies of Victorian Britain were able to tackle serious social problems that eluded a market solution but in which it would have been dangerous to involve the state: the reclamation of prostitutes, for example. Private philanthropy also provided a useful arena for the exercise of the Christian values of compassion, mercy, and service,[78] as well as an opportunity for businessmen, many of them still excluded from an effective political role because of religious restrictions or franchise limitations, to demonstrate their social importance.[79]

At a deeper level, charities succeeded in tempering and softening the rigour of market forces, so contributing to the stability of society as a whole, just as family and home life were supposedly doing. Significantly, the Christian economist Chalmers always insisted that philanthropy be based on the family as a unit, rather than operate on 'functional' lines. Most Victorians agreed.[80]

If the world of private charity was indeed a realm apart, like the home, this might explain why women played so prominent a role in philanthropic activities throughout the entire nineteenth century.[81] True, much of this philanthropic work was local and on a small scale.[82] Yet it was precisely in this kind of environment that women would feel themselves most 'at home' and might be expected to show their effectiveness.

Finally, the harsh stringency of the poor-law system (in theory, if not always in practice) and the impersonality of its administration made it highly desirable that there should be a sphere within which there could be discrimination. The virtue of charity was supposed to be that, as well as exhibiting a 'superior economy

[76] O. Checkland, *Philanthropy in Victorian Scotland: Social Welfare and the Voluntary Principle* (Edinburgh, 1980), 2–3.   [77] Finlayson, *Citizen, State, and Social Welfare*, 81, 92.

[78] On the insistence of the Christian churches that businessmen must systematically devote part of their profits to philanthropic causes, see E. J. Garnett, ' "Gold and the Gospel": Systematic Beneficence in Mid-Nineteenth Century England', in W. J. Sheils and D. Wood (eds.), *The Church and Wealth*, Studies in Church History, xxiv (1987), 347–58.

[79] R. J. Morris, 'Voluntary Societies and British Urban Elites, 1780–1850', *Historical Journal*, 26 (1983), 95–118. See the interesting discussion in B. Harrison, 'Philanthropy and the Victorians', in id., *Peaceable Kingdom* (Oxford, 1982), 229. On philanthropy as a symptom of social insecurity, E. W. Sager, 'The Social Origins of Victorian Pacifism', *Victorian Studies*, 23 (1979–80), 214–15.

[80] Incidentally, the Webbs' later flouting of this axiom in their famous Poor Law Minority Report played a large part in its discrediting: what the Webbs saw as 'the break-up of the Poor Law', their many opponents saw as a 'break-up of the family'.

[81] F. K. Prochaska, *Women and Philanthropy in Nineteenth-Century England* (Oxford, 1980); A. Summers, 'A Home from Home—Women's Philanthropic Work in the Nineteenth Century', in S. Burman (ed.), *Fit Work For Women* (London, 1979), 33–63. See Ch. 7.

[82] L. Davidoff and C. Hall, *Family Fortunes: Men and Women of the English Middle Class, 1780–1850* (London, 1987), 434. See also S. Conway, 'The Politicization of the Nineteenth-Century Peace Society', *Historical Research*, 66 (1993), 267–8.

of administration',[83] it gave individual donors an opportunity to develop their personalities by exercising their powers of *choice*—a choice both over the *field* of philanthropy in which to specialize and also over the *people* who were to be helped. 'Voluntary charity, guided by discretion', declared Thomas Spencer, 'draws out the best feelings in him that gives, and in him that receives, but money taken by force from some and given without that care which is exercised by the man who relieves at his own cost, is invariably the cause of mischief.'[84]

His nephew carried the argument one stage further, suggesting that a sharp distinction needed to be drawn between the imperatives of 'justice', which was blind to personal character and circumstances, and the imperatives of 'beneficence', where 'character' was the determining factor both in its 'positive' and 'negative' expressions ('charity' and 'mercy', respectively). Precisely because the state, as an agency of 'justice', could do nothing except ensure that citizens received only that to which they were entitled by an impartial interpretation of the rules, there were, in Spencer's view, many types of suffering which only the voluntary society was in a position to alleviate.[85] Indeed, Spencer thought that voluntary beneficence *might* even be 'adequate to achieve all those mitigations [of suffering] that [were] proper and needful'.[86] At the very least, private philanthropy served the community in ways which public action never could.

So much for the first interpretation. It has much to recommend it. However, the boundary between the state and philanthropic activity could not be quite so easily demarcated. For a start, as Norman McCord has shown, 'in practice official and unofficial activity for the care of the poor were controlled by much the same people'.[87] Moreover, many voluntary societies (those run by the anti-slavery campaigners and later by the temperance reformers, for example), far from keeping a distance between themselves and the state, sought to goad Parliament or government into taking up their own particular legislative or administrative panaceas.[88]

Moreover, even when the private society professed its intention of 'ploughing its own furrow', in practice it often encroached, unwittingly in most cases, upon the work of the public authorities, causing confusion, overlap, and waste. These problems were particularly liable to occur when it came to dealing with poverty

[83] M. O'Reilly, 'On The Superior Economy of Administration of Voluntary as Distinguished from Legal Charity', *Transactions of the National Association for the Promotion of Social Science*, 1861, 660–8. The 1858 Workhouse Visiting Society allowed volunteers into workhouses—in part because this was an economy measure! (F. Prochaska, *The Voluntary Impulse: Philanthropy in Modern Britain* (London, 1988), 35). [84] T. Spencer, *New Poor Law*, 8.

[85] Spencer, *Principles of Ethics*, in id., *Synthetic Philosophy*, ii. 270–5. See T. S. Gray, 'Herbert Spencer's Theory of Social Justice—Desert or Entitlement?', *History of Political Thought*, 2 (1981), 175–6. For further refinements of this distinction, see below.

[86] Cited in Gray, 'Spencer's liberalism', 123. One should underline the caveat 'proper and needful'. On Spencer's accompanying doubts about the usefulness of much private philanthropy, see below.

[87] N. McCord, 'The Poor Law and Philanthropy', in Fraser (ed.), *New Poor Law*, 100.

[88] D. Eastwood, 'Men, Morals and the Machinery of Social Legislation, 1790–1840', *Parliamentary History*, 13 (1994), esp. 199–201, 205.

and pauperism. Hence Goschen's Minute of 20 November 1869 which emphasized how important it was 'to avoid the double distribution of relief to the same persons, and, at the same time, to secure that the most effective use should be made' of voluntary funds. Goschen wanted 'to mark out the separate limits of the Poor Law and of charity respectively, and [to find out] how it is possible to secure joint action between the two'. While the Poor Law dealt with 'the totally destitute', Goschen thought that charities should organize goods and services for the poor—for example, in the form of the redemption of articles from pawn—though they should *not* provide *gifts* of food or money.[89]

Now, of course, underlying the Goschen Minute was the clear implication that many charitable bodies were operating along the wrong lines and inadvertently doing harm rather than good. That is why, despite the claims of the ideologists of private philanthropy, their activities could not be shielded against the kind of utilitarian critique which had earlier been directed against the old poor law.

Take, for example, the argument that private citizens should be allowed freedom in the exercise of their benevolence because this was a way of developing the moral fibre of the donor. The argument was open to objections on two counts. First, it seemed to relegate to a minor position the objective needs of those in pressing need of practical help. Second, both the utilitarian and the political economist could condemn this approach as likely to encourage the would-be philanthropist in irresponsible self-indulgence.[90]

There were good grounds for the latter complaint. After all, throughout the nineteenth century one encounters many well-to-do philanthropists, often females, who openly proclaimed that the cause they were espousing had given shape and meaning to otherwise aimless or frivolous lives.[91] Such philanthropy might well satisfy the emotional needs of the well-to-do. But it arguably led, at best, to a tinkering with social problems instead of getting at their root causes, and, at worst, to the infliction of considerable long-term harm.

In any case, why was dependence on the state so much more degrading than the receipt of charitable assistance? The Victorian middle class struggled to resolve this question—often rather unconvincingly. William Chance, for example, admitted that charity might be 'demoralizing if bestowed carelessly and indiscriminately', but he claimed that it had the advantage of being 'uncertain'![92]

Many devotees of political economy, unpersuaded by such sophistry, fretted at the prospect that untrammelled philanthropic choice was allowing the evils of the

[89] Cited in S. Webb and B. Webb, *English Poor Law Policy* (London, 1963; first pub. 1910), 144–5.
[90] Greg, 'Charity', 78–9. The *Westminster Review* went so far as to allege that many private charities were 'kept up for the imperfectly concealed purpose of making places for people who cannot find occupations anywhere else' (Anon., 'The Philanthropy of the Age and its Relation to Social Evils', *Westminster Review*, 91 (1869), 445).
[91] e.g. the prison reformer, Matilda Wrench (quoted in A. Summers, '"In a few years we shall none of us that now take care of them be here": Philanthropy and the State in the Thinking of Elizabeth Fry', *Historical Research*, 66 (1993), 140). Many more examples can be found in Finlayson, *Citizen, State, and Social Welfare*, 49–50.   [92] Chance, *Treatment of the Poor*, 141.

old allowance system, apparently ended in 1834, to creep back in. Thus Greg bitterly complained that the New Poor Law had achieved much and would have achieved more, 'had not blind charity . . . interfered to prevent the free and full action of those thoroughly sound, though stern principles of right and justice, on which it was founded'. Unfortunately, he lamented,

we are becoming foolishly soft, weakly tender, irrationally maudlin, unwisely and mischievously charitable. Under the specious mask of mercy to the criminal and benevolence to the wretched, we spare our own feelings at the cost of the most obvious principles of morality, the plainest dictates of prudence, the dearest interests of our country.[93]

Similarly the *Saturday Review* complained that 'all shame of begging seem[ed] to have disappeared', as thousands of mendicants flooded into the capital. The 'capricious benevolence' of the rich had brought about a situation in which 'the mendicant's profession [was] becoming as general and as gambling [*sic*] as a stock-jobber's'.[94]

It was this 'capricious benevolence' which many advocates of the market economy, among them Bagehot[95] and Fawcett, so disliked. 'Any scheme, however well-intentioned it may be', argued Fawcett, 'will indefinitely increase every evil it seeks to alleviate if it lessens individual responsibility by encouraging the people to rely less upon themselves and more upon the state.' The 'manly fellows', of whom he was one, felt that even John Stuart Mill, with his 'sentimental', 'feminine' side, could not entirely be absolved from fostering these regrettable attitudes.[96] It was a point which James Fitzjames Stephen made more bluntly in a letter to his sister-in-law, in which he complained that Mill had deserted 'the proper principles of rigidity and ferocity' upon which the great utilitarian philosopher had been brought up.[97]

But Mill, too, frequently railed against what he saw as the excesses of sentimental philanthropy, for which, he ruefully conceded, silly women bore much of the blame. 'Unenlightened and shortsighted benevolence', he complained, were sapping 'the very foundations of the self-respect, self-help, and self-control which are the essential conditions both of individual prosperity and of social virtue.' Mill felt that women were less likely to make this mistake once they had acquired responsibility for the practical management of schemes of beneficence. However, 'a woman born to the present lot of women, and content with it, how should

---

[93] Greg, 'Charity', 63–4.

[94] 'Pauperism, Charity, and the Poor-Law', *Saturday Review*, 25 Dec. 1869, pp. 812–13. Greg thought that private philanthropy had stimulated the 'trade' of begging so powerfully that it now possessed as many sub-branches as the cotton industry! (Greg, 'Charity', 73).

[95] See W. Bagehot, *Physics and Politics* (Boston, Mass., 1956; first pub. 1872), 137–8.

[96] Cited in Collini, *Public Moralists*, 185.

[97] Stephen to E. Cunningham, 12 Sept. 1872, cited in J. A. Colaiaco, *James Fitzjames Stephen and the Crisis of Victorian Thought* (New York, 1983), 124. Stephen's own creed was aptly described by Frederic Harrison as 'Calvinism *minus* Christianity' ('The Religion of Inhumanity', *Fortnightly Review*, 19 (1873), 677, cited in ibid., 160).

she appreciate the value of self-dependence?'[98] Indeed, as Brian Harrison rightly observes, 'Mill made female sentimentality one of his major reasons for enfranchising women; political experience might render their philanthropy more discriminating.'[99]

Herbert Spencer felt even greater despair at what was happening in the philanthropic world. Unless charities were administered with much greater care, he warned, the connection between cause and effect would become obliterated, causing individuals to abandon responsibility for their own behaviour: 'To separate pain from ill-doing is to fight against the constitution of things, and will be followed by far more pain', he warned.[100] Voluntarily organized poor relief, he conceded, was less objectionable than public relief, but it was objectionable all the same: 'For though the vitiating influences of coercion are now avoided the vitiating influences of proxy-distribution remain.'[101] 'May we not by frequent aid to the worthy render them unworthy?', Spencer asked: 'are we not almost certain by helping those who are already unworthy to make them more unworthy still?' Worse still, such misplaced benevolence was manufacturing a class of 'undeserving poor' who would transmit their weaknesses to their offspring.[102]

The question of how to 'regulate our pecuniary beneficence' so as to 'avoid assisting the incapable and the degraded to multiply' seemed to Spencer to be 'almost insurmountable', since attempts to stop the unworthy from propagating their kind would simply lead to a great increase in illegitimacy. 'Evil has been done and the penalty must be paid', he grimly concluded: 'Cure can come only through affliction.'[103] Note that the message was all the harsher in that Spencer, believing evolutionary progress to entail the continuous purging of the unfit, did not really have the confidence of ideologues like Smiles that individuals could raise themselves in the world by the pursuit of 'self-improvement'.

By the 1860s, 'sentimental' philanthropic societies were coming in for a torrent of abuse.[104] Some political economists even viewed employer paternalism

---

[98] J. S. Mill, *The Subjection of Women,* ed. S. Mansfield (Arlington Heights, Ill., 1980; first pub. 1869), 88–9. J. D. Milne expressed a similar point of view, but less provocatively (*Industrial Employment of Women in the Middle and Lower Ranks,* 2nd edn. (London, 1870; first pub. 1857), 43).

[99] Harrison, 'Philanthropy and the Victorians', 246. On female zealotry and its contrast with the calculating approach of the 'trading politician', see A. Tyrrell, '"Woman's Mission" and Pressure Group Politics in Britain (1825–60)', *Bulletin of the John Rylands Library,* 63 (1980), 223–4.

[100] H. Spencer, *The Man Versus the State,* ed. D. Macrae (London, 1969; first pub. 1884), 83.

[101] Spencer, *Principles of Ethics,* in id., *Synthetic Philosophy,* ii. 381–2. These sentiments clearly fit with his observations on the role of 'charity' and 'mercy', outlined above.

[102] Spencer, *Man Versus the State,* 83.

[103] Spencer, *Principles of Ethics,* in id., *Synthetic Philosophy,* ii. 392–4. Ricardo had earlier argued, in similar vein, that the country could 'never get into a good system after so long persevering in a bad one but by much previous suffering of the poor' (Ricardo to Trower, 27 Jan. 1817, *The Works and Correspondence of David Ricardo,* ed. P. Sraffa (Cambridge, 1952), vii. 125, cited in S. Hollander, 'Ricardo and the Corn Laws: A Revision', *History of Political Economy,* 9 (1977), 11).

[104] See Revd W. G. Blaikie, 'On the Collisions of Benevolence and Social Law', *Transactions of the National Association for the Promotion of Social Science, 1863,* 707–8.

suspiciously.[105] It may perhaps be true, as the historian, Patrick Joyce, puts it, that employer paternalism was the 'logical outcome of *laissez-faire* ideology and not its logical opposite', since paternalistic practice 'developed within the matrix of strongly held *laissez-faire* notions of what the relations of employer and worker should be'.[106] However many contemporaries were more inclined to *contrast* philanthropy and 'business' than to explore the links between them.

Who was providing the greater practical help for his dependants, they asked: the employer who aimed for economic success or the employer who deliberately set out to be a philanthropist? The Revd W. G. Blaikie diplomatically observed that a useful social role could be played by *both* types: 'Each may derive very important lessons from the other; and the prevalence of a friendly spirit between them will at once dispose them to learn from each other, and enable them to work comfortably and advantageously into each other's hands.'[107] But William Ellis boldly claimed that 'the noblest duty that [could] be performed by man towards his fellow-men, [was] the prevention of destitution, by averting its causes—the Vices' —which was what successful capitalists were doing.[108] Indeed, according to the *Westminster Review*, it was really

of much less consequence that a man should expend large sums in charity or upon luxuries than that he should be regular in paying his bills; for it is less desirable that he should encourage unlimited expectations than that he should contribute to increase the sense of security among the industrial classes.

Along with successful capitalists, political economists were celebrated as the true philanthropists. 'Their philanthropy may indeed take a different form from vulgar charity', wrote the contributor to the *Westminster Review*, 'but it is a difference not between hardness and benevolence, but between scientific and unscientific ways of being benevolent. . . . It is not political economy on the one side, and the Christian religion on the other', but rather knowledge versus ignorance.[109] Ellis agreed: 'The economist . . . with his more comprehensive intelligence and his

[105] In S. Smiles's view employers must set a good example, without being patronizing (*Thrift* (London, 1886), 179, 192–210).

[106] P. Joyce, *Work, Society and Politics: The Culture of the Factory in Later Victorian England* (Brighton, 1980), 138. See Samuel Greg's description of how he attempted in his cotton mill to prevent 'benevolence being poisoned into a fountain of moral mischief' (*Two Letters to Leonard Horner, Esq., on The Capabilities of the Factory System* (London, 1840), 26). Cynics might argue that the paternalists hoped to encourage self-reliance but not so much as to foster true independence and upward mobility (see B. Hilton's review of D. Roberts, *Paternalism in Early Victorian England* (New Brunswick, NJ, 1979), in *Historical Journal*, 24 (1981), 771).

[107] Blaikie, 'Collisions', 710–12. For further discussion of this dilemma, Garnett, 'Gold and the Gospel', 353–5.

[108] W. Ellis, *Education as a Means of Preventing Destitution* (London, 1851), 81–2.

[109] 'Political Economy', *Westminster Review*, 84 (1865), 119, 128. *The Economist*, too, believed that money was a far more reliable indicator of obligation than 'benevolence or hospitality' ('The Morality of Trade and of Law', *The Economist*, 23 June 1855, pp. 671–2).

more considerate benevolence, feels that it is his duty to care for a future as well as for the present race of labourers.'[110]

Education, in particular, would achieve far more than any quantity of philanthropic endeavour—or so the political economists believed. 'The really well-trained, educated, and intelligent', declared Chadwick, bore distress better than the ignorant: 'they are the last to come upon charitable relief lists, and the first to leave them. They are most easily helped.'[111] But, before the working man could be educated, members from the higher social orders who were trying to help him also needed educating, if they were really to 'do good'.

Ironically, it was the misapplication of their beloved principle of competition which particularly worried the stern advocates of political economy. They feared that a kind of 'Gresham's Law' might be operating, whereby bad charities drove out the honest ones. Medical missions, in particular, attracted criticism for their alleged discouragement of thrift.[112] Admittedly, as Brian Harrison puts it, 'philanthropists, like entrepreneurs, were seen as undertaking society's risk-taking free of charge—as pioneering philanthropic inventions with the ingenuity and energy which also inspired their commercial innovations'.[113] But while to some Victorians this development was a cause for rejoicing, others worried at the high price being exacted from society. For competition, the merits of which were usually trumpeted, seemed to some 'political economists' to be decidedly out of place in the sphere of philanthropy, where its effect was to set up rivalries between organizations seeking to outbid one another by an ostentatious display of ambition and generosity. As Spencer noted, the evil was often 'intensified by sectarian competition'.[114] Charles Trevelyan agreed: every religious sect 'distrusts, more or less, the method of the rest, and all distrust the political economists', he complained.[115]

It was because she had feared that an unchecked growth of organized benevolence might take place that the youthful Harriet Martineau had broadly opposed *all* philanthropy, as well as calling for the abolition of the poor law:

If the abuses of the pauper system were abolished, and the wisest of all possible measures substituted, its operation would be impaired if the public persisted in giving alms and maintaining soup charities, and other well-meaning institutions which do little but harm.

---

[110] Ellis, *Education*, 136.

[111] E. Chadwick, 'Address on Economy and Trade', *Transactions of the National Association for the Promotion of Social Science, 1864*, 80.

[112] K. J. Heasman, 'The Medical Mission and the Care of the Sick Poor in Nineteenth-Century England', *Historical Journal*, 7 (1964), 238.

[113] Harrison, 'Philanthropy and the Victorians', 229–30. Harrison also notes that two aspects of philanthropic work often conflicted, fund-raising, and expert knowledge of the subject matter: 'entrepreneurs' might be highly competent in the former, but have 'erroneous' views about the latter (ibid., 243).   [114] Spencer, *Principles of Ethics*, in id., *Synthetic Philosophy*, ii. 383.

[115] R. Humphreys, *Sin, Organised Charity and the Poor Law in Victorian England* (Basingstoke, 1995), 53.

Why devote so much money to charity, she had asked, when a 'truly effectual benevolence' would work instead for the reduction of taxes, the direct cause of most suffering and misery?[116]

In *Cousin Marshall* Martineau was prepared to make an exception to this harsh rule only in the case of 'the relief of sudden accidents and rare infirmities': charitable work which was unlikely to lead to an increase in dependency.[117] It was precisely this kind of doctrinaire approach to social problems which had earlier caused the pious Chalmers to worry over the danger of demoralizing the Scottish people by providing them with their Bibles *gratis*: 'the habit of purchasing is extinguished, and this society of ours, like the institution of the poor rates, leaves the people of the land in greater want, and poverty, and nakedness than ever'.[118]

But the abolitionist approach to philanthropic work, like the parallel campaign to achieve the total abolition of all publicly funded poor relief, was largely abandoned by the 1830s, no doubt because it seemed to fly in the face of both morality and prudence. Indeed, the 1830s and 1840s saw a massive expansion of philanthropic provision, at a time when expenditure on the poor law was more or less steadily falling. In London alone, 279 charities were founded in the first half of the century, another 144 in the 1860s.[119] Hence the disquiet being expressed in the 1860s and 1870s.

What was to be done about a development apparently so replete with peril? Some questioned the current mania for 'societies' and 'associations'. Even Cobden had probably not needed the help of the Anti-Corn Law League when he set out to achieve free trade, argued one contributor to the *Westminster Review*: voluntary reform of all kinds would run much more smoothly if individuals fell back on their own unaided judgement.[120] Archbishop Whately set a sterling example in this respect, since, according to an admirer, 'he abhorred systematic charity, like an ultra-political economist as he was'. Whately's daughter concurred, writing that her father gave generously to the necessitous, not on a system, but 'on the spur of the occasion, called forth by peculiar instances of want and peculiar calls for sympathy'.[121]

However, most critics of the excesses of philanthropy wanted the organizations responsible for them to be, not so much *abolished*, as *more intelligently administered*, with a view to preventing their members rushing out, unprepared, into encounters with the poor. From the establishment of Visiting Societies in the 1840s through to the Charity Organization Society (COS), founded in 1869, there was thus a constant emphasis on the importance of *training*. By the end of the century this

[116] H. Martineau, 'On the Duty of Studying Political Economy', in id., *Miscellanies*, 2 vols. (Boston, 1836), i. 275–6, 279, 281.   [117] Martineau, *Cousin Marshall*, 130.
[118] Cited in M. T. Furgol, 'Chalmers and Poor Relief: An Incidental Sideline?', in A. C. Cheyne (ed.), *The Practical and the Pious: Essays on Thomas Chalmers (1780–1847)* (Edinburgh, 1985), 121.
[119] Humphreys, *Sin, Organised Charity and Poor Law*, 52.
[120] 'Philanthropy of the Age', 451.
[121] [H. Merivale], 'Archbishop Whately', *Edinburgh Review*, 120 (1864), 405; E. J. Whately, *Life and Correspondence of Richard Whately, DD* (London, 1875), 246–7.

often meant the inculcation of the kind of skills (case work, for example), which we now associate with the profession of social worker. But for most of the Victorian period, reformers concerned themselves less with vocational training, in the modern sense, than with fostering an appropriate social *attitude*. 'We shall . . . never get the desired reform in charitable almsgiving', thought Chance, 'until every aspirant for holy orders has to pass an examination in the principles which under-lie all *true* charity, before he is admitted to the ministry.'[122] In other words, he wanted charitable work, as much as public policy, to be grounded in the prin-ciples of political economy (though kept quite separate from any kind of sectarian proselytism).

Octavia Hill, one of the founders of the Charity Organization Society, held clear views about what this entailed. In her opinion, the time was approaching when 'gifts' were beginning 'to back up insufficient wages, like the oudoor relief system under the old poor-law'. The supply of 'necessaries' to the poor, she argued, was undermining their self-reliance and 'simply making a present to employers by low-ering wages'. The answer was to devote 'not money, but thought and time, and knowledge, and sympathy, and love, to the poor'.[123] Indeed, the more that class divisions in the larger cities widened as a result of residential segregation and social zoning, the more important it seemed that these face-to-face meetings were organ-ized through systematic home visiting and other contrived attempts at 'the prac-tice of neighbourliness', undertaken by properly trained charitable workers.

What political economists meant by a proper training was learning to exercise an iron control over one's emotions. Spencer never tired of expounding this theme. Greg, too, thought that there was a fundamental distinction between

two classes of philanthropists—the feelers and the thinkers—the impulsive and the systematic—those who devote themselves to the relief or the mitigation of existing misery, and those who, with a longer patience, a deeper insight, and a wider vision, endeavour to prevent its recurrence and perpetuation by an investigation and eradication of its causes.[124]

Again like Spencer, Greg found the whole question of charitable provision an agonizing one: 'To the conscientious and the thoughtful the path of philanthropy is one of briars and thorns.' But one field of endeavour recommended itself to him as doing good 'without the violation of any moral principle or economic rule', and that was 'the providing and pointing out of safe and profitable investments for the savings of the frugal and industrious among the humbler classes':

It combines all the requisites and avoids nearly all the prohibitions which mark out the legitimate path of philanthropic aid. It interferes with no individual action: it saps no

---

[122] W. Chance suggested the desirability of passing an examination in the first Report of the 1834 Poor Law Commission and in the Goschen Circular, among other things (*Treatment of the Poor*, 164).

[123] O. Hill, 'The Importance of Aiding the Poor without Almsgiving', *Transactions of the National Association for the Promotion of Social Science, 1869*, 592, 592–3. On Octavia Hill, J. Lewis, *Women and Social Action in Victorian and Edwardian England* (Aldershot, 1991), 24–82.

[124] 'English Socialism', in Greg, *Essays on Political and Social Science*, i. 461.

individual self-reliance. It prolongs childhood by no proffered leading-strings: it valetudinarizes energy by no hedges or walls of defence, no fetters of well-meant paternal restriction.[125]

THRIFT AND SELF-HELP

Greg's polemic shows that, to quote Prochaska, 'the distinction between a philanthropic society and a mutual aid society is less clear cut than is sometimes assumed'.[126] Linking both types of organization were the premises of political economy. After all, the primary moral taught by political economy was the importance of helping the poor and the disadvantaged in ways which promoted self-reliance and discouraged dependency. Earlier in the century Mrs Marcet had criticized unsystematic charity, blaming it for causing more poverty than it cured, but she had gone on to recommend private philanthropy which took the form of encouraging thrift—in other words, the establishment of benefit clubs, friendly societies, and savings banks, all of which were nurseries of 'prudential habits'.[127] Most plebeian friends of political economy agreed—even if, like Francis Place, they wanted working-class improvement to be self-generated, not imposed from above by Evangelical bullying.[128]

Yet most political economists and the popularizers of their creed inclined to the view that the habit of thrift was not innate but would have to be cultivated. 'Wise economy is not a natural instinct, but the growth of reflection, and often the product of experience', wrote Smiles. 'Prodigality is much more natural to man', and so manual workers had to 'be trained in good habits'.[129] To inculcate the values of providence and thrift thus became Smiles's main mission in life.[130]

By mid-Victorian times the gospel of self-help had generated its own parables and homilies, which, unconsciously no doubt, mimicked those of organized religion, among them exemplary tales of redemption, featuring former wastrels and drunkards who had later become paragons of thrift.[131]

However, perhaps because the likelihood of backsliding among the poor seemed so great, even the promotion of thrift was pursued with some caution. Collectivist

[125] 'Investments for the Working Classes', ibid., 389–90. See H. Spencer's similar observations in *Social Statics, or The Conditions Essential to Human Happiness Specified* (London, 1868; first pub. 1850), 356–7.

[126] Prochaska, *Voluntary Impulse*, 30. Similarly Finlayson, *Citizen, State, and Social Welfare*, 44.

[127] Marcet, *Conversations*, 148–50, 155.

[128] B. Harrison, 'Two Roads to Social Reform: Francis Place and the "Drunken Committee" of 1834', *Historical Journal*, 11 (1968), 295.

[129] Cited in P. Johnson, 'Class Law in Victorian England', *Past & Present*, 141 (1993), 164. The same applied to gambling, drinking, and divorce (ibid., 168). See, too, Smiles, *Thrift*, 2.

[130] Smiles's classic encomium on providence is to be found in *Self-Help: With Illustrations of Conduct and Perseverance* (London, 1910; first pub. 1859), 345–52.

[131] Thus the President of the CWS regaled the Royal Commission on Labour in 1892 with an edifying tale of a heavy drinker who had been 'saved' after his wife had become a member of the store (P. H. J. H. Gosden, *Self-Help: Voluntary Associations in the 19th Century* (London, 1973), 206).

expressions of 'self-help', like trade unionism, naturally incurred suspicion. Hence Martineau, while praising co-operative stores, denounced trade unions as a 'tyranny', 'a social anomaly almost incredible in England', and 'a calamity well-nigh intolerable' to capitalists and labourers alike.[132] Friendly societies enjoyed a better reputation with the political economists and even with Herbert Spencer,[133] but the fact that these bodies often met in public houses and had rituals involving communal drinking stood as a blot against their name.[134]

By contrast, savings banks, with their individualistic rhetoric of self-help, were almost universally praised, uniting, as they did, 'evangelicals with classical economists, and social reformers with advocates of retrenchment'.[135] Gladstone preened himself over his part in setting up the Post Office Savings Bank, a measure which, far from being a piece of 'grandmotherly legislation', had, he said, 'help[ed] the people by enabling the people to help themselves'.[136] All the same, it is significant that for most of the nineteenth century the withdrawal terms which the Post Office Savings Bank laid down for its mainly working-class depositors were distinctly harsher than those facing the middle-class customers of the clearing banks: the aim being, as one minister admitted, 'to withdraw from men the temptation of spending their money by interposing a little difficulty and delay in getting it out of the banks'.[137] Moreover, as in all mutual-aid organizations, there was a risk that fraudulent officials might disappear with the funds.[138]

Yet, compared with other forms of philanthropic activity, savings banks seemed to present little danger. But the mere existence of such facilities by itself was not enough. For it was generally recognized that some sort of line had first to be drawn between those capable of pulling themselves up by their boot-straps and those who were so 'helpless' that they required—perhaps had an entitlement to—support

---

[132] [Martineau], 'Co-operative Societies in 1864', *Edinburgh Review*, 120 (1864), 420. Smiles, too, was worried about trade unions, though he admired other forms of working-class association, esp. the co-operative movement, building societies, freehold land societies, savings banks, and, with reservations, friendly societies (*Thrift*, 99–122).

[133] 'Specialized Administration' (1871), in Spencer, *Man Versus the State*, 302.

[134] Finlayson, *Citizen, State, and Social Welfare*, 77. But some commentators urged middle-class philanthropists not to worry too much about the association of mutual aid societies with public houses (C. Hardwick, 'Friendly or Benefit Societies', *Transactions of the National Association for the Promotion of Social Science, 1858*, 640–1). See also H. Perkin, *The Origin of Modern English Society 1780–1880* (London, 1969), 381–4, and S. Cordery, 'Friendly Societies and the Discourse of Respectability in Britain, 1825–1875', *Journal of British Studies*, 34 (1995), 35–58.

[135] Eastwood, 'Men, Morals and Machinery', 201–2.

[136] H. C. G. Matthew, *Gladstone: 1875–1898* (Oxford, 1995), 321. These remarks were made to railway savings bank depositors on 19 June 1890.

[137] The Minister was Ayrton (Johnson, 'Class Law', 151–4, esp. 154). Moreover, Eastwood shows that originally government effectively subsidized savings banks by guaranteeing a rate of interest above market level, the idea being that working-class investors would have a stake in their native land. But the economy drive of Joseph Hume brought about a lowering of the rate in 1828, and it then fell *below* the market rate in the 1840s—an intriguing case of 'economy' clashing with, and overcoming, 'providence' ('Men, Morals and Machinery', 203–4).

[138] Finlayson, *Citizen, State, and Social Welfare*, 77. This was perhaps a partial reason for Greg's preference for the life assurance company as a channel of thrift (*Essays on Political and Social Science*, i. 406).

from others.[139] Even Harriet Martineau showed a genuine sympathy for the Lancashire workmen hit by the cotton famine, and never suggested that their problems could be solved by self-help or the application of the lessons of political economy![140] But where was the line to be drawn?

Chalmers had earlier suggested that it perhaps did no harm to provide gratuitous treatment for the sick, since such provision would not encourage others to fall ill;[141] on the other hand, the incentive to insure against the possibility of sickness might be undermined if such help were provided too easily. Moreover, on which side of this all-important dividing line did other disadvantaged groups fall—widows and the mentally ill, for example? No consensus ever emerged on such questions. What did become clear, however, was that self-help and thrift would never entirely displace philanthropic activities of a more conventional kind. Hence the importance of purging charitable work of the grosser 'abuses' that currently disfigured it.

THE COS AND THE LIMITATIONS OF
VICTORIAN PHILANTHROPY

We have seen that 'scientific' charity frowned on the mere doling out of goods and money. Instead, the better-off were urged to develop habits of self-reliance among the poor, where possible. But this could not simply be done by *preaching*. It also required the socially privileged to set a good example and to cultivate 'friendly' relationships with the poor through direct personal contact.

The harsh treatment often meted out to the dependent poor by those who viewed social problems in this way was lightly camouflaged by the use of a traditionally 'religious' language. 'It is the old truth, on which Christianity is based, of "Love one another"', gushed Smiles. 'Giving money, blankets, coats, and such-like, to the poor—where the spirit of sympathy is wanting,—does not amount to much.'[142] But how much real love and sympathy was involved in the activity of bodies like the COS?

The paradoxical nature of the COS's welfare work has been fully documented elsewhere, but its bearings on the subject-matter of the present chapter deserve some discussion. Convinced that poverty (inadequate income) would be reduced to very small dimensions once the scourge of 'pauperism' (a diseased mental condition) had been vanquished,[143] the activists of the COS gave priority to rooting

[139] G. H. Ford analyses the way this features as one of the moral dilemmas in *Bleak House* in 'Self-Help and the Helpless in Bleak House', in R. H. Rathburn and M. Steinmann (eds.), *From Jane Austen to Joseph Conrad* (Minneapolis, 1958), 92–105.

[140] C. Midgley, *Women against Slavery: The British Campaigns, 1780–1870* (London, 1992), 183.

[141] See below, p. 194.   [142] Smiles, *Thrift*, 180–1.

[143] Significantly, the COS, according to R. Humphreys, held Chalmers in awe, some of its members seeing him as a 'spiritual ancestor' (*Sin, Charity and Poor Law*, 58).

out various abuses, such as mendicancy on the part of the recipients and financial misconduct on the part of charity fund-raisers. Unfortunately, in the process, the spirit of 'charity' (in the Christian sense of 'love') was inevitably lost.[144] More fundamentally, the utilitarian assumptions of the COS generated a concern for 'scientific philanthropy', which threatened to turn its agents into bureaucratic administrators, a transformation which made a mockery of the claim that 'charity' was somehow superior to the cold and impersonal state.[145]

Perhaps, too, 'organized charity' was something of a contradiction in terms. Voluntary societies, however slackly they were run, ministered to the emotional needs of their members and subscribers, who wanted to maintain the maximum of operational autonomy: they were thus unlikely to welcome attempts by 'outsiders' (whether bodies like the COS or government) to 'organize' them in the light of some rational, centralized plan. The chaos of the charitable world against which the utilitarians railed was an essential part of its appeal.

In other ways, too, many subscribers refused to observe the ground rules being laid down by those who advocated a more 'scientific' charity. The COS wanted assistance directed exclusively towards the 'deserving' poor. In so far as this meant helping those who were willing and capable of regaining an 'independent' life, it required the most efficient possible distribution of resources—that is to say, the concentration of help on recipients who would tangibly *benefit* from help. But it was very often the most pitiable cases which attracted attention: and these tended to be poor people who were the least 'deserving', judged by the utilitarian ethic which defined the goodness or badness of an action solely by its *consequences*. As one experienced observer of charitable activities in Liverpool shrewdly commented: 'The more acute the sense of guilt, the more numerous, degraded and desperate must be those to be served, till workers came to vie with each other in seeking out hitherto unknown degrees of horror and difficulty in their work, to the consternation of organized charity.'[146]

Worse still, there remained a residual sympathy for certain categories of social outcast, in particular 'travellers' and tramps, despite the attempt by 'experts' to bring these 'deviants' under community control. Goschen told Parliament that 'it would be impossible effectively to deal with the most pressing evils of vagrancy unless the public guarded themselves against the exercise of indiscriminate charity'.[147] Unfortunately, the romanticization of the 'traveller's' lifestyle by writers

---

[144] Even O. Hill complained that the tone of the COS was getting 'harder, the alienation deeper'. She wanted charity to be 'a witness of real love' (Lewis, *Women and Social Action*, 45).

[145] W. Bagehot had foreseen this process when he had earlier written: 'Philanthropy must submit to the machinery of philanthropy' ('Faith and Business', *Saturday Review*, 7 (1 Jan. 1859), 10–11, in N. St J. Stevas (ed.), *Collected Works of Walter Bagehot* (1986), xiv. 217). Evangelical advocates of 'systematic benevolence' made a heavy use of analogies with business life in their addresses to their lay audience (Garnett, 'Gold and the Gospel', 349).

[146] M. B. Simey, *Charitable Effort in Liverpool in the Nineteenth Century* (London, 1951), 105.

[147] 13 May 1870, cited in T. J. Spinner, *George Joachim Goschen: The Transformation of a Victorian Liberal* (Cambridge, 1973), 31.

like George Borrow and Robert Louis Stevenson may have encouraged the very opposite.[148]

But, more important than all these factors combined, was the failure of political economy and utilitarianism to discredit the older ethical codes which insisted on the intrinsic value of certain kinds of philanthropic behaviour, quite regardless of their *consequences*. In fact, no account of Victorian philanthropy is adequate which cannot find a place for the play of kindness, compassion, and disinterested 'good deeds'. Many of these philanthropists and would-be philanthropists were alienated by the constant reiteration of the dangers of pauperization: one lady said that she 'scarcely dared to offer "a cup of beef-tea to a sick neighbour for fear of demoralizing him and offending against the canons of political economy and the organisation of charity" '.[149]

Rejecting the orthodoxies of the day, many middle-class philanthropists drew instead upon an eighteenth-century concept of 'benevolence' which celebrated spontaneous acts of kindness to others. Here the hero was the humane, kindly gentleman, memorably presented by Dickens in a variety of fictional guises (from Mr Pickwick to John Jarndyce), in all of whom generosity was a kind of natural gift, an instinct of goodness. (Mill's later commendation of 'altruism' was superficially similar, but, in reality, very different, because it involved a measure of *calculation*.)

This doctrine of benevolence could be combined without too much difficulty with a latitudinarian Bible-based Christianity, as the case of Dickens shows. The parable of the Good Samaritan, which dominated the moral imagination of Victorian Christendom, clearly underlies a novel like *Bleak House*, in which the touchstone of character is how its fictional actors treat the crossing-sweeper Jo, who, viewed rationally, is quite beyond the reach of *social* redemption (though, despite his religious 'ignorance', he is eminently redeemable by God's grace).

Admittedly many Christians, especially Roman Catholics and those Protestants affected by the Evangelical Revival, had difficulty in going along with the Dickensian view of the world because they believed strongly in Original Sin and so could accept no portrayal of human nature which assumed or even hinted at man's innate goodness. To them, charity was, instead, a *duty*—a duty owed to one's conscience and to God. Yet they, too, rejected the proposition that charity was a rational venture aimed at promoting the greatest happiness of the greatest

---

[148] M. A. Crowther, 'The Tramp', in R. Porter (ed.), *Myths of the English* (Cambridge, 1992), 109. Crowther shows that severe vagrancy policies had little effect, partly because they seemed to conflict with specific Christian teachings, but also because they 'upset sensibilities cultivated within the literary tradition'.

[149] Cited in Finlayson, *Citizen, State, and Social Welfare*, 54, 79. See also Humphreys, *Sin, Charity and Poor Law*, 111. George Eliot was therefore drawing attention to a conundrum very familiar to many well-to-do women of her age in her depiction of Dorothea sitting down in the library 'before her particular little heap of books on political economy and kindred matters, out of which she was trying to get light as to the best way of spending money so as not to injure one's neighbours, or—what comes to the same thing—so as to do them the most good' (*Middlemarch*, Penguin edn. (London, 1965; first pub. 1871–2), ch. 83, p. 863).

number.[150] Indeed, even a Christian economist like Bishop Sumner later had doubts about the morality of the New Poor Law, calling on his readers to remember that 'we are every one members one of another' (Romans 12: 5) and intimating that some Christians, in their enthusiasm for political economy, had neglected more well-tried methods for dealing with the results of sin, such as the obligation on the rich to minister to the poor.[151]

Yet *some* Evangelicals continued to protest that they saw no contradiction between the dictates of Christianity and the principles of political economy. Theirs was a religion which emphasized divine 'justice', rather than divine 'benevolence', and this facilitated an ideological accommodation with the new materialistic creeds. Here, for example, is Chalmers providing his own peculiar gloss on Christ's miracles of mercy:

The thing more particularly to be remarked upon is, the difference of procedure between His relief of want and His relief of disease. There are only two recorded instances of His having fed the people miraculously when they happened to be overtaken with hunger—for on a third occasion He declined so to gratify their wishes (John 6: 26, 27). There are innumerable instances, on the other hand, of His having cured the diseased miraculously, and not one instance recorded of His having declined one application of it. . . . A public charity for the one tends to multiply its objects—because it enlists the human will on the side, if not of poverty, at least of the dissipation and indolence which leads to poverty. A public charity for the other will scarcely, if ever, enlist the human will on the side of disease.[152]

This way of interpreting the Christian Gospel was later carried over into the COS by some of those Anglicans who supported its programme. 'The marvel of Christ's life is his repression of his powers of benevolence', declared one clergyman, in a sermon delivered at Oxford University in 1868.[153]

But the very extravagance of such claims suggests one reason why they did not carry total conviction even with those to whom they were addressed. It would take much more than this to convince a Bible-reading people that Jesus Christ was a Benthamite Utilitarian born before His time! The writings of the pioneering feminist, Bessie Raynes Parkes, illustrate the point. 'It has been asserted that "the sermon on the mount forms the basis for the soundest system of political economy" ', she wrote, 'but so far does this appear to me to be from the truth, that it is the discrepancy between the two dispensations which constitutes one great difficulty

---

[150] A conundrum for the Christian was whether one could act benevolently towards someone for whom one felt no affection (T. A. Roberts, *The Concept of Benevolence: Aspects of Eighteenth-Century Moral Philosophy* (London, 1973), 111).

[151] Extract from Sumner's *A Charge Addressed to the Clergy of the Diocese of Chester* (London, 1844), cited in Soloway, *Prelates and People*, 187–8. Significantly, the address was made against the backdrop of Chartist disturbances.

[152] Chalmers, 'Political Economy of the Bible', 47. Greg preferred to argue the case on secular grounds, but he too invoked the divine command 'that if any man would not work, neither should he eat' as proof that political economy was merely 're-echoing Christianity and common sense' (Greg, 'English Socialism', in *Essays on Political and Social Science*, i. 477). Similarly Spencer in *Man Versus the State*, 83.   [153] Cited in Jones, *Outcast London*, 247.

of legislation, and renders the conscientious discharge of private charity a matter of much care.'[154] Significantly, Parkes invoked 'the story of the good Samaritan, who, when he saw that the stranger was wounded, did not stop to speculate on the best way of rendering roads secure from thieves, but *went to him and bound up his wounds*'.[155]

An awful warning of another way in which political economy, taken literally, could destroy natural affection was provided by Dickens through his portrayal of that unspeakable paragon of self-improvement, Bitzer, in *Hard Times*. Bitzer, it will be recalled, had prudently contrived to incarcerate his elderly mother in the workhouse:

It must be admitted that he allowed her half a pound of tea a year, which was weak in him: first, because all gifts have an inevitable tendency to pauperize the recipient; and, secondly, because his only reasonable transaction in that commodity would have been to buy it for as little as he could possibly give, and sell it for as much as he could possibly get; it having been clearly ascertained by philosophers that in this is comprised the whole duty of man—not a part of man's duty, but the whole.[156]

As a satire on utilitarianism and political economy, *Hard Times* is often unfair. But it is none the less emotionally persuasive.

CONCLUSION

Despite being fashioned to deal with a rather different sort of problem from the one confronting the urban areas of mid-Victorian Britain, in its own terms the New Poor Law did more or less 'work': for a whole generation the receipt of public assistance was stigmatized, many poor people were deterred from going on to the rates at all, and the burden of local taxation was rigorously contained.

But for many middle-class Victorians, the New Poor Law had disquieting aspects which they only tolerated because of the existence of a vast network of philanthropic bodies capable of dealing in a more merciful and discriminating way with human disadvantage and suffering.

Yet the pessimistic Greg had a point when he protested that, unless the 'lessons of political economy' were also brought to bear upon *private* philanthropic provision, the objectives of the New Poor Law would never be realized. One possible

---

[154] B. R. Parkes, *Essays on Woman's Work* (London, 1865), 225. One of the most difficult of all questions in modern society, she added, was 'in what way the principle of benevolence, having its root in the principle of Christianity, can be brought in well and wisely as a counteractive of the evil or the selfish dealings of men?' (ibid., 226–7).

[155] Ibid., 102. On the revealing differences between the evangelical concept of 'systematic benevolence' and the ideology of the COS, see Garnett, 'Gold and the Gospel', 355–6.

[156] C. Dickens, *Hard Times*, Chapman & Hall edn. (n.d.; first pub. 1854), bk. 2, ch. 1, p. 373.

'solution', favoured by Harriet Martineau and others, was the total 'abolition' of
all alms-giving, but this was a completely impractical notion—hence the quest
for a 'scientific' approach to charity which would check the harmful impulses of
'capricious benevolence'. But, as we have seen, those who set out to 'organize'
charity in this way found themselves thwarted and frustrated at every turn: powerful traditions, doctrines, and vested interests stood in the way of their plans. As
a consequence 'scientific philanthropy' was never seriously put into practice.

This was not merely the result of a 'failure of the will'. For insoluble dificul-
ties lay at the heart of the entire enterprise. How could the voluntary principle be
reconciled with the attempt to plan philanthropic provision? And how could the
short-term emotional needs of donors be gratified without imperilling the long-
term interests of the community? Finally, which categories of disadvantaged person could be helped without undermining work incentives, savings incentives, and
family values?

Presumably the relentless propagandizing in favour of 'independence', self-reliance,
and thrift must have done something to influence the behaviour patterns of
the poor. At any rate, the late Victorian expansion of the various self-help organizations like friendly societies can be cited as proof that a significant sector of
the working population had 'internalized' the values of a popularized political
economy.[157]

But self-help was crippled by its own inherent inconsistencies. Given the
assumption that prudence and forethought did not come naturally to the working
classes, these values had to be deliberately propagated: the poor had to be persuaded, cajoled, even, if need be, coerced into habits of self-reliance. However,
self-reliance once having been achieved, it became very difficult for middle-class
moralists to control the expressions which it then took. In theory 'mutual aid'
seemed an admirable way in which relatively poor people pooled their resources
in order to avoid reliance upon the state. But, as the history of both trade unionism and of the co-operative movement shows, such ventures could, over time,
develop in ways which directly threatened the values and the practices of a market society.

This raises a wider dilemma. The voluntary society, by acting as a barrier to
the expansion of the state, was meant to strengthen and broaden the sphere of
market transactions. But, as the case of education demonstrates, 'voluntaryism'
often ended up challenging important commercial interests: after all, the subsidized schooling provided by the big voluntary societies directly competed with
the work of the totally autonomous fee-paying 'adventure schools'.[158]

There are other ways in which the competition of self-help organizations sometimes damaged 'producer interests'. For example, GPs strongly disliked friendly
societies (for which many doctors were obliged to work) because they saw these

[157] For a sceptical view see P. Mandler, in P. Mandler (ed.), *The Uses of Charity: The Poor on Relief in the Nineteenth-Century Metropolis* (Philadelphia, 1990), 1–2, 15.
[158] G. R. Searle, *Entrepreneurial Politics in Mid-Victorian Britain* (Oxford, 1993), Ch. 7.

bodies as manifestations of 'patient power' threatening their own hard-won earnings.[159] The co-operative store posed an even greater threat. Co-operation was widely admired for its role in freeing working-class customers from the snare of 'tick' and providing an outlet for modest savings. But, of course, the appearance of such stores in a particular town was very bad news indeed for many small shopkeepers.

However, commercial interests tended to have the last laugh. For by the closing decades of the nineteenth century, profit-making businesses like the industrial insurance companies had started to undermine the position of 'self-help' organizations and voluntary charities alike. To the apostles of thrift, this was a somewhat worrying trend. For, as Finlayson notes, although industrial insurance societies claimed that their collectors 'helped to foster habits of providence and self-reliance among the poorest sections of the community, least able, or likely, to be provident, . . . the real purpose of the visit was a business one; and the regularity of the visit pointed to the assumption that without it, no savings would be made'.[160]

Indeed, the final irony is that, undermined by this sort of commercial competition, the older self-help organizations, like friendly societies, continued to atrophy, until ultimately, as José Harris observes, a reluctant state was dragged in to serve the many social needs which the market, by itself, had proved incapable of meeting.[161]

[159] A. Digby, *Making a Medical Living: Doctors and Patients in the English Market for Medicine, 1720–1911* (Cambridge, 1994), 51, 122.   [160] Finlayson, *Citizen, State, and Social Welfare*, 64.
[161] Harris, *Private Lives*, 12.

9
Principle, Profits, and Patriotism

FREE TRADE AND MORAL PROGRESS

From the very start, political economy had had a cosmopolitan bias. In his theory of comparative advantage David Ricardo had asserted that the 'advanced' nations were becoming mutually interdependent at an economic level as a result of the international division of labour, and it seemed that this development was also being furthered by the internationalization of the *investment* markets.

Mrs Marcet was therefore speaking for most political economists when she made 'Mrs B.' tell Caroline that 'instead of struggling against the dictates of reason and nature, and madly attempting to produce everything at home, countries should study to direct their labours to those departments of industry for which their situation and circumstances are best adapted'. Her precocious pupil draws the 'correct' lesson: 'The more I learn upon this subject, the more I feel convinced that the interests of nations, as well as those of individuals, so far from being opposed to each other, are in the most perfect unison', she observes.[1]

Henry Reeve explained in greater detail in the *Edinburgh Review* why economic changes were transforming relationships between states in this advantageous way:

Mechanical ingenuity has rendered many of the restrictions and limitations of former times physically impracticable, since railroads and electric telegraphs cannot be placed under the laws of blockade. Nation is united to nation by a thousand ties of interest and intimacy never known before. . . . The enormous development of modern trade, the infinite varieties and facilities of intercourse, and the ramifications by which every want of human society is supplied, have rendered it physically impossible to act otherwise than by general rules founded on public principles.[2]

An apologist of the new factory system like Andrew Ure never doubted that industrialization acted as a force for world peace:

Nations, convinced at length that war is always a losing game, have converted their swords and muskets into factory implements and now contend with each other in the bloodless but still formidable strife of trade. They no longer send troops to fight on distant fields but

---

[1] Mrs Marcet, *Conversations on Political Economy: In Which The Elements of That Science Are Familiarly Explained* (London, 1839; first pub. 1816), 359, 363.

[2] [H. Reeve]: 'The Orders in Council on Trade during War', *Edinburgh Review*, 100 (July 1854), 193–4, 218.

fabrics to drive before them those of their old adversaries in arms, and to take possession of a foreign mart.[3]

Cobden eloquently expounded a similar thesis, predicting that free trade would break down the barriers separating nations—'barriers, behind which nestle[d] the feelings of pride, revenge, hatred, and jealousy, which every now and then burst their bounds, and deluge[d] whole countries with blood'.[4] This vision of free trade inexorably leading to the establishment of international peace and harmony became elevated in Cobden's mind into a quasi-religion. Writing in his diary on 14 June 1860, he declared the central tenet of his faith: 'It is only by the greater diffusion of knowledge in the science of political economy, that men will cease to covet their neighbour's land, from the conviction that they may possess themselves of all that it produces by a much cheaper, as well as honester, process than by war and conquest.'[5] 'No free trade in cutting throats', was Cobden's slogan.[6]

John Stuart Mill, too, invoked the theory of comparative advantage in support of free trade, laying particular emphasis on its *moral* desirability: free trade, he argued, was not only 'the principal guarantee of the peace in the world' but also, more generally, provided 'the great permanent security for the uninterrupted progress of the ideas, the institutions, and the character of the human race'.[7] This was the orthodox claim. Indeed, to an extreme individualist like the young Herbert Spencer, putting restrictions on commercial intercourse could *never* be justified: 'The moral law', he writes in *Social Statics*, 'is cosmopolite—is no respecter of nationalities: and between men who are the antipodes of each other, either in locality or any thing else, there must still exist the same balance of rights as though they were next-door neighbours in all things.'[8]

Not surprisingly, then, free trade formed an element, albeit a subordinate one, in the ideology of the Peace Society.[9] The belief that free trade would bring with it not only financial benefits but also world peace similarly lay at the centre of the creed professed by the Anti-Corn-Law League, one of its publicists, Cooke Taylor, declaring that he found it 'an invariable rule that free and equitable trade always

---

[3] A. Ure, *The Philosophy of Manufactures* (1835), cited in J. D. Y. Peel, *Herbert Spencer: The Evolution of a Sociologist* (1971), 196.

[4] Speech of 28 Sept. 1843 (J. Bright and J. E. T. Rogers (eds.), *Speeches on Questions of Public Policy by Richard Cobden, MP* (London, 1908; first pub. 1870), i. 40).

[5] J. Morley, *The Life of Richard Cobden* (London, 1896; first pub. 1881), ii. 302–3.

[6] Cited in F. H. Hinsley, *Power and the Pursuit of Peace: Theory and Practice in the History of Relations between States* (Cambridge, 1963), 97. W. D. Grampp, *The Manchester School of Economics* (London, 1960), 118.

[7] Cited in O. Kurer, 'John Stuart Mill on Government Intervention', *History of Political Thought*, 10 (1989), 472.

[8] H. Spencer, *Social Statics, or The Conditions Essential to Human Happiness Specified* (London, 1868; first pub. 1855), 326.

[9] S. Conway, 'The Politicization of the Nineteenth-Century Peace Society', *Historical Research*, 66 (1993), 275.

was a bond of peace and that the spirit of monopoly—particularly when it assumed the shape of territorial aggrandizement, became the frequent source of wars'.[10]

Many Christian theologians, including Malthus and Chalmers, viewed free trade as part of God's plan for the world, interference with which was a kind of impiety;[11] and a Christian missionary like David Livingstone, writing in the aftermath of the Repeal of the Corn Laws, could scornfully refer to the earlier trade restrictions as 'a remnant of heathenism'.[12] Livingstone and Bishop Samuel Wilberforce, too, celebrated commerce both as an agency for diffusing the Gospel among uncivilized peoples and also as an instrument for the opening-up of new overseas markets for British goods like cotton clothing. In this way, as one historian notes, many Victorian Churches 'marketed their gospel to the world as the commodity of surpassing value, confident that providence would honour a faithful performance of their duty with a substantial return on their investment'.[13]

Nevertheless, it is important to remember that the 'imperialism of free trade' was supposed to be an entirely *peaceful* process. So while missionaries denounced the Opium Wars for having dealt a severe blow to public morality,[14] most political economists were equally insistent that warfare was not only a crime against humanity but also folly: in the modern world, they believed, fighting could serve no rational purpose.

Henry Maine, it will be recalled, had contended that individual freedom and progress were guaranteed by acceptance of the principles of political economy, which in their turn rested on the prior establishment of 'free contract' and the institution of private property.[15] From this he deduced that a people like the Irish peasantry, lacking a developed sense of contract, were incapable of reaching informed judgements or of managing their own affairs intelligently.[16]

But it was more common for Victorian theorists to use Maine as 'proof' that in the modern world violence and compulsion were destined to be supplanted by discussion, bargaining, and consent—in international as well as in industrial relations. 'Man, in his originally barbarous state, took everything he wanted from his neighbour by force or fraud, the strong always preying on the weak', argued one contributor to the Social Science Congress; but 'civilization introduced the principle of exchange of commodities in opposition to this predatory instinct; and society advanced in proportion as exchange triumphed over force.'[17]

---

[10] Cooke Taylor to Cobden, 29 Nov. 1842, cited in R. F. Spall, jun., 'Free Trade, Foreign Relations, and the Anti-Corn-Law League', *International History Review*, 10 (1988), 409. This article provides a good resumé of the free traders' attitude to international relations.   [11] See Ch. 2.

[12] B. Stanley, ' "Commerce and Christianity": Providence Theory, The Missionary Movement, and the Imperialism of Free Trade, 1842–1860', *Historical Journal*, 26 (1983), 82.

[13] Ibid., 76.   [14] Ibid., 79–80.

[15] G. Feaver, *From Status to Contract: A Biography of Sir Henry Maine 1822–1888* (London, 1969), 55, 215. See Ch. 3.   [16] Ibid., 216. Maine later became an ardent Unionist.

[17] T. J. Dunning, 'On the Principle of Exchange in Relation to Lock-Outs', *Transactions of the National Association for the Promotion of Social Science, 1866*, 795. This formed part of the speaker's case about the illegitimacy of lock-outs.

Those who subscribed to this two-stage model of historical evolution therefore wanted the realm of tradition, custom, and hereditary privilege to be replaced by a fluid, competitive social order in which merit and achievement would receive their due reward without reference to accidents of birth or status, and they were confident in their belief that a world dominated by contractual relationships formed by supposedly 'free', autonomous citizens was morally preferable to the values of the old, discredited 'feudal' civilizations.[18]

This is what Walter Bagehot had in mind when he coined his famous phrase, 'government by discussion'. In optimistic mood, Bagehot upheld the superiority of trading over warfare, seeing the transition from the one to the other as an aspect of 'social evolution'. 'As the trade which we now think of as an incalculable good' was in earlier times thought to be 'a formidable evil and destructive calamity', so, he argued, 'war and conquest, which we commonly and justly see to be evils now, [were] in that age often singular benefits and great advantages'. Yet in present-day societies, Bagehot contended, progress was no longer achieved by warfare but 'by the competition of customs' and by an ever-widening commercial intercourse.[19]

Unfortunately, not only were some benighted foreigners yet to acquire these 'enlightened' views on matters of trade, but it seemed that even British ministries contained self-styled free traders who could not entirely be trusted to live up to their principles. So the mid-Victorian generation was well aware of the paradox later to be dramatized by Norman Angell: war might well be 'the Great Illusion', but that did not mean that it would not necessarily occur.

THE EVIL OF 'MILITARISM'

Many Radicals felt these anxieties with particular acuteness. In their view, the trouble with contemporary Britain was that the state was out of kilter with civil society: its political institutions, which still bore the imprint of a militaristic past, were thus quite inappropriate to a people largely employed in peaceful commercial competition.

Forgetting the dependence of British trade 'upon the stability afforded by the European state system',[20] doctrinaire free traders maintained that government had no role whatever to play in commercial policy: 'To commerce, the fostering care of statesmen and legislators is a withering blight . . . Freedom, perfect and entire, freedom is all that is wanted', declared the *Anti-Corn-Law League Circular* in October 1839. Commercial codes and treaties

[18] The links between political economy and a severe judicial interpretation of contract (with its concomitant, the decline of equity) deserve closer attention. A good starting point is W. R. Cornish and G. de N. Clark, *Law and Society in England 1750–1950* (London, 1989), 201–2, 215–20.

[19] W. Bagehot, *Physics and Politics* (Boston, Mass., 1956; first pub. 1872), 156.

[20] Spall, 'Free Trade', 431. Spall sees this as 'a basic inconsistency in League philosophy on foreign relations'.

have always contained within them the seeds of war and misery; remove the barriers which these have raised, and the nations of the earth, like separate bodies, having chemical affinity for each other, would speedily rush together and, in a common union of interest, would forget their hatreds and animosities.[21]

Cobden went further, claiming that those who held political power and social influence—members of the court, the great landowners, army and navy officers, and so on—had a sinister interest in fomenting international discord and war, and that many ordinary citizens, brought up to reverence 'feudal' values, were simply out of touch with commercial reality and the 'truths' of political economy. Herbert Spencer agreed: 'If, for the last four or five centuries', he wrote, 'the civilized world, instead of having been engaged in invasions and conquests, had directed its attention to the real sources of wealth—industry and commerce, science and the arts—long since would our nobility have found that they were mere drones in the hive, and long since would they have ceased to glory in their shame.'[22] That is why the Radicals so passionately wanted to 'modernize' the country's system of government and administration with the aim of bringing it into line with its expanding capitalist economy.

Should the armed services themselves be overhauled? Political economists boasted that their 'science' had much to teach statesmen on how 'to determine the real cost to a nation of any given military system'.[23] But what in practice did this mean?

Adam Smith had expressed a preference for a standing army rather than a part-time militia because (unlike earlier republican theorists) he wanted the commercial principle of the division of labour to be applied to government and thought professional armies were less likely to disrupt ordinary economic activity.[24] Smith's argument was that, as the art of war became increasingly technical and 'mechanical', its practice necessarily devolved upon a particular class of citizens with the time and inclination to make it their full-time occupation:

Into other arts the division of labour is naturally introduced by the prudence of individuals, who find that they promote their private interest better by confining themselves to a particular trade, than by exercising a great number. But it is the wisdom of the state only which can render the trade of a soldier a particular trade, separate and distinct from all others. A private citizen who, in time of profound peace, and without any particular encouragement from the public, should spend the greater part of his time in military exercises,

[21] Ibid., 417.

[22] H. Spencer, 'The Proper Sphere of Government' (1843), in J. Offer (ed.), *Herbert Spencer: Political Writings* (Cambridge, 1994), 23.

[23] T. E. Cliffe Leslie, *The Military System of Europe Economically Considered* (Belfast, 1856), 3. Leslie was Professor of Jurisprudence and Political Economy at Queen's, Belfast.

[24] J. Robertson, 'The Legacy of Adam Smith: Government and Economic Development in the *Wealth of Nations*', in R. Bellamy (ed.), *Victorian Liberalism: Nineteenth-Century Political Thought and Practice* (London, 1990), 25.

might, no doubt, both improve himself very much in them, and amuse himself very well; but he certainly would not promote his own interest. It is the wisdom of the state only which can render it for his interest to give up the greater part of his time to this peculiar occupation.[25]

A professional army, raised on voluntary lines, certainly had much to commend it, not least its cheapness: it required no large body of private soldiers to pay, and officers could be attracted by appeals to 'honour' rather than through lavish cash incentives—indeed, the low salary would discourage gentlemen from taking to soldiering with the intention of profiting from it, which was another of its advantages.[26] Conversely few political economists had a good word to say for the obvious contemporary alternative, a Continental-style conscript army. Such an institution, Cliffe Leslie claimed, would result in 'the loss of the skilled labour, invention and productive enterprise that [were] dissipated and directed from their natural channels, and of the steady habits of application to business that [were] not permitted to be formed in early life'.[27] And Samuel Laing, who strongly disliked what he had seen of the Prussian Army during his foreign travels, declared that 'a public trained in the habits of military life [were], also, bad consumers, as well as bad producers' because 'as consumers, they [did] not bring into the home market the almost fastidious and finical taste for, and estimate of fine workmanship, superior material, and perfect finish, which [was] a principal element in the superiority of one manufacturing country over another'.[28]

However, some significant voices were raised in opposition to the prevalent orthodoxy. Leading members of the Manchester School, for example, pointed out that if Britain really did wish to engage in Continental wars, there were some advantages in raising an army by conscription, since this would force the middle classes in industrial areas like West Yorkshire to fight in the wars for which they were excitedly clamouring.[29] But Cobden, of course, continued to see war as a relic from more barbarous times, to be avoided at almost any cost. Moreover, like other Radicals, he feared that professional armies, whether composed of volunteers or of conscripts, all tended to acquire an unhealthy influence over government, which they then used to benefit their own personnel at the expense of the community they claimed to be defending. The youthful Spencer went even further, arguing that military forces of any kind were *unnecessary* since an effective resistance to aggression could be organized without resorting to government agencies![30]

---

[25] A. Smith, *An Inquiry into the Nature and Causes of The Wealth of Nations*, ed. E. Cannan (Chicago, 1976; first pub. 1776), bk. 5 ch. i, p. 219.

[26] This is the main theme of Leslie's *Military System*, which cites the theories of N. Senior (*An Outline of the Science of Political Economy* (New York, 1965; first pub. 1836), 214–15), who in turn draws on Smith (*Wealth of Nations*, bk. 1, ch. 10, p. 122).

[27] Cliffe Leslie, *Military System*, 11.

[28] S. Laing, *Notes of a Traveller, on the Social and Political State of France, Prussia, Switzerland, Italy and Other Parts of Europe* (London, 1854; first pub. 1842), 76.

[29] G. R. Searle, *Entrepreneurial Politics in Mid-Victorian Britain* (Oxford, 1993), 100.

[30] Spencer, 'Proper Sphere of Government', 25.

THE CRIMEAN WAR

The Crimean War, however, suggested that not all free-trade Radicals could be relied upon to stick to their principles at times of patriotic excitement. For in 1854, many Radicals who believed in principle that fighting was an economically irrational activity nevertheless embraced war against the hated Tsarist regime of Russia, which they saw as a moral crusade. Even Harriet Martineau, pleased though she was over the exposure of aristocratic inefficiency, broadly supported the Allied cause.[31] This schism within Radicalism can be traced back to the French Invasion scare of 1852,[32] but its existence was dramatized two years later when Cobden, Bright, and other members of the Manchester School were deserted by many of those whom they had once regarded as their closest supporters.

Cobden had made the mistake of underestimating the strength of conventional patriotism, which drew upon values like chivalry, courage, duty, and self-sacrifice which still possessed, if not a universal, at least a very wide appeal. Throughout the eighteenth century the 'country' opposition had upheld a 'republican' concept of 'virtue', derived from a study of classical literature, which condemned the mere pursuit of wealth as productive of effeminacy, luxury, and corruption; against these evils the sole protection was said to be the public-spirited citizen, willing and able to defend the *patria* by force of arms.[33] Such values, suitably updated, were now being disseminated by the modernized public schools, and even the Radicals were not immune to their appeal.

Moreover, there was another version of 'nationalism', one rooted in an explicit rejection of Cobden's philosophy of the market, to which some mid-Victorian Radicals subscribed. Thus, according to George Dawson: 'A nation ha[d], as it were, a life and being in, but higher than, the individuals. It was a truer symbol, Britannia, seated with her spear and helmet, on the penny-piece, than to hold that a nation should be but a mere bundle of individuals.'[34] Many Radicals also took pride in the British legacy of 'freedom' and wished to extend it, if need be by armed intervention, to peoples like the Poles, the Hungarians, and the Italians, as they struggled against injustice and alien oppression.[35]

Given the existence of this range of attitudes to foreign policy, it is hardly surprising that, once the Crimean War had broken out, the anti-war Radicals found themselves (unfairly) denounced as vulgar materialists, indifferent to anything that could not be measured in pecuniary terms, and even as traitors. For example, Sturge, the Quaker pacifist, a corn factor by trade, had his motives held up to ridicule, especially over the Peace Society slogan, 'War and Dear Bread' (corn factors, of course, had long enjoyed the reputation of being war profiteers).[36]

---

[31] V. K. Pichanick, *Harriet Martineau: The Woman and Her Work 1802–76* (Ann Arbor, 1980), 207–8.   [32] M. Taylor, *The Decline of British Radicalism, 1847–1860* (Oxford, 1995), 217.
[33] Preface.
[34] Cited in M. C. Finn, *After Chartism: Class and Nation in English Radical Politics, 1848–1874* (Cambridge, 1993), 168.   [35] Ibid., 91. Also, Taylor, *Decline of British Radicalism*, ch. 6.
[36] A. Tyrrell, *Joseph Sturge and the Moral Radical Party in Early Victorian Britain* (London, 1987), 213. Sturge found himself attacked by Harriet Martineau and denounced by a former employee.

Critics also pointed out the seeming illogicality of Bright's willingness for disputes between the two sides of industry to be 'fought out' to a conclusion, while denying *nations* this mode of resolving their differences. Bright's views were in defiance of the moral instincts of most of his fellow-countrymen, who inclined to the opposite solution.[37]

The case of Samuel Smiles shows how attractive patriotism could still be to many Radicals and one-time Radicals. True, Smiles warned that 'a nation [might] be very big in point of territory and population, and yet be devoid of true greatness'. 'The people of Israel were a small people', he observed, while, conversely, the mighty Roman Empire had eventually collapsed because of the corruption of its people. But Smiles also believed that, 'as there is an ignoble, so is there a noble patriotism—the patriotism that invigorates and elevates a country by noble work'.[38] Under the threat of a French invasion (which Cobden thought pure scaremongering got up by Britain's war party), Smiles enrolled in the Volunteers, a movement which he welcomed for providing a training school in disciplined citizenship. Significantly, Wellington and other military leaders find a place in the pantheon of 'heroes' celebrated in *Self-Help*.

Was this merely yet one more example of Smiles's 'apostasy'? Or was there a more deep-seated incompatibility between the doctrines of economic individualism and self-help, on the one hand, and conventional patriotism, on the other? Indeed, what precisely did political economy suggest that a government should do in the sphere of commercial policy, once war had broken out with a country which had formerly been a close trading partner? This dilemma, which had stirred up considerable controversy during the latter stages of the Napoleonic Wars, resurfaced with a vengeance after Britain had sent its expeditionary force to the Crimea in 1854.

POLITICAL ECONOMY AND THE CONDUCT OF WAR

Once war had broken out, there were three positions which upholders of orthodox political economy could logically adopt, and all three had their backers.

The first and simplest strategy was neutralism or pacifism, the avoidance of war at almost any sacrifice. During the Napoleonic Wars such a line had been pursued, not only by many popular Radicals, but also by Brougham, leader of the Philosophical Whigs and a staunch devotee of political economy. In the course of

---

[37] S. Hollander, *The Economics of John Stuart Mill*, ii, *Political Economy* (Oxford, 1985), 978. This gibe was made by the *Examiner*, reporting on a socialist conference at which Bright had denounced Tribunals of Commerce and Courts of Arbitration as 'impertinences'. For a sympathetic view of the 'rationality' of Cobden and Bright, A. J. P. Taylor, *The Trouble Makers: Dissent Over Foreign Policy 1792–1939* (London, 1957), 56–62.   [38] S. Smiles, *Character* (London, 1871), 28–9.

his spirited campaign against the Government's Orders-in-Council,[39] Brougham drew attention to the many unacceptable consequences of war: gaols filled with debtors, 'poor houses crowded with objects of mendicity', and some counties in which, so great was the distress, people were 'driven even to insurrection'.[40] Brougham thus thought peace desirable on political, economic, and moral grounds: categories which seem not to have been clearly separated in his mind.

Later, during the Crimean War, John Bright attacked government policy in a series of speeches which similarly blended economic and moral arguments. Posing as a 'commercial' Member, he vividly brought the costs of war home to the attention of the House:

Every man connected with trade knows how much trade has suffered, how much profits in every branch of trade—except in contracts arising out of the war—have diminished, how industry is becoming more precarious and the reward for industry less, how the price of food is raised, and how much there is of a growing pressure on all classes, especially upon the poorest of the people.[41]

The Manchester School also believed that the United States, with its negligible expenditure on armaments and its foreign policy based upon non-interventionism, would before long emerge as the most powerful trading nation in the world—at Britain's expense. 'Do you believe', Bright warned,

that when the capital of the greatest banking-house in Lombard Street can be transferred to the United States on a small piece of paper in one post, that the imposition of 75,000,000l of taxation over and above the taxation of an equal population in the United States will not have the effect of transferring capital from this country to the United States, and, if capital, then trade, population, and all that forms the bone and sinew of this great empire?

Such set-backs, Bright added, were likely to be permanent, since 'when a nation has gone a step backwards it is difficult to restore it to its position; if another nation has passed it in the race, it is almost impossible for it to regain the ground it has lost'.[42]

Yet, even in Radical circles, Bright's was a minority position.[43] For, granted that there was substance in his warnings, it remained unclear what in practice a government could reasonably be expected to do if the actions of another power faced it with a situation where the only alternatives were the surrender of vital national interests, on the one hand, or going to war, on the other.

---

[39] On this issue, see C. W. New, *The Life of Henry Brougham to 1830* (Oxford, 1961).

[40] Hansard, 2nd ser., xxi, 1101, 1115: 3 Mar. 1812.

[41] Hansard, 3rd ser., cxxxviii, 1620: 7 June 1855. In addition, by the latter stages of the war taxes had increased and the Treasury had been forced to resort to loans—considered by orthodox economists to be 'bad housekeeping'.   [42] Ibid., 1624-5.

[43] Initially Radicals had been reassured by Gladstone's 1854 budget, which seemed to demonstrate that it was possible to pursue the war in harmony with free trade principles (Taylor, *Decline of British Radicalism*, 233-4).

Hence, the second strategy, which simply accepted the occasional necessity of fighting, but treated this as an 'emergency' during which the normal dictates of political economy would have to be *suspended*. Once the Crimean War had broken out, even Reeve, despite his strong sense of the economic interdependence of all advanced commercial nations, phlegmatically argued such a case:

Whilst our fleets are equipped for foreign seas, and our troops sent forth for foreign service, with that energy which the active operations of war demand, a change of almost equal magnitude takes place in many of the internal duties of the State and of the community. The national finances are no longer regulated with strict economy, but a lavish though inevitable expenditure dissipates in a few months the savings of former years, and the hope of further reductions in taxation. The laws of trade are to a certain extent suspended, and every national interest becomes subordinate to the one paramount object of distressing and weakening the enemy.[44]

Some MPs deduced from this that the sooner the war ended, the better for all concerned, but that, in the interim, the utmost ruthlessness should be shown in its prosecution. During the Crimean War, W. Henry Watson, MP for Hull, an important shipping and commercial centre, denounced any suggestion 'that blockade should be entirely done away with, and that free trade should be allowed in time of war as in time of peace': 'Let us have either one thing or another. Certainty was essential to commerce on occasions like the present. Either let us have free trade, or let there be a blockade, and let it be strictly enforced.'[45]

The Economist broadly agreed. War, it felt, was at best 'a hateful and horrible alternative', which a country should only take with great reluctance on occasions when it had a 'just and necessary cause'. However, it continued:

having been forced into it, it is our bounden duty to take whatever steps are the most likely to bring it to an early close. And better by far that we should submit for a short time to more severe sacrifices, than allow it to linger on for an indefinite period. Humanity and policy alike dictate that course which, at whatever cost or temporary inconvenience, will soonest rescue us from the horrors of war and restore to us the blessings of peace.[46]

Others were prepared to say outright that in wartime *all* considerations of economic advantage should be discarded in favour of the higher imperative of patriotism. Hence, when they read the Order-in-Council of April 1854 which, in effect, legalized trade with Russia except through the blockaded ports, many businessmen reacted with amazement and dismay.[47] The mercantile MP, R. Porrett Collier, MP for Plymouth, urged war *à l'outrance*:

Did any man suppose that they were to enter upon a war without incurring serious injury to themselves? Were they to go about their affairs in the usual manner, to pass their Reform

[44] [Reeve], 'Orders in Council', 193.   [45] Hansard, cxxxvi, 1704, 1706: 20 Feb. 1855.
[46] *The Economist*, 30 Sept. 1854, p. 1062. This piece may well have been written by its editor, James Wilson. Reeve later repeated these sentiments ('Orders in Council', 225).
[47] O. Anderson, *A Liberal State at War: English Politics and Economics During the Crimean War* (London, 1967), 255. The French also reacted with consternation.

Bills, and busy themselves with matters of external legislation, and if they had any surplus cash to spare expend it in crumpling up the Emperor of Russia? If they were not prepared for the sacrifices of war they ought never to have undertaken it. If they were not prepared for the sacrifices of war they had better conclude peace at once, and on whatever terms they could make. But should it be said of this country that it hesitated not to sacrifice the lives of the best and bravest of its children in the cause of liberty, that it could contemplate with comparative calmness the calamities of the battle-field and the hospital, but that there was one thing it could not contemplate without agony and despair, and that was a rise in the price of tallow? . . . If they were only prepared to carry on the war in that spirit, they were rightly called a nation of shopkeepers, and they had better stay at home [Mr Bright: Hear, hear!].[48]

Lord Albermarle, presenting a petition from the merchants, manufacturers, and bankers of Bristol, conceded that political economy and war were 'incompatible with each other' since 'war implie[d] a negative of all trade'.[49] Very well, then: for the duration of the national emergency, the interests of trade would have to be subordinated.

Mockery of penny-pinching businessmen came from the most unlikely sources. The *Illustrated London News*, normally a mouthpiece for the commercial community in its struggle against privileged aristocrats, joined in the hue and cry:

Can we do nothing but make railroads and cotton goods? Are we indeed a nation of miserable bunglers? And are we so demoralized by a long peace—so soaked and sodden in the fat of commercial speculation—that we have lost the robust and manly virtues of our ancestors?

The paper went on to sneer at those who would 'sacrifice the national honour for the sake of a miserable percentage on a running transaction',[50] while *Punch* published a piece, 'the Russian Pig Market', which was directed at war profiteers who had the audacity to trade with the hated enemy while gallant soldiers were dying on the battlefield.[51]

These attacks on 'unpatriotic' traders seem to prefigure the much more virulent outcry which later broke out, in somewhat similar circumstances, during the First World War. But, of course, mid-Victorian governments did not have the competence, even if they had had the desire, to enforce a measure like the Trading With The Enemy Acts of 1914. Short of pulling out of the war entirely, the Aberdeen ministry, and Palmerston's government which followed it, consequently had no real alternative but to adopt the third strategy, which sought to combine an effective prosecution of the war with a modified version of 'business as usual'.

But what would this mean in practice? J. L. Ricardo, a railway director and financier (and, incidentally, a nephew of the famous political economist), wrote a book entitled *The War Policy of Commerce* (1855), the substance of which he also

[48] Hansard, cxxxvi, 1670: 20 Feb. 1855. By profession Collier was a lawyer, though he represented a mercantile constituency. See, too, the remarks of Thomas Alexander Mitchell, MP for Bridport, himself a Russian merchant (ibid., 1678).   [49] Ibid., cxxxvii, 1860: 27 Apr. 1855.
[50] *Illustrated London News*, 17 Feb. 1855, pp. 145–6.   [51] *Punch*, 6 Oct. 1855, p. 139.

expounded from his seat in the Commons. Ricardo had a simple solution to all difficulties: let commercial activities proceed as usual without any attempt at government interference, even if this meant the continuation of the flourishing trade between Britain and Russia; for past experience, he believed, had shown that attempts at regulation always tended to damage British commercial interests quite as much as those of the 'enemy'. As Olive Anderson notes, such was the rigidity of Ricardo's free-trade faith that it led him to deprecate the very notion of economic warfare.[52] Meanwhile, Cliffe Leslie was urging a total abandonment of the policy of blockade: 'let us seek in political science instead of in the usage of former wars our views of national policy and international law', he implored.[53]

However, as so often happened, enthusiastic amateurs in political economy were more doctrinaire than the true 'experts'. Nassau Senior, for one, accepted that questions of government policy could not be settled by reference to general economic principles.[54] And another professor of political economy, George Rickards, declared: 'It is quite possible to injure the future and lasting interests of the nation by an over-strained dread of subjecting posterity to obligations'; after all, it was better 'to succeed by a mortgaged patrimony than to an exhausted estate'.[55]

In her masterly study of the impact of the Crimean War on British society and politics, Anderson claims that the ministerial ethos of mid-Victorian Britain was, in general, pragmatic and empirical. Whatever its subsequent reputation, the Crimean War, she insists, was in no way a 'Free Trade war'.[56] At the same time, she also emphasizes the point that the language in which the war's rights and wrongs were debated owed much to memories of what had happened during the struggle against Napoleon.

In an attempt to breach Napoleon's Continental System, the British Government of the day had passed a series of highly controversial Orders-in-Council, which forbade all commercial transactions with French ports or with ports under enemy control—except to merchants who had been given a licence dispensing them from the general prohibition.

The objections against such a licensing system were threefold. First, as George Canning, then speaking from the backbenches, declared in the momentous Commons debate of 1812, restrictions for the purpose of retaliation might in certain circumstances be acceptable, but not if they were intended as a way of prosecuting commercial rivalries: they 'were most perfect as they approached towards a belligerent measure, and receded from a commercial one'.[57] Canning suspected the Government of using the Orders in an attempt to achieve the long-term crippling of the French economy, an objective which those versed in political economy thought both illegitimate and likely to prove counter-productive. Brougham

---

[52] Anderson, *Liberal State at War*, 257.   [53] Ibid., 257.   [54] Ibid., 187.
[55] G. K. Rickards, *The Financial Policy of War: Two Lectures on the Funding System and on the Different Modes of Raising Supplies in Time of War* (London, 1855), esp. 73.
[56] Compare R. C. Binkley, *Realism and Nationalism, 1852–1871* (New York, 1935), 176–7.
[57] Hansard, 2nd ser., xxi, 1140, 1147: 3 Mar. 1812.

felt little confidence in ministers in their 'capacity of tradesmen' and said that he 'trembled' for the consequences 'of leaving our commerce to such management'.[58]

Second, not content with these strictures, Brougham went on to denounce the Orders-in-Council on more general grounds. For example, he warned that they might well end up embroiling the United Kingdom with hitherto friendly 'neutral' states: a warning seemingly borne out with the outbreak of the Anglo-American War of 1812. (James Cropper, the Liverpudlian merchant who later became a leading figure in the anti-slavery movement, had similar fears.)[59]

But there was yet another consideration. Brougham went to great pains to demonstrate that the Orders-in-Council stood wide open to corruption and evasion: they had, he claimed, established a system which had begun in forgery, was being continued by perjury, and would end in enormous frauds.[60] In short, alleged Brougham, British merchants were being debauched and demoralized:

I shall soon be ashamed of the title which I hope still to boast, a representative of free, independent, honest British traders. . . . Let it be no longer said that England, whose merchants in former and happier times were held in universal estimation for probity and honour, have forfeited a character by the preservation of which alone they can claim a just right to the privileges of humanity.[61]

The responsible minister put up a stout defence of his department. But posterity long remembered the charges of Brougham's indictment.

It was almost certainly with the earlier debate of March 1812 in mind that Edward Cardwell, the main architect of the Aberdeen Coalition's wartime measures, distinguished between measures which were protectionist and those that were retaliatory in intent. Cardwell favoured the use of blockade, but he dismissed a system based on customs regulations as a 'suicidal policy'.[62] This became government policy when on 11 April 1854 the Privy Council rejected licensing as likely to foster fraud, privilege, and monopoly.[63] On this score at least, J. L. Ricardo found it possible to support the ministry. Warning against any return to the 'miserable economical doctrines displayed in the Orders in Council' of 1806–7, he agreed with Cardwell that it was 'inexpedient . . . to create competition to ourselves, and that it was far easier to lose a market for our goods than it was to recover it again'.[64]

However cautious and pragmatic his conduct, Cardwell nevertheless declared his reluctance to discard entirely the 'lessons of political economy', even in the midst of a protracted war. 'If doctrines be true, then the more important the crisis, the more serious the consequence of departing from them, the more you are

---

[58] Ibid., 1107–8.
[59] D. B. Davis, *Slavery and Human Progress* (New York, 1984), 180. On Cropper, see Ch. 4.
[60] Hansard, 2nd ser., xxi, 1110: 3 Mar. 1812.   [61] Ibid., 1114.
[62] Ibid., cxxxvi, 1690–1: 20 Feb. 1855.   [63] Anderson, *Liberal State at War*, 254–5.
[64] Hansard, cxxxvi, 1701–2: 20 Feb. 1855. Reeve, too, argued that the earlier licensing system had led to the conferral of privileges which were against the wider public interest ('Orders in Council', 217–18).

bound in reason and prudence to adhere to them', he declared: 'How can you show that that which is commercially injurious would be politically expedient?'[65] As Henry Reeve observed, the challenge was thus to find a way of accommodating the country's commercial interests without their being allowed to shape wider policy:

The measures we have now passed in review are calculated to promote our national interests in the widest sense by keeping up that industrial activity and commercial prosperity which are the principal resources of the country—by enabling us liberally to apply our national wealth to the contest—and by removing many of those vexatious and oppressive restrictions which aggravated the evils of war to this community, and served to embroil us with the other Powers of the world.[66]

The Allied governments had accordingly agreed 'to leave the operations of trade as much as possible to their natural course, subject only to the positive operations of war'—in other words, the blockade would continue, but there would be no licences.[67]

As with the handling of the Drink Question,[68] the drawing-up of a policy of wartime economic management was gradually settled on a compromise basis. High-flown principles were often invoked, but often they served as a cloak concealing the play of self-interest. Many of the merchants who spoke out in the parliamentary debates certainly had ulterior motives. For example, during the Napoleonic Wars, protestors against the Orders-in-Council were often MPs representing commercial or industrial districts which stood to benefit directly from a change in policy.[69] The same thing happened during the Crimean War.[70]

As for governments, they faced a difficult dilemma. They had to strike an appropriate balance between diplomatic and military considerations. Too strict a blockade risked drawing neutral states into the war on the enemy side and might damage the country's commercial interests—interests which, as Reeve had observed, underpinned Britain's position as a global power. On the other hand, too lenient a policy risked misunderstanding even in the relatively sophisticated environment of the House of Commons, and few senior statesmen were prepared to draw down upon their heads the accusation that they were undermining the dignity and the interests of the nation for the 'low' purpose of commercial advantage.

What the Crimean War showed was that though there was a theoretic case for applying the principles of political economy to the task of economic management in war, in practice this was impossible without so affronting the moral sensibilities of MPs and voters as to endanger the existence of government itself. The fact

---

[65] Hansard, cxxxvi, 1696–7: 20 Feb. 1855.   [66] 'Orders in Council', 225.
[67] Ibid., 218.   [68] See Ch. 10, pp. 250–2.   [69] Hansard, 2nd ser., xxi, 1162: 3 Mar. 1812.
[70] One backbench MP, Viscount Duncan, had the frankness to admit that he was trying to advance the economic welfare of his Scottish constituents (ibid., cxxxvi, 1704: 20 Feb. 1855). On the self-interest accompanying the apparent patriotism of the Russian merchants, Anderson, *Liberal State at War*, 256–7.

that ministers like Cardwell and James Wilson,[71] both devotees of political economy, felt obliged to temper theory with expediency is particularly telling, illustrating as it does that reasons of public morality forbade the wholesale importation of axioms from that science into the consideration of major issues of war and peace. As we will see in the next chapter, there were other aspects of public life which had similarly to be placed in a kind of 'reserved area'.

THE INTERNATIONAL MARITIME QUESTION

After the ending of the Crimean War the issue of whether the dictates of political economy could be combined with an effective defence of national interests lost much of its urgency. But one facet of this problem came into even sharper relief with the postwar signing of the Paris Declaration (1856), which defined the rights of belligerent powers to seize private property at sea belonging to an enemy power or to ships visiting enemy ports.[72] Britain, as the world's dominant naval power, had always sought maximum freedom to exploit its advantage by using the weapon of blockade. But to many political economists, and to some prominent members of the shipping interest (for example, the Liverpool Chamber of Commerce), this was a barbaric practice which needed to be abolished for reasons both of morality and economic expediency. So strongly did Cobden feel on the subject that, aided by old Anti-Corn Law League activists like Henry Ashworth, he devoted much of the remaining years of his life to agitating for a change in international law.[73]

The international maritime question whipped up emotions to fever pitch. Defenders of Britain's traditional methods of warfare felt that if the reformers had their way, vital national interests would be jeopardized. But to many businessmen and those steeped in political economy, the liability of private property at sea to seizure and confiscation seemed to be an affront to modern civilization.[74] It reminded John O'Hagan of the old savage practice of enslaving prisoners of war.[75] The critics were all the more horrified when British ministers stubbornly defended this 'abuse' despite the public protests of the United States government. Britain's official stance, alleged Henry Ashworth, ran counter to 'the enlightened character of the age, the more humane spirit of the times, and our high Christian professions', as well as being against the interests of the commercial community.[76]

---

[71] There were, however, policy differences between the two men (Anderson, *Liberal State at War*, 263–4).   [72] Hinsley, *Power and the Pursuit of Peace*, 232–3.

[73] Searle, *Entrepreneurial Politics*, 153–6.

[74] e.g. 'The Laws of War', *Westminster Review*, 94 (1870), 386.

[75] J. O'Hagan, 'Should the Private Property of Citizens of a Belligerent State be Protected from Capture at Sea?', *Transactions of the National Association for the Promotion of Social Science, 1861*, 752.

[76] H. Ashworth, 'International Maritime Law and Its Effects Upon Trade', ibid., 1864, 597.

True, the Paris Declaration did bring about what some saw as a small step towards a more enlightened future by abolishing the right of privateering. But others, like O'Hagan, argued that if the plunder of private property continued to have the sanction of the law of nations, then such dirty work was best left to the privateer:

It was, no doubt, a detestable trade—an odious mixture of the gambler and the pirate. Still, for the ignoble task of tracking, hunting down, and seizing some defenceless brig or schooner, the privateer, nerved by selfish desire, and undisturbed by any higher aim, was, I say, more likely to be effective than the regular cruisers of the State with whom such employment is only casual, to whom it must be contemptible, and who of course are always liable to be called away to some more honourable duty.[77]

Ashworth agreed: the effect of the Paris Declaration, he grumbled, was 'merely to dispossess the privateers of the privilege they had heretofore enjoyed, and to secure to government ships a monopoly of the plunder'.[78] Given all the dangers, Ashworth claimed that henceforward the only safe policy for a British government to pursue was one of rigid non-intervention.[79]

Cobden took a wider view. Britain, as a global economic power, could only exercise its right of blockade at the risk of damaging its own interests, he declared: 'of what use . . . is a weapon of offence which recoils with double force on ourselves?'[80]

Free trade, in the widest definition of the term, means only the division of labour, by which the productive powers of the whole earth are brought into mutual co-operation. If this scheme of universal dependence is to be liable to sudden dislocation whenever two governments choose to go to war, it converts a manufacturing industry, such as ours [*sic*], into a lottery, in which the lives and fortunes of multitudes of men are at stake.[81]

Once again, Cobden was identifying the claims of humanity with security of property. But the British government was no more impressed by this line of reasoning than they were by his approach to foreign policy in general.

THE NOTION OF A 'JUST WAR'

International relations in the nineteenth century differed somewhat from the other spheres of policy examined in this book. Usually the direct application of market principles to a particular policy area provoked complaints that, in the search for cheapness and profits, moral 'goods' were being ignored or sacrificed. But this was not really the case with questions of peace and war since, as we have seen, the proponents of universal free trade held out the prospect of world peace, the

---

[77] O'Hagan, 'Private Property of Citizens', 751.
[78] Ashworth, 'International Maritime Law', 597.   [79] Ibid., 603.
[80] R. Cobden, 'A Letter to Henry Ashworth, Esq.' (1862), in *The Political Writings of Richard Cobden* (London, 1886), 386.
[81] Ibid., 389. See also Cobden to Sumner, 23 Jan. 1862, in J. A. Hobson, *Richard Cobden: The International Man*, ed. N. Masterman (London, 1968; first pub. 1919), 26).

brotherhood of man, and the enrichment of human life through the mutually beneficent intercourse of peoples and of nations—all morally attractive ideals. If the free traders found themselves under criticism at all, it was as 'theoreticians' ignorant of the complexities of international relations or as credulous and sentimental philanthropists prepared to take risks with vital national interests in pursuit of their ideals.

Even so, the Cobdenites successfully held the moral high ground so long as they could plausibly claim that commercial progress and free trade were agencies of human betterment. But what if the principle of competition should prove to be at variance with moral duty? A revealing episode took place in 1850 when Cobden took part in an agitation against the Tsar's attempts to raise a loan in London; the proceeds of this loan, alleged the critics, would shore up a tyrannical regime and foster a bellicose Russian foreign policy. But Cobden's stance laid him open to the reiterated charge that he was violating his own free-trade principles: ' "Why won't you let us lend our money in the dearest market, and borrow in the cheapest?" ', asked the critics: ' "Why not have free trade in money as well as in everything else?" '

Cobden replied that people were, of course, free to invest their money anywhere. All he was doing was asserting his right, 'as a free man in a free country', to meet his 'fellow-citizens in public assembly like the present, to try and warn the unwary against being deceived by those agents and money-mongers in the city of London who will endeavour to palm off their bad securities on us if they can'. If people chose to ignore this good advice, let them take the consequences.[82] Characteristically, though, Cobden insisted that bankrolling the Tsar would be a risky and unsound investment. In his appeal to anyone who had 'a conscience which [was] proof against one per cent', Cobden could therefore base his case 'on the ground of morality, on the ground of political economy, on political grounds, and on the ground of personal safety and security' by presenting the projected Russian Loan as a 'most nefarious attempt' on the public's 'credulity and their pockets'.[83] In this instance, then, Cobden continued to insist that, as always, morality went hand in hand with commercial prudence: violate the former and pecuniary loss would result.

However, as we have seen, the Cobdenites had much greater difficulty in squaring this particular circle when it came to deciding what to do about slavery and slave-grown produce.[84] For a while, free traders were able to unite around the desirability of the voluntary boycott, which, as one historian puts it, was 'a badge of "purity" and a mark of earnestness'.[85] But though such activities might soothe the troubled conscience, by the middle of the century it was becoming increasingly, though grudgingly, accepted that slavery might have to be *suppressed by force*

---

[82] Speech of 18 Jan. 1850 (Bright and Rogers (eds.), *Speeches by Cobden*, ii. 406).

[83] Security, he argued, depended upon the life of an individual: 'In thus lending your money, you place it upon a volcano' (ibid., 414).   [84] Ch. 4.

[85] D. Turley, *The Culture of English Antislavery 1780–1860* (London, 1991), 78.

if it were ever to disappear from the face of the earth. Hence, once the American Civil War had broken out, British abolitionists, despite being confused by the North's initial refusal to come out explicitly against slavery, rallied strongly to Lincoln's banner—especially after the issuing of the Emancipation Proclamation of September 1862.

What of the political economists themselves? John Bright had favoured the North from the start, as did Harriet Martineau who wrote editorials in its support in the *Daily News*.[86] However, Cobden for a long time refused to shift his position. Although personally detesting slavery, he continued to believe that it must be left to collapse under the weight of its own contradictions. Moreover, his sympathies in some respects inclined him to favour the 'free trade' South over the protectionist North.[87] Finally, Cobden deprecated the use of violence in the pursuit of social progress: in fact, he endorsed the South's right to secede from the Union and was dismayed by the attempt to prevent this by force.[88]

But Cobden had adopted a stance that was morally and politically impossible, and before the Civil War had ended he had come into line with Bright and mainstream Radical opinion. There had always been Radicals who argued that war might be justified in, say, overthrowing a tyrannical regime: hence the support which some Radicals gave the Aberdeen and Palmerston governments during the Crimean War. But the cause of the slaves in the American South had even greater appeal, and few British free traders could resist this call on their conscience. Yet, as time would show, Cobden had had good reason for fearing that a precedent was being set which would later be used by Radical campaigners to justify armed intervention in far less worthy causes.

CONCLUSION

Once the link was severed between free trade, non-intervention, and morality, the free traders quickly saw the ground disappear from under their feet; for their activities could then be construed as a grubby quest for personal wealth. The Cobdenite Radicals had always run the risk of being accused of spurning the patriotic virtues of bravery, gallantry, the spirit of self-sacrifice, and so on. Lord Palmerston, for example, had memorably taunted Bright during the Crimean War with calculating whether the cost of submitting to a foreign invasion would exceed the cost of fighting a war and being prepared to opt for the former if this seemed likely to produce a profit![89] Such slurs were unfair on Bright. They were also unfair on

---

[86] C. Midgley, *Women against Slavery: The British Campaigns, 1780–1870* (London, 1992), 178. Martineau stuck with the old line that abolition would increase planters' profits because free labour was more productive than the slave system (ibid., 179).

[87] Cobden to Sumner, 3 Dec. 1861, in Hobson, *Cobden*, 350.

[88] Searle, *Entrepreneurial Politics*, 156–8.

[89] J. Ridley, *Lord Palmerston* (London, 1970), 427–8.

Cobden, who probably valued free trade because he saw it as the pathway to world peace, rather than embracing world peace in the hope of material rewards. 'It may be objected that I appeal to low motives in thus dwelling upon the pecuniary view of the question', Cobden wrote privately to Sturge: 'True: but if the New Testament has failed to inspire Christians with faith in the principles of peace, I may surely be excused if I demonstrate how costly is their reliance for defence upon the spirit of war.'[90]

None the less, there was a certain plausibility in the charge that the free traders were mercenary moneygrubbers. For the Cobdenite world-view was a cosmopolitan one which celebrated the movement of goods and services across national frontiers: it vindicated the citizen's right to buy in the cheapest and sell in the dearest market, the whole world over. Investors were accorded the same freedom. Thus in discussing the propriety of sending capital abroad, McCulloch had given due weight to the power of patriotism, but he had also argued that 'the love of country' had its limits, 'the love of gain [being] a no less powerful and constantly operating principle'.[91]

Cobden would presumably have found McCulloch's formulation misleading. The apparent conflict between personal gain and national benefit, most free marketeers maintained, only applied in the short run. It was a mercantilist fallacy to believe that the increased prosperity of one country could only be achieved at the expense of another. The beauty of free trade was that it operated as a mechanism for harmoniously reconciling the material needs of peoples and individuals throughout the advanced commercial world: narrow patriotism militated against that enlarged and intelligent conception of the national interest to which the Cobdenites subscribed.

This antipathy to conventional 'patriotism' meant that the Cobdenite advocates of *laissez-faire* often seemed, 'perhaps unconsciously to themselves, to hold that it [was] the first duty of a [true] patriot to assume his Government to be in the wrong, until it [could] be absolutely demonstrated that it is in the right'.[92] But the Cobdenites contended that in the long run it was invariably the vociferous patriots who inflicted greater damage on the national interest.

Unfortunately, as in so many other spheres of policy, neither governments nor peoples could always afford to take the long-term view. Faced by, say, Tsarist aggression, it made little sense to point out that violence was ultimately self-defeating. Similarly, the proposition that all nations would benefit from peace and free trade made considerable sense at a theoretical level. But Lord Redesdale, way back in the late 1820s, had pointed to its major drawback when he observed that 'a general system of free trade [could] only be founded upon the establishment of universal and constant peace, and universal and constant good will of man to man, and [was]

[90] Cobden to Sturge, 16 Sept. 1844, *Cobden Papers*, Add Mss 43656, fo. 53.
[91] J. R. McCulloch, *The Principles of Political Economy* (Edinburgh, 1825), 385.
[92] R. Williams, 'Laissez-Faire', *Fraser's Magazine*, 1 (1870), 81.

utterly inconsistent with the present condition of mankind divided into various states, under various governments'.[93]

The Radicals were also weakened by the failure of Gladstone to share their approach to international relationships. In some respects, it is true, Gladstone was close to Cobden. Free trade, he believed, was a very 'powerful agent in consolidating and in knitting together the amity of nations'. But Gladstone linked this to a High Church view of God's plan for harmonious mutual intercourse between nations, which he sought to achieve through the 'Concert of Europe'. As Colin Matthew puts it, for Gladstone, 'foreign policy was not, as it was for the Radicals, corrupt dealings between landed castes, but rather the means by which European nations communicated for the public good'.[94] Nor did Gladstone shrink from the use of military and naval intervention, which he saw 'as a natural part of the maintenance of the civilized order of the world'.[95]

Finally, from mid-century onwards the whole climate of international relations was changing in ways which the Manchester School Radicals found disturbing. In the optimistic climate following the Repeal of the Corn Laws they could still assume that other nations would shortly follow the British precedent and seek for themselves the blessings of free trade. The Anglo-French Treaty of 1860 seemed to be a step in precisely this direction. But, as we have seen, even the Northern American States, from which much better might have been expected, had disappointed the admiring Cobden by sharply raising their tariffs in the early 1860s. Over the next three decades many Continental States followed suit, compounding the offence (in Cobdenite eyes) by increasing their expenditure on armaments.

Thus the Spencerian belief that history was moving from a social order grounded in compulsion to one grounded in peaceful commercial competition had to face up to the possibility that for years to come disastrous wars might still break out between economically advanced countries. As a rueful F. W. Hirst later remarked, what Adam Smith had not sufficiently realized was the omnipresent danger that civilized nations would apply their wealth to the machinery of destruction.[96] This was a terrifying prospect, since the wars to which such military rivalries might lead threatened to bring in their wake, not only vast human suffering, but also 'wasteful' armaments expenditure, a distortion of fiscal policy, the disruption of normal trading patterns, injury to private property, and, not least, a corruption of public morals.[97] By the 1870s the international outlook was decidedly grim.

Indeed, Herbert Spencer himself, though he continued to predict the inevitable triumph of the industrial type of civilization, conceded that in many societies no

---

[93] B. Gordon, *Economic Doctrine and Tory Liberalism 1824–1830* (London, 1979), 61.

[94] H. C. G. Matthew, *Gladstone: 1809–1874* (Oxford, 1988; first pub. 1986), 181.

[95] Matthew also points out that every Cabinet Gladstone had sat in since 1843 had dispatched a military expedition somewhere (H. C. G. Matthew, *Gladstone: 1875–1898* (Oxford, 1995), 123).

[96] F. W. Hirst, *The Political Economy of War* (London, 1915), 11.

[97] Pichanick, *Martineau*, 58.

such developmental path had occurred and that some societies might never escape from the militant stage at all. Spencer had the misfortune to live long enough to see in the unified German State a strange symbiosis of industrial society and militarism: a phenomenon which, if his theories had been true, could never have arisen.[98] Nor was this all, since, like Cobden, Spencer saw traces of the militant society even in advanced commercial countries like Britain. As Tim Gray puts it, it therefore remained unclear whether international peace really would finally establish itself through the operation of immutable law, or whether, on the contrary, there was a 'rhythm', whereby the two different types of society—the military and the industrial—alternated.[99]

The free traders suffered many disappointments during the course of the nineteenth century over their failure to implement their principles in the face of intractable difficulties. But their philosophy of international relations was more decisively discredited than any other aspect of their creed—destroyed, in fact, by the very historical processes they had once so confidently invoked.

[98] Peel, *Herbert Spencer*, ch. 9.

[99] T. Gray, 'Herbert Spencer's Liberalism—From Social Statics to Social Dynamics', in Bellamy (ed.), *Victorian Liberalism*, 126. Peel argues that, in his later writings, Spencer 'tended to take the militant/industrial distinction as non-evolutionary, one which partially cross-cuts a more evolutionary classification' (*Herbert Spencer*, 205).

10

Moral Reform

Most Christians in Victorian Britain had no difficulty in accepting that morality and law would not always coincide. For example, only the most doctrinaire Sabbatarians, including the Lord's Day Observance Society, founded in 1831, suggested that people could or even should be made moral or religious by Act of Parliament. As W. R. Greg observed, 'It is a common mistake with many excellent men, to suppose that, because any action is wicked and mischievous, it necessarily follows that it is desirable to proceed against it by legal means, or forcible repression.'[1] But neither, it was agreed, should Parliament force its citizens into immorality, nor should it create circumstances likely to encourage social behaviour widely regarded as immoral.[2]

But how, if at all, could such moral constraints be reconciled with the operation of a free market? This proved to be an acute dilemma for many Victorians, particularly for those businessmen who proudly identified themselves as convinced free traders yet who, as Christians (often but not always Dissenters), subscribed to a strict moral code of conduct. The dilemma became an acute one in the 1850s since this was when the earlier emphasis on 'moral suasion' gave ground before campaigns which aimed at legislative restriction and prohibition. As Brian Harrison puts it, 'While in some spheres in the 1850s *laissez-faire* principles seemed widely accepted, in the religious world they were being resoundingly challenged.'[3]

The 'moral reformers' of mid-Victorian Britain set out to suppress or discourage a number of 'immoral' practices: most notably, cruelty to animals, sexual vice, betting and gaming, Sabbath-breaking, and the various abuses associated with the trade in alcoholic beverages.

From the viewpoint of this book, the campaign against cruel sports can largely be ignored because the resultant controversy revolved almost entirely around the propriety and expediency of interfering in the traditional pastimes of the people.[4] It threatened no *major* vested interests—except perhaps over measures like the

---

[1] He went on to liken prostitution to 'vices, like bad temper, hatred, malice, and covetousness, which, however noxious, it is not a part of the duty of government actively to repress or punish' (W. R. Greg, 'Prostitution', *Westminster Review*, 53 (1850), 489, 493–4).

[2] Plumptre, a Sabbatarian, claimed that a Bill to allow Sunday travelling on the Scottish railways 'was really an attempt to make the people irreligious by Act of Parliament' (Hansard, civ, 841: 25 Apr. 1849).   [3] B. Harrison, 'The Sunday Trading Riots of 1855', *Historical Journal*, 8 (1965), 220.

[4] See B. Harrison, 'Animals and the State in Nineteenth-Century England', *English Historical Review*, 88 (1973), 786–820.

'Dogs Employed in Drawing' Bill, which provoked Joseph Hume, an ardent free trader, to speak out on behalf of the equally wretched human beings whose livelihood happened to depend on the labour of dogs.[5]

In fact, when it came to cruelty to animals for the purpose of human 'amusement', the political economists were divided. John Stuart Mill, in his *Principles of Political Economy*, declared it to be 'the grossest misunderstanding of the principles of liberty' to treat 'the infliction of exemplary punishment on ruffianism practised towards these defenceless creatures . . . as a meddling by Government with things beyond its province'.[6] However, probably most of his fellow economists took Hume's view of the matter.[7]

SEXUAL 'VICE'

'Vice' constituted a far more serious problem for those seeking to discover the limits within which market competition could legitimately take place. Sexual favours were, of course, a purchasable commodity in Victorian Britain, human bodies, female, male, and infantile, being on sale in every sizeable centre of population.[8] Indeed, the huge (if unquantifiable) army of prostitutes operating in Victorian London (to say nothing of other provincial cities[9]) testifies to the entrepreneurial energy that had gone into satisfying the population's sexual appetites, in all their diversity.

Moreover, a certain portion of the 'vice trade' was being organized along thoroughly modern commercial lines, as Gladstone discovered when, having rescued a young and beautiful prostitute, described by himself as being 'at the top of the tree', he was told by the proprietor of the brothel in which the girl worked: 'I feel justified in asking you to pay the heavy account.'[10] According to a contemporary

---

[5] Hansard, lxvii, 1287: 22 Mar. 1843. In the case of cruel sports like cock-fighting, presumably members of certain occupational groups (e.g. publicans) stood to make some pecuniary loss.

[6] Cited in Harrison, 'Animals and the State', 816.

[7] Ibid., 813–14, 816. John Bright, too, refused to join the campaign (ibid., 818).

[8] See the graphic account of the 'market' in child prostitutes in E. M. Sigsworth and T. J. Wyke, 'A Study of Victorian Prostitution and Venereal Disease', in M. Vicinus (ed.), *Suffer and Be Still: Women in the Victorian Age* (Bloomington, Ind., 1972), 77–99.

[9] Until recently it was argued that prostitution peaked in the early 1840s in many industrial towns (D. J. V. Jones, *Crime, Protest, Community and the Police in Nineteenth-Century Britain* (London, 1982), 25). In York, numbers went on rising up to 1860, according to F. Finnegan (*Poverty and Prostitution: A Study of Victorian Prostitution in York* (Cambridge, 1979), 69). M. Mason, however, has suggested that the ratio of prostitutes to population fell in the course of the 19th c. and that many contemporary estimates ludicrously exaggerated their number (*The Making of Victorian Sexuality* (Oxford, 1994), 76–82). See also B. Littlewood and L. Mahood, 'Prostitutes, Magdalenes and Wayward Girls: Dangerous Sexualities of Working-Class Women in Victorian Scotland', *Gender and History*, 3 (1991), 161.

[10] R. Pearsall, *The Worm in the Bud: The World of Victorian Sexuality* (London, 1971; first pub. 1969), 314–15. Gladstone's guilty fascination with erotic literature and street-walkers is well known. For the latest account, R. Jenkins, *Gladstone* (London, 1995), esp. 101–15.

estimate (probably exaggerated), prostitution in London alone absorbed more than £8 million a year, of which nearly six-and-a-half million pounds found its way into the pockets of the brothelkeepers.[11]

Pornography, too, was, a thriving branch of the publishing industry, with its London base in Holywell Street, off Fleet Street, where a wide range of 'dirty books' and obscene prints could be purchased, some home-produced, some imported in bulk (mainly from France). Here was material varied enough to gratify every conceivable sexual taste.[12] As Lord Campbell, the author of the 1857 'Sale of Obscene Books, etc' Act, informed their Lordships, 'a considerable capital was engaged in the trade', which employed agents as commercial travellers the length and breadth of the country; the newly instituted penny post was also utilized to advertise the wares which were on offer and to invite people 'to come, and see and purchase'.[13] Likewise a doctor wrote in 1857 of commercial houses that were 'exclusively devoted to this kind of merchandise', employing an army of hawkers who 'spread these pictures and books all over the kingdom'.[14] Steven Marcus claims that during the middle and later decades of the nineteenth century, 'pornographic writings were produced and published in unprecedented volume—it became in fact a minor industry'.[15] Indeed, as W. T. Stead later noted, the London underworld formed 'a strange inverted world . . . the same, yet not the same, as the world of business and the world of politics'.[16]

Prior to 1830, many pornographic productions had served a social or political purpose: for example, there were close links between 'libertinism' and 'libertarianism', both of which aimed to subvert established religious or political authority. But thereafter, pornography assumed a more recognizably 'modern' form, under the direction of entrepreneurs such as George Cannon, Edward Duncombe, and the remarkable William Dugdale, who 'dominated the "smut" market until the 1870s', when a new generation of professionals entered the trade.[17] These men's 'goods' offered the reader nothing but private titillation.[18]

There was another aspect of nineteenth-century pornography in Britain which conventional opinion was bound to find particularly distasteful. Contrary to the received wisdom, argues one historian, the key to Victorian pornography was not

[11] W. Tait, *Magdalenism: An Inquiry into the Extent, Causes, and Consequences of Prostitution in Edinburgh* (Edinburgh, 1840), 145. [12] Pearsall, *Worm in the Bud*, ch. 8.
[13] Hansard, cxlvi, 327: 25 June 1857.
[14] Cited in Sigsworth and Wyke, 'Victorian Prostitution', 84.
[15] S. Marcus, *The Other Victorians: A Study of Sexuality and Pornography in Mid-Nineteenth Century England* (London, 1969; first pub. 1966), 286.
[16] B. Harrison, 'Underneath the Victorians', *Victorian Studies*, 10 (1967), 239.
[17] I. McCalman, *Radical Underworld: Prophets, Revolutionaries and Pornographers in London, 1795–1840* (Cambridge, 1988), 211–15, 235.
[18] According to one authority, pornography became 'more vicious and specialised' in the early 19th c. See the full and interesting account of the trade in D. Thomas, *A Long Time Burning: The History of Literary Censorship in England* (London, 1969), esp. 192.

flagellation (*le vice anglais*) but what he calls 'incestuous burlesque'.[19] Through its endless depictions of couplings between nephew and aunt, parents and children, and so on, this literature not only transgressed the boundaries of sexual acceptability, it also struck at the very root of the 'ideology of domesticity' by inverting all approved family relationships. Well might Marcus write that 'the view of human sexuality as it was presented in the subculture of pornography and the view of sexuality held by the official culture were reversals, mirror images, negative analogues of one another'.[20]

Not surprisingly, therefore, prostitution and pornography found few if any articulate defenders: these two trades, unlike that of the butcher (famously celebrated by Adam Smith), went unsung, although in their own way they, too, exemplified the 'wonders' which market forces could perform.[21] Sexual vice, of course, was almost universally condemned as morally and socially *unacceptable*; indeed, the more blatantly commercial its expression, the greater the disgust that was provoked.[22]

At the forefront of the organizations setting out to crush the nefarious sex trade was the 'Society for the Suppression of Vice' (commonly known as the 'Vice Society'), a predominantly Evangelical body that had been founded in 1802.[23] While many philanthropists hoped to 'reclaim' those prostitutes they thought redeemable, the Vice Society and other vigilante groups set their sights on the suppression of brothels.[24] In the late 1840s some MPs and peers wanted to make the 'seduction' of young females a criminal offence,[25] and during the 1880s, at the height of the 'social purity' agitation, the harrying of prostitutes intensified; certain zealots even harboured the ambition of outlawing fornication![26] The Vice Society, partly through the influence which it wielded over the newly formed police force, also tried hard to shut down the pornography trade, and one of its spokesmen claimed

[19] Ibid., 274. Thomas also notes the popularity of pornographic fables which depict teachers seducing their pupils, and vice versa (p. 278), as well as other 'perversions', all of which 'serve to displace procreative processes which, in the end, might lead to the constitution or the reconstitution of family life' (274).   [20] Marcus, *The Other Victorians*, 286.

[21] Of course, it could be said that a kind of 'division of labour' operated in many brothels.

[22] Chapman defined prostitution as 'a public and promiscuous traffic of their own persons carried on by women for the sake of gain' ([J. Chapman], 'Prostitution in Relation to the National Health', *Westminster Review*, 92 (1869), 183).

[23] For the complicated relationship between the Vice Society and the 'Proclamation Society', M. Mason, *The Making of Victorian Sexual Attitudes* (Oxford, 1994), 69–72.

[24] E. J. Bristow, *Vice and Vigilance: Purity Movements in Britain since 1700* (Dublin, 1977), 56. However, Mason shows that in its early years the Vice Society was more concerned to prosecute Sabbath-breakers and the organizers of lotteries than to suppress various kinds of sexual immorality (*Sexual Attitudes*, 73). On 'Magdalenism', ibid., 82–115.

[25] An 'Act to Protect Women Under Twenty-One From Fraudulent Practices to Procure Their Defilement' was passed in 1849, though it was rarely used (Bristow, *Vice and Vigilance*, 61). Mason shows that the authors of such measures often confused 'seduction' with 'procurement' (*Sexual Attitudes*, 74–6). See, too, Sigsworth and Wyke, 'Victorian Prostitution', 85, 88.

[26] On the National Vigilance Association (NVA), see Bristow, *Vice and Vigilance*, 112–21. On the anti-Contagious Diseases campaigner and Liberal MP, H. J. Wilson, one of the zealots in question, J. R. Walkowitz, *Prostitution and Victorian Society: Women, Class, and the State* (Cambridge, 1980), 141.

in 1838 that the number of establishments in London selling obscene goods had been reduced from ninety to twenty-three as a result of its efforts.[27]

So emotive an issue was 'vice' that many lost their heads completely when discussing it. Thus Lord Campbell, the Lord Chief Justice, exasperated by the practical difficulties raised by some peers during the passage of his Obscene Publications Bill (critics had quite reasonably called for a clearer definition of 'obscenity'), turned on Lord Lyndhurst, the former Tory Lord Chancellor, and accused him of showing zeal for the 'filthy' produce of Holywell Street and upholding the cause of 'free trade in obscene publications'.[28] Lyndhurst, who was very deaf, did not hear this insult, but his friends were later kind enough to tell him what had been said, and a parliamentary wrangle ensued.[29]

Faced by such moral crusades, most advocates of 'political economy' instinctively held back. Of course, there were certain sexual 'offences' so disgusting that all could unite in demanding that the state banned them: for example, violent sexual assaults (outside the family), gross indecency in public places, and sexual trafficking involving young children (i.e. the 'White Slave Trade'). The last practice anyway stood condemned in the eyes of the political economist since it implicated those too young to form valid or meaningful contracts.[30] But was it wise to carry the campaign against sexual vice any further?

Some political economists thought that it was. After all, the prostitute, by embodying 'an unnatural form of femininity',[31] seemed a threat to both conventional morality and public order. For as well as spreading contagious disease (a topic to which we will return shortly), prostitution encouraged a wide range of other antisocial activities. William Tait, a Scottish doctor who had made a careful study of prostitution in Edinburgh, claimed that 'perhaps a fourth part of the sum expended for [its] support . . . , [was] obtained by fraudulent means', many of the 'presents' given by the shop assistants and apprentices to their favoured 'ladies' having been procured dishonestly. There were, in addition, 'the thieves, thimblers, swindlers, etc' who dwelt in brothels and 'share[d] the booty with the females who live[d] in them'. Tait also waxed eloquent about sons defrauding their fathers; businessmen going bankrupt; and many other promising young men being distracted from their professional careers—all as a result of the corrupting power of prostitution.[32]

---

[27] Bristow, *Vice and Vigilance*, 45; Thomas, *A Long Time Burning*, 189, 197, 212, 282–5.

[28] Hansard, cxlvi, 333–4, 336–7: 25 June 1857. Lord Brougham was another sceptic.

[29] Ibid., 1357–8: 13 July 1857.

[30] Greg, who was hostile to any attempt to criminalize prostitution itself, wrote: any 'carnal connexion with children of tender years, *with or without consent*, is a high crime and misdemeanour' (Greg, 'Prostitution', 487). Of course, a lot depended upon what was meant by 'tender years'. It was only with the Criminal Law Amendment Act of 1885 that the age of consent was raised to 16.

[31] L. Nead, *Myths of Sexuality: Representations of Women in Victorian Britain* (Oxford, 1988), 100.

[32] Tait, *Magdalenism*, 180. While deploring prostitution and calling for the clearing of the streets and the suppression of brothels, Tait did also provide a sober explanation of the reasons why many young girls took up this occupation. Since prostitution was not itself an offence, many prostitutes were arrested on other charges, including stealing from the person and being drunk and disorderly (Jones, *Crime, Protest, Community and Police*, 25–6, 107, 165). On prostitutes and brothel-keepers stealing

A similar indictment could be made against the pornography trade, around which other petty crimes circled—including what Mayhew called 'the Sham Indecent Street-Trade', in which swindlers sold passers-by allegedly obscene material, which was actually quite innocuous.[33]

Prostitution may have upset conventional notions of propriety in an even more fundamental way. For, as Lynda Nead notes, although the purchase and sale of sexual favours was largely regulated by the law of supply and demand, the prostitute 'distorted' the normal operations of the market because she stood 'as worker, commodity and capitalist', thereby blurring 'the boundaries of bourgeois economics in the same way that she [tested] the boundaries of bourgeois morality'.[34]

There were other aspects of prostitution which directly concerned the political economist *qua* political economist. For on its fringes, as John Duguid Milne showed, there existed large numbers of sempstresses and slop workers who had been driven to eke out their earnings by selling their bodies. As a result, they could 'afford to work at lower wages than [were] adequate to support them; and by the fall in wages so caused, the rest of their class [were] driven to the same resort'—an apparent case of competition in the labour market being distorted by 'unfair' trading practices.[35] Milne's own belief was that, if the general industrial status of women could be improved, 'honest' sempstresses would eventually raise their degraded sisters to their own level, rather than be dragged down by them, and that, as for the 'true' prostitutes, they were not in rivalry with anyone else.[36] But few contemporaries shared his optimism.

All of this provided a shocking revelation of human wickedness and depravity. But what in practice could be done about it? Some political economists, including the outspoken W. R. Greg, subscribed to the view, widely held by police, magistrates, and most Members of Parliament, that, since prostitution had been in operation since the start of recorded history, it was unlikely to disappear quickly in the face of voluntary or legislative opposition, and therefore should largely be left alone, except when it blatantly threatened public order or public decency.[37] Taking 'dirty books' out of circulation was probably going to be no easier.

---

from clients, see Finnegan, *Poverty and Prostitution*, 116–24. Other wayward working-class girls found themselves driven into penitentiaries where they were given instruction in, for example, domestic service, in the hope that they might later become model workers as well as model females (Littlewood and Mahood, 'Prostitutes, Magdalenes and Wayward Girls', 164–7).

[33] Thomas, *A Long Time Burning*, 272. According to Marcus, the egregious Dugdale was also a swindler, confidence-trickster, and would-be blackmailer (*The Other Victorians*, 68–77).

[34] Nead, *Myths of Sexuality*, 98–9.

[35] J. D. Milne, *Industrial Employment of Women in the Middle and Lower Ranks*, 2nd edn. (London, 1870; first pub. 1857), 239–42.   [36] Ibid., 241–3.

[37] See Mason's discussion of Greg as a representative of what he calls 'classic moralism', an anti-utopian view of the world which rejected the 'puritanical prudery' of those who sought to strengthen police powers against prostitutes, so leaving 'the door open to a degree of acceptance, however sullen, of sexual transgression' (*Sexual Attitudes*, 48–61). In Greg's view, 'few men—incalculably few—are truly celibate by nature or by choice' (W. R. Greg, *Why Are Women Redundant?* (London, 1869), first published in *National Review* (Apr. 1862), 27).

Moreover, political economists had particular reasons of their own for trying to rein in the 'moral interventionists'. For as a group they prided themselves on placing reason before emotion, and this general dislike of 'enthusiasm' tended to set them at odds with puritanical zealotry. Then, too, most political economists harboured a gut suspicion of any action, however well intentioned, that produced an increase in police powers or that imperilled the individual's freedom. Hume, for one, saw societies for the prosecution of vice as 'little better than conspiracies against the liberty of the subject'.[38]

The 1857 Obscene Publications Bill well illustrates this point.[39] A measure to which Mr Pritchard, Secretary of the Vice Society, had made a contribution[40] did not inspire much confidence in these circles, and the Bill met stout criticism from free-trade MPs like Roebuck, James White (Cobden's friend), and John Locke, partly on libertarian, partly on practical, and partly on 'class grounds'.[41] After all, the prosecution of booksellers meant, in practice, resort to such dangerous expedients as employment of informers, entrapment, police raids, and sequestration of property. Though he said he was as concerned as anyone to stop 'the abominable traffic' in pornography, Roebuck expressed the strongest objection to the *methods* being advocated.[42]

The Liberal MP, Richard Monckton Milnes (who just happened to own an extensive library of erotica![43]), raised another pertinent objection, citing the case of reputable booksellers in the metropolis who were worried lest 'in a trade where so much competition existed, the Bill, if passed, would enable any man, hostilely disposed towards them, to give information, and declare upon oath, that he knew they had some obscene books in their possession'.[44] This, of course, resembled the anxieties elicited by the prospect of adulteration legislation.[45] Nor were these anxieties misplaced, since after the 1857 Act the police and their helpers often indulged in questionable behaviour. Indeed, despite serving six prison sentences, Dugdale himself enjoyed one delicious moment of revenge when he brought a successful action against the Vice Society, whose agents had broken into his premises and removed certain of his books—illegally.[46]

Moreover, free traders would have observed that the periodic police drives against prostitutes seldom achieved their objectives. The intention was usually to clear a

---

[38] B. Harrison, 'State Intervention and Moral Reform in Nineteenth-Century England', in P. Hollis (ed.), *Pressure From Without in Early Victorian England* (1974), 303.

[39] Thomas, *A Long Time Burning*, 261–3.   [40] Hansard, cxlvi, 1355–6: 13 July 1857.

[41] E.g. while the legislation threatened the humble trader who *sold* obscene books or prints, its sponsor made it quite clear that there was no question of criminalizing the *ownership* of such material, which no doubt came as a great relief to wealthy roués who had amassed considerable libraries of erotica. The class bias in mid-Victorian animal welfare legislation was even more blatant.

[42] Hansard, cxlvii, 1482: 12 Aug. 1857.   [43] Thomas, *A Long Time Burning*, 286.

[44] Hansard, cxlvii, 1479: 12 Aug. 1857. There was also the question of the fate of the property seized by the police. Lord Campbell suggested that if the prosecution succeeded, the sequestrated property should be treated in the same way as commercial goods that had not paid duty (ibid., cxlvi, 328–9: 25 June 1857).   [45] See Ch. 5, p. 92.

[46] Thomas, *A Long Time Burning*, 280–1.

particular urban neighbourhood of a 'nuisance' that was causing public embarrassment and depressing local property values—in itself a good pretext for intervention in the eyes of most political economists.[47] But attempts to crack down on the night haunts of prostitutes did not *solve* the problem, they merely *displaced* it, often driving the girls, along with their protectors and clients, into hitherto 'respectable quarters'.[48]

To the reflective political economist, there was a still more fundamental reason for the failure of such exercises. Greg pointed this out in a famous article on 'Prostitution', published in the *Westminster Review* in 1850: 'To endeavour forcibly to cut off the supply of prostitutes while the demand for them continues unchecked, must be futile, as both experience and reasoning might teach us.'[49] Citing what he regarded as a disastrous precedent—the attempt to suppress the slave trade forcibly by means of the Africa Squadron—Greg argued that if there was a powerful enough demand for a commodity, that demand would always be met, often in a 'worse' form than the one which had goaded well-meaning 'reformers' into attempting suppression.[50]

The most thorough investigation of prostitution in Victorian times was undertaken by William Acton, who started off from the same premise as Greg: that prostitution existed and flourished 'because there [was] a demand for the article supplied by the agency'. But, continued Acton, though supply was 'regulated by demand, and demand [was] the practical expression of an ascertained want', want and demand could be 'either natural or artificial'. Articles of luxury, for example, were 'the objects of artificial demand, which depends not merely on the want, but is actually increased by the supply; that is to say, the desire for these articles grows with the possession and enjoyment of them.'[51] Prostitution was just such a luxury. Male desire supplied the want, which prostitution met—though in a 'perverted' way, since sexual intercourse was intended for mutual satisfaction, not to be made a 'matter of commerce'.[52]

Nevertheless Acton was prepared to admit, as did Greg, that 'a woman if so disposed may make profit of her own person, and . . . the State has no right to prevent her'.[53] Government should instead try to do three things: create conditions in which the demand for prostitutes did not exist, protect the vulnerable,

[47] Bristow, *Vice and Vigilance*, 56. The main concern of the police was with order and decorum in the streets and public spaces; soliciting, prior to the passing of the Criminal Law Amendment Act of 1885, was only an offence if it 'annoyed' passers-by (R. D. Storch, 'Police Control of Street Prostitution in Victorian London: A Study in the Contexts of Police Action', in D. H. Bayley (ed.), *Police and Society* (London, 1977), 50–1, 53).

[48] Walkowitz, *Prostitution*, 42. See Greg 'Prostitution', 490.

[49] Greg, 'Prostitution', 490. Similarly there were critics of the Permissive Bill who questioned why the prohibitionists were trying to prevent the sale of a commodity (alcohol), the consumption of which was perfectly legal (A. E. Dingle, *The Campaign for Prohibition in Victorian England: The United Kingdom Alliance 1872–1895* (London, 1980), 25). [50] Greg, 'Prostitution', 489–90.

[51] W. Acton, *Prostitution Considered in Its Moral, Social, and Sanitary Aspects*, 2nd edn. (London, 1870, repr. 1972; first pub. 1857), 161–2. On Acton, see Mason, *Sexual Attitudes*, 60–1.

[52] Acton, *Prostitution*, 162–3. [53] Cited in Marcus, *The Other Victorians*, 5.

and remove 'temptations'. Acton also recommended a regime of 'healthy bodily exercise and mental application' as the 'true remedy' for men's 'morbid excitement'.[54]

It may seem surprising that Acton did not view early marriage as a possible solution to the difficulty. Neither did Greg. Why might this have been so? There is an obscure but much discussed passage in Greg's article which seems to concede that early marriage was one way of satisfying men's powerful sexual drives, but that, unfortunately, this would have economically undesirable consequences: precisely the point that political economists were always making.[55]

Theoretically, of course, the use of contraceptives within marriage would have allowed socially and economically ambitious young men to marry at an earlier age, so rescuing them from the sexual temptations graphically described in Greg's article, without having to incur the crippling expenses of parenthood. However, as Mill's youthful escapade had earlier shown,[56] conventional Victorian opinion, and its agents, the police, clearly regarded contraception as a far greater social evil than prostitution. Since the alternative to marriage, 'illicit intercourse', was also unacceptable (the purity of upper-class females had to be preserved if they were to play their allotted role as the chaste custodians of the domestic sanctuary), prostitution came to be viewed as a regrettable but inevitable social 'fact'.[57]

Now, in fairness to Greg, it must be said that his piece on 'Prostitution' contains no direct reference to delayed marriages. On the other hand, as we have seen, Greg shared with most political economists the conviction that 'prudence' was needed in the fight against poverty. The *Westminster Review* article also shows Greg's total hostility to the idea of casual promiscuity and his even greater disgust at anything that smacked of an 'intrigue with a married woman': something, he observes, which 'is condemned, by Christian and worldly moralists alike, as a violation of vows, a deception of confidence, and a cruel destruction of domestic felicity'—a clear endorsement of the conventional domestic ideology.[58]

It seemed, then, that, for several reasons, prostitution was here to stay. Yet prostitution, as Greg and Acton well understood, was creating a public health problem by spreading venereal disease. Did the State have an obligation to protect the public against such hazards?

Acton thought that, though the State should certainly not 'encourage' prostitution, it could not be indifferent to its consequences. He justified this belief by drawing a distinction between lawful and unlawful trading: 'The mere fact of endeavouring to trade with . . . bad fish, or meat, or the false weights, is an offence against the law', he writes.[59] There was, he reasoned, a parallel 'between the case

---

[54] Acton, *Prostitution*, 163.   [55] Walkowitz, *Prostitution*, 42–3.   [56] Ch. 7.
[57] Walkowitz, *Prostitution*, 42–3. On whether delayed marriages among 'gentlemen' lay behind the alleged growth of prostitution in early 19th c. Britain, see Storch, 'Police Control', 53–4. The link was certainly drawn at the time by a number of commentators, including the *Lancet* (Sigsworth and Wyke, 'Victorian Prostitution', 85–6).   [58] Greg, 'Prostitution', 481.
[59] Acton, *Prostitution*, 218.

of a dishonest trader and a diseased prostitute' in that both were inflicting an injury upon the public.[60] Admittedly, the injury was being directly incurred by men engaging in 'immoral transactions' who perhaps 'deserved' their fate. But contagious diseases also exposed the innocent to the risk of infection. And so the State was entitled to intervene in the name of the 'public good'.[61] These were the grounds on which both Acton and Greg advocated the regulation of prostitution along Continental lines, before later giving strong support to the ill-fated Contagious Diseases (CD) Acts.

The trouble with the CD Acts was that, by regulating prostitution, they gave it a kind of state approval, and, not surprisingly, this triggered off a campaign of passionate moral protest—a campaign in which the ill-used prostitute was sometimes emotively equated with the slave.[62] Little need be said here of this agitation, raising, as it does, issues which fall outside the scope of the book. In a sense the CD Acts were only incidentally about prostitution anyway, their principal purpose being one of 'public hygiene': the protection of HM's soldiers and sailors against infection. Yet, even as a sanitary device, the CD Acts were open to one powerful objection: they provided for the compulsory detention, inspection, and treatment of female prostitutes, but not of their male clients. It was this 'double standard' which so angered Mrs Josephine Butler and her supporters (many of them men).

The 'double standard' may have been *morally offensive*, but it had a rationale behind it. For as Paul McHugh has argued, 'examining women periodically while leaving men alone was, in one sense, logically defensible (the women were selling their services, the State therefore regulated the transaction without troubling the purchaser)'.[63] This was precisely the point of Acton's parallel between infected prostitutes and bad fish.

How many political economists were convinced by this sort of logic? Some must have been, but probably most shrank from following their principles to such a conclusion. Mill, for one, had predictably come out, from the very start, as a violent opponent of the CD Acts, and Harriet Martineau, anxious to uphold the dignity of women, gave the authority of her name to the repeal campaign.

True, it was possible, on utilitarian grounds, to construct a plausible case for the CD Acts by invoking the precept of the 'greatest happiness of the greatest number': the short-term distress which the Acts occasioned would be justified by

---

[60] Ibid., 218–19. The *Lancet*, which also supported the CD Acts, drew an analogy between the government's duty to restrain the actions of diseased prostitutes and its duty 'to interfere with a railway when in a dangerous condition' (Sigsworth and Wyke, 'Victorian Prostitution', 97).

[61] Acton, *Prostitution*, 219–20.

[62] Acton himself argued that 'to license prostitution is to license sin, and in measure to countenance it. Recognition is not license, and has neither the appearance nor the effect of encouraging vice' (ibid., 206). Unfortunately for Acton, few contemporaries found this distinction meaningful. On the 'slave-woman' analogy, see Ch. 4.

[63] P. McHugh, *Prostitution and Victorian Social Reform* (London, 1980), 261.

the long-term public good.[64] On the other hand, as we have seen, to those brought up in the market traditions of political economy, State intervention of any sort immediately aroused suspicion, particularly when, as in the case of the CD Acts, it could be demonstrated that heavy-handed State action was resulting in infringements of personal liberty. Significantly enough, the campaign against the CD Acts attracted large numbers of advanced Radicals, horrified by what they saw as the brutal pretensions of 'aristocratic' doctors. The Acts also reinforced their dislike of the military establishment. Mill, for example, was scandalized by 'the idea of keeping a large army in idleness and vice and then keeping a large army of prostitutes to pander to their vices'.[65]

The agitation of the 'repealers' sent a powerful message to government about the political dangers of meddling with such emotional subjects as prostitution. It also gave a new fillip to the venerable cause of 'voluntaryism'. Josephine Butler herself endorsed this creed, even though she knew that it amounted in practice to the condoning of 'free trade in vice'.[66]

Significant, too, is the fact that when Mill gave his evidence to the 1870–1 Royal Commission on the Operation of the Contagious Diseases Acts, he not only spoke about the threat to liberty, the degradation of women, and the blow that the Acts had inflicted upon public morality: he also branded the attempt to reduce the risk of a client's contracting syphilis from a prostitute as an undesirable shielding of the individual against the consequences of his wrongdoing.[67] He developed this argument in a private letter:

To soldiers and ignorant persons it cannot but seem that legal precautions taken expressly to make that kind of indulgence safe, are a license to it. There is no parallel case of an indulgence or pursuit avowedly disgraceful and immoral for which the government provides safeguards. A parallel case would be the supplying of stomach pumps for drunkards, or arrangements for lending money to gamblers who may otherwise be tempted into theft in moments of desperation, and thus injure their wives and families.[68]

[64] This, of course, presupposed that the Acts really *were* producing the beneficial consequences which their advocates claimed for them—a highly dubious claim (ibid., 152–3, 249).

[65] Mill to W. T. Malleson, 18 Jan. 1870, in J. S. Mill, *Collected Works*, ed. F. E. Mineka and D. N. Lindley (Toronto, 1984), xvii. 1688. Mill wanted to try instead the experiment of 'the military education of all classes' or having a married army.

[66] Butler favoured the prosecution of pornographers and brothel-keepers and the raising of the age of consent, but she equally firmly adhered to the cause of the *voluntary* reclamation of the prostitute, having what Harrison calls 'a libertarian horror of officialism' ('State Intervention and Moral Reform', 313).

[67] McHugh, *Prostitution*, 63–4. Mill's evidence is given in full in J. M. Robson (ed.), *Complete Works of John Stuart Mill*, 21 (Toronto, 1986), 351–71. esp. 355, 358, 371. 'I do not see how that which makes illicit indulgence of that sort safe, and is supposed to do so, can be prevented from gaining some degree of encouragement to it' (p. 371). Mill recognized the necessity of public action which dealt with the *consequences* of particular pieces of wrongdoing, but did not think that this should take the form of facilitating such actions beforehand (p. 358).

[68] Mill to J. Nichol, 29 Dec. 1870, in Mill, *Collected Works*, xvii. 1791. This emotional utterance totally ignored Acton's point about venereal disease afflicting guilty and innocent alike.

This was only one of many instances in which Christian traditionalists found themselves in improbable agreement with political economists, the two groups united
by the belief that 'as a man sows, so shall he reap'.

GAMBLING AND BETTING

Gambling and betting, too, presented a problem to those anxious to establish free-
market relationships. Not only was there a major industry centring upon horse-
racing and gentlemen's gaming clubs, but for much of the eighteenth and early
nineteenth century the State had raised a substantial portion of its revenue from
lotteries.[69] However, with the Evangelical Revival gathering momentum, the moral
propriety of *all* forms of gambling and betting came into question. Thus in 1819
Mr Lyttelton moved for suppression of the State lottery, arguing that 'a spirit of
gambling, injurious, in the highest degree, to the morals of the people, [was] encouraged and provoked', which weakened 'the habits of industry' and diminished 'the
permanent sources of the public revenue', as well as encouraging other types of
gambling.[70] It was attitudes such as these which contributed to the final ending of
the State lottery in 1826.

As social disapproval spread,[71] the State moved to disassociate itself from
other forms of gambling, egged on by various vocal moralistic pressure groups.
For example, the 'Vice Society' conducted a strong campaign against betting and
gaming, which it associated with other sins like drunkenness, Sabbath-breaking,
and whoring.[72] In a sermon preached at Cheltenham parish church during race
week in June 1827 the Revd F. Close roundly condemned gambling as 'a vice
which appear[ed] to be growing and increasing in our land', a vice which was
'more preeminently destructive both of body and soul, than any other which Satan
ever devised for the ruin of mankind'. Gambling, he argued, was productive
of 'envy, malice, revenge, the lust of money, pride, contention, cruelty, and, as
we have on one occasion known, murder!'; similarly, race meetings promoted

---

[69] See J. Raven, 'The Abolition of the English State Lotteries', *Historical Journal*, 34 (1991), 371–8.
There is much of interest on the history of early lotteries in R. Munting, *An Economic and Social
History of Gambling in Britain and the USA* (Manchester, 1996), 13–14, 55–7. On the early development of gambling on horses, C. Chinn, *Better Betting with a Decent Feller: Bookmaking, Betting and
the British Working Class 1750–1990* (London, 1991); M. Clapson, *A Bit of a Flutter: Popular Gambling
and English Society, c.1823–1961* (Manchester, 1992).
[70] J. Ashton, *The History of Gambling in England* (New York, 1968; first pub. 1899), 238–9.
Wilberforce took a prominent part in the parliamentary enquiry of 1808 (Munting, *Gambling*, 57).
[71] See the strictures against the gaming halls—'sinks of iniquity'—in the anonymous book, *The
Gambler's Scourge* (London, 1824), cited in E. B. Perkins, *Gambling in English Life* (London, 1950), 11.
[72] R. Munting, 'Social Opposition to Gambling in Britain: An Historical Overview', *International
Journal of the History of Sport*, 10 (1993), 298.

'prostitution and licentiousness, drunkenness and strife', broke up families, and ruined the poor. Why, the racecourse, said the preacher, was even more sinful than the theatre![73]

There was also a *secular* case against gambling, likely to appeal to political economists. This held that gambling was an irrational activity that not only pandered to greed and selfishness but also weakened respect for property, since property could only legitimately be acquired by gift or exchange.[74] As with prostitution, gambling and gaming were frequently linked to swindling and petty theft.[75] Moreover, in the words of one historian, 'it was a matter of perpetual scandal to the man of business that the society gambler would honour his gaming debts though scorning to the last the claims of the honest tradesman among his creditors, while betting among the lower orders was regarded as a constant threat to property and social order'.[76]

At a deeper level, too, gambling caused offence. Herbert Spencer, for example, argued that it involved 'the obtainment of pleasure at the cost of another's pain', so violating the spirit of 'fellow-feeling'.[77] George Eliot's Dr Lydgate viewed gambling 'as if it had been a disease' and likened its temptations to those of drink: 'He had said to himself that the only winning he cared for must be attained by a conscious process of high, difficult combination tending towards a beneficent result.'[78] Similar attitudes engendered anxiety over the propriety of Stock Exchange speculation.[79] In Roger Munting's words: 'The reliance on chance to determine income and fortune flew in the face of the work ethic and the spirit of capitalism.'[80]

Politicians found themselves in a dilemma. The Report of the 1844 Select Committee informed them that 'betting, to the extent to which it is now carried out, so far from being necessary to the maintenance of Racing is greatly injurious to it'.[81] In reality, as everyone knew, horse-racing was inextricably bound up with

[73] Revd F. Close, *The Evil Consequences of Attending the Race Course Exposed: A Sermon Preached in the Parish Church of Cheltenham, 17 June 1827*, 3rd edn. (London, 1827), 8–10. See Chinn, *Better Betting*, 60–1.
[74] D. Dixon, *From Prohibition to Regulation: Bookmaking, Anti-Gambling, and the Law* (Oxford, 1991), 49–50.
[75] The 1844 Select Committee of the House of Lords into Gaming heard evidence that punters were sometimes drugged and robbed while on the premises and made the victims of a variety of swindles. It was also suspected that persons who frequented gambling houses sometimes stole from their employers or committed other offences against property (*Third Report of the House of Lords into Laws Respecting Gaming, 1844*, vi, esp. pars. 92, 112, 113, 116).
[76] P. Bailey, *Leisure and Class in Victorian England: Rational Recreation and the Contest for Control, 1830–1885* (1978), 23–4, 134.
[77] H. Spencer, *The Principles of Ethics*, in id., *The Synthetic Philosophy of Herbert Spencer*, Westminster edn. (New York, 1892–6), i. 530.
[78] G. Eliot, *Middlemarch*, Penguin edn. (1965; first pub. 1871–2), ch. 66, pp. 720–1.
[79] See Ch. 5, pp. 81–6.
[80] Munting, *Gambling*, 29. By contrast, in earlier centuries chance was widely viewed as 'the hand of God' (ibid., 4). See also Clapson, *A Bit of a Flutter*, 20.
[81] *Third Report of Lords Select Committee on Gaming*, p. v.

gambling, but, being the 'sport of kings', it had the good fortune to enjoy royal patronage.[82]

Parliament's response to the moralistic outcry was to pass the 1845 Gaming Act, which declared all gambling contracts legally unenforceable—a measure which was anyhow needed for practical reasons since the courts had become clogged up with such cases. Further legislation followed in 1853 and 1854 giving the police powers to close betting shops and gaming houses.[83] However, the government acted cautiously and without the guidance of any very clear principle. The Attorney-General admitted in 1853 that he did not want to interfere with private betting, which he regarded as 'legitimate', his only quarrel being with betting at *open* houses.[84] Yet neither did he approve of the suggestion that betting houses be licensed, something which he declared 'would be discreditable to the Government, and would only tend to increase the mischief instead of preventing it'.[85]

Meanwhile other kinds of gambling, particularly the mass betting industry centred upon horse-racing, continued to grow, helped by improved communications —even though off-course betting was still not allowed.[86] As for the 'vices' of the rich, these were practised in private houses and in exclusive clubs without hindrance from the police, so confirming the widely held view that the operation of the law was being grossly distorted by class bias.[87]

Gambling and betting thus inhabited a twilight world in mid- and late-Victorian Britain. *The Times* might, on one occasion, have commended the 'usefulness' of betting on the ground that it made 'people give their attention, think what they are about, form the soundest opinion they can, sift the counter-statements, weigh their own words, prepare for events, and realize them when they come'.[88] On the whole, however, gambling and betting were not treated as though they formed a 'respectable' branch of trade. At the same time, despite being subjected to some restrictions, no serious moves were made to criminalize them.

The nature of the dilemma becomes clear from Mill's agonizing in *On Liberty*. 'Fornication . . . must be tolerated, and so must gambling', he mused, 'but should a person be free to be a pimp, or to keep a gambling-house? The case is one of those which lie on the exact boundary line between two principles, and it is not

[82] Munting, 'Social Opposition to Gambling', 300, 298.

[83] Ibid., 298–300; R. Munting, 'Betting and Business: The Commercialisation of Gambling in Britain', *Business History*, 31 (1989), 67–8; Munting, *Gambling*, 23; Clapson, *A Bit of a Flutter*, 22–3; Dixon, *Prohibition*, 38–9. These Acts were cited as a precedent by Lord Campbell when he introduced his Obscene Publications Bill (Hansard, cxlvi, 328: 25 June 1857).

[84] Ibid., cxxix, 87–8: 11 July 1853.   [85] Ibid., 88.   [86] Dixon, *Prohibition*, 43.

[87] Legal restrictions, argued many moralists, were most needed for the protection of the vulnerable: the young, the ill-educated, and the poor (Munting, *Gambling*, 24). Ironically, however, there is evidence to suggest that it was the middle classes who favoured the most irrational (i.e. 'aleatory') forms of gambling (like roulette and other casino games), while the working classes were drawn to forms of betting in which knowledge and judgement played a part and where the risks were correspondingly reduced (i.e. 'agnostic gambling') (D. C. Itzkowitz, 'Victorian Bookmakers and Their Customers', *Victorian Studies*, 32 (1988), 26–30).

[88] 'Derby Day', 30 May 1868, cited in Chinn, *Better Betting*, 75.

at once apparent to which of the two it properly belongs.'[89] Mill eventually came down on the side of government non-intervention.[90]

William Acton dealt with the issue more lucidly. Gambling, he observed, was

immoral and its public practice prohibited, so much so, that not only are public gaming tables suppressed, but even wagering on horse races is prohibited in the streets, and in public-houses. If any man, therefore, loses his money gambling, he has only himself to thank for his folly; and had he not engaged in an immoral transaction, he would have been secure against the loss.

Yet, however wrong gambling might be, argued Acton, its popularity meant that it would be 'quite impossible for the law to put it down'. From this it followed that if money was 'unfairly won at games of chance, the cheat [was] liable to punishment for obtaining money under false pretences'.

According to Acton, the state's policy towards gambling, like its policy towards prostitution, therefore observed two principles. First, the law insisted on 'fair play, that what is actually given should correspond with what is professed to be given'. Second, in the case of both gambling and prostitution, the law reasonably decreed that persons who persisted in immoral actions should 'not do it in such a manner as to place temptation in the way of the thoughtless and ignorant'—hence legislation to protect minors.[91]

But because legal prohibitions like the criminalization of gaming houses proved so ineffectual, the emphasis gradually switched from legislation to the work of 'moral suasion', a development which found favour with the political economists, who, though they had their own reasons for wanting to discourage patterns of behaviour seemingly at odds with the requirements of a modern commercial society, shrank from outright prohibition.

THE SUNDAY TRADING QUESTION

By contrast, two issues arose in the middle years of the century which caused a perplexing conflict of loyalties: the campaign for restrictions on Sunday trading and the growing movement to curb, or even ban, the sale of intoxicating liquor. In both cases the existing law prescribed restrictions which were residues of the older, pre-commercial society (the laws restricting Sunday trading dated back to

---

[89] J. S. Mill, *On Liberty*, Everyman edn. (1910; first pub. 1859), 154.

[90] Mill saw the desirability of suppressing gaming houses (and brothels) but was struck by the apparent illogicality of 'punishing the accessory, when the principal is (and must be) allowed to go free; of fining or imprisoning the procurer, but not the fornicator—the gambling-house keeper, but not the gambler' (ibid., 155).   [91] Acton, *Prostitution*, 219–20.

the reign of Charles II).[92] But should these restrictions be intensified, as the campaigners wanted, or else relaxed or even abolished? And how could the conflicting demands of morality and economic freedom be reconciled?

The Sunday Trading Question came into prominence as the result of the convergence of two separate developments: first, the growth of sabbatarianism itself,[93] and, second, a need to clear the confusion surrounding the law. This resulted in a number of legislative initiatives, notably the ill-fated scheme of Lord Robert Grosvenor and later the Bills introduced by the 'Christian Socialist', Tom Hughes. Perhaps inevitably these measures drew fire from both flanks: from people who wanted to extend and from people who wanted to restrict Sunday trading. Hence, Hughes's 1867 measure, denounced in some quarters as an intolerable interference with freedom of trade, was categorized by another MP as 'a Bill for the licensing of public trading on the Sunday'.[94]

The Church of England was badly divided. Its doctrine allowed Sunday trading for any one of three purposes: works of piety, works of necessity, and works of charity (or mercy).[95] But, of course, these principles were susceptible to a variety of interpretations. As Francis Bacon had earlier observed: 'It is an easy and compendious thing to call for the observation of the Sabbath-day . . . ; but what actions and works may be done upon the Sabbath, and in what cases . . . is a matter of great knowledge and labour, and asketh much meditation and conversation in the Scriptures, and other helps which God hath provided and preserved for instruction.'[96] Time had not made Bacon's dilemma any easier to resolve. In Victorian Britain, even the episcopacy was split, with some bishops viewing the Bills brought in by Grosvenor and Hughes as a reasonable compromise, while others complained of betrayal.

This formed part of a wider argument within Christianity as to whether 'rules of perfection' should be *imposed* on the mass of humanity. On the one side, there were those like the Archbishop of Canterbury who thought that 'though it would be better, no doubt, to brave all the consequences of an adherence to the Divine command, it would . . . be too much to expect such heroic virtue from the mass of mankind', even if 'persons of high Christian principle would brave all consequences and would resolve, in spite of any loss they might sustain, to refrain

[92] As one MP privately commented: 'The Law of Charles 2d. is unworkable. Magistrates inflict nominal penalties': Trelawny diary, 6 July 1870, T. A. Jenkins (ed.), *The Parliamentary Diaries of Sir John Trelawny, 1868–73*, Camden Fifth Series (London, 1994), iii. 409.

[93] J. Wigley, *The Rise and Fall of the Victorian Sunday* (Manchester, 1980).

[94] Hansard, clxxxvii, 582: 15 May 1867.

[95] Percival, in his *Medical Ethics*, declared that medical men had a duty to observe the Sabbath, 'so far as is compatible with the urgency of the cases under their charge' (T. Percival, *Medical Ethics: Or, a Code of Institutes and Precepts Adapted to the Professional Conduct of Physicians and Surgeons* (Manchester, 1803), 49).

[96] K. Thomas, 'Cases of Conscience in Seventeenth-Century England', in J. Morrill, P. Slack, and D. Woolf (eds.), *Public Duty and Private Conscience in Seventeenth-Century England: Essays Presented to G. E. Aylmer* (Oxford, 1993), 35.

from selling on the Sabbath Day'.[97] Other ecclesiastics took a less flexible line; could what was morally wrong be economically right, they asked?

The friends of the working classes were similarly split, partly depending upon whether it was the interest of the consumer or that of the trader which was uppermost in their minds. The situation was rendered more complex still by divisions *within* the trading community. For whereas many small dealers and street hawkers needed the opportunity to make money on a Sunday, other traders, including many of the better-off shopkeepers, wanted at least one day in the week free from irksome toil. In Harrison's view, this led to 'a confrontation on the Sunday Question . . . between, on the one hand, the large shopkeeper, smaller shopkeepers anxious for Sunday rest, shop assistants, and Evangelicals, and, on the other, Sunday marketeers, their customers, radicals and infidels'.[98]

The wider issue of sabbatarian restriction was still further complicated by the intrusion of demands for 'rational recreations'. Free traders were active during the mid-1850s in the foundation of the National Sunday League: indeed, Roebuck, Mill, and James Heywood saw its work as occupying 'the place towards Religious Liberty that the Anti-Corn Law League did towards true commerce', to quote Harrison's words.[99] Moreover, it was the doctrinaire free trader, Joseph Hume, who urged the opening of the British Museum on Sunday with the argument that such a reform would 'be productive of benefit to the morals of the people' by providing them, for the first time, with 'places of rational instruction and amusement', as an alternative to the public house.[100]

But one man's moral right was another man's desecration of the Sabbath, and Hume's stand made him very unpopular with his Scottish constituents—nor did he help his cause by publicly describing the Scottish people as more immoral than the English, despite the stricter Sunday restrictions which operated north of the border![101] In fact, Hume found himself in the awkward position of declaring that Sunday was 'special', yet trying to sponsor recreational activities which meant that some poor people might have to work seven days a week.[102]

What position did the political economists and their latter-day disciples adopt on the more general issue of Sunday working? As Thomas Hughes reminded Parliament in 1867, Adam Smith himself was on record as describing Sunday as 'an institution of inestimable value, apart from all claim to its Divine authority'.[103]

---

[97] Hansard, clxxxiii, 343: 3 May 1866.

[98] Harrison, 'Sunday Trading Riots', 222. As so often in the area of 'moral reform', what purported to be a point of principle was often an expression of some interest, but the motives of individuals are hard to disentangle.   [99] Harrison, 'State Intervention and Moral Reform', 303.

[100] Hansard, lv, 721: 14 July 1840. Sabbatarians and temperance reformers also clashed from time to time. The leader of the teetotal faction, for example, offended the sabbatarians because he saw Sunday morning as the best time at which to disseminate his literature (L. L. Shiman, *Crusade Against Drink in Victorian England* (Basingstoke, 1988), 68).   [101] Hansard, civ, 843: 25 Apr. 1849.

[102] Wigley, *Victorian Sunday*, 77.

[103] Hansard, clxxxvii, 577: 15 May 1867. His view was shared by Gladstone: (Trelawny diary, 18 Apr. 1871, Jenkins (ed.), *Trelawny Diaries*, Camden Fifth Series, iii. 428).

On the other hand, most economists had a visceral dislike of all moralistic restrictions: 'The plain fact is, we meddle too much with one another', grumbled Roebuck.[104] It must also be significant that in six parliamentary divisions on the 1855 Sunday Trading Bill, doctrinaire free traders consistently voted against restriction, as, indeed, they had done when faced by similar measures in the 1840s.[105]

For the essence of the free-trade case was that individuals should be left to exercise their own consciences on how they chose to spend their Sundays and that legislative *prohibitions* were wrong because buyers and sellers knew their own interests best. 'Why should not persons be allowed to do what they pleased if they did not inconvenience anybody else?', asked the Radical MP, John Locke:

Working men who objected to buying after nine [the deadline set in the Bill before the House] were quite at liberty to abstain from doing so, but why should they ask Parliament to prohibit it? They must be excessively fond of legislation, and must think that Parliament, even though it had Reform to deal with, was in want of a job.[106]

Free traders added that, in order to survive, many working folk could not *afford* to lie in bed on Sundays. According to one MP, 'the small trades-people looked at the question on very narrow grounds, talked of their little ones, and the loss of profits'.[107] Moreover, it was pointed out that some traders and customers would probably break a law which seemed to them merely an artificial impediment to their freedom of action.[108] Indeed, any distortion of the market risked inhibiting commercial progress: Joseph Locke made the telling point that restrictions on Sunday rail travel would benefit only postilions![109] In short, to quote the words of another Liberal MP, Massey, *all* regulation of trade

was unsuited to the genius of the present day, which discountenanced the principle of giving crutches and artificial helps to persons in the exercise of their callings. Tradesmen ought to be left entirely to their own individual guidance in such matters; and, if a man felt that he required recreation on Sunday, or had religious scruples to carrying on his business on that day, he ought not to object to make any little sacrifice that might be incidental to his pursuit of health or pleasure, or that might be involved in obedience to the dictates of his conscience.[110]

---

[104] Hansard, xxviii, 155: 26 May 1835.

[105] Harrison, 'Sunday Trading Riots', 222. Indeed, Harrison goes further, arguing, more generally, that moral reformers as a whole were 'vigorously opposed by all who drew crudely individualist conclusions from their reading of political economy, or who assumed that *laissez faire* principles applied universally' (Harrison, 'State Intervention and Moral Reform', 302).

[106] Hansard, clxxxix, 36, 39: 24 July 1867.

[107] See Serjeant Gaselee's amusing account of his debates on the issue with a hairdresser (ibid., 38).

[108] Truck, and all the abuses associated with that discredited system, might return, it was claimed (ibid., cxxxviii, 1915: 13 June 1855).

[109] Ibid., civ, 833: 25 Apr. 1849. Joseph Locke was a Liberal MP. He is not to be confused with his parliamentary colleague, John Locke.   [110] Ibid., cxxxviii, 1913: 13 June 1855.

Well might the Lord's Day Observance Society lambast 'that political economy which it is the disgrace of the present age to view as coincident with political morality'.[111]

But the free traders did not get things all their own way. For their opponents did not consist exclusively of religious zealots who rested their case on a literal reading of the Bible and were resistant to any kind of reasoned argument. In some respects, more formidable were the 'reformers' who contended that most people *wanted* Sunday to be kept 'special' but could not achieve this so long as a minority of irresponsible traders insisted on conducting business seven days a week: hence, only the imposition of general rules would allow them to have their way— precisely the argument that had earlier been used by many advocates of factory legislation.[112]

Thus R. Macfie said that the 1869 Sunday Trading Bill then before the House 'would enable respectable tradesmen who had been accustomed to close their shops on Sundays in a Christian country to continue to do so'.[113] Two years earlier Lord Claud Hamilton had used a similar argument, calling the Sunday Trading Bill

a simple response to the demands of thousands and tens of thousands of tradesmen in the metropolis, respectable fathers of families, who sought to be protected from the obligation, which competition at present imposed upon them, of keeping open their shops upon Sunday, and be thus enabled to enjoy his rest on the Sabbath and to look after the morals and welfare of his children and dependents.

'This was no attempt to enforce the religious observance of the Sabbath', he claimed.[114]

Some restrictionists took up the free traders' argument about how retailers were often obliged by necessity to work on a Sunday, but then proceeded to turn the argument on its head by using it to show the importance of imposing general rules so as to protect the God-fearing man from the competition of the less scrupulous.[115] Lord Chelmsford could thus portray a Sunday Trading Bill as a means of reconciling tradesmen's consciences with their 'pecuniary interests'.[116]

Such pleading cut no ice with religious traditionalists who refused to accommodate faint-hearted Christians 'who were afraid of obeying God's commandments, lest by so doing they might suffer in pocket'.[117] But other Christians were happy

[111] Harrison, 'State Intervention and Moral Reform', 303. Few Churchmen shared Trollope's belief that observance of the Sabbath was not one of *Christ's* commands (Anthony Trollope, *The New Zealander*, ed. N. J. Hall (Oxford, 1965; written 1855–6), 91–2).

[112] Whately distinguished between handicraft-work, in which more could be done in seven days than in six, and retailing, in which the same volume of business was transacted over the week: if *one* shopkeeper stayed open, he might gain an advantage over his rivals, but if *all* did so, no one would gain. In the latter case, legislative restriction would therefore serve the greater good (E. J. Whately, *Life and Correspondence of Richard Whately, DD* (London, 1875), 335).

[113] Hansard, cxciv, 562: 3 Mar. 1869.   [114] Ibid., clxxxvii, 586: 15 May 1867.

[115] Ibid., clxxxiii, 338: 3 May 1866.   [116] Ibid., 1039: 17 May 1866.

[117] Ibid., clxxxvii, 591: 15 May 1867 (Henley). The Evangelical, Richard Raikes, urged observance of the Sabbath in order not to bring about the wreckage of British commerce by incurring the divine wrath. But even Raikes admitted that 'the epistolary intercourse between different parts of this

to bolster their sabbatarianism with arguments about the importance of allowing the citizen to make a really free choice. 'It is not that we want a law to compel the observance of the day', wrote Hugh Stowell:

What we need, is a law to restrain men in authority from forcing their dependents to violate the day. It is not that you can make men religious by act of parliament; but you can, by legislative enactment, restrict employers from constraining those whom they employ to be irreligious.[118]

Charles Kingsley carried this argument one stage further. The London tailors, he noted, were liable to dismissal if they did not agree to work on a Sunday:

Why not? Is there anything about the idle day in seven to be found among the traditions of Mammon? When the demand comes, the supply must come; and will, in spite of foolish auld-warld notion about keeping days holy—or keeping contracts holy either, for indeed, Mammon has no conscience—right and wrong are not words expressible by any commercial laws yet in vogue; and therefore it appears to earn this wretched pittance is by no means to get it.[119]

There was also a *business case* for sabbatarian restrictions. This took two forms. First, it was sometimes argued that a reduction of the working week brought about by a complete cessation of labour on the Sabbath would increase productivity and thus be of 'decided pecuniary advantage to the employers'. A variation of this argument had earlier been employed by some of the spokesmen for the factory Short Time movement. However, it is rare to encounter it in mid-Victorian sabbatarianism.[120]

Much more common is the second contention which treated the observance of the Sabbath as a touchstone of 'character' and so as a guarantor of business probity—an important consideration in the 1850s when the general public was so preoccupied with commercial fraud. Thus, H. A. Boardman, author of *The Bible in the Counting-House* (1854), could write:

If just conceptions of the Deity are essential to sound morality, then must it be admitted that the Sabbath is one of the main buttresses of the public morals . . . Dealing with men in the masses, those who observe this day . . . will usually be found on the side of industry, frugality, honesty, intelligence, and good citizenship; while those who habitually profane it, will generally be more or less addicted to idleness, fraud, prodigality, swearing, intemperance, or other vices. The true way to secure trustworthy clerks and faithful warehouse-men, to gather around your great establishments a body of subordinates and

empire, which is essential to commerce, cannot be carried on without the employment of [some] individuals on the Sunday' (*On Christian Humility as Applicable to the Practice of the World* (London, 1825), ch. 4).

[118] H. Stowell, *A Model for Men of Business: Or, Lectures on the Character of Nehemiah* (London, 1854), 292.

[119] C. Kingsley, 'Cheap Clothes and Nasty', in id., *Alton Locke: Tailor and Poet* (1895; first pub. 1850), p. lxxiii.   [120] Wigley, *Victorian Sunday*, 77.

helpers who can be relied upon in all exigencies, and who will do your work thoroughly and cheerfully, is, to encourage all in your employ to honour the Sabbath. Loyalty to God is the best guarantee of fidelity to man.[121]

Stowell delivered a similar message, telling the exemplary story of an employer who dismissed a pious clerk for his obstinate refusal to work on a Sunday, only to reinstate him when he discovered that none of his replacements were so honest and reliable: the moral of the story was 'that God honours those who honour Him by honouring His day'.[122] There actually existed a published volume of 'Sabbath Documents' chronicling the doings of God-fearing businessmen who had been richly rewarded even in this life for their reverential attitude towards the Lord's Day.[123]

Finally, observance of the Sabbath, it was claimed, restored the businessman to his family circle for at least one day in the week and enabled him to 'abstract his mind from his speculations, his risks, and his responsibilities',[124] a necessary step if the honourable vocation of a merchant was not to degenerate into sharp practice, dishonesty, and 'mammon-worship'. (Sabbatarian practices, of course, were said to count for nothing in God's eyes if they simply involved an observance of *forms*: 'The shutters on a Sabbath may close the shop against the world, and yet the world be not shut out from the heart of the shopman.'[125])

Thus the free-trade case for leaving the observance of the Sabbath to the private conscience was countered by arguments for legislative restrictions which rested, not just on the authority of the Bible and the teaching of the Church, but also on considerations of individual freedom and the need to foster a healthy business morality.

The result was gridlock. None of the compromise measures for rationalizing the archaic sabbatarian laws reached the statute book. It was too dangerous to attempt tighter legislative restrictions, as the riots of 1855 showed. But neither did the doctrinaire free-market case succeed in converting Parliament.

In these circumstances the only way forward lay through 'Social Sabbatarianism', which demanded of its members their *voluntary* abstention from Sunday amusements. The advantage of this solution, as John Wigley shows, was that it 'allowed MPs to reconcile their *laissez-faire* principles with their religious values, for no legislation was called for, merely the defence of the *status quo*'.[126]

In the long run, of course, it was changing social habits, not legislation or pressure-group activities, which determined how the majority of the British people observed Sunday. Meanwhile, sabbatarianism was important because, as Brian Harrison argues, it was one of a number of issues in the middle decades of the

---

[121] Revd H. A. Boardman, *The Bible in the Counting-House: A Course of Lectures to Merchants* (London, 1854), 240.
[122] Stowell, *Model for Men of Business*, 301–2.
[123] Revd J. B. Owen, *Business Without Christianity* (London, 1855), 32–3.
[124] Stowell, *Model for Men of Business*, 255, 291.   [125] Owen, *Business Without Christianity*, 7.
[126] Wigley, *Victorian Sunday*, 71–2.

nineteenth century where 'free traders were embarrassed by demands that the claims of morality should override *laissez-faire* principle'.[127] In other words, it demonstrated that, in a religious country like Victorian Britain, there were limits beyond which the free-market ideology could not be pushed.

THE LIQUOR QUESTION

A similar predicament surrounded the selling of alcoholic liquor. Should there be a free market in such drinks, subject only to regulations affecting weights and measures, purity, and the like? Or did alcohol present such moral dangers that society needed to restrict its sale and even its use? The problem with alcohol, then and now, is that it is at one and the same time an attractive and nutritious beverage,[128] a medicine, a commodity which since time immemorial has been central to important social rituals and ceremonies like weddings, and a powerful mood-enhancing drug which, taken in excess, can have various harmful social consequences.

It is the latter aspect of alcohol, obviously, which explains why the sale of liquor has always been restricted to vendors who possess a licence granted by the magistrates. However, in nineteenth-century Britain there was a free-trade lobby which mounted a powerful challenge to all such restrictions. Why, they asked, should beer and wine not be sold on the same basis as other commodities like bread? No one seriously denied that alcohol could be abused or that public drunkenness threatened decency and order. But the free marketeers blamed many of these evils on a misconceived regulatory regime.

Nor did free traders approve of the imposition of punitively high taxes on alcoholic drinks, since they thought that, as with indirect taxes generally, such dues merely encouraged smuggling, which was itself an offence against social and commercial morality, as Adam Smith had shown.[129] McCulloch took up this theme in his 'Remarks upon the Wine and Brandy Trade', which painted a grim picture of how high duties on alcoholic drinks bred 'a contempt for the enactments of the Legislature' and diffused 'predatory and ferocious habits among the peasantry'.[130] In any case, commercial progress, in time, would automatically lead to moral progress,

---

[127] Harrison, 'Sunday Trading Riots', 222.

[128] One commentator thought that, taken in restricted doses, alcohol was 'a most valuable medicine-food' ([F. E. Anstie], 'Does Alcohol Act as Food?', *Cornhill Magazine*, 6 (1862), 329).

[129] A. Smith, *An Inquiry into the Nature and Causes of The Wealth of Nations*, ed. E. Cannan (Chicago, 1976; first pub. 1776), bk. 5, ch. 2, pp. 351–2.

[130] [J. R. McCulloch]. 'Remarks upon the Wine and Brandy Trade', *Edinburgh Review*, 45 (1826), 169–73, esp. 173. These remarks applied to the former state of affairs in Ireland prior to the recent reduction of the duties on Scottish and Irish spirits. McCulloch wanted a similar reduction in the duties on *foreign* spirits, which he claimed would considerably improve the public revenue, 'give peace to extensive districts', and 'suppress one of the most fruitful sources of crime and atrocity' (ibid., 173).

or so it was claimed, since modern industry required its workforce to be both educated and sober.[131]

'Free trade in drink' was first attempted with the Beer Act of 1830 and finally
abandoned when Liverpool's 'free licensing scheme' collapsed in the 1860s.[132] The
origins of the 1830 Beer Act can be traced back to the Radicals' suspicion of the
power traditionally wielded by magistrates (a facet of what they saw as 'old corruption'), allied to a more general dislike of monopoly. Joseph Hume propounded
the free-trade case in all its vigour in a speech calling for the lowering of the duty
on spirits:

he allowed that the immediate effect of making spirits cheap might be morally injurious,
yet it would not long continue so; for it was always the case, with reference to any dear
article, that when accidental circumstances enabled the poorer classes to obtain it, they gratified
themselves to excess; but as soon as it became easily accessible, it was comparatively
neglected.[133]

'Good wages and low prices were the best security for good conduct', he later
remarked.[134]

Hume's fellow MP, Robert Slaney, agreed that the general principle that the
demand for goods ought to regulate the number of vendors should be applied to
the sale of alcoholic beverages as well as to every other commodity.[135] The advocates of 'free trade in beer' accordingly attacked their opponents for upholding a
'vested interest'[136] and accused the big brewers, whose tied houses had come to
dominate the trade, of exploiting their monopoly position.[137]

Hume and Slaney had the backing of the *Edinburgh Review*, in which Sydney
Smith lambasted the licensing system as a gross piece of discrimination against
the 'common people':

The benefit of that principle of competition which is so useful to the rich, ought not to be
withheld from the poor. To withhold that competition, is to establish monopoly; monopoly
enhances the prices of refreshments to the stationary and the travelling poor; deteriorates
the quality of those refreshments; and renders those who dispense them indifferent whether
their conduct is satisfactory to their guests.

---

[131] B. Harrison, 'Philanthropy and the Victorians', in id., *Peaceable Kingdom* (Oxford, 1982), 230.

[132] I am obviously indebted, in the paragraphs that follow, to B. Harrison's *Drink and the Victorians: The Temperance Question in England 1815–1872* (London, 1971), esp. ch. 3, pp. 251, 348–51.

[133] Hansard, x, 362: 23 Feb. 1824. Hume affected to see no difference between the duty on spirits and the duty on silks. [134] Ibid., xiii, 136: 25 Apr. 1825.

[135] Ibid., xix, 857: 21 May 1828. But Slaney accepted that the publican should be required to give security for good conduct. [136] Ibid., xxiv, 402: 4 May 1830.

[137] The point was made by Sydney Smith, who said that as a consequence of 'monopoly', public houses were being bought up in large numbers by big brewers, who then forced 'trash' down the throats of the poor ([S. Smith], 'Licensing of Alehouses', *Edinburgh Review*, 44 (1826), 447). However, as Lord Malmesbury pertinently observed, if this so-called monopoly in fact derived from 'the great command of capital enjoyed by the principal brewers', then 'this kind of monopoly would always pre-vail' (Hansard, xxv, 996–7: 6 July 1830).

Subjecting the poor to this system was 'to rule them upon the principles of a very odious tyranny', said Smith. The 'one cure', he concluded, was to 'make the trade in hospitality as open as the trade in sugar, requiring certificates of character, and visiting abuse with penalties and disqualification'.[138]

It was convictions like these that underlay the 1830 Beer Act, which made it easy for beer-sellers to open up a retail outlet in return for the modest outlay of two guineas. The Act's rationale had earlier been explained by Smith as follows:

If the trade in public houses were free; there would be precisely the number wanted; for no man would sell liquor to his ruin;—and not only that, but they would be carried on by the people best qualified for the business. The lazy and the rude man would be supplanted by the active and the civil man,—as he is in all other trades which are left to the wholesome principle of competition.[139]

Within a few years of its enactment, some 35,000 beerhouses had appeared, many of them badly managed enterprises selling a cheap but highly adulterated product.[140] By the mid-Victorian period, public opinion had on the whole come to regret the Beer Act, and the measure was effectively emasculated, stage by stage, until a private Bill of 1869 killed it outright.[141] Posterity has, on the whole, been no more sympathetic. 'It is hard to find a redeeming feature of this debauch', wrote the Webbs in their history of liquor licensing.[142] But, then, the Webbs had double cause for censoriousness, since they were inveterate enemies of the free market *and* highly puritanical in their social mores.[143] The latest historians of the brewing industry have assessed the legislation more judiciously: 'a curious mixture of up-to-date political economy and old-fashioned Georgian indifference to the social consequences of legislation', is their verdict.[144]

The second major attempt at securing 'free trade in drink', the so-called free-trade licensing system, involved only two cities: Wolverhampton and, more importantly, Liverpool, where the key figure was that doughty Cobdenite, Robertson Gladstone, William's elder brother.[145] Here the magistrates' bench was dominated between 1862 and 1866 by Radical Liberals who issued licences to all applicants of good character, irrespective of any assessment of the neighbourhood's drinking needs, in the hope that the number of retail stores could be safely left to the law of supply and demand.[146] In a letter to *The Times* the Liverpudlian merchant prince

---

[138] [Smith], 'Licensing of Alehouses', 441–57, esp. 452, 456, 457.　　　[139] Ibid., 446.

[140] Harrison, *Drink and the Victorians*, 81–2.　　　[141] Harrison, *Drink and the Victorians*, 247–51.

[142] S. Webb and B. Webb, *The History of Liquor Licensing in England Principally From 1700 to 1830* (London, 1963; first pub. 1903), 127.

[143] Significantly, the Webbs, later on in the same work, referred to 'the wonderful story of the growth of Temperance organisations and their effect in changing public opinion' (ibid., 144).

[144] T. R. Gourvish and R. G. Wilson, *The British Brewing Industry 1830–1980* (Cambridge, 1994), 22, 15–22. See also Harrison, *Drink and the Victorians*, 81.

[145] On Robertson Gladstone, see G. R. Searle, *Entrepreneurial Politics in Mid-Victorian Britain* (Oxford, 1993), esp. 58–9.

[146] Harrison, *Drink and the Victorians*, 251; P. T. Winskill and J. Thomas, *History of the Temperance Movement in Liverpool and District* (Liverpool, 1887), 68–9.

(and Liberal MP), William Rathbone, forcefully put the case for throwing the trade open on equal terms to all wishing to enter:

An open licensing system would deprive the publicans of the monopoly profits by the aid of which they can supply their premises with every kind of adventitious attraction such as no other shopkeeper can afford . . . , [thus destroying] the monopoly out of which many of the moral and all the political evils of the trade now arise.[147]

A contributor to the *Westminster Review*, after expressing approval of the Beer Act, similarly welcomed the principle underlying free licensing: 'If people like to set up public-houses where they are not wanted, let them do so at their peril; they will soon close them', he argued: the only safeguard needed was an assurance that publicans would enforce respectability in their establishments.[148]

But the Liverpool scheme, controversial from the start, threw the town into uproar. Opponents declared the magistrates' actions both illegal and at variance with the wishes of local people. Moreover, as in the aftermath of the Beer Act, the statistics seemed to show an alarmingly sharp rise in drunkenness, though the 'free licensers' hotly queried their accuracy.[149] In an attempt to silence the critics, Robertson Gladstone persuaded sympathetic magistrates to compile 'a black or drunkards' list' containing the names and addresses of all who were convicted of drunkenness, to be published every Thursday in the *Liverpool Mercury*.[150] But this bid to cope with a grave social problem by combining competition with publicity —both popular Radical nostrums—did not win over the doubters. In 1866 the whole scheme was wound up.

True, 'free trade in licensing' enjoyed *some* support in the parliamentary Liberal Party among doctrinaire marketeers. Their number included Robert Lowe, who later protested that 'the experiment of free trade in the retail trade of intoxicating liquors ha[d] never been tried on a sufficient scale and for a sufficient time to furnish us with data on which we can rely'.[151] Interestingly enough, there are also suggestions that William Gladstone was a sympathizer. Thus in a Commons debate of 1865 Roebuck insinuated that the Chancellor had fallen under the influence of his brother,[152] while, more tellingly, Henry Bruce, the Home Secretary in Gladstone's first ministry who had responsibility for licensing legislation, later penned a private letter in which he irritably complained that the Prime Minister 'care[d] for nothing but "free-trade", which the House won't have'.[153]

Perhaps Gladstone's free-trade sympathies can also be seen in his earlier authorization of 'grocers' licenses', which had dismayed most of his Nonconformist supporters as well as the temperance lobby. The temperance historian, Winskill,

---

[147] Letter to *The Times*, 21 May 1872, cited in E. F. Rathbone, *William Rathbone: A Memoir* (London, 1905), 257–60. Curiously, he had earlier been an opponent.
[148] 'Drunkenness Not Curable by Legislation', *Westminster Review*, 64 (1856), 483.
[149] P. T. Winskill, *The Temperance Movement and Its Workers* (1892), iii. 136.
[150] Ibid., 163.
[151] R. Lowe, 'The Birmingham Plan of Public-House Reform', *Fortnightly Review*, 21 (1877), 6.
[152] Hansard, clxxvii, 650: 24 Feb. 1865.   [153] J. Morley, *Life of Gladstone* (1903), ii. 390.

describes this innovation as 'one of the most fatal mistakes ever made by an enlightened statesman' and implies that Gladstone must have been 'afflicted with some mental obliquity of vision' when he sponsored it.[154] But the publicans also reacted angrily, realizing the Gladstone was deliberately seeking to undermine the monopoly which the existing licensing system was conferring upon them. Indeed, Gladstone openly conceded that he disliked the status quo because it led both police and magistrates to hold back from using their full powers of control in the face of public-house disorders out of a feeling that this would be unfair to a 'vested interest'.[155]

The grocers' licence scheme was a subtle one which eluded easy labelling. 'Was it a free trade or a protective measure?', asked one perplexed MP.[156] In a sense, it was neither, but perhaps it leant more to the free-trade side.

TEMPERANCE

Meanwhile, what position did Cobden and Bright take up on the drink question? In the event, they did not, as might have been expected, give their whole-hearted support to the free licensing schemes of Robertson Gladstone, their ally in so many other Radical crusades. Instead both men gradually devised their own rather different solution to the drink problem.

As a matter of personal hygiene Cobden and Bright largely refrained from the imbibing of alcoholic beverages, but they did not object to alcohol as such. In fact, Cobden later came to regard the light wines of France as beneficial to health and morals—and certainly preferable to spirits and the fortified wines of Spain and Portugal, then the well-to-do Englishman's favourite tipples.[157] It was therefore appropriate that the famous 'Cobden Act of 1860', which lowered the customs duties on many French imports including table wines, should later have contributed to the spread of more moderate drinking habits. Cobden was also able to present his 1860 measure as an important step in the direction of improving Anglo-French relations and, through it, the promotion of world peace: moral goals which were welcomed on both political and self-interested grounds by many of the businessmen who subscribed to the ideology of free trade.

---

[154] Winskill, *Temperance Movement and Its Workers*, iii. 134–5. H. Carter concludes that, with the grocers' licence, Gladstone made 'the same lamentable error' as Parliament had done in 1830 (*The English Temperance Movement: A Study in Objectives* (London, 1933), 133).

[155] Hansard, clvii, 1307: 26 Mar. 1860. The measure also allowed a special wine licence to be conferred on refreshment houses. Gladstone thought that temperance was best promoted by encouraging people to drink wine rather than spirits and by 'offering the people the means of reasonable access to the refreshing influences of liquor in conjunction with the meals they are required to take' (ibid., 1314).

[156] Ibid., clviii, 1035: 10 May 1860.

[157] Harrison, *Drink and the Victorians*, 248–9; N. C. Edsall, *Richard Cobden: Independent Radical* (Cambridge, Mass., 1986), 349.

But by adopting this strategy Cobden not only distanced himself from the Liverpudlian 'free licensers': he also gravely disappointed many other erstwhile admirers who had now joined the prohibitionist camp. In a sense, Cobden was remaining true to the ethos of the early nineteenth-century temperance movement, which had accepted the relative harmlessness of beer, drunk in moderation, while seeking to discourage spirit drinking. In this attempt to suppress, not drinking as such, but drunkenness, the temperance movement placed the onus of responsibility on the purchaser to exercise self-control: 'If the drunkard had not bought, the seller would not have sold.'[158]

Something of this view of the world carried over into 'teetotalism', whose adherents took the 'pledge' never to touch alcohol in any form.[159] This went much further than the earlier insistence on moderation, but it was similar in that it still left the crucial decisions to the individual conscience. Female activists may have advised other women to reject all marriage proposals from men who were not teetotal,[160] a very powerful form of 'moral suasion'! Yet teetotallers retained the expectation that individuals, unaided, would have to win their own private battle against temptation.

The material rewards for so doing were said to be considerable. Teetotalism, like sexual continence and providence, was portrayed as a means whereby the poor but honest workman could rise in the world, even to the point of becoming a capitalist in his own right, through the practice of those quintessentially Smilesian virtues, perseverance and forethought. Indeed, Smiles himself urged working men to avoid the 'self-imposed taxation' involved in drinking intoxicants.[161] Nor was it accidental that self-help and sobriety should be linked in this way: after all, self-help clearly *presupposed* sobriety, and, in its absence, social progress was unlikely to be achieved.[162]

The wider economic advantages to be derived from this quest hardly needed stressing. 'No investment in benevolent work yields a better return than that which aims at the removal and prevention of our national intemperance', claimed the National Temperance League.[163] Indeed, some employers, teetotallers themselves, would employ only total abstainers, particularly when it came to jobs which

---

[158] Shiman, *Crusade Against Drink*, 10–15.

[159] Joseph Livesey, for one, always put self-control at the centre of his creed (Harrison, *Drink and the Victorians*, 214–18).

[160] A. Tyrrell, ' "Woman's Mission" and Pressure Group Politics in Britain (1825–60)', *Bulletin of the John Rylands Library*, 63 (1980), 220.

[161] B. Harrison, ' "A World Of Which We Had No Conception": Liberalism and the English Temperance Press: 1830–1872', *Victorian Studies*, 13 (1969), 143.

[162] For further discussion of the links between sobriety, on the one hand, and thrift, on the other, see Ch. 8. It may be significant that the *British Temperance Advocate*, the organ of the National Temperance Society, was edited by Thomas Spencer, the uncle and mentor of Herbert Spencer (Harrison, 'A World Of Which We Had No Conception', 136–7). On the relationship between the two Spencers, see Ch. 8.

[163] Cited in Harrison, 'Philanthropy and the Victorians', 223. See also J. B. Brown, 'The Pig or the Stye: Drink and Poverty in Late Victorian England', *International Review of Social History*, 18 (1973), 383.

entailed residence in their own home.[164] Yet if economic progress owed so much to abstinence, was there not a case for *imposing* it on the entire community by Act of Parliament?

PROHIBITION

This further step was taken in 1853 with the founding of the United Kingdom Alliance (UKA). Henceforward, *voluntary* renunciation of alcoholic drinks was partially displaced by a more aggressive anti-drink crusade which aimed either at total 'prohibition' (on the model of the 'Maine Law') or at a localized ban on the sale of alcohol, under the terms of the 'Permissive Bill'—the UKA's own favoured solution.[165]

'Prohibitionism', in all its manifestations, was obviously the polar opposite of 'free trade in drink', but it was also at odds with the older temperance movements. As Lilian Shiman puts it,

prohibition meant a fundamental change in method as well as in policy. It meant a change of focus from the drinker to the seller of intoxicating beverages. Self-control, the basis on which the teetotal movement was built, was of little importance to the prohibitionist.[166]

The source of evil was no longer located within the breast of each individual: it was projected outward on to the brewers and publicans who lived by the liquor trade.[167]

This change of direction offended John Stuart Mill, who had the strongest of objections to the Maine Law on both libertarian and free-trade grounds. The sale of alcoholic drinks, Mill conceded, was indeed a 'social act', but he thought restriction an intolerable infringement, not so much of the liberty of the seller, as of the liberty of buyer and consumer.[168] Mill did recognize the right of the state to impose conditions and to require guarantees from drink vendors, but that is as far as he would go:

Almost every article which is bought and sold may be used in excess, and the sellers have a pecuniary interest in encouraging that excess; but no argument can be founded on this,

---

[164] Shiman, *Crusade Against Drink*, 40–1. However, some employers did the very opposite, in the interest of harmony among their workforce, since they knew how unpopular teetotal workmen often were with their mates (ibid.).

[165] The American state of Maine had introduced prohibition in 1853. The 'Permissive Bill' favoured by the UKA would have given ratepayers the power to ban the sale of alcohol anywhere in their locality, if they achieved a five-sixths majority. Note that 'local option', with which the Permissive Bill was often confused, differed in that its prime purpose was merely to make the licensing authority accountable to local electors. On the parliamentary fate of the successive Permissive Bills, Dingle, *Prohibition*. On the activities of the UKA, D. A. Hamer, *The Politics of Electoral Pressure: A Study in the History of Victorian Reform Agitations* (Hassocks, 1977), chs. 9–13.

[166] Shiman, *Crusade against Drink*, 76.   [167] Ibid., 41.   [168] Mill, *On Liberty*, 145.

in favour, for instance, of the Maine Law; because the class of dealers in strong drinks, though interested in their abuse, are indispensably required for the sake of their legitimate use.[169]

More basic still was the objection that the Permissive Bill involved an assault on property rights. The veteran Radical, Sir John Trelawny, complained that its advocates were proposing 'to ruin a great industry without compensation', a course of action that was little less than robbery.[170]

In 1877 a similar line of argument was deployed by Robert Lowe to refute the plan concocted by a group of Birmingham Radicals who sought a compulsory reduction in the number of public houses. Lowe denounced this project as a repudiation of the spirit of 1846 and also as rank confiscation, since the liquor trade, in his opinion, was 'as legitimate as any other'. In any case, Lowe thought it no more possible to regulate drinking than eating. 'We profess ourselves quite unable to understand how that which is economically so utterly wrong can be socially so entirely right', he exploded. Free competition in the articles they consumed was 'the charter of the poor'. Moreover, argued Lowe, 'it seems to us the vainest thing in the world to suppose that by placing a trade on a basis economically false, and therefore morally wrong, you can ever arrive at a good result'.[171] Ham-fisted attempts to muddle together commercial policy and 'police' could only result in illegitimate restraints of trade.[172]

An article in the *Westminster Review* in 1856 put the position of the free marketeers very clearly. Its author admitted that drunkenness was 'the curse of England—a curse so great that it far eclipse[d] every other calamity under which we suffer'. However, restrictions like the Maine Law were said to be 'an evil worse than that of drunkenness', because their effect would be 'to increase the sphere of State government, and to deaden the sense of individual responsibility'. The sale of alcohol, claimed the *Westminster Review*, bore no resemblance to lotteries, betting houses, brothels, nuisances, coining money, and slavery, all of which were 'wholly wrong', 'wrong *ab initio*'. There might, indeed, be a case for continuing with restrictions on opening hours in licensed premises, an interference with trade which was 'economically wrong, but still expedient'. Apart from that, though, the *Westminster Review* saw no feasible remedy other than the encouragement of rational recreations and of thrift: 'If we teach a man to save money, to feel the pleasure of being the owner of a few pounds in the savings-bank, we teach him control . . . , [and thus] to abhor the prodigal extravagance which ruins drunkards.'[173]

[169] Mill thought the State entitled to impose restrictions and to require guarantees from dealers in alcohol, since the promoting of intemperance was 'a real evil' (ibid., 155).

[170] Trelawny's diary, 13 July 1870, in Jenkins (ed.), *Trelawny Diaries*, Camden Fifth Series, iii. 411. Trelawny also raised the issue of 'class legislation'.

[171] Lowe, 'Birmingham Plan', 1–9.

[172] John Chapman had earlier drawn parallels between the Maine Law and the campaign to 'regulate' the medical profession, which he equally disliked ('Medical Despotism', *Westminster Review*, 65 (1856), 560).

[173] 'Drunkenness Not Curable by Legislation', 463, 464, 474, 480–1, 484, 489–90.

Yet the prohibitionists stood resolutely by their beliefs. Members of the UKA often pleaded the case of disadvantaged women and children, the 'victims' of alcohol abuse, in an attempt to demonstrate that drunkenness had uniquely harmful social consequences.[174] 'Our battle is against wife-beating, and other violent crime', said another prohibitionist orator in 1865.[175] Here, it seemed, was yet one more manifestation of an 'intolerable' evil, justifying the suspension of the ordinary laws of political economy.

Prohibitionists also stressed the *economic* benefits which the success of their cause would bring in its train. Perhaps this partly explains why the Alliance drew important support from the ranks of the textile manufacturers, to many of whom it seemed self-evident that sobriety would increase industrial competitiveness and help working people to become 'little capitalists'.[176] Workmen, it was claimed, were wasting their money on drink when they might have been purchasing more cotton shirts![177] There was surely a strand of self-interest in a manufacturers' prohibitionism which thus linked 'moral progress' to the prospect of higher profits.[178]

But wider considerations than the profitability of industry were involved. Most prohibitionists genuinely believed that alcohol was the prime cause of poverty. Even pioneering socialists like Keir Hardie and Philip Snowden, though convinced that heavy drinking was more often a consequence than a cause of penury and degradation, supported coercive temperance measures because they did not see how a beer- and whisky-sodden working class could ever fight effectively for its own emancipation.[179] Alcohol was also blamed for a wide range of social and personal ills, such as insanity, crime, and sexual depravity—ills which not only inflicted misery on the families affected but also involved the wider community in heavy costs.

All these arguments appear in the writings of one of the UKA's leading spokesmen, the Nonconformist cotton spinner, William Hoyle. In a book significantly entitled, *Our National Resources; And How They Are Wasted. An Omitted Chapter in Political Economy*, Hoyle blamed the current depression in his industry 'mainly, if not entirely' on 'the improvident and unproductive character of our labour and expenditure, especially in reference to the articles of intoxicating drinks'.[180]

---

[174] Moral reformers tended, as a group, to treat the working class in this way. Thus the RSPCA argued in 1846 that the 'uneducated man' was 'after all but a child in the maturity of his physical powers'.(Harrison, 'State Intervention and Moral Reform', 301).

[175] B. Harrison, 'A Genealogy of Reform in Modern Britain', in C. Bolt and S. Drescher (eds.), *Anti-Slavery, Religion and Reform: Essays in Memory of Roger Anstey* (Folkestone, 1980), 141.

[176] Harrison, *Drink and the Victorians*, 220–1; on the prominent role played in the Alliance by first-generation Lancashire textile manufacturers, see Dingle, *Prohibition*, 181–2, 196–8. The headquarters of the Alliance was in Manchester.

[177] Some workmen suspected that the 'hidden agenda' in the advocacy of temperance by their employers was a move to reduce wages (Shiman, *Crusade against Drink*, 40).

[178] D. W. Gutzke, *Protecting the Pub: Brewers and Publicans against Temperance* (Woodbridge, 1989), 35.   [179] Brown, 'The Pig or the Stye', 390–4.

[180] W. Hoyle, *Our National Resources; And How They Are Wasted. An Omitted Chapter in Political Economy* (London, *c*.1871), p. x.

According to Hoyle, heavy drinking led not only to drunkenness, but also to waste, destitution, crime, pauperism, insanity, accidents, premature death, and much else. But for the liquor traffic, he added, the poor and police rates 'need not, at the outside, be more than a fourth of what they now [were]'.[181] The magnitude of the problem meant that it was no longer enough to rely on the slow process of education: 'The virtue that will withstand the evils will put them away.'[182]

Liberal thinkers and politicians found themselves compelled by the drink problem to redefine some of their most basic beliefs. The dramatic transformations to which this could give rise is evident from the history of Edward Baines, a Congregationalist, staunch free trader, and one-time 'voluntaryist', who nevertheless came in time to accept the necessity of legislative restriction. Baines denied any intention of interfering 'with the liberty of the working man' but said he *did* want 'to enfranchise him from the worst of bondage, to improve his condition, as well as that of his wife and family'.[183]

A similar line of reasoning led T. H. Green into assigning the state a much larger role in national life than his early- and mid-Victorian predecessors would have thought tolerable. Green aimed not simply to prevent the excessive drinking of one man from injuring others who relied upon him, but also to save that man from himself by removing needless occasions of temptation—his point being that, while voluntary reform was desirable, it was 'not the part of a considerate self-reliance to remain in presence of a temptation merely for the sake of being tempted'. Moreover, reasoned Green, just as no man could be allowed to sell himself into slavery, it scarcely seemed permissible to let him enslave himself to drink.[184]

Older Radicals stuck to their guns and mocked these newfangled ideas. In a speech to the Commons in 1871 John Locke reiterated his belief that there were 'too many attempts by hon. Members to make the people slaves by Act of Parliament', and he mocked Jacob Bright who had recently advocated restraining 'the sale of liquors at a particular time when nobody wanted to drink':

If nobody wanted to drink during the time referred to, where was the occasion for this Bill? Why that perpetual 'meddling and muddling' system, which was so much favoured by certain hon. Members of that House, who were always saying that the condition of the people must be ameliorated—that the people generally were fools, and that they alone were the Solons, the lawmakers, and lawgivers who would arrange all those matters for them.[185]

---

[181] Ibid., 87.   [182] Ibid., 146. See Shiman, *Crusade Against Drink*, 18–20.

[183] Hansard, ccvii, 375: 21 June 1871. Earlier in his career he had supported Buckingham's motion to set up the 'Drunken Committee', but he generally relied on educational effort, rather than state coercion (B. Harrison, 'Two Roads to Social Reform: Francis Place and the "Drunken Committee" of 1834', *Historical Journal*, 11 (1968), 277.

[184] T. H. Green, 'Lecture on Liberal Legislation and Freedom of Contract' (1880), in R. L. Nettleship (ed.), *Works of Thomas Hill Green* (London, 1888), iii. 384–6. In his *Lectures on The Principles of Political Obligation* (London, 1883) Green presented the 'unrestrained traffic in deleterious commodities' as something which the state could and should curb in the interests of future generations (p. 210).   [185] Hansard, ccvii, 382: 21 June 1871.

However, by 1871 such sentiments were beginning to look somewhat dated.

Finally, the prohibitionists put forward what was in some ways their most persuasive argument when they denied that alcohol was an ordinary commodity which market forces could safely regulate. The demand for drink, they asserted, was artificially created by those who traded in it—unlike, say, the demand for bread.[186] In fact, the essential difficulty surrounding alcohol, claimed the 'Alliance', was that it could not 'be solved by appeal to the general law of supply and demand' since alcohol was an article 'which create[d] and stimulate[d] an appetite in itself', so that 'the thirst for drink [was] never satiated by indulgence'.[187] Such arguments were extensively used in the 1860s—testimony to the power still exercised by the free-trade principle but also to the importance attached by 'reformers' to modifying that principle.[188]

Prohibitionists anyhow denied that drinkers were the rational and mobile beings assumed in the market model constructed by the political economists. One of their spokesmen actually called for habitual drunkards to be treated as though they were insane.[189] More plausibly, it could be argued that the public authorities had a right to curtail trading in substances and activities that were *addictive*, such as alcohol, opium, or gambling.[190]

For all these reasons many erstwhile free marketeers eventually came round to the conclusion that the sale of alcoholic beverages was one of the few areas in which monopoly was *good*.[191] At least, they felt, the creation of a public monopoly was preferable to the private monopoly enjoyed by the brewers with their tied houses.[192] Hence by the 1870s an advanced Radical like Joseph Chamberlain could advocate the so-called Gothenburg Scheme, which concentrated responsibility for the purchase and control of drink in the hands of the local authorities.[193] If the 1830 Beer Act had a lesson to teach, some now reasoned, this was the folly of stimulating competition when this could only result in disastrous social and moral consequences.

[186] Harrison, *Drink and the Victorians*, 349–50.

[187] Executive of the UKA, Manchester, 'The Licensing System', *National Association for the Promotion of Social Science (1866)*, 614. This echoed the argument earlier used, in 1846, by the reformer, Stanley Pope, who claimed that in the drink trade 'demand does *not* limit and regulate supply; supply *does* create and increase the demand' (Harrison, 'State Intervention and Moral Reform', 304).

[188] Bruce, too, used this argument, not of course in support of the Permissive Bill or of Local Veto, but in the course of sponsoring his own much more moderate measure (Carter, *English Temperance Movement*, 146).

[189] J. A. Symonds, 'Uncontrolled Drunkenness: What Legislative Measures Might be Proposed to Deal with Cases of Uncontrolled Drunkenness?', *Transactions of the National Association for the Promotion of Social Science, 1869*, 417.

[190] This particular analogy was later drawn by J. A. Hobson, in B. S. Rowntree (ed.), *Betting and Gambling: A National Evil* (London, 1905), 302.

[191] Harrison, *Drink and the Victorians*, 349–50. But, as we have seen elsewhere, the case of the drink trade was not unique.

[192] Opponents saw this 'monopoly' as the source of widespread social and political corruption (Gutzke, *Protecting the Pub*, 51–2).

[193] J. B. Brown, 'The Temperance Career of Joseph Chamberlain, 1870–1877: A Study in Political Frustration', *Albion*, 4 (1972), 29–44.

But few senior politicians wanted to touch the Gothenburg Scheme. Instead, there was a compromise in the form of Bruce's 1872 Licensing Act, which subjected the drink trade to strict controls, but otherwise allowed it freedom of operation. Ironically, these restrictions would have been even more stringent if the temperance 'fanatics', in their pursuit of 'perfection', had not sabotaged Bruce's original scheme.[194]

In fairness to the free traders, one should observe that those who had contended that the drink problem would be self-correcting if only ignorant legislators had the sense to leave well alone, were, in the long run, at least partially vindicated. For though changing patterns of leisure (owing little or nothing to government action) certainly did not work to the long-term advantage of the sabbatarians, they *did* lead from the late 1870s onwards to a fall in the *per capita* consumption of alcohol, a process that was probably assisted by the cheapening and purification of non-alcoholic beverages, such as tea, coffee, and cocoa. This was in line with the predictions of Herbert Spencer, who viewed moderation in eating and drinking as a sign of social progress (in America, he said, even *temperate* drinking now stood condemned), but who never favoured *legislative* interventions of any kind.[195] As Lowe had forcefully argued, the spread of forethought and providence might be slow, but it offered the only hope of lasting progress.[196]

That, however, was true only in the long run. Governments had to deal with social problems as they arose with a view to devising short-term solutions, and politicians did not have the luxury of sitting on their hands and doing nothing, once the public conscience had been stirred and public order seemed imperilled.

CONCLUSION

In the end, as with the sabbatarian question, prostitution, and gambling, the conflict between the conflicting imperatives of morality and economics prevented any clear-cut solution to the drink problem. Public authorities prudently steered clear of the 'Gothenburg system', the furore surrounding the CD Acts serving as a warning of the fate that might befall a government which attempted to 'organize' activities regarded by many of its citizens as sinful or disgraceful.

Yet neither was free trade allowed to rip. We have seen how doctrinaire free traders had always insisted that attempts to stamp out 'immorality' would fail if aimed simply at stopping the supply of the objectionable substance. Even interventions that took the form of punitively taxing a commodity, they argued, had

---

[194] Dingle, *Prohibition*, 30–3. Even so, the 1872 Bill left the drink trade with a sense of grievance which was to shape its political behaviour for at least another generation.

[195] Spencer, *Principles of Ethics*, in id., *Synthetic Philosophy*, i. 435–7. For Spencer's contemptuous dismissal of Prohibitionism, see *The Man Versus the State*, ed. D. Macrae (London, 1969; first pub. 1884), 93.   [196] Lowe, 'Birmingham Plan', 1–9.

adverse consequences: providing a pretext for smuggling, for example, and tempting otherwise respectable citizens to break the law. The more drastic step of prohibiting sales entirely was likely to do still greater long-term social harm. Try, by all means, to influence consumer demand, but do not otherwise meddle with the operation of the market, they pleaded. This argument was used in mid-Victorian times against attempts at closing down gaming clubs, criminalizing prostitution, and enforcing prohibition—just as in more recent years the argument has been revived by free marketeers wanting to liberalize the sale and use of 'banned substances'.

But taking the free-trade case to its logical conclusion affronted the moral sensibilities of the Victorian middle classes, as the experiment in 'free licensing' shows. Indeed, the extravagant language used by some of the proponents of 'freedom' merely provoked a reaction, which led in time to a more sceptical and thoughtful understanding of the drawbacks to pursuing a free-market solution to complex social problems.

Members of the so-called Drunken Committee, set up by the anti-slavery crusader, John Silk Buckingham, were ahead of their time when they confidently declared: 'The *right* to exercise legislative interference for the correction of any evil which affects the public weal, cannot be questioned, without dissolving society into its primitive elements.'[197] But a quarter of a century later such sentiments had become commonplace. Indeed, when the journalist, Robert Williams, wrote his famous 1870 article setting down the necessary limits to *laissez-faire*, it was to the drink question that he devoted much of his attention before baldly concluding that the government had a duty '*to repress all such acts as involve open and defiant scandal to ordinary morality*'.[198]

Of course, that did not happen, either, in any simple sense, and the more fanatical 'moral reformers' suffered quite as many defeats as did their free market adversaries. Yet some of the objections to unrestricted competition used by sabbatarians, temperance reformers, and the 'vice squad' duly made their way into general political argument, where they were sometimes put to uses which their originators had neither intended nor foreseen: for example, with the late Victorian expansion of advertising, there were many commodities other than alcoholic beverages for which it could plausibly be said that demand had been 'artificially' created.

Meanwhile, confronted with calls to put down some shocking 'evil', most mid-Victorian policy-makers saw the wisdom of looking for compromises with which a majority of the population felt more or less comfortable. Only one thing was crystal clear: market competition, by itself, had not provided a satisfactory answer to the complex dilemmas thrown up by an advanced commercial society.

---

[197] Harrison, 'Two Roads to Social Reform', 278.
[198] R. Williams, 'Laissez-Faire', *Fraser's Magazine*, 1 (1870), 79.

11

'Authority' and the Market

It is often claimed that the British are a pragmatic people, uninterested in the abstract dogmas which have preoccupied other nations like the French. W. R. Greg once observed to John Morley 'how surprised and disappointed he was by the indifference of public men, even the giants like Peel, to anything like general views and abstract principles of politics or society'.[1] But other Victorian intellectuals saw things differently. 'No nation in the world is so logical as the English nation', claimed James Fitzjames Stephen in 1866:

Once get it well convinced of the truth of a general principle ... and it will do anything. For instance, the English nation believes in political economy, and the consequence is that it is the only nation in the world which has established free trade. The New Poor Law and the Bank Charter Act were based upon the principles of the same science.[2]

When did this faith in political economy reach its zenith? Some historians argue that the foundations of the subject were laid early in the nineteenth century when the educated classes, less confident about capitalist growth than they later became, were still hedging market principles around with precepts and practices inherited from older orders of authority; but that with the triumph of free trade in 1846, followed by the rapid economic expansion and relative social stability of the following decades, market liberalism established its ascendancy—before new doubts set in during the late 1870s and 1880s.

Arrogant dogmatism is indeed the hallmark of much mid-Victorian political economy. In 1869 Henry Fawcett pityingly dismissed those foolish enough to challenge the absolute validity of his 'science': 'in a few pages of Adam Smith the fallacy of protection was demonstrated as clearly as any proposition of Euclid', he observed.[3] Similarly Herbert Spencer treated hostility to political economy as a form of primitive superstition and likened contemporary attacks on its practitioners to the earlier attempts by theologians to refute astronomers' accounts of the solar system.[4] If some mid-nineteenth-century political economists felt so sure that their 'science' embodied a set of universal truths, this, as Howard Temperley shrewdly observes, may be because liberals of their generation did not see 'capitalism' as a

[1] J. Morley, 'W. R. Greg: A Sketch', *Macmillan's Magazine*, 48 (1883), 120.
[2] J. F. Stephen, 'Mr Matthew Arnold and His Countrymen', *Saturday Review*, 18 (1864), 684, cited in J. A. Colaiaco, *James Fitzjames Stephen and the Crisis of Victorian Thought* (New York, 1983), 19–20.
[3] H. Fawcett, 'Address on Economy and Trade', *Transactions of the National Association for the Promotion of Social Science, 1868*, 113.
[4] H. Spencer, *The Study of Sociology* (London, 1873), 153. See, too, H. Spencer, *Social Statics, or The Conditions Essential to Human Happiness Specified* (London, 1868; first pub. 1855), 331.

'system' like slavery or feudalism: in their eyes, it was neither more nor less than 'an emancipation from traditional restraints, a liberation of energies, a letting go'.[5]

However, one could argue that it was at an earlier period, in the 1820s and 1830s, that belief in the virtues of an untrammelled market flourished in its most naïve form. Sydney Smith's support of the total deregulation of the sale of alcohol[6] is only one example of the simple doctrinaire approach which characterized many of the contributions to the *Edinburgh Review* in the 1820s. In 1832 the youthful Harriet Martineau well caught the innocence of the age with her claim that the 'science' of political economy had already reached completion: a confident assertion which contrasts with the more cautious observations which she made towards the end of her life.[7]

Writing in 1865, Bessie Rayner Parkes observed that thirty years earlier people had been so bewitched with political economy's 'clearness, its firm granite basis of thought, the unerring certainty of its law in action, that the best and most benevolent thinkers placed the future of the human race at its feet'. But subsequent experience, she felt, had 'done much to undeceive us'.[8]

As this book has shown, doubts developed over quite how the laws of political economy could be applied to practical problems. Even a confident exponent of the 'science' like Robert Lowe once admitted: 'There is a point where the doctrine of *laissez-faire* ceases to be applicable, as in the case of children. As to when that point is reached, honest and able men may reasonably differ.'[9]

Nor was it self-evident that human beings always understood their own best interests in the way that both utilitarianism and political economy presupposed. 'The uncultivated cannot be competent judges of cultivation', said Mill in one of his most famous dictums.[10] Doctors likewise argued that patients were incapable of judging professional competence—an argument, the wider implications of which Robert Williams explored in a famous article of 1870:

A man is the best judge of his own interests in those cases only where he has some special knowledge. A country gentleman can buy his own horses, but he must take the qualifications of his physician upon trust, and he is absolutely incompetent to decide upon the solvency of a company in which he may wish to take shares, or of an insurance office in which he may wish to effect a policy.[11]

In all these matters, Williams thought, the state could legitimately intervene to lay down acceptable standards of professional service, to protect an ignorant public from exploitation or maltreatment. Intervention in the market might also be

---

[5] H. Temperley, 'Capitalism, Slavery and Ideology', *Past & Present*, 75 (1977), 118.
[6] Ch. 10.
[7] V. K. Pichanick, *Harriet Martineau: The Woman and her Work 1802–76* (Ann Arbor, 1980), 49.
[8] B. R. Parkes, *Essays on Woman's Work* (London, 1865), 227.
[9] R. Lowe, 'Attacks on Political Economy', *Nineteenth Century*, 4 (1878), 868.
[10] J. S. Mill, *Principles of Political Economy* (London, 1848), in id., *Collected Works*, ed. J. M. Robson (Toronto, 1965), iii. 947.   [11] R. Williams, 'Laissez-Faire', *Fraser's Magazine*, i (1870), 75.

permissible when 'demand' was fuelled by addiction, since the market required consumers that were capable of free and rational choice.[12]

There was another difficulty. Even those sympathetic to political economy could see that, though the self-correcting mechanisms of the market might *eventually* produce beneficial outcomes, this would be of little value to the current generation. 'The instincts of humanity', argued Bessie Parkes, 'refuse to sanction the immediate sacrifice of human life to the slow working out of an economical law.'[13] Thus were Spencerian warnings about taking short-term views stood on their head. Robert Williams, once again, made the point very well:

When we say that free competition must ultimately rid the market of inferior goods, we forget that life is often too short for fraud to be properly exposed. Honesty would be the best policy, and the interests of buyer and of seller would be identical, if we all lived for some two or three hundred years. As it is, life is so short that it is often the most lucrative course for the vendor to pursue a quick career of what practically amounts to fraud, and then to retire upon his gains and leave the buyer in the lurch.

Williams complained that 'economists in their demonstrations disregarded the element of time altogether'.[14]

However, the main anxiety revolved around whether a reliance upon untrammelled market forces was compatible with the maintenance of moral values, like truth and honesty. By mid-century this no longer seemed self-evident. 'Free trade was never intended to apply to any system which has untruth stamped upon it', argued one speaker at the Social Science Association, in a debate about legislative measures to curb the adulteration of food and drink.[15] Hence the attempts to distinguish legitimate trade from 'trafficking'—attempts which gradually led most defenders of a market economy to accept the necessity of banning the sale and purchase of a variety of commodities in the interest of public morality. The assault on slavery was especially important because it created a precedent adopted later in the century by other crusaders against 'evil'. There could be no legitimate 'property in vice', be its owners slaveholders or publicans.

Moreover, the principle of competition, it became realized, was sometimes misapplied, as happened when philanthropists sought to steal an advantage over rival organizations by offering more generous terms to their 'clients'.[16] Similarly, even so conscientious and respectful a student of political economy as James Graham insisted that competition should play no part in medical accreditation, since this merely resulted in the different licensing bodies underbidding one another and thus driving down standards.[17] The *moral* case against allowing market forces free play was also frequently voiced. Thus temperance workers called for efforts 'to

---

[12] See Ch. 10.   [13] Parkes, *Woman's Work*, 239.   [14] Williams, 'Laissez-Faire', 76.
[15] P. Bevan, 'What Legislative Measures Ought to be Taken to Prevent the Adulteration of Food, Drink, and Drugs', *Transactions of the National Association for the Promotion of Social Science, 1870*, 391.   [16] See Ch. 8.
[17] Hansard, lxxvi, 1897–8: 7 Aug. 1844. See Ch. 6.

put an end to that base competition downwards' which they saw as the defining feature of the drink trade,[18] a cry echoed by other reformers shocked by the prevalence of adulteration or by the hardships suffered by workers in the 'sweated industries'.[19]

There was thus a delicate balancing act to be performed if the claims of morality were to be reconciled with the teaching of political economy. Bessie Parkes wrestled strenuously with this problem. Her starting point was that 'in our extremely complex state of civilisation, where the consequences of any movement act and react beyond our ken, some comprehension of the natural social laws under which the world [was] governed [was] necessary, even to the success of religious activity'.[20] However, she continued, political economy meant

the rule of true self-interest; it is in itself neither moral nor immoral; it represents the laws by which we are swayed in dealing for ourselves and for our families with the outward world of strangers, of whom we know nothing. The more our circle of interest and affection enlarges, the farther recedes that boundary beyond which we treat other human beings scientifically, without any self denial. The mother denies herself for her children; the good mistress for her servants; the good master eases within certain possible limits the burdens of his workpeople, and spends upon them much of the profit which he acquires through their labor; the good clergyman considers his whole parish as his family; and so the principle of getting everything as cheap as possible may gradually be leavened by a far nobler principle; and in an ideal nation Political Economy and Christianity might work together in the relation of master and slave.[21]

Many other middle-class Victorians shared the perception that political economy was dangerous—dangerous, that is, unless linked to a source of unquestioned authority which could adjudicate on those many occasions when morality clashed with market principles. Given the failure of the ideologists of capitalism to resolve such predicaments, traditional élite groups, among them the leaders of the Christian Churches, found themselves being thrust forward into a policing role.

RELIGIOUS AUTHORITY

Contemporary satirists sometimes portrayed religious provision as a kind of commercial speculation: one thinks of Thackeray's fictional character, Charles

---

[18] W. T. Gardiner, 'Uncontrolled Drunkenness: What Legislative Measures might be Proposed to Deal with Cases of Uncontrolled Drunkenness?', *Transactions of the National Association for the Promotion of Social Science, 1869*, 422–3.

[19] See Ch. 5. On the distortion of the market under the impact of prostitution, see Ch. 7.

[20] Parkes, *Woman's Work*, 225.

[21] [B. R. Parkes], 'The Opinions of John Stuart Mill', *English Woman's Journal*, 6 (Sept. 1860), 7.

Honeyman, a fashionable preacher who had bought Lady Whittlesea's Chapel in Mayfair, a chapel ('the shop overhead') that was symbolically situated over a wine-vault.[22]

In some respects, the activities of the Churches did indeed mimic the operations of the market. For example, one can see a kind of division of labour at work within Christianity. Sects and churches proliferated, actively competing against one another for the allegiance of the faithful. Economic individualism was thus paralleled, after a fashion, by a religious outlook which emphasized the sovereignty of the conscience, turning each Christian into a kind of consumer who could 'shop around' in search of the form of worship which best suited his individual needs: in a word, 'voluntaryism'. The commitment of so many Non-conformist ministers to the cause of the Anti-Corn Law League, too, suggests that a close ideological affinity existed between those assailing the 'land monopoly' in the name of political economy, and those assailing the 'Anglican monopoly' in the name of 'religious freedom'.[23]

Moreover, these 'voluntaryists' could cite Adam Smith himself in their support. Religious teachers, according to Smith, might 'either depend altogether for their subsistence upon the voluntary contributions of their hearers; or . . . derive it from some other fund to which the law of their country may entitle them; such as a landed estate, a tythe [*sic*] or land tax, an established salary or stipend'. Smith's predictable conclusion was that the exertion and zeal of ministers were 'likely to be much greater in the former situation than in the latter'.[24] As with physicians and lawyers, therefore, the fate of 'ecclesiastics' might

safely be entrusted to the liberality of individuals, who are attached to their doctrines, and who find benefit or consolation from their spiritual ministry and assistance. Their industry and vigilance will, no doubt, be whetted by such an additional motive; and their skill in the profession, as well as their address in governing the minds of the people, must receive daily increase, from their increasing practice, study, and attention.[25]

Yet Smith also saw the other side to the argument.[26] The legislator, he suggested, would be ill-advised to encourage the competitive zeal of the clergy of

[22] W. M. Thackeray, *The Newcomes* (London, 1855), in *The Works of William Makepeace Thackeray* (London, 1898), viii. 29–30, 117, 258, 463, *passim*. See J. McMaster, *Thackeray: The Major Novels* (Manchester, 1971), 159–61.

[23] As Adam Smith had earlier observed: 'The laws concerning corn may every where be compared to the laws concerning religion', *An Inquiry into the Nature and Causes of The Wealth of Nations*, ed. E. Cannan (Chicago, 1976; first pub. 1776), bk. 4, ch. 5, p. 48).   [24] Ibid., bk. 5, ch. 1, p. 309.

[25] Ibid., 312.

[26] See the discussion in N. Rosenberg, 'Some Institutional Aspects of the *Wealth of Nations*', *Journal of Political Economy*, 68 (1960), 557–70; G. M. Anderson, 'Mr. Smith and the Preachers: The Economics of Religion in the *Wealth of Nations*', *Journal of Political Economy*, 96 (1988), 1066–88; C. G. Leathers and J. P. Raines, 'Adam Smith on Competitive Religious Markets', *History of Political Economy*, 24 (1992), 499–513; A. M. C. Waterman, *Revolution, Economics and Religion: Christian Political Economy, 1798–1833* (Cambridge, 1991), 230.

different sects, because 'each ghostly practitioner, in order to render himself more precious and sacred in the eyes of his retainers', would seek to 'inspire them with the most violent abhorrence of all other sects' and to 'continually endeavour, by some novelty, to excite the languid devotion of his audience'. Smith feared that this would prejudice public order: 'Customers will be drawn to each conventicle by new industry and address in practising on the passions and credulity of the populace.'[27] It was also a matter of historical record, Smith noted, that 'violent religious controversy' and 'political faction' had a tendency to reinforce one another[28] —thereby jeopardizing that domestic tranquillity so essential to a prosperous commercial society.

Looking to the American colonies, Smith conceded that in a country where there was a *multiplicity* of sects, each entertaining 'some peculiar tenets of its own', the 'interested and active zeal of religious teachers' would be of great benefit and no harm would result since, no one sect being in a position to force its dogmas on its rivals, all would learn the virtues of moderation and toleration, and law-makers would soon understand the need to treat them impartially. If the Independents had emerged victorious from the English Civil War, Smith felt, England might now be in the same happy situation as prevailed in Pennsylvania.[29]

Yet the Independents had *not* emerged victorious from the Civil War, and so the dangers of sectarian competition to which Smith had drawn attention had to be taken seriously. We have already noted that many political economists expressed dismay at the damage being inflicted on the organization of a 'scientific' philanthropy by competing churches vying for donations and members.[30] Some went on to argue that a well-ordered society was therefore best served by an endowed religion.

Naturally such arguments appealed to the likes of Chalmers and Whately, both of whom were ministers in a state church. Religion and learning were not 'exposed to sale in a shop, or [had] to undergo, in some form or other, a process of marketing', wrote Chalmers, but that did not mean that religion and learning were any less conducive to national prosperity: on the contrary, a church establishment powerfully subserved 'industry and the enjoyment of its fruits'. Chalmers could thus portray the Church, with its wealth and privileges, as highly 'useful'.[31]

Although Nonconformists dismissed as sophistry Chalmers's case for an Establishment, they, too, were anxious to protect religion from the commercial pressures of the outside world. This can be seen in the movement for the abolition of pew rents, upon which many chapels (as well as Anglican Churches) had traditionally relied to pay their minister. If pew rents had a justification other than narrow financial expediency, it was that a judiciously arranged pricing mechanism would protect the well-to-do from the embarrassment of coming into close proximity with the flea-ridden expectorating poor. However, such considerations failed to prevail against the objection that it was 'un-Christian' to discriminate against

---

[27] Smith, *Wealth of Nations*, bk. 5, ch. 1, p. 312.   [28] Ibid., 313.   [29] Ibid., 314–15.
[30] Ch. 8.   [31] T. Chalmers, *On Political Economy* (New York, 1968; first pub. 1832), 341–3.

poor people by placing the provision of religious worship on to a commercial footing, as pew-renting was doing.[32]

Thus even those early-nineteenth-century clergymen who 'doubled up' as political economists took care to exempt the Church itself from those market transactions they were generally so eager to validate. And there was widespread support
for Chalmers's main contention: that, in matters of faith and morals, some *external* centre of authority was needed to provide a commercial society with spiritual
guidance.

How effective the Christian Churches actually were in influencing the behaviour
of businessmen is, of course, quite another matter. The moralistic homilies which
clergymen customarily delivered often amounted to little more than pietistic
piffle.[33] Moreover, it is arguable that general admonitions to 'behave well' merely
led, in many cases, to unintentional hypocrisy of the kind acutely analysed by George
Eliot in her portrayal of the banker, Bulstrode.[34] Yet only an utter cynic would
deny that 'business evangelism' made *some* contribution to curbing the play of
acquisitive greed by arousing the businessman's sense of guilt and by holding up
high standards of commercial probity.

The case of the Sturges, who were Quaker corn-merchants, is instructive. In
1856 Joseph Sturge wrote anxiously to his brother about the 'temptations' presented by the highly speculative trade from which they both earned their livelihood. And in an earlier despairing outburst he had referred to the necessity of
making 'reparation to Society and those still connected with us by exhibiting an
example of true moderation in Trade (not living to trade but trading to live) and
conducting the business on the principle of strict Xtian equity and uprightness'.
Joseph Sturge, for one, tried very hard to live up to these lofty ideals.[35]

In a few instances the Christian Churches actually imposed spiritual sanctions
on their flock, as happened in March 1868 when the Bloomsbury Baptist chapel
examined S. M. Peto, whose London, Chatham to Dover Railway Company had
earlier gone bankrupt. Despite the fact that their numbers included the chapel
treasurer and a lay deacon who was himself a businessman, the investigators struggled to make sense of the recent bankruptcy proceedings. None the less, they ended
up by formally censuring Peto, on the ground that, although he had done nothing specifically dishonest, they could not 'declare our brother to have been free
from blame'.[36]

[32] Nonconformity, and particularly Wesleyan Methodism, was slower to start a movement to 'free'
the pews than the Church of England (K. S. Inglis, *Churches and the Working Classes in Victorian
England* (London, 1963), 48–57, 106–7). [33] Ch. 2.

[34] G. Eliot, *Middlemarch*, Penguin edn. (London, 1965; first pub. 1871–2), ch. 61, pp. 665, 667–8.

[35] A. Tyrrell, *Joseph Sturge and the Moral Radical Party in Early Victorian Britain* (London, 1987),
31. As a corn merchant, Sturge felt that temptations had been particularly acute when the Sliding
Scale of the Corns Laws had been in operation, which is why he greeted their abolition with relief
(ibid., 30–2). See, too, E. J. Garnett, 'Aspects of the Relationship Between Protestant Ethics and Economic
Activity in Mid-Victorian England', D.Phil thesis (Oxford, 1986), Ch. 2. See also Ch. 5, p. 80.

[36] P. L. Cottrell, 'Sir Samuel Morton Peto', in D. J. Jeremy (ed.), *Dictionary of Business Biography*
(London, 1985), iv. 651.

In 1825 the Society of Friends endeavoured, more ambitiously, to cut off disaster at source by issuing a code of conduct designed to shield the Christian businessman from temptation by warning against 'deviating from safe and regular methods
of business' and drawing attention to the perils of succumbing to the desire
'rapidly to enlarge [one's] possessions'.[37]

Admittedly, some businessmen who vaunted a social conscience may have acted
from motives that were not entirely disinterested. For example, it has been suggested that most of the high-minded merchants and manufacturers who worshipped
in Manchester's Cross St Unitarian Chapel were prosperous and highly esteemed
figures, whose 'humanitarianism' took the form of trying to kill off competition
from a new cohort of small capitalists who were cutting costs by mistreating their
workforce.[38] Cynics have also noted that an *affectation* of virtue was sometimes
indispensable to worldly success. This was particularly true of bankers, who
needed to inspire total trust in their clients. As Norman Russell puts it, the Victorian
banker's duty was 'to seem above reproach, impeccable in his public and private
life, and aloof from any breath of scandal. . . . The hallmarks of a banker's public
character were an outwardly grave and calm aspect, and a shunning of personal
ostentation.'[39] But human beings invariably act from a mixture of motives which
are difficult to disentangle, and it would be a mistake totally to discount the
Christian businessman's claims to be acting under divine guidance.

Christian morality also left its mark in a wider sense, since even secular theorists tended to invoke moral rules of conduct for the regulation and moderation
of economic conduct: rules largely deriving from traditional religious teaching. The
point can be illustrated by examining the writings of Samuel Smiles.

Smiles started off from the premise that some of the finest qualities of human
nature were 'intimately related to the right use of money; such as generosity, honesty, justice, and self-denial; as well as the practical virtues of economy and providence'. Yet he also recognized that these virtues had their counterpart in 'avarice,
fraud, injustice, and selfishness, as displayed by the inordinate lovers of gain; and
the vices of thoughtlessness, extravagance, and improvidence, on the part of those
who misuse and abuse the means entrusted to them'.[40] A proper balance had therefore to be struck between saving and spending, thrift and generosity.

Self-Help, with its emphasis on 'character', is certainly not a proto-Thatcherite
manifesto, written in praise of the entrepreneur and his values.[41] Neither can Smiles's
ideas accurately be presented as 'political economy, translated into a few simple

[37] Tyrrell, *Sturge*, 31–2.
[38] J. Seed, 'Unitarianism, Political Economy and the Antinomies of Liberal Culture in Manchester,
1830–1850', *Social History*, 7 (1982), 8–9.
[39] Cited in N. Russell, *The Novelist and Mammon: Literary Responses to the World of Commerce in
the Nineteenth Century* (Oxford, 1986), 75. On the other hand, as a gentleman, neither could the banker
afford to skimp (ibid., 77–8).   [40] S. Smiles, *Thrift* (London, 1886), p. v.
[41] See the attacks on Keith Joseph's interpretation in E. M. Sigsworth (ed.), *In Search of Victorian
Values* (Manchester, 1988), 12–13, 31–2.

dogmatic propositions', as Marxists once believed.[42] In fact, Smiles insists that the main goal in life should *not* be the amassing of great wealth, but rather the attainment of the kind of 'independence' which allows a man to help family and friends. 'Comparatively few people can be rich', Smiles reasons, 'but most have it in their power to acquire, by industry and economy, sufficient to meet their personal wants.'[43] The man with personal savings could 'neither be bought nor sold': he was 'the centre of his own little world'.[44]

In the writings of Harriet Martineau, the cult of 'independence' achieves an almost messianic fervour:

Is it a delusion that I stand here a happier (I don't mean a better) man than you, because I can stretch out my hands and say, 'Not a penny of another man's money has touched these palms?' Is it a mistake to think that my children look up to their superiors with different eyes from the little creatures that live on charity; neither downcast like the humbled, nor bold like the hardened? . . . Here I stand, and I defy any body to despise me.[45]

Incidentally, Martineau practised what she preached by turning down the offer of a state pension, an action warmly commended by Herbert Spencer, another defender of the autonomous individual.[46]

But though this ideology of 'independence' assumed the sovereignty of conscience, it did not encourage *moral relativity*. On the contrary, the emphasis on duty and character and the commendation of honesty, persistence, and prudence, assumed the existence of a set of moral axioms possessing universal validity, which all 'right-thinking' citizens could freely accept. And such a wide-ranging social consensus did probably exist after the passing of the 1870 Education Act, which, in José Harris's view, 'made a generalized Christian morality more nearly universal than ever before or since'.[47]

POLITICAL LEADERSHIP

Just as some early Victorian prelates actively promulgated political economy, so, too, did some prominent figures from within the *political* establishment. True, Cobden and other class-conscious northern industrialists raged at the stupidity shown by the aristocratic governments of the day. But this was in many ways unfair. For, as Gregory Claeys puts it, 'while the language of natural rights was

[42] A. Tyrrell, 'Class Consciousness in Early Victorian Britain: Samuel Smiles, Leeds Politics, and the Self-Help Creed', *Journal of British Studies*, 9 (1970), 115.
[43] Smiles, *Thrift*, pp. vi, 15, 21.   [44] Ibid., 16, 21.
[45] H. Martineau, 'The Parish', in id., *Poor Laws and Paupers Illustrated* (London, 1831), 196.
[46] Memo of 1889, in D. Duncan, *The Life and Letters of Herbert Spencer* (London, 1908), 289–90. Spencer contrasted 'the nobility of the political economist, who is supposed to be by nature hard and prosaic', with the meanness of the poet Tennyson who had taken a state pension.
[47] J. Harris, *Private Lives, Public Spirit: A Social History of Britain 1870–1914* (Oxford, 1993), 178.

appropriated by nineteenth-century working-class radicals in particular', 'much Whiggism came to be defined by an adherence to Benthamite utilitarianism and classical political economy'.[48]

In the early decades of the century, Henry Brougham, through his active involvement in the *Edinburgh Review*, had provided the key link between the Whig leadership and the (predominantly Scottish) school of political economists. Thereafter, the main nerve-centre of political economy was London's Political Economy Club, to which some businessmen belonged but which also attracted many members from the traditional world of landed society and government: for example, Lord Althorp and Lord Lansdowne, both of whom also spent much time in the company of Nassau Senior.[49]

Professional men also figured prominently in the affairs of the Political Economy Club, and lawyers, in particular, were quick to latch on to the basic premises of the new science, a development in which Brougham once again played an influential role. In fact, by the middle of the century a new generation of judges was emerging well-versed in the classical texts of political economy, and the rise of legal formalism and a severe presentation of the concept of freedom of contract were often buttressed by the authority of Smith and Ricardo. In fact, lawyers like Lord Justice Bramwell were still clinging obstinately to some of the axioms of early nineteenth-century political economy long after these had gone out of favour among economists and other social scientists.[50]

One lawyer, whose enthusiasm for the 'dismal science' led him to join the Political Economy Club before going on to achieve prominence in politics, was Robert Lowe, a lifelong hero-worshipper of Adam Smith. Lowe could justly boast that he had shown a willingness throughout his career to follow the 'science' of political economy, as he understood it, wherever this might lead and whatever short-term unpopularity might be incurred; indeed, Lowe was rather proud of having no business interests which might have warped his judgement. For, like many theorists among the contemporary Radical Right, Lowe believed that 'producers' enjoyed an unfair advantage over 'consumers', since the latter were dispersed and incapable of united action—and hence stood in need of protection.[51]

For their part, most political economists were willing enough to collaborate with aristocratic politicians. From David Hume's and Adam Smith's time onwards it had been recognized that commercial society could flourish under a diversity of

[48] G. Claeys, 'The French Revolution Debate and British Political Thought', *History of Political Thought*, 11 (1990), 59–80, esp. 62.

[49] The links between the economists and some of the Whig magnates are interestingly discussed in P. Mandler, *Aristocratic Government in the Age of Reform: Whigs and Liberals 1830–1852* (Oxford, 1990). See also M. Bowley, *Nassau Senior and Classical Economics* (London, 1937), pt. 2, ch. 2. Also important in the establishment of *The Economist* was 'the Aristocracy's Adam Smith', Lord Radnor (R. K. Huch, *The Radical Lord Radnor: The Public Life of Viscount Folkestone, Third Earl of Radnor (1779–1869)* (Minneapolis, 1977), ch. 10).

[50] P. S. Atiyah, *The Rise and Fall of Freedom of Contract* (Oxford, 1979), 380, 387.

[51] G. R. Searle, *Entrepreneurial Politics in Mid-Victorian Britain* (Oxford, 1993), 320–1.

different political systems.[52] Moreover, in party matters, political economists tended to hold cautious views, being especially careful to keep a distance between themselves and the 'entrepreneurial Radicals'. McCulloch, for example, may have hated the Tories, but he loathed Radicalism; and, though he admired some of the Liberal Conservatives, notably Peel, his main allegiance was to the progressive Whigs associated with the *Edinburgh Review*, a journal to which he made regular contributions.[53] W. R. Greg was another important mediator between the worlds of political economy and high politics, since he shared with the Whigs an impatience with sentimentality, a willingness to use the authority of the state to override class and sectional interests, and a preoccupation with administrative competence.[54]

The case of James Wilson, who founded *The Economist* in 1843 and served as its first editor, is also instructive. Wilson idolized Adam Smith as the chief discoverer of the principle of *laissez-faire*, but his writings otherwise seem to own less to the British school of political economy than to the French economist Frédéric Bastiat and his theory of a natural 'harmony of interests' between all social classes.

Such was Wilson's commitment to the liberation of the market that he was prepared to co-operate with anyone who subscribed to his philosophy. For if free trade and *laissez-faire* benefited all mankind, what reason was there for supposing that even the great landowners, or at least their more intelligent members, would not champion the new creed? In fact, *The Economist* sought to apply its doctrinaire principles to public life in ways which often brought it into conflict with manufacturing interests—for example, it wanted the total abolition of the country's patent laws and dismissed businessmen's calls for their improvement as an improper attempt to escape the beneficent sway of market forces. Wilson himself served, in a junior capacity, in a succession of Whig-dominated Ministries.[55]

Yet the leading statesmen who espoused the doctrines of political economy and formed alliances with its adherents tended to hold forcefully to conceptions of the State which transcended the restricted sphere of liberty in commercial matters. The point can be well illustrated by reference to Lowe. No senior politician had a more ardent commitment to the 'principles' of political economy or a more fervent belief in the market as a solvent of contemporary difficulties. Civil servants who were not conversant with the writing of Adam Smith, he once opined, did not deserve to hold their positions. But that did not make Lowe at all happy about handing over public offices to businessmen who might well have axes of their own to grind. Thus when the scandals of the Crimean War threw up a pressure group,

[52] S. Collini, D. Winch, and J. Burrow, *That Noble Science of Politics: A Study in Nineteenth-Century Intellectual History* (Cambridge, 1983), 30.

[53] D. P. O'Brien, *J. R. McCulloch: A Study in Classical Economics* (London, 1970), 19, 101–3.

[54] One historian, J. P. Parry, has even located Greg, along with James Fitzjames Stephen, among the 'Whig-Liberals' (*Democracy and Religion: Gladstone and the Liberal Party 1867–75* (Cambridge, 1989; first pub. 1986), 76–7. But Parry concedes that Greg, like Stephen and Lowe, placed 'a greater emphasis on the role of the intellect in the direction of national affairs than many whig-liberals'.

[55] Searle, *Entrepreneurial Politics*, 45–9.

the Administrative Reform Association (ARA), which agitated for a reform of Whitehall geared to making it easier for businessmen to become civil servants, bringing their commercial expertise with them, Lowe was not convinced. Nor was Lowe in any way averse to drawing upon the authority of government to supplement the working of the market, when he deemed this necessary.[56]

The Whig patricians, to an even greater degree, reshaped the meaning of political economy in the light of their own understanding of the wider needs of society, which centred upon the importance of 'integrating and harmonizing different classes and interest groups within the political nation', under enlightened aristocratic leadership.[57]

Gladstone also had a complex relationship with political economy. For although, after 1845, free trade assumed in his eyes the basis of a new morality, he continued to derive from his religious convictions a sensitive understanding of the role of national churches and, through them, the particularities of local communities,[58] while, as Colin Matthew explains, 'there was always a strong *étatist* element in Gladstone which lay ambivalently and uneasily side-by-side with his fiscal liberalism'.[59] Nor was such an emphasis unpalatable to many of the political economists themselves, as the story of mid-Victorian civil service reform shows.

REFORM OF THE CIVIL SERVICE AND THE MAKING OF THE MODERN STATE

Most market liberals no more wanted to subordinate the operations of the state to the imperatives of political economy than they desired to make the activities of the Church subservient to their creed. On the contrary, they usually accorded state officials their own 'protected' sphere, often bracketing them with professional men. 'The divine, the physician, the soldier, ministers of state, and magistrates' were all 'unproductive labourers', wrote Mrs Marcet in her *Conversations*; yet all these personages rendered useful services to the community:

There is no greater stimulus to industry than security of property; justice is therefore essentially necessary to encourage productive labour; and the legislator and magistrate, though they do not immediately produce commodities, are as necessary to their production as the labours of the husbandman or artisan; and these different species of labour constitute one of the most useful branches of the division of labour.[60]

---

[56] Ibid., ch. 3.
[57] J. Parry, *The Rise and Fall of Liberal Government in Victorian Britain* (New Haven, 1993), 3.
[58] H. C. G. Matthew, *Gladstone: 1875–1898* (Oxford, 1995), 193.
[59] H. C. G. Matthew, *Gladstone: 1809–1874* (Oxford, 1988; first pub. 1986), 76, 169.
[60] Mrs Marcet, *Conversations on Political Economy: In Which The Elements of That Science Are Familiarly Explained* (London, 1839; first pub. 1816), 277.

Adam Smith had earlier adopted a similar stance.

In other words, most dedicated marketeers saw that commerce and industry needed an infrastructure of public services: services which private individuals would have no incentive to provide but which could more efficiently be directed by municipal authorities or by the state. As Mrs Marcet acknowledged, such services obviously included the defence of the realm and the administration of justice, but perhaps they also extended to sanitary measures and to the provision of a state-run telegraph system. Whether elementary education should fall within the public sector or be left for market forces to supply remained one of the main bones of contention in mid-Victorian Britain.[61] But, as Brian Harrison puts it, state intervention in education and in the regulation of the liquor trade could both be portrayed as essential to the well-being of contemporary capitalism: for only if ignorance and drunkenness were removed, could 'the free-acting, atomistic society' be made to work.[62]

Even someone so committed to doctrines of *laissez-faire* as Martineau was prepared for the state to assume quite extensive responsibility not only in education, but also in the arts and sciences and in the area of public works.[63] The Manchester School, by contrast, tended to be more cautious. Cobden, for example, took his mistrust of the 'intrigue and corruption' which he associated with all government institutions to quite extraordinary lengths.[64] But, regardless of where exactly state boundaries were to be drawn, nearly all spokesmen for the new commercial society believed such boundaries to be necessary—and demanded that, once established, they must be respected.

For it was widely recognized that there were certain operations which it would be *morally* offensive for anyone but the public authorities to mount. Thus Adam Smith had argued against a resort to mercenary armies, though he acknowledged the possibility of this option.[65] The purchase of commissions similarly attracted opprobrium, because this involved a kind of market transaction in an area of national life where trading, in any shape or form, was judged illegitimate. 'Purchase and professional qualification are antagonistic and incompatible principles', declared Charles Trevelyan: 'We must take our choice of them.'[66]

The British prided themselves on being the most 'progressive' commercial society in Europe. But what distinguished them from their continental neighbours, as one historian puts it, was 'the absence of a sprawling, tentacular state apparatus'

---

[61] Searle, *Entrepreneurial Politics*, ch. 7.

[62] B. Harrison, 'Philanthropy and the Victorians', in id., *Peaceable Kingdom: Stability and Change in Modern Britain* (Oxford, 1982), 235.

[63] H. Martineau, *The Moral of Many Fables* (London, 1834), 128–32.

[64] See S. Conway, 'The Politicization of the Nineteenth-Century Peace Society', *Historical Research*, 66 (1993), 282.   [65] In fact, he favoured a professional standing army (Ch. 9).

[66] C. E. Trevelyan, *The Purchase System in the British Army* (London, 1867), cited in P. J. Corfield, *Power and the Professions in Britain 1700–1850* (London, 1995), 193. On the purchase system, A. Bruce, *The Purchase System in the British Army, 1660–1871* (London, 1980).

produced by the sale of offices and tax farming.[67] Indeed, at the very moment
when the entrepreneurial radicals were seeking to widen the market and introduce
market principles into many fields of public policy, there was pressure to create a
public domain from which commercial practice and commercial ethics would be
totally *excluded*. Thus the entrepreneurial radicals expressed horror at the survival
of the old custom of buying and selling votes in parliamentary elections—an 'abuse'
which they associated with Old Corruption and 'feudalism'.

Nor did the political economists and their friends generally favour subcontracting
public services to private industries or companies: Bentham made few converts to
his idea of a 'National Charity Company', run on joint-stock lines, through which
the management of poor relief could be farmed out.[68] His scheme for a 'model
prison', based on the principle of 'contract management', fared no better, the critics
objecting that where 'pecuniary advantage [was] made the most prominent object
of attention, the experiment of reformation could not be fairly tried'.[69] Prison reformers like John Howard were seeking to move in the very *opposite* direction, by ending
the kind of 'commercial' regime common in eighteenth-century prisons, where the
keepers derived most of their income from a series of fees and charges levied on the
prisoners; they called instead for a public service manned by salaried functionaries.[70]

There was also general rejoicing in Radical and free trade circles in 1833 when
the Whig government deprived the East India Company of its monopoly of trade
and navigation with China, leaving it largely free to concentrate on its administrative functions, under loose Whitehall control. For the accepted wisdom was that
government and trading should be kept in separate compartments in order to protect society against corruption.

Finally, given the prevalence of the anxieties over how best to curb business
malpractice, it seemed important to maintain public authorities that could act in
a disinterested way. As we saw in Chapter 5, the prospect of *municipal councils*
assuming responsibility for suing traders who broke the law on adulteration was
vigorously contested by those who pointed out that many urban councils were
dominated by tradesmen who might be tempted to exploit such powers in order
to injure their rivals. There was thus a paradoxical situation. The northern middle
class of mid-Victorian Britain tended to view local government more favourably
than central government, because, while the hated 'aristocratic state' was relatively
impervious to their influence, they could reasonably hope to capture municipal

---

[67] Cited in P. Harling and P. Mandler, 'From "Fiscal-Military" State to Laissez-Faire State,
1760–1850', *Journal of British Studies*, 32 (1993), 47–52. Adam Smith himself had disapproved of 'tax
farming' (*Wealth of Nations*, bk. 5, ch. 2, pp. 434–5).

[68] J. R. Poynter, *Society and Pauperism: English Ideas on Poor Relief 1195–1834* (London, 1969), 132.
For further details, R. G. Cowherd, *Political Economists and the English Poor Laws: A Historical Study
of the Influence of Classical Economics on the Formation of Social Welfare Policy* (Athens, Oh., 1977),
91–2.

[69] M. Ignatieff, *A Just Measure of Pain: The Penitentiary in the Industrial Revolution, 1750–1850*
(London, 1978), esp. 109–12; J. Semple, *Bentham's Prison: A Study of the Panopticon Penitentiary* (Oxford,
1993), esp. 275.   [70] Ignatieff, *Just Measure of Pain*, 36–8.

councils. But was a council controlled by local manufacturers, merchants, and shop-keepers the sort of body best suited to 'policing' a modern commercial society? Curbs on business malpractice seemed, rather, to require a 'neutral' *state*, staffed by a cadre of 'disinterested' officials.

It was Robert Lowe, as Chancellor of the Exchequer, who eventually drew up the Order-in-Council of 1870 which threw open most civil service departments to recruitment based on open competitive examinations. But this reform, a belated embodiment of the recommendations made in the earlier Northcote-Trevelyan report,[71] was designed to erect an almost impassable barrier between private commerce and industry, on the one hand, and government and administration, on the other. The market model once espoused by the ARA was rejected in favour of the creation of a new aristocracy of service, selected from the largely classics-trained graduates of the older universities.[72]

Even a critic of open competitive examinations such as James Fitzjames Stephen conceded that there was some strength in the claim that this recruitment mechanism would end jobbery and so raise the moral tone of public life.[73] Similarly, Bagehot, who started off as a sceptic,[74] had come round by 1870 to acknowledging that the British had devised a system for shielding the country from one of the gravest dangers facing a 'democracy', 'the danger of making the administrative patronage the prize of either political party'.[75]

Now, this development can be viewed in one of two ways. It can be seen as a defeat for entrepreneurial radicalism and as a triumph for older pre-industrial values and ideals. It may be significant that Spencer positively disliked civil service examinations: youths, he argued, were 'being educated in such ways that they may pass them and get employment under Government', with the result 'that men who might otherwise reprobate further growth of officialism, [were] led to look on it with tolerance, if not favourably, as offering possible careers for those dependent on them and those related to them'.[76]

However, there is also a strong case for saying that the late-Victorian civil service in fact proved to be generally acceptable to the majority of class-conscious businessmen because the latter recognized, not always consciously perhaps, that the market needed to be regulated and balanced by a civil service in which 'merit' rather than birth reaped its due reward (hence, the use of open examinations), but in which, as in the professions, an ethic of service prevailed, not a desire for profit. Late-Victorian government had its weaknesses, but it was comparatively free from the scandal and corruption which had discredited the business community earlier

---

[71] 'The temptation to jobbery, and the danger of decidedly improper appointments being made, [was] also considerably less' if *young* men were recruited to civil service, said the Northcote-Trevelyan report (p. 9).   [72] Searle, *Entrepreneurial Politics*, ch. 5.

[73] [J. F. Stephen], 'Competitive Examinations', *Cornhill Magazine*, 4 (1861), 692, 704–5.

[74] W. Bagehot, 'Competitive Tests for the Public Service', *The Economist*, 20 (1862), cited in N. St J. Stevas (ed.), *Collected Works of Walter Bagehot* (1974), vi. 73.

[75] W. Bagehot, 'The Revolution in the Civil Service', *The Economist*, 11 June 1870, ibid., 77.

[76] H. Spencer, *The Man Versus the State*, ed. D. Macrae (London, 1969; first pub. 1884), 94.

in the century.[77] Even before the Northcote-Trevelyan reforms had come fully into effect, Trollope could celebrate the honesty of civil servants: men who were 'not constrained to mix any chicory with their coffee'.[78]

The classical economists appreciated the advantages of such a disinterested source of authority, as do some members of the modern 'Chicago School'. 'The organization of economic activity through voluntary exchange', writes Milton Friedman, 'presumes that we have provided, through government, for the maintenance of law and order to prevent coercion of one individual by another, the enforcement of contracts voluntarily entered into, the definition of the meaning of property rights, [and] the interpretation and enforcement of such rights.'[79] Arguably such functions can best be performed by a state machinery that is not itself directly implicated in ordinary market transactions. Many mid-Victorian political economists would thus have agreed with James Wilson, who proclaimed during the Crimean War outcry against aristocratic incompetence that 'legislation and Government require[d] some talents different from those which succeed at the desk or in the factory.'[80]

THE NEW PATERNALISM?

There remains to be discussed another very important mid-Victorian response to the moral anxieties raised by capitalism. This is the ideology known to historians as the 'new paternalism': that mania for works outings, tea parties, and welfare provisions by which some employers, especially those in the textile industry, sought to stabilize their relationship with their 'hands'.[81] Running parallel with these welfare initiatives were attempts on the part of some manufacturers to fashion a more collaborative relationship with the trade unions—in the interests of an industrial harmony which might, in the long run, promote greater productivity.

Such projects sometimes led to clashes with the custodians of the truths of political economy. Thus, after Fawcett had delivered to his audience at the 1859 Social

[77] Scandal multiplied in the early 20th c., however (G. R. Searle, *Corruption in Modern British Politics, 1895–1930* (Oxford, 1987)).

[78] What dishonesty there was, he added, was purely personal ([A. Trollope], 'The Civil Service as a Profession', *Cornhill Magazine*, 3 (1861), 216–17). However, Trollope by no means approved of most of the late Victorian reforms to the service (*The Three Clerks* (London, 1989; first pub. 1857), 561–8).

[79] M. Friedman, *Capitalism and Freedom* (Chicago, 1962), 27, cited in J. Evensky, 'Ethics and the Classical Liberal Tradition in Economics', *Journal of Political Economy*, 24 (1992), 66, where it is argued that Smith himself had come to realize that 'only in a community of ethical individuals [could] the invisible hand do its job properly' (p. 61).

[80] *The Economist*, 28 Apr. 1855, 449. Mill, who combined his career as a writer with a clerkship at the East India Company. similarly realized the limitations of the market.

[81] P. Joyce, *Work, Society and Politics: The Culture of the Factory in Late Victorian England* (Brighton, 1980), ch. 4; R. Price, *Labour in British Society: An Interpretative History* (London, 1986), 59–67; N. Kirk, *The Growth of Working Class Reformism in Mid-Victorian England* (London, 1985), 292–300.

Science Congress an address in which he seemed to be treating labour as a commodity and welcoming industrial conflict as a necessary stage in the determination of a proper wage level, W. E. Forster, the worsted manufacturer, expressed his dissent. Speaking as a practical employer, Forster argued that his own priority was not to cheapen labour but rather to 'get his work done well, and to pay such wages as would best accomplish that object'.[82] His fellow woollen magnate, Edward Akroyd, the creator of the model community of Akroydon in Halifax, took a broadly similar approach. 'Political economy will not help us to avoid strikes and their attendant evils', he said. 'Nay, the danger is aggravated by the rigid application of this science.'[83]

But 'progressive' Liberal capitalists who thought in these terms realized that, though their activities were an 'enlightened' way of creating industrial harmony and stability and so of boosting profits, they could also be represented as a conspiracy against the consuming public, since the latter might have to pay for the concessions in the form of higher prices.[84]

Similar disagreements broke out in the mid-Victorian years over the value of trade unions. Most political economists continued to view these 'combinations' as a potentially dangerous conspiracy against the general public. But by the late 1850s many manufacturers knew better than to treat labour as though it were a mere commodity since they had come to appreciate the benefits that might accrue from co-operating with trade union leaders. To a manufacturer like William Felkin of Nottingham, good industrial relations had always mattered more than the quest for cheapness.[85] Hence, when political economists raised objections to this sort of collaboration, many businessmen responded by sneeringly referring to 'pedants' and 'professors'.[86]

These clashes partly reflect two different perspectives on the world. Political economy, from the start, had had a 'consumerist' bias. 'Consumption is the sole end and purpose of all production', declares Adam Smith in the *Wealth of Nations*, 'and the interest of the producer ought to be attended to, only so far as it may be necessary for promoting that of the consumer.'[87] Later political economists took up the refrain. 'Consumption is the great end and object of all human industry', writes McCulloch: 'Production is merely a means to attain an end.'[88]

[82] *Transactions of the National Association for the Promotion of Social Science, 1859*, 716. However, Forster and others probably failed to understood fully what Fawcett was saying (G. Becattini, 'Henry Fawcett and the Labour Question', in L. Goldman (ed.), *The Blind Victorian: Henry Fawcett and British Liberalism* (Cambridge, 1989), 125–30).

[83] *Transactions of the National Association for the Promotion of Social Science, 1859*, 720.

[84] 'As a political economist myself', said Akroyd defensively, 'I am fully aware of the objections which may be justly raised against any unwise interruptions of the ordinary channels of supply and demand' (*Transactions of the National Association for the Promotion of Social Science, 1857*, 529).

[85] R. Church, *Economic and Social Change in a Midland Town: Victorian Nottingham 1815–1900* (London, 1966), 327–31.

[86] See Forster's condescending remarks about Ricardo in ' "Strikes" and "Lock-Outs" ', *Westminster Review*, 61 (1854), 140.   [87] Smith, *Wealth of Nations*, bk. 4, ch. 8, p. 179.

[88] J. R. McCulloch, *The Principles of Political Economy* (Edinburgh, 1825), 390. Chalmers agreed: 'The end of all production is consumption. The *terminus ad quem* of all labour, is the enjoyment of those who buy its products; whether these shall be material or immaterial' (*On Political Economy*, 335).

Businessmen who embodied 'producer interests' necessarily saw things differently. Indeed, many of them looked with a somewhat sceptical eye on political economy, with its model-building and its supposedly universal 'laws'. To a mid-Victorian businessman the approach of the political economist might well be very interesting, even illuminating. But he had needs, some practical, some moral, which political economy could in no way satisfy. To take only the most obvious of points, many Victorian businessmen were devout practising Christians. However keen they might be on profit-maximization, they seldom operated as 'economic man' was supposed to do, because they were conscious of their social obligations and religious duties.[89]

Northern manufacturers were particularly keen to give the lie to those who were denouncing them as heartless money-grubbers. This is obvious from the propaganda put out by the Association of Chambers of Commerce, with its preoccupation with 'mercantile honour'.[90] Many successful capitalists from the manufacturing towns also suffered from feelings of social and personal insecurity which tempered their entrepreneurial ambition. Because their sense of self-worth was bound up with the new communities which they had 'adopted',[91] they spent much time and energy, particularly from the 1850s onwards, in trying to bring beauty and dignity to their cities—through the construction of civic buildings, the establishment of public parks, the endowment of museums and libraries, and by sundry voluntary good works.

Thus the class feeling of many members of the urban middle class found expression in an intense pride in 'their' city, of which the obverse was jealousy and dislike of rival urban centres. All this forms part of what Anthony Howe has called 'the moralization of the capitalist',[92] that attempt on the part of some manufacturers to live up to a heroic Carlylean ideal of what a true 'captain of industry' might be. Hence, too, the desire on the part of some businessmen to overcome the barriers which still made it difficult for them to get into Parliament: they wanted to demonstrate that they were something other than second-class citizens and hoped that the urban communities they represented might bask in the reflected glory of their personal success.

In their quest to harmonize the ethics of the pulpit with the ethics of the counting-house, thoughtful mid-Victorian Christian merchants and manufacturers pursued a variety of complicated strategies, among them 'employer paternalism'. However, far from being helpful, the very idiom of 'classical' political economy was positively damaging to the esteem of the manufacturing class, and one reason

[89] Searle, *Entrepreneurial Politics,* 308–15; D. Roberts, *Paternalism in Early Victorian England* (New Brunswick, NJ, 1979), ch. 7.
[90] Well might W. L. Sargant ask what evidence there was for supposing that businessmen as a class were any more acquisitive or money-conscious than, say, lawyers—or even landed 'gentlemen' (W. L. Sargant, *Essays of a Birmingham Manufacturer* (1869), i. 42).
[91] For a penetrating analysis of the Bradford 'millocrats', see T. Koditschek, *Class Formation and Urban Industrial Society: Bradford, 1750–1850* (Cambridge, 1990), pt. 2.
[92] A. Howe, *The Cotton Masters 1830–1860* (Oxford, 1984), 314.

why some businessmen remained chary of it was that they did not want their opponents (from landed society and from within their own workforce) to brand them as worshippers of Mammon, as Carlyle and Ruskin had done. Nor had political economy much to offer those who were animated by civic pride.

On the other hand, even in the 1830s and 1840s there existed a distinctive body of writing which reflected, much more faithfully than Smith, Ricardo, or even McCulloch, the social perspectives of the manufacturing class. Its style was the antithesis of political economy, being polemical not scientific, and descriptive rather than analytical. This literature also tended towards the celebration of the particular (a town, a region, an industrial process), avoiding the formulation of supposedly universal 'laws'. Among its most important texts we might mention: Charles Babbage's *Economy of Machinery and Manufactures* (1832),[93] Andrew Ure's *Philosophy of Manufactures* (1835), Cooke Taylor's *Tour of the Manufacturing Districts* (1842), Edward Baines's *The Social, Educational and Religious State of the Manufacturing Districts* (1843), and William Felkin's *History of the Machine-Wrought Hosiery and Lace Manufactures* (1867).[94]

The 'new paternalist' ideology also took the form of portraying industrial society as a kind of 'family', in which factory owners and managers exercised a kindly supervision and control over their dependants. Arthur Helps, influenced by Carlyle on the one hand and by the Christian Socialists on the other, eloquently expounded this ideal:

I believe that the parental relation will be found the best model on which to form the duties of the employer to the employed; calling, as it does, for active exertion, requiring the most watchful tenderness, and yet limited by the strictest rules of prudence from intrenching [*sic*] on that freedom of thought and action which is necessary for all spontaneous development. . . . [For] the rule of a father . . . is the type of all good government, that under which the divine jurisdiction has been graciously expressed to us.[95]

However, was this a feasible option? Henry Fawcett, for one, thought not, arguing that it was impossible to revive the old master–servant relationship: 'the relations of employers and employed are now purely commercial', he argued: 'if an attachment exists between them, it must be based upon some identity of pecuniary interests'.[96] Yet despite Fawcett's reservations, political economy and paternalism for long continued their uneasy coexistence. Why did this happen?

[93] Babbage has been called 'the Arthur Young of the machinery age' (R. M. Romano, 'The Economic Ideas of Charles Babbage', *History of Political Economy*, 14 (1982), 402).

[94] See Stanley Chapman's introductory observations in W. Felkin, *History of the Machine-Wrought Hosiery and Lace Manufactures* (London, 1967; first pub. 1867), p. xv.

[95] A. Helps, *The Claims of Labour. An Essay on the Duties of the Employers to the Employed*, 2nd edn. (London, 1845), 153–4, 157.

[96] Hence his support for co-operation (H. Fawcett, 'Co-operative Societies; Their Social and Economical Aspects', *Macmillan's Magazine*, 2 (1860), 439–40). For an interesting discussion of the contradictions within the ideology of paternalism, C. Gallagher, *The Industrial Reformation of English Fiction, 1832–1867* (Chicago, 1985), 120.

Some historians argue that Victorian liberal thought was constructed around the concept of contract but that contractual vocabulary was dropped in favour of images of the family ('organicism') when it came to legitimizing the existence of *hier-archy*. In Greta Jones's words, the Victorians 'intertwined the language of political and legal equality with that of the family to find a means of reconciling the fact of subordination with the precepts of a system which theoretically rejected it'.[97]

This observation undoubtedly applies to issues of gender as well as to issues of race: as Catherine Hall puts it, 'the family of man has always been constituted through hierarchy and inequalities of power'.[98] Indeed, we have seen that while Mill and his circle used a modified concept of contract to advocate changes which would enhance women's status and authority *vis à vis* their male relatives, the ideology of domesticity served to justify women's continuing *dependence*.

But, paradoxically, the position is reversed when one comes to capitalist competition, for here a strict theory of contract was frequently employed to oppose workers' rights, while resort to an organic view of society suggested ways in which the harsher aspects of competition might humanely be tempered and modified, in the interests of the weak and the vulnerable.

Perhaps, however, it would be a mistake to contrast the two concepts quite so starkly. Hobsbawm and Rudé, in analysing early-nineteenth-century agrarian society, have persuasively argued that it was the *combination* of political economy and paternalism which was so useful to the dominant economic class:

its rulers wanted [the English countryside] to be both capitalist and stable, traditionalist and hierarchical. In other words, they wanted it to be governed by the universal free market of the liberal economist . . . but only to the extent that suited nobles, squires and farmers; they advocated an economy which implied mutually antagonistic classes, but did not want it to disrupt a society of ordered ranks.[99]

A similar *mélange* can be found in the attitude of the governing classes to the problems of *urban and industrial* Britain.

Political economy and 'organicism' likewise coexisted and interreacted in the ideology advanced by the apologists for capitalism. In early Victorian Manchester, the culture of the liberal middle class, argues John Seed, 'was not . . . some simple and unified world of ideas predicated on political economy and utilitarian philosophy, a viciously philistine form of religious dissent and naked self-interest'; on the contrary, it successfully appropriated elements of conservative culture (Gothic architecture, for example). But, Seed adds, 'the language of organic ties and patriarchal authority, the gestures of paternalist philanthropy, and so on— should not be seen as the abdication of liberalism but as signs of its ambition and

[97] G. Jones, *Social Darwinism and English Thought* (Brighton, 1980), 144.
[98] C. Hall, ' "From Greenland's Icy Mountains . . . to Afric's Golden Sand": Ethnicity, Race and Nation in Mid-Nineteenth Century England', *Gender and History*, 5 (1993), 217.
[99] E. J. Hobsbawm and G. Rudé, *Captain Swing* (London, 1969), 47.

power to absorb and subordinate alternative sources of meaning, its capacity for adaptation'.[100]

The writings of Mrs Gaskell show one way in which political economy could be made more palatable by having an older paternalist ideology engrafted upon it. In her early novel, *Mary Barton* (1848), Gaskell declares that she 'knew nothing of Political Economy, or the theories of trade' and that she had simply 'tried to write truthfully'. But by the time of *North and South* (1854–5), Gaskell's position has shifted: she now accepts the basic truths of political economy, but urges the masters to temper the justice of their position by humane behaviour. This attempt at synthesizing two quite different 'discourses', the abstract language of political economy and human narrative, is central to the novel, just as it was central to many attempts to make political economy more widely acceptable by showing that it had a 'heart'.[101]

However, employer paternalism was not merely a 'fiction'. When Fawcett pronounced the death of the 'old master–servant relationship', he was writing later in the century, by which time industrial communities had become more atomized than they were in the early Victorian Manchester analysed by Seed or imaginatively re-created in Gaskell's 'Milton'. Nevertheless, for good or ill, employer authority, like the still pervasive influence of Church and State, continued to restrain the operations of the market and to moderate the dominance of a market-oriented view of the world throughout the entire nineteenth century—and beyond.

CONCLUSION

Only in recent years has market liberalism broken free from all these restrictions and claimed its right to rule the world. This is largely because the various sources of 'authority' described above now lack the power which they had in mid-Victorian Britain to hold acquisitive individualism in check. 'Employer paternalism', which once had a basis in practice as well as in theory, could only operate within small and medium-sized firms, many family-owned, which were deeply rooted in a particular locality. The boards of contemporary multinational corporations, by contrast, shift capital around the world in a search for profit, with scant concern for the welfare of employees or suppliers; provincial pride and social conscience play little part in the calculations of those who direct them, just as they are largely absent from the strategies of investors, whether individual or corporate.

---

[100] Seed, 'Unitarianism', 11, 25. Compare the view of M. Wiener, *English Culture and the Decline of the Industrial Spirit 1850–1980* (Cambridge, 1981).

[101] In this paragraph, I am indebted to the very stimulating article by S. Dentith: 'Political Economy, Fiction and the Language of Practical Ideology in Nineteenth-Century England', *Social History*, 8 (1983), 195–6.

This move towards a global market has coincided with declining memberships and a loss of self-confidence on the part of the Churches and with a dwindling of the authority of Christianity. Few clergymen now take it upon themselves to provide direct spiritual guidance to the business community, and the Churches' periodical warnings about the corroding effect of greed and cupidity seem to emanate from the margins of society, not, as in Victorian times, from its heart.

Moreover, although the State now commands resources vastly more powerful than it had at its disposal 150 years ago, its capacity to control and 'tame' the forces of capitalism has been weakened by a decline in the respect accorded to 'public service'. Market forces and commercial practices have now invaded nearly all areas of policy, from prison management to hospital care. With the effective dismantling of the Northcote-Trevelyan-style civil service through the establishment of 'next step' agencies and the like, even the boundary between the public and the private sphere has become blurred.

More than that, Thatcherism, it has truly been said, has 'turned the free market from an economic theory into a social ethos—and in the process liberated large sections of society from the weight of deference and lack of self-confidence that had previously kept them submissive'.[102] The aggressive individualism thereby unleashed has changed family relationships in profound ways, many of them beneficial, but as a result the family itself has lost much of its former effectiveness as a protector of its members against the harsher pressures of the business world—despite the belated and doomed crusade to restore 'family values'. Citizenship, too, is acquiring new meanings, as, with government approval, the community is progressively broken down into a mass of atomized 'customers'.

Far from curbing and controlling these developments, the British State has positively encouraged them. The 'consumers capitalism' advocated by Mrs Thatcher and her followers has given priority to consumer choice over almost all other social goods. Unfortunately, modern Conservatives, it has been justly observed, 'have no coherent view of the functions and limits of market institutions'.[103] In the absence of such a theory, governments have, largely unwittingly, spent the last decade and a half undermining or marginalizing the institutions and belief systems which once kept rampant individualism under some sort of control.

Intelligent middle-class Victorians, slowly, haltingly, acquired an appreciation of the complexity of the social and ethical codes upon which a market-driven economy ultimately relies for its success. Capitalism, they learnt, requires a particular balance between acquisitiveness and probity: tilt the balance too much in one direction, and social (even economic) disaster threatens. Thus, whatever their personal motivation, those working in nineteenth-century Britain for the 'moralization' of the market probably contributed to the long-term stability of the capitalist order. These are insights which, admittedly in a radically new context, may have to be rediscovered.

---

[102] L. Siedentor, 'A Nation Stuck in Selfish Mode', *The Independent*, 14 Oct. 1993.
[103] J. Gray, 'Down and Out in Blackpool', *The Guardian*, 4 Oct. 1993.

Bibliography

OFFICIAL PAPERS

Hansard Parliamentary Debates, 2nd and 3rd series (all references in notes are to 3rd series, unless stated otherwise).
Third Report of the House of Lords into Laws Respecting Gaming, 1844, vol. vi.
Report from Select Committee on Adulteration of Food, &tc (1856).

NEWSPAPERS AND JOURNALS

All the Year Round
Blackwood's Magazine
Cornhill Magazine
The Economist
English Woman's Journal
Edinburgh Review
Fraser's Magazine
Household Words
Lancet
Macmillan's Magazine
Nineteenth Century
North British Review
Quarterly Review
Saturday Review
The Times
Transactions of the National Society for the Promotion of Social Science
Westminster Review

PRIMARY SOURCES

ACTON, W., *Prostitution Considered in Its Moral, Social and Sanitary Aspects*, 2nd edn. (1870, repr. 1972; first pub. 1857).
ANDERSON, J., *Observations on Slavery Particularly With a View to Its Effect on the British Colonies, in the West Indies* (Manchester, 1789).
ANON., *Free Trade in Negroes* (London, 1849).
BAGEHOT, W., *Lombard Street*, 12th edn. (London, 1906; first pub. 1873).
—— *Physics and Politics* (Boston, Mass., 1956; first pub. 1872).

BAINES, E., *The Social, Educational and Religious State of the Manufacturing Districts* (London, 1843).

—— *The Value of the Sabbath to the Working Classes* (London, 1854–5).

BOARDMAN, REVD H. A., *The Bible in the Counting-House: A Course of Lectures to Merchants* (London, 1854).

BODICHON, B. L. S., *Objections to the Enfranchisement of Women Considered* (London, 1866).

—— *Reasons for the Enfranchisement of Women* (London, 1866).

BOURNE, H. R. F., *The Romance of Trade* (London, 1871).

BRIGHT, J., and ROGERS, J. E. T. (eds.), *Speeches on Questions of Public Policy by Richard Cobden, MP*, 2 vols. (London, 1908; first pub. 1870).

BROUGHAM, H., *An Inquiry Into the Colonial Policy of the European Powers* (Edinburgh, 1803).

BUSHNELL, H., *Sermons on Living Subjects* (London, 1872).

BUTLER, J. E. (ed.), *Woman's Work and Woman's Culture* (London, 1869).

—— *Personal Reminiscences of a Great Crusade*, 2nd edn. (London, 1898).

CAIRNES, J. E., *On the Best Means of Raising the Supplies for a War Expenditure* (London, 1854).

—— *The Slave Power: Its Character, Career and Probable Designs*, 2nd edn. (London, 1863).

CARLYLE, T., *Past and Present*, Ward, Lock & Co. edn. (1910; first pub. 1843).

—— *Latter-Day Pamphlets* (London, 1850).

CHALMERS, T., *The Application of Christianity to the Commercial and Ordinary Affairs of Life In A Series of Discourses* (Glasgow, 1820).

—— *The Christian and Civic Economy of Large Towns*, 3 vols. (London, 1821–6).

—— *On Political Economy* (1832; reprinted, New York, 1968).

—— *On the Power, Wisdom and Goodness of God as Manifested in the Adaptation of External Nature to the Moral and Intellectual Constitution of Man* (London, 1853; first pub. 1833).

CHANCE, W., *Our Treatment of the Poor* (London, 1899).

CHAPMAN, J., *The Medical Institutions of the United Kingdom: A History Exemplifying the Evils of Over-Legislation* (London, 1870).

CLARKSON, T., *An Essay on the Slavery and Commerce of the Human Species . . .* (London, 1785).

CLIFFE LESLIE, T. E., *The Military System of Europe Economically Considered* (Belfast, 1856).

CLOSE, REVD F., *The Evil Consequences of Attending the Race Course Exposed: A Sermon Preached in the Parish Church of Cheltenham, 17 June 1827*, 3rd edn. (London, 1827).

COBDEN, R., *The Political Writings of Richard Cobden* (London, 1886).

COLERIDGE, S. T., ' "Blessed are ye that sow beside all Waters!"': A Lay Sermon Addressed to the Higher and Middle Classes on the Existing Distresses and Discontents' (1817), in R. J. White (ed.), *The Collected Works of Samuel Taylor Coleridge, vi, Lay Sermons* (1972), 119–230.

CONDER, J., *Wages or the Whip: An Essay On the Comparative Cost and Productiveness of Free and Slave Labour* (London, 1833).

COWAN, C., *The Danger, Irrationality, and Evils of Medical Quackery* (London, 1839).

CROPPER, J., *A Letter Addressed to the Liverpool Society for Promoting the Abolition of Slavery, On the Injurious Effects of High Prices of Produce, and the Beneficial Effects of Low Prices, On The Condition of Slaves* (Liverpool, 1823).

DARWIN, C., *The Descent of Man*, 2nd edn. (1874, rev. 1899; first pub. 1871).

DICKENS, C., *American Notes for General Circulation*, Chapman & Hall edn. (n.d.; first pub. 1842).

—— *Bleak House*, Chapman & Hall edn. (n.d.; first pub. 1852–3).

—— *Hard Times*, Chapman & Hall edn. (n.d.; first pub. 1854).

—— *Little Dorrit*, Chapman & Hall edn. (n.d.; first pub. 1855–7).

—— *Great Expectations*, Chapman & Hall edn. (n.d.; first pub. 1861).

ELIOT, G., *The Mill on the Floss*, Blackwood edn. (Edinburgh, 1878; first pub. 1860).

—— *Middlemarch*, Penguin edn. (1965; first pub. 1871–2).

ELLIS, S. S., *The Women of England, Their Social Duties and Domestic Habits*, 9th edn. (London, 1839).

—— *The Daughters of England, Their Position in Society, Character and Responsibilities* (London, 1842).

ELLIS, W., *Outlines of Social Economy* (London, 1846).

—— *Progressive Lessons in Social Science*, 2nd edn. (London, 1862; first pub. 1850).

—— *Education as a Means of Preventing Destitution* (London, 1851).

—— *A Layman's Contribution to the Knowledge and Practice of Religion in Common Life* (London, 1857).

EVANS, D. M., *The Commercial Crisis of 1847–48*, Newton Abbott edn. (1969; first pub. 1849).

—— *Facts, Failures and Frauds: Revelations Financial Mercantile Criminal* (New York, 1968; first pub. 1859).

—— *The History of the Commercial Crisis 1857–1858 and the Stock Exchange Panic of 1859* (London, 1859).

FAWCETT, M. G., *Tales in Political Economy* (London, 1874).

FELKIN, W., *History of the Machine-Wrought Hosiery and Lace Manufactures* (London, 1967; first pub. 1867).

FRANCIS, J., *Chronicles and Characters of the Stock Exchange* (London, 1849).

—— *A History of the English Railway: Its Social Relations and Revelations, 1820–1845*, 2 vols. (London, 1851).

GASKELL, E., *North and South* (London, 1854–5).

—— *Wives and Daughters* (Oxford, 1987; first pub. 1864–6).

GREEN, T. H., 'Lecture on Liberal Legislation and Freedom of Contract', in R. L. Nettleship (ed.), *Works of Thomas Hill Green*, 3 vols. (1880), iii. 365–86.

—— *Lectures on the Principles of Political Obligation* (London, 1883).

GREG, S., *Two Letters to Leonard Horner, Esq., on the Capabilities of the Factory System* (London, 1840).

GREG, W. R., *Past and Present Efforts for the Extinction of the African Slave Trade* (London, 1840).

—— *The Creed of Christendom; Its Foundations and Superstructure* (London, 1851).

—— *Essays on Political and Social Science, Contributed Chiefly to the Edinburgh Review*, 2 vols. (London, 1853).

—— *Why Are Women Redundant?* (London, 1869).

—— *Enigmas of Life* (London, 1872).

HARDY, T., *The Life and Death of the Mayor of Casterbridge*, New Wessex edn. (1975; first pub. 1886).

HASSALL, A. H., *Food and Its Adulterations* (London, 1855).

HASSALL, A. H., *Adulterations Detected: Or, Plain Instructions For the Discovery of Frauds in Food and Medicine* (London, 1857).

HELPS, SIR A., *The Claims of Labour: An Essay on the Duties of the Employers to the Employed*, 2nd edn. (London, 1845).

HOYLE, W., *Our National Resources; And How They Are Wasted: An Omitted Chapter in Political Economy* (London, c.1871).

JENKINS, T. A. (ed.), *The Parliamentary Diaries of Sir John Trelawny, 1858–1865*, Camden Fourth Series, xl (London, 1990).

—— *The Parliamentary Diaries of Sir John Trelawny, 1868–73*, Camden Fifth Series (London, 1994), iii. 329–513.

KINGSLEY, C., *Alton Locke: Tailor and Poet* (London, 1895; first pub. 1850).

LAING, S., *Notes of a Traveller, on the Social and Political State of France, Prussia, Switzerland, Italy and other Parts of Europe* (London, 1854; first pub. 1842).

LALOR, J., *Money and Morals: A Book For The Times* (London, 1852).

LYTTELTON, REVD W. H., *Sins of Trade and Business* (London, 1874).

MACAULAY, T. B., 'Francis Bacon' (July 1837), in id., *Critical and Historical Essays*, 2 vols., Everyman edn. (London, 1907), ii. 290–398.

McCULLOCH, J. R., *The Principles of Political Economy* (Edinburgh, 1830; first pub. 1825).

—— *Considerations on Partnerships with Limited Liability* (London, 1856).

MACKAY, T., *A History of the English Poor Law* (London, 1904).

MAINE, H. S., *Ancient Law* (London, 1861).

MALTHUS, T., *An Essay on The Principle of Population*, 1st edn. (London, 1798).

MARCET, MRS, *Conversations on Political Economy: In Which The Elements of That Science Are Familiarly Explained* (London, 1839; first pub. 1816).

MARTINEAU, H., *Cousin Marshall* (London, 1832).

—— *Demarara: A Tale* (London, 1832).

—— *Weal and Woe in Garveloch* (London, 1832).

—— *Poor Laws and Paupers Illustrated* (London, 1833).

—— *The Moral of Many Fables* (London, 1834).

—— 'On the Duty of Studying Political Economy', in id., *Miscellanies*, 2 vols. (Boston, 1836), i. 272–88.

—— *Society in America*, 3 vols. (London, 1837), i. 148–54.

MARX, KARL, and ENGELS, FREDERICK, *Selected Works*, 2 vols. (Moscow, 1958).

MILL, J. S., *Principles of Political Economy* (London, 1848), in *Collected Works*, ii and iii, ed. J. R. Robson (Toronto, 1965).

—— *On Liberty*, Everyman edn. (1910; first pub. 1859).

—— *Considerations on Representative Government*, Everyman edn. (1910; first pub. 1861).

—— *The Subjection of Women*, ed. S. Mansfield (Arlington Heights, Ill., 1980; first pub. 1869).

—— *Collected Works of John Stuart Mill*, 33 vols. (Toronto, 1965–91).

MILNE, J. D., *Industrial Employment of Women in the Middle and Lower Ranks*, 2nd edn. (London, 1870; first pub. 1857).

MORRIS, A. J., *Religion and Business: Or Spiritual Life in One of its Secular Departments* (London, 1853).

NEATE, C., *Two Lectures on Trades Unions, Delivered in the University of Oxford in the Year 1861* (Oxford, 1862).

Owen, Revd J. B., *Business Without Christianity* (London, 1855).

Parkes, B. R., *Essays on Woman's Work* (London, 1865).

Percival, T., *Medical Ethics: Or, a Code of Institutes and Precepts Adapted to the Professional Conduct of Physicians and Surgeons* (Manchester, 1803).

Rae, J., *Life of Adam Smith* (New York, 1965; first pub. 1895).

Raikes, R., *Considerations on the Alliance between Christianity and Commerce* (London, 1825; first pub. 1806).

—— *On Christian Humility as Applicable to the Practice of the World* (London, 1825).

Reade, C., *Hard Cash: A Matter-of-Fact Romance* (New York, n.d.; first pub. 1863).

Ricardo, D., *The Principles of Political Economy and Taxation*, ed. D. Winch (London, 1987; first pub. 1817).

—— *The Works and Correspondence of David Ricardo*, 11 vols., ed. P. Sraffa (Cambridge, 1952).

Ricardo, J., *The War Policy of Commerce* (London, 1855).

Richmond, W., *Economic Morals: Four Lectures* (London, 1890).

Rickards, G. K., *The Financial Policy of War: Two Lectures on the Funding System and on the Different Modes of Raising Supplies in Time of War* (London, 1855).

Ritchie, J. E., *Thoughts on Slavery and Cheap Sugar: A Letter to the Members and Friends of the British and Foreign Anti-Slavery Society* (London, 1844).

Ruskin, J., *Unto This Last* (London, 1862).

Sargant, W. L., *Essays of a Birmingham Manufacturer* (London, 1869).

Senior, N. W., *An Outline of the Science of Political Economy* (New York, 1965; first pub. 1836).

Shirreff, E., *Intellectual Education and Its Influences on the Character and Happiness of Women* (London, 1858).

Smiles, S., *Self-Help: With Illustrations of Conduct and Perseverance* (1910; first pub. 1859).

—— *Lives of the Engineers*, 3 vols. (London, 1862).

—— *Character* (London, 1871).

—— *Thrift* (London, 1886).

Smith, A., *An Inquiry into the Nature and Causes of The Wealth of Nations*, ed. E. Cannan (Chicago, 1976; first pub. 1776).

Smith, B. L., *Women and Work* (London, 1857).

Spencer, H., *Social Statics, or The Conditions Essential to Human Happiness Specified* (London, 1868; first pub. 1850).

—— *The Study of Sociology* (London, 1873).

—— *The Data of Ethics* (London, 1894; first pub. 1879).

—— *The Principles of Sociology*, 3 vols. (1876–96), in id., *Synthetic Philosophy of Herbert Spencer*, Westminster edn. (New York, 1892–6).

—— *The Man Versus the State*, ed. D. Macrae (London, 1969; first pub. 1884).

—— *The Principles of Ethics*, 2 vols. (1879–93) (1891–3), in id., *Synthetic Philosophy of Herbert Spencer*, Westminster edn. (New York, 1892–6).

—— *Essays, Scientific, Political, and Speculative*, 3 vols. (London, 1893).

Spencer, T., *Objections to The New Poor Law Answered* (London, 1841).

Stephen, J. F., *Liberty, Equality, Fraternity*, ed. R. J. White (Cambridge, 1967; first pub. 1873).

Stephen, L., *Life of Henry Fawcett* (London, 1885).

STEWART, D. (ed.), *The Works of Adam Smith, Ll.D.* (London, 1811).

STOWELL, H., *A Model for Men of Business; Or Lectures on the Character of Nehemiah* (London, 1854).

TAIT, W., *Magdalenism: An Inquiry into the Extent, Causes, and Consequences of Prostitution in Edinburgh* (Edinburgh, 1840).

THACKERAY, W. M., *The Great Hoggarty Diamond* (London, 1841).

—— *The Diary of C. Jeames De La Pluche* (1845–6), in *The Works of William Makepeace Thackeray*, vol. iii (London, 1898).

—— *The Newcomes* (1855), in *The Works of William Makepeace Thackeray*, vol. viii (London, 1898).

THOMSON, H. B., *The Choice of a Profession* (London, 1857).

TROLLOPE, A., *The New Zealander*, ed. N. J. Hall (Oxford, 1965; written 1855–6).

—— *The Three Clerks* (Oxford, 1989; first pub. 1857).

URE, A., *The Philosophy of Manufactures: Or, an Exposition of the Scientific, Moral, and Commercial Economy of the Factory System of Great Britain* (London, 1835).

WARREN, S., *The Moral, Social and Professional Duties of Attornies and Solicitors* (London, 1848).

WHATELY, E. J., *Life and Correspondence of Richard Whately, DD* (London, 1875).

WHATELY, R., *Introductory Lectures on Political Economy: Delivered at Oxford, 1831* (London, 1847).

WILBERFORCE, S., *An Appeal to the Religion, Justice, and Humanity of the Inhabitants of the British Empire on Behalf of the Negro Slaves in the West Indies* (London, 1823).

WILKINSON, J. J. G., *Unlicensed Medicine* (London, 1855).

WRIGHT, T. ['The Journeyman Engineer'], *Some Habits and Customs of the Working Classes* (London, 1867).

—— ['The Journeyman Engineer'], *The Great Unwashed* (London, 1868).

SECONDARY WORKS

BOOKS

ABEL-SMITH, B., and STEVENS, R., *Lawyers and the Courts: A Sociological Study of the English Legal System 1750–1965* (London, 1967).

ANDERSON, O., *A Liberal State at War: English Politics and Economics During the Crimean War* (London, 1967).

ARMYTAGE, W. H. G., *A. J. Mundella 1825–1898* (London, 1951).

ASHTON, J., *The History of Gambling in England* (New York, 1968; first pub. 1899).

ASHWORTH, J., *Slavery, Capitalism and Politics in the Antebellum Republic*, i, *Commerce and Compromise, 1820–1850* (Cambridge, 1995).

ATIYAH, P. S., *The Rise and Fall of Freedom of Contract* (Oxford, 1979).

BAILEY, B., *The Resurrection Men: A History of the Trade in Corpses* (London, 1991).

BAILEY, P., *Leisure and Class in Victorian England: Rational Recreation and the Contest for Control, 1830–1885* (London, 1978).

BELLAMY, R. (ed.), *Victorian Liberalism: Nineteenth-Century Political Thought and Practice* (London, 1990).

BERG, M., *The Machinery Question and the Making of Political Economy, 1815–48* (Cambridge, 1980).

BERLANT, J. L., *Profession and Monopoly: A Study of Medicine in the United States and Great Britain* (Berkeley, 1975).

BIAGINI, E. F., *Liberty, Retrenchment and Reform: Popular Liberalism in the Age of Gladstone, 1860–1880* (Cambridge, 1992).

BINKLEY, R. C., *Realism and Nationalism, 1852–1871* (New York, 1935).

BLACKBURN, H., *Women's Suffrage: A Record of the Women's Suffrage Movement in the British Isles With Biographical Sketches of Miss Becker* (New York, 1971; first pub. 1902).

BLYTH, E. K., *Life of William Ellis* (London, 1889).

BOLT, C., *The Anti-Slavery Movement and Reconstruction: A Study in Anglo-American Co-operation 1833–77* (London, 1969).

—— and DRESCHER, S. (eds.), *Anti-Slavery, Religion and Reform: Essays in Memory of Roger Anstey* (Folkestone, 1980).

BOWLEY, M., *Nassau Senior and Classical Economics* (London, 1937).

BOYLAN, T. A., and FOLEY, T. P., *Political Economy and Colonial Ireland* (London, 1992).

BRISTOW, E. J., *Vice and Vigilance: Purity Movements in Britain since 1700* (Dublin, 1977).

BROWN, J. M., *Dickens: Novelist in the Market-Place* (London, 1982).

BROWN, S. J., *Thomas Chalmers and the Godly Commonwealth in Scotland* (Oxford, 1982).

BRUCE, A., *The Purchase System in the British Army, 1660–1871* (London, 1980).

BRUNDAGE, A., *The Making of the New Poor Law: The Politics of Inquiry, Enactment and Implementation, 1832–39* (London, 1978).

BURMAN, S. (ed.), *Fit Work for Women* (London, 1979).

BURN, W. L., *The Age of Equipoise: A Study of the Mid-Victorian Generation* (London, 1964; repr. 1968).

BURNETT, J., *Plenty and Want: A Social History of Diet in England from 1815 to the Present Day* (London, 1966).

BURTON, H., *Barbara Bodichon 1827–1891* (London, 1949).

BYNUM, W. F., LOCK, S., and PORTER, R. (eds.), *Medical Journals and Medical Knowledge: Historical Essays* (London, 1992).

CARTER, H., *The English Temperance Movement: A Study in Objectives* (London, 1933).

CHECKLAND, O., *Philanthropy in Victorian Scotland: Social Welfare and the Voluntary Principle* (Edinburgh, 1980).

CHEYNE, A. C. (ed.), *The Practical and the Pious: Essays on Thomas Chalmers (1780–1847)* (Edinburgh, 1985).

CHINN, C., *Better Betting with a Decent Feller: Bookmaking, Betting and the British Working Class 1750–1990* (London, 1991).

CHURCH, R., *Economic and Social Change in a Midland Town: Victorian Nottingham 1815–1900* (London, 1966).

CLAPSON, M., *A Bit of a Flutter: Popular gambling and English Society, c.1823–1961* (Manchester, 1992).

CLIVE, J. *Scotch Reviewers: The 'Edinburgh Review', 1802–1815* (London, 1957).

COCKS, R. J. C., *Sir Henry Maine: A Study in Victorian Jurisprudence* (Cambridge, 1988).

COLAIACO, J. A., *James Fitzjames Stephen and the Crisis of Victorian Thought* (New York, 1983).

COLE, H., *Things For the Surgeon: A History of the Resurrection Men* (London, 1964).

COLLINI, S., *Public Moralists: Political Thought and Intellectual Life in Britain, 1850–1930* (Oxford, 1991).

COLLINI, S., WINCH, D., and BURROW, J., *That Noble Science of Politics: A Study in Nineteenth-Century Intellectual History* (Cambridge, 1983).

CORFIELD, P. J., *Power and the Professions in Britain 1700–1850* (London, 1995).

CORNISH, W. R., and CLARK, G. DE N., *Law and Society in England 1750–1950* (London, 1989).

COWHERD, R. G., *Political Economists and the English Poor Laws: A Historical Study of the Influence of Classical Economics on the Formation of Social Welfare Policy* (Athens, Oh., 1977).

DAVENPORT-HINES, R. P. T. (ed.), *Speculators and Patriots: Essays in Business Biography* (London, 1986).

DAVIDOFF, L., and HALL, C., *Family Fortunes: Men and Women of the English Middle Class, 1780–1850* (London, 1987).

DAVIS, D. B., *The Problem of Slavery in Western Culture* (London, 1966; repr. 1970).

—— *The Problem of Slavery in the Age of Revolution, 1770–1823* (Ithica, NY, 1975).

—— *Slavery and Human Progress* (New York and Oxford, 1984).

DIAMOND, A. (ed.), *The Victorian Achievement of Sir Henry Maine: A Centennial Reassessment* (Cambridge, 1991).

DIGBY, A., *Making a Medical Living: Doctors and Patients in the English Market for Medicine, 1720–1911* (Cambridge, 1994).

DINGLE, A. E., *The Campaign for Prohibition in Victorian England: The United Kingdom Alliance 1872–1895* (London, 1980).

DIXON, D., *From Prohibition to Regulation: Bookmaking, Anti-Gambling, and the Law* (Oxford, 1991).

DRESCHER, S., *Econocide: British Slavery in the Era of Abolition* (Pittsburgh, 1977).

—— *Capitalism and Antislavery: British Mobilization in Comparative Perspective* (London, 1986).

DRIVER, C., *Tory Radical: The Life of Richard Oastler* (New York, 1946).

DUMAN, D., *The Judicial Bench in England 1727–1875: The Reshaping of a Professional Elite* (London, 1982).

—— *The English and Colonial Bars in the Nineteenth Century* (London, 1983).

DUNCAN, D., *The Life and Letters of Herbert Spencer* (London, 1908).

EDSALL, N. C., *The Anti-Poor Law Movement, 1834–44* (Manchester, 1971).

—— *Richard Cobden: Independent Radical* (Cambridge, Mass., 1986).

ELLIOT, A. D., *Life of Lord Goschen 1831–1907* (London, 1911).

ELSHTAIN, J. B., *Public Man, Private Woman: Women in Social and Political Thought* (Oxford, 1981).

ERICKSON, A. B., *The Public Career of Sir James Graham* (Oxford, 1952).

FEAVER, G., *From Status to Contract: A Biography of Sir Henry Maine 1822–1888* (London, 1969).

FIDO, M., *Bodysnatchers: A History of the Resurrectionists, 1742–1832* (London, 1988).

FINER, S. E., *The Life and Times of Sir Edwin Chadwick* (London, 1952).

FINLAYSON, G., *Citizen, State, and Social Welfare in Britain 1830–1990* (Oxford, 1994).

FINN, M. C., *After Chartism: Class and Nation in English Radical Politics, 1848–1874* (Cambridge, 1993).

FINNEGAN, F., *Poverty and Prostitution: A Study of Victorian Prostitution in York* (Cambridge, 1979).

FLADELAND, B., *Abolitionists and Working-Class Problems in the Age of Industrialization* (Baton Rouge, La., 1984).

FONTANA, B., *Rethinking the Politics of Commercial Society: The Edinburgh Review, 1802–1832* (Cambridge, 1985).

FOREMAN-PECK, J., and MILLWARD, R., *Public and Private Ownership of British Industry 1820–1990* (Oxford, 1994).

FRANCIS, M., and MORROW, J., *A History of English Political Thought in the Nineteenth Century* (London, 1994).

FRASER, D. (ed.), *The New Poor Law in the Nineteenth Century* (London, 1976).

FRIEDMAN, M., *Capitalism and Freedom* (Chicago, 1962).

GALBRAITH, J. K., *A History of Economics: The Past as the Present* (London, 1987; repr. 1989).

GALLAGHER, C., *The Industrial Reformation of English Fiction: Social Discourse and Narrative Form 1832–1867* (Chicago, 1985).

GLENDINNING, V., *Trollope* (London, 1992).

GOLDMAN, L. (ed.), *The Blind Victorian: Henry Fawcett and British Liberalism* (Cambridge, 1989).

GORDON, B., *Political Economy in Parliament, 1819–1823* (London, 1976).

—— *Economic Doctrine and Tory Liberalism, 1824–1830* (London, 1979).

GOSDEN, P. H. J. H., *Self-Help: Voluntary Associations in the 19th Century* (London, 1973).

GOURVISH, T. R., and WILSON, R. G., *The British Brewing Industry 1830–1980* (Cambridge, 1994).

GRAMPP, W. D., *The Manchester School of Economics* (London, 1960).

GREEN, D. G., *Working-Class Patients and the Medical Establishment: Self-Help in Britain from the Mid-Nineteenth Century to 1948* (Aldershot, 1985).

GUTZKE, D. W., *Protecting the Pub: Brewers and Publicans against Temperance* (Woodbridge, 1989).

HAMER, D. A., *The Politics of Electoral Pressure: A Study in the History of Victorian Reform Agitations* (Hassocks, 1977).

HARRIS, J., *Private Lives, Public Spirit: A Social History of Britain 1870–1914* (Oxford, 1993).

HARRISON, B., *Drink and the Victorians: The Temperance Question in England 1815–1872* (London, 1971).

HECKSCHER, E. F., *The Continental System: An Economic Interpretation* (Oxford, 1922).

HERSTEIN, S. R., *A Mid-Victorian Feminist, Barbara Leigh Smith Bodichon* (New Haven, 1985).

HILTON, B., *The Age of Atonement: The Influence of Evangelicalism on Social and Economic Thought 1795–1865* (Oxford, 1988).

HIMMELFARB, G., *The Idea of Poverty: England in the Early Industrial Age* (London, 1984).

HINSLEY, F. H., *Power and the Pursuit of Peace: Theory and Practice in the History of Relations between States* (Cambridge, 1963).

HIRST, F. W., *The Political Economy of War* (London, 1915).

HOBSBAWM, E. J., and RUDÉ, G., *Captain Swing* (London, 1969).

HOBSON, J. A., *Richard Cobden: The International Man*, ed. N. Masterman (London, 1968; first pub. 1919).

HOLCOMBE, L., *Victorian Ladies at Work* (Newton Abbot, 1973).

HOLCOMBE, L., *Wives and Property: Reform of the Married Women's Property Law in Nineteenth-Century England* (Oxford, 1983).

HOLLANDER, S., *The Economics of John Stuart Mill*, ii, *Political Economy* (Oxford, 1985).

HOLTON, S. S., *Feminism and Democracy: Women's Suffrage and Reform Politics in Britain 1900–1918* (Cambridge, 1986).

HOSTETTLER, J., *Thomas Wakley: An Improbable Radical* (Chichester, 1993).

HOUGHTON, W., *The Victorian Frame of Mind 1830–1870* (New Haven, 1957).

HOWE, A., *The Cotton Masters 1830–1860* (Oxford, 1984).

HUCH, R. K., *The Radical Lord Radnor: The Public Life of Viscount Folkestone, Third Earl of Radnor (1779–1869)* (Minneapolis, 1977).

HUMPHREYS, R., *Sin, Organised Charity and the Poor Law in Victorian England* (Basingstoke, 1995).

HURWITZ, E. F., *Politics and the Public Conscience: Slave Emancipation and the Abolitionist Movement in Britain* (London, 1973).

HUTTON, W., *The State We're In* (London, 1995).

IGNATIEFF, M., *A Just Measure of Pain: The Penitentiary in the Industrial Revolution, 1750–1850* (London, 1978).

INGLIS, K. S., *Churches and the Working Classes in Victorian England* (London, 1963).

JAGGAR, A. M., *Feminist Politics and Human Nature* (Brighton, 1983).

JAY, E., and JAY, R. (eds.), *Critics of Capitalism: Victorian Reactions to 'Political Economy'* (Cambridge, 1986).

JENKINS, R., *Gladstone* (London, 1995).

JEREMY, D. (ed.), *Business and Religion in Britain* (Aldershot, 1988).

JONES, D. J. V., *Crime, Protest, Community and Police in Nineteenth-Century Britain* (1982).

JONES, G. S., *Outcast London: A Study in the Relationship between Classes in Victorian Society* (Oxford, 1971).

JONES, G., *Social Darwinism and English Thought: The Interaction Between Biological and Social Theory* (Brighton, 1980).

JOYCE, P., *Work, Society and Politics: The Culture of the Factory in Later Victorian England* (Brighton, 1980).

—— *Visions of the People: Industrial England and the Question of Class, 1848–1914* (Cambridge, 1991).

KENT, S. K., *Sex and Suffrage in Britain, 1860–1914* (Princeton, 1987).

KIRK, H., *Portrait of a Profession: A History of the Solicitors' Profession, 1100 to the Present Day* (London, 1976).

KIRK, N., *The Growth of Working Class Reformism in Mid-Victorian England* (London, 1985).

KNOTT, J., *Popular Opposition to the 1834 Poor Law* (London, 1986).

KODITSCHEK, T., *Class Formation and Urban-Industrial Society: Bradford, 1750–1850* (Cambridge, 1990).

LAMBERT, R., *Sir John Simon 1816–1904 and English Social Administration* (London, 1963).

LANGFORD, P., *A Polite and Commercial People: England 1727–1783* (Oxford, 1989).

LEDBETTER, R., *A History of The Malthusian League 1877–1927* (Columbus, Oh., 1976).

LESTER, V. M., *Victorian Insolvency: Bankruptcy, Imprisonment for Debt, and Company Winding-up in Nineteenth-Century England* (Oxford, 1995).

LEVINE, P., *Victorian Feminism 1850–1900* (London, 1987).

—— *Feminist Lives in Victorian England: Private Roles and Public Commitment* (Oxford, 1990).

Lewis, J. (ed.), *Before the Vote Was Won: Arguments For and Against Women's Suffrage* (London, 1987).

—— *Women and Social Action in Victorian and Edwardian England* (Aldershot, 1991).

Lloyd, C., *The Navy and the Slave Trade: The Suppression of the African Slave Trade in the 19th Century* (London, 1949).

Longmate, N., *The Waterdrinkers: A History of Temperance* (London, 1968).

Loudon, I., *Medical Care and the General Practitioner, 1750–1850* (Oxford, 1986).

Lubenow, W. C., *The Politics of Government Growth: Early Victorian Attitudes Toward State Intervention, 1833–1848* (Newton Abbot, 1971).

Manchester, A. M., *A Modern Legal History of England and Wales, 1750–1950* (London, 1980).

Mandler, P., *Aristocratic Government in the Age of Reform: Whigs and Liberals 1830–1852* (Oxford, 1990).

—— (ed.), *The Uses of Charity: The Poor on Relief in the Nineteenth-Century Metropolis* (Philadelphia, 1990).

Marcus, S., *The Other Victorians: A Study of Sexuality and Pornography in Mid-Nineteenth Century England* (London, 1966; repr. 1969).

Marshall, T., *Murdering to Dissect: Grave-Robbing, Frankenstein and the Anatomy Literature* (Manchester, 1995).

Mason, M., *The Making of Victorian Sexual Attitudes* (Oxford, 1994).

—— *The Making of Victorian Sexuality* (Oxford, 1994).

Mathieson, W. L., *Great Britain and the Slave Trade, 1839–65* (New York, 1967).

Matthew, H. C. G., *Gladstone: 1809–1874* (Oxford, 1986; repr. 1988).

—— *Gladstone: 1875–1898* (Oxford, 1995).

McCalman, I., *Radical Underworld: Prophets, Revolutionaries and Pornographers in London, 1795–1840* (Cambridge, 1988).

McHugh, P., *Prostitution and Victorian Social Reform* (London, 1980).

McMaster, J., *Thackeray: The Major Novels* (Manchester, 1971).

McMaster, R. D., *Trollope and the Law* (Basingstoke, 1986).

Meadowcroft, J., *Conceptualizing the State: Innovation and Dispute in British Political Thought 1880–1914* (Oxford, 1995).

Meek, R. L., *Economics and Ideology and Other Essays: Studies in the Development of Economic Thought* (1967).

Menefee, S. P., *Wives for Sale: An Ethnographic Study of British Popular Divorce* (Oxford, 1981).

Midgley, C., *Women against Slavery: The British Campaigns, 1780–1870* (1992).

Mineka, F. E., *The Dissidence of Dissent: The Monthly Repository, 1806–1838* (Chapel Hill, NC, 1944).

Montgomery, M. E., *'Gilded Prostitution': Status, Money, and Transatlantic Marriages, 1870–1914* (London, 1989).

Morley, J., *The Life of Richard Cobden*, 2 vols. (London, 1896; first pub. 1881).

—— *Life of Gladstone* (London, 1903).

Munting, R., *An Economic and Social History of Gambling in Britain and the USA* (Manchester, 1996).

Nead, L., *Myths of Sexuality: Representations of Women in Victorian Britain* (Oxford, 1988).

New, C. W., *The Life of Henry Brougham to 1830* (Oxford, 1961).

O'Brien, D. P., *J. R. McCulloch: A Study in Classical Economics* (London, 1970).

OFFER, J. (ed.), *Herbert Spencer: Political Writings* (Cambridge, 1994).

PARKER, C. S. (ed.), *Sir Robert Peel from his Private Papers*, 3 vols. (London, 1899).

PARRY, J. P., *Democracy and Religion: Gladstone and the Liberal Party 1867–75* (Cambridge, 1986; repr. 1989).

—— *The Rise and Fall of Liberal Government in Victorian Britain* (New Haven, 1993).

PARRY, N., and PARRY, J., *The Rise of the Medical Profession: A Study of Collective Social Mobility* (London, 1976).

PAUL, E. F., *Moral Revolution and Economic Science: The Demise of Laissez-Faire in Nineteenth-Century British Political Economy* (Westport, Conn., 1979).

PEARSALL, R., *The Worm in the Bud: The World of Victorian Sexuality* (London, 1969; repr. 1971).

PEEL, J. D. Y., *Herbert Spencer: The Evolution of a Sociologist* (London, 1971).

PERKIN, H., *The Origin of Modern English Society 1780–1880* (London, 1969).

—— *The Rise of Professional Society: England since 1880* (London, 1989).

PERKINS, E. B., *Gambling in English Life* (London, 1950).

PETERSON, M. J., *The Medical Profession in Mid-Victorian London* (Berkeley, 1978).

PETRIE, G., *A Singular Iniquity: The Campaigns of Josephine Butler* (London, 1971).

PICHANICK, V. K., *Harriet Martineau: The Woman and Her Work 1802–76* (Ann Arbor, 1980).

POCOCK, J. G. A., *Virtue, Commerce and History* (Cambridge, 1985).

POLLOCK, J., *Wilberforce* (London, 1977).

POOVEY, M., *Uneven Developments: The Ideological Work of Gender in Mid-Victorian England. Women in Culture and Society* (Chicago, 1988).

PORTER, R., *Disease, Medicine and Society in England, 1550–1860* (London, 1987).

—— *Health for Sale: Quackery in England, 1660–1850* (London, 1989).

POYNTER, J. R., *Society and Pauperism: English Ideas on Poor Relief, 1795–1834* (London, 1969).

PRICE, R., *Labour in British Society: An Interpretative History* (London, 1986).

PROCHASKA, F. K., *Women and Philanthropy in Nineteenth-Century England* (Oxford, 1980).

—— *The Voluntary Impulse: Philanthropy in Modern Britain* (London, 1988).

RATHBONE, E. F., *William Rathbone: A Memoir* (London, 1905).

READ, D., *Cobden and Bright: A Victorian Political Partnership* (London, 1967).

RENDALL, J., *The Origins of Modern Feminism: Women in Britain, France and the United States, 1780–1860* (Basingstoke, 1985).

—— (ed.), *Equal or Different: Women's Politics 1800–1914* (Oxford, 1987).

—— *Women in an Industrializing Society: England 1750–1880* (Oxford, 1990).

RICHARDSON, R., *Death, Dissection and the Destitute* (1987; repr. 1989).

RIDLEY, J., *Lord Palmerston* (London, 1970).

ROBB, G., *White Collar Crime in Modern England: Financial Fraud and Business Morality, 1845–1929* (Cambridge, 1992).

ROBBINS, L., *The Theory of Economic Policy in English Classical Political Economy* (London, 1952).

ROBERTS, D., *Paternalism in Early Victorian England* (New Brunswick, NJ, 1979).

ROBERTS, T. A., *The Concept of Benevolence: Aspects of Eighteenth-Century Moral Philosophy* (1973).

RODGERS, B., *The Battle Against Poverty, i, From Pauperism to Human Rights* (London, 1968).

ROSSI, A. S. (ed.), *John Stuart Mill and Harriet Taylor Mill: Essays on Sex Equality* (Chicago, 1970).

ROUTH, G., *The Origin of Economic Ideas* (White Plains, NJ, 1975).

ROWNTREE, B. S. (ed.), *Betting and Gambling: A National Evil* (London, 1905).

RUSSELL, N., *The Novelist and Mammon: Literary Responses to the World of Commerce in the Nineteenth Century* (Oxford, 1986).

SANDERS, V. (ed.), *Harriet Martineau: Selected Letters* (Oxford, 1990).

SEARLE, G. R., *Corruption in Modern British Politics, 1895–1930* (Oxford, 1987).

—— *Entrepreneurial Politics in Mid-Victorian Britain* (Oxford, 1993).

SEMMEL, B., *The Rise of Free Trade Imperialism: Classical Political Economy, the Empire of Free Trade, and Imperialism 1750–1850* (Cambridge, 1970).

—— *John Stuart Mill and the Pursuit of Virtue* (New Haven, 1984).

SEMPLE, J., *Bentham's Prison: A Study of the Panopticon Penitentiary* (Oxford, 1993).

SHATTOCK, J., and WOLFF, M. (eds.), *The Victorian Periodical Press: Samplings and Soundings* (Leicester, 1982).

SHIMAN, L. L., *Crusade Against Drink in Victorian England* (Basingstoke, 1988).

SIGSWORTH, E. M. (ed.), *In Search of Victorian Values* (Manchester, 1988).

SIMEY, M. B., *Charitable Effort in Liverpool in the Nineteenth Century* (Liverpool, 1951).

SMITH, K. J. M., *James Fitzjames Stephen: Portrait of a Victorian Rationalist* (Cambridge, 1988).

SMITH, R. G., *Regulating British Medicine: The General Medical Council* (Chichester, 1992).

SOCKWELL, W. D., *Popularizing Classical Economics: Henry Brougham and William Ellis* (New York, 1994).

SOLOWAY, R. A., *Prelates and People: Ecclesiastical Social Thought in England 1783–1852* (London, 1969).

—— *Birth Control and the Population Question in England, 1877–1930* (Chapel Hill, NC, 1982).

SPINNER, T. J., JUN., *George Joachim Goschen: The Transformation of a Victorian Liberal* (Cambridge, 1973).

SPRIGGE, S. S., *The Life and Times of Thomas Wakley* (London, 1897).

STEVAS, N. St J. (ed.), *Collected Works of Walter Bagehot*, 15 vols. (London, 1965–85).

TAYLOR, A. J. P., *The Trouble Makers: Dissent Over Foreign Policy 1792–1939* (London, 1957).

TAYLOR, M., *The Decline of British Radicalism, 1847–1860* (Oxford, 1995).

TEMPERLEY, H., *British Antislavery 1833–1870* (Harlow, 1972).

TENNYSON, G. B. (ed.), *A Carlyle Reader: Selections from the Writings of Thomas Carlyle* (Cambridge, 1984).

THOMAS, D., *A Long Time Burning: The History of Literary Censorship in England* (London, 1969).

TURLEY, D., *The Culture of English Antislavery 1780–1860* (London, 1991).

TYRRELL, A., *Joseph Sturge and the Moral Radical Party in Early Victorian Britain* (London, 1987).

UGLOW, J., *Elizabeth Gaskell* (London, 1993; repr. 1994).

VICINUS, M. (ed.), *Suffer and Be Still: Women in the Victorian Age* (Bloomington, Ind., 1972).

—— *Independent Women: Work & Community for Single Women 1850–1920* (Chicago, 1985).

WADDINGTON, I., *The Medical Profession in the Industrial Revolution* (Dublin, 1984).

WALKOWITZ, J. R., *Prostitution and Victorian Society: Women, Class, and the State* (Cambridge, 1980).

WALVIN, J. (ed.), *Slavery and British Society 1776–1846* (London, 1982).

WALVIN, J., *Black Ivory: A History of British Slavery* (London, 1992).

WATERMAN, A. M. C., *Revolution, Economics and Religion: Christian Political Economy, 1798–1833* (Cambridge, 1991).

WEBB, S., and WEBB, B., *The History of Liquor Licensing Principally in England From 1700 to 1830* (London, 1963; first pub. 1903).

—— —— *English Poor Law Policy* (London, 1963; first pub. 1910).

WEISS, B., *The Hell of the English: Bankruptcy and the Victorian Novel* (Lewisburg, 1986).

WIENER, M., *English Culture and the Decline of the Industrial Spirit 1850–1980* (Cambridge, 1981).

WIGLEY, J., *The Rise and Fall of the Victorian Sunday* (Manchester, 1980).

WILTSHIRE, D., *The Social and Political Thought of Herbert Spencer* (Oxford, 1978).

WINCH, D., *Adam Smith's Politics: An Essay in Historiographic Revision* (Cambridge, 1978).

—— *Malthus* (Oxford, 1987).

—— *Riches and Poverty: An Intellectual History of Political Economy in Britain, 1750–1834* (Cambridge, 1996).

WINSKILL, P. T., *The Temperance Movement and Its Workers*, 4 vols. (London, 1892).

—— and THOMAS, J., *History of the Temperance Movement in Liverpool and District* (Liverpool, 1887).

WOODROOFE, K., *From Charity to Social Work in England and the United States* (London, 1962).

YATES, G. G., *Harriet Martineau On Women* (New Brunswick, NJ, *c.*1985).

ARTICLES AND UNPUBLISHED PAPERS

ANDERSON, G. M., 'Mr. Smith and the Preachers: The Economics of Religion in the *Wealth of Nations*', *Journal of Political Economy*, 96 (1988), 1066–88.

ANNAS, J., 'Mill and the Subjection of Women', *Philosophy*, 52 (1977), 179–94.

BARTRIP, P., 'The *British Medical Journal*: A Retrospect', in W. F. Bynum, S. Lock, and R. Porter (eds.), *Medical Journals and Medical Knowledge: Historical Essays* (1992), 126–45.

BIAGINI, E. F., 'British Trade Unions and Popular Political Economy, 1860–1880', *Historical Journal*, 30 (1987), 811–40.

—— 'Popular Liberals, Gladstonian Finance and the Debate on Taxation, 1860–1874', in E. F. Biagini and A. J. Reid (eds.), *Currents of Radicalism: Popular Radicalism, Organised Labour and Party Politics in Britain, 1850–1914* (Cambridge, 1991), 134–62.

BLAUG, M., 'The Classical Economists and the Factory Acts—A Re-examination', in A. W. Coats (ed.), *The Classical Economists and Economic Policy* (London, 1971), 104–22.

BOSTETTER, M., 'The Journalism of Thomas Wakley', in J. H. Wiener (ed.), *Innovators and Preachers: The Role of the Editor in Victorian England* (Westport, Conn., 1985), 275–92.

BRENT, R., 'God's Providence: Liberal Political Economy as Natural Theology at Oxford 1825–62', in M. Bentley (ed.), *Public and Private Doctrine* (Cambridge, 1993), 85–107.

BRIGHTFIELD, M. F., 'The Medical Profession in Early Victorian England, as Depicted in the Novels of the Period (1840–1870)', *Bulletin of History of Medicine*, 35 (1961), 238–56.

BROWN, J. B., 'The Temperance Career of Joseph Chamberlain, 1870–1877: A Study in Political Frustration', *Albion*, 4 (1972), 29–44.

—— 'The Pig or the Stye: Drink and Poverty in Late Victorian England', *International Review of Social History*, 18 (1973), 380–95.

BRUNDAGE, A., 'The Making of the New Poor Law *Redivivus*: Debate', *Past & Present*, 127 (1990), 183–6.

CAMPBELL, T. D., and ROSS, I. S., 'The Utilitarianism of Adam Smith's Policy Advice', *Journal of History of Ideas*, 42 (1981), 73–92.

CASSELL, R. D., 'Lessons in Medical Politics: Thomas Wakley and the Irish Medical Charities, 1827–39', *Medical History*, 34 (1990), 412–23.

CHECKLAND, S. G., 'The Propagation of Ricardian Economics in England', *Economica*, 16 (1949), 40–52.

—— 'The Advent of Academic Economics in England', *The Manchester School of Economic and Social Studies*, 19 (1951), 43–70.

CLAEYS, G., 'The French Revolution Debate and British Political Thought', *History of Political Thought*, 11 (1990), 59–80.

—— 'The Origins of the Rights of Labor: Republicanism, Commerce, and the Construction of Modern Social Theory in Britain, 1796–1805', *Journal of Modern History*, 66 (1994), 249–90.

CONWAY, S., 'The Politicization of the Nineteenth-Century Peace Society', *Historical Research*, 66 (1993), 267–83.

CORDERY, S., 'Friendly Societies and the Discourse of Respectability in Britain, 1825–1875', *Journal of British Studies*, 34 (1995), 35–58.

COTTRELL, P. L., 'Sir Samuel Morton Peto', in D. J. Jeremy (ed.), *Dictionary of Business Biography* (London, 1985), iv. 644–53.

COWEN, D. L., 'Liberty, Laissez-Faire and Licensure in Nineteenth-Century Britain', *Bulletin of History of Medicine*, 43 (1969), 30–40.

CROWTHER, M. A., 'The Tramp', in R. Porter (ed.), *Myths of the English* (Cambridge, 1992), 91–113.

DENTITH, S., 'Political Economy, Fiction and the Language of Practical Ideology in Nineteenth-Century England', *Social History*, 8 (1983), 183–99.

DRESCHER, S., 'Public Opinion and the Destruction of British Slavery', in J. Walvin (ed.), *Slavery and British Society 1776–1846* (London, 1982), 22–48.

DUMAN, D., 'The Creation and Diffusion of a Professional Ideology in Nineteenth-Century England', *Sociological Review*, 27 (1979), 113–38.

—— 'Pathway to Professionalism: The English Bar in the Eighteenth and Nineteenth Centuries', *Journal of Social History*, 13 (1980), 615–28.

DUNKLEY, P., 'Paternalism, The Magistracy and Poor Relief in England, 1795–1834', *International Review of Social History*, 24 (1979), 371–97.

—— 'Whigs and Paupers: The Reform of the English Poor Laws, 1830–1834', *Journal of British Studies*, 20 (1981), 124–42.

EASTWOOD, D., 'The Making of the New Poor Law *Redivivus*: Debate', *Past & Present*, 127 (1990), 186–94.

—— 'Men, Morals and the Machinery of Social Legislation, 1790–1840', *Parliamentary History*, 13 (1994), 190–205.

EVENSKY, J., 'The Evolution of Adam Smith's Views on Political Economy', *History of Political Economy*, 21 (1989), 123–45.

—— 'Ethics and the Classical Liberal Tradition in Economics', *History of Political Economy*, 24 (1992), 61–77.

FELTES, N. N., 'Community and the Limits of Liability in Two Mid-Victorian Novels', *Victorian Studies*, 17 (1973–4), 355–69.

FIELDEN, K., 'Samuel Smiles and Self-Help', *Victorian Studies*, 12 (1968), 155–76.

FORD, G. H., 'Self-Help and the Helpless in *Bleak House*', in R. C. Rathburn and M. Steinmann (eds.), *From Jane Austen to Joseph Conrad* (Minneapolis, 1958), 92–105.

FOREMAN-PECK, J., 'Sleaze and the Victorian Businessman', *History Today*, 45 (1995), 5–8.

GARNETT, E. J., 'Aspects of the Relationship Between Protestant Ethics and Economic Activity in Mid-Victorian England', D.Phil thesis (Oxford, 1986).

—— ' "Gold and the Gospel": Systematic Beneficence in Mid-nineteenth-Century England', in W. J. Sheils and D. Wood (eds.), *The Church and Wealth*, Studies in Church History, xxiv (1987), 347–58.

—— 'Hastings Rashdall and the Renewal of Christian Social Ethics, *c*.1890–1920', in J. Garnett and C. Matthew (eds.), *Revival and Religion Since 1700: Essays for John Walsh* (London, 1993), 297–316.

—— and HOWE, A. C., 'Churchmen and Cotton Masters in Victorian England', in D. J. Jeremy (ed.), *Business and Religion in Britain* (Aldershot, 1988), 72–94.

GILLESPIE, N. C., 'Divine Design and the Industrial Revolution: William Paley's Abortive Reform of Natural Theology', *Isis*, 81 (1990), 214–29.

GILMOUR, R., 'The Gradgrind School: Political Economy in the Classroom', *Victorian Studies*, 11 (1967), 148.

GOLDMAN, L., 'The Origins of British "Social Science": Political Economy, Natural Science and Statistics, 1830–1835', *Historical Journal*, 26 (1983), 587–616.

GOLDSTROM, J. M., 'Richard Whately and Political Economy in School Books 1833–80', *Irish Historical Studies*, 15 (1966–7), 131–46.

GORDON, S., 'The London *Economist* and the High Tide of Laissez Faire', *Journal of Political Economy*, 63 (1955), 461–88.

GOURVISH, T. R., 'The Rise of the Professions', in T. R. Gourvish and A. O'Day (eds.), *Later Victorian Britain, 1867–1900* (1988), 13–35.

GRAMPP, W. D., 'Classical Economics and its Moral Critics', *History of Political Economy*, 5 (1973), 359–74.

GRAY, J. N., 'Spencer on the Ethics of Liberty and the Limits of State Interference', *History of Political Thought*, 3 (1982), 465–81.

GRAY, T. S., 'Herbert Spencer's Theory of Social Justice—Desert or Entitlement?', *History of Political Thought*, 2 (1981), 161–86.

GREEN, S., 'Archbishop Frederick Temple on Meritocracy, Liberal Education and the Idea of a Clerisy', in M. Bentley (ed.), *Public and Private Doctrine* (Cambridge, 1993), 149–67.

GROSS, I., 'The Abolition of Negro Slavery and British Parliamentary Politics 1832–3', *Historical Journal*, 23 (1980), 63–85.

HALL, C., 'The Butcher, the Baker, the Candlestickmaker: The Shop and the Family in the Industrial Revolution', in E. Whitelegg *et al.* (eds.), *The Changing Experience of Women* (Oxford, 1982), 2–16.

—— ' "From Greenland's Icy Mountains . . . to Afric's Golden Sand": Ethnicity, Race and Nation in Mid-Nineteenth Century England', *Gender and History*, 5 (1993), 212–30.

HARDING, B., 'Transatlantic Views of Speculation and Value, 1820–60', *Historical Research*, 66 (1993), 209–21.

HARLING, P., and MANDLER, P., 'From "Fiscal-Military" State to Laissez-Faire State, 1760–1850', *Journal of British Studies*, 32 (1993), 44–70.

HARRIS, I., 'Paine and Burke: God, Nature and Politics', in M. Bentley (ed.), *Public and Private Doctrine* (Cambridge, 1993), 34–62.

HARRISON, B., 'The Sunday Trading Riots of 1855', *Historical Journal*, 8 (1965), 219–45.

—— 'Religion and Recreation in Nineteenth-Century England', *Past & Present*, 38 (1967), 98–125.

—— 'Underneath the Victorians', *Victorian Studies*, 10 (1967), 239–62.

—— 'Two Roads to Social Reform: Francis Place and the "Drunken Committee" of 1834', *Historical Journal*, 11 (1968), 272–300.

—— '"A World Of Which We Had No Conception": Liberalism and the English Temperance Press: 1830–1872', *Victorian Studies*, 13 (1969), 125–58.

—— 'Animals and the State in Nineteenth-Century England', *English Historical Review*, 88 (1973), 786–820.

—— 'State Intervention and Moral Reform in Nineteenth-Century England', in P. Hollis (ed.), *Pressure From Without in Early Victorian England* (1974), 289–322.

—— 'A Genealogy of Reform in Modern Britain', in C. Bolt and S. Drescher (eds.), *Anti-Slavery, Religion and Reform: Essays in Memory of Roger Anstey* (Folkestone, 1980), 119–48.

—— 'Philanthropy and the Victorians', in id., *Peaceable Kingdom: Stability and Change in Modern Britain* (Oxford, 1982), 217–59.

HART, J. T., 'The *British Medical Journal*, General Practitioners and the State 1840–1990', in W. F. Bynum, S. Lock, and R. Porter (eds.), *Medical Journals and Medical Knowledge: Historical Essays* (London, 1992), 228–47.

HEASMAN, K. J., 'The Medical Mission and the Care of the Sick Poor in Nineteenth-Century England', *Historical Journal*, 7 (1964), 230–45.

HELMSTADTER, R. J., 'W. R. Greg: A Manchester Creed', in R. J. Helmstadter and B. Lightman (eds.), *Victorian Faith in Crisis: Essays on Continuity and Change in Nineteenth-Century Religious Belief* (1990), 187–222.

HOLLANDER, S., 'Ricardo and the Corn Laws: A Revision', *History of Political Economy*, 9 (1977), 1–47.

—— 'On Malthus's Population Principle and Social Reform', *History of Political Economy*, 18 (1986), 187–235.

HONT, I., and IGNATIEFF, M., 'Needs and Justice in the *Wealth of Nations*: An Introductory Essay', in I. Hont and M. Ignatieff (eds.), *Wealth and Virtue: The Shaping of Political Economy in the Scottish Enlightenment* (Cambridge, 1983), 1–44.

ITZKOWITZ, D. C., 'Victorian Bookmakers and Their Customers', *Victorian Studies*, 32 (1988), 7–30.

JOHNSON, P., 'Class Law in Victorian England', *Past & Present*, 141 (1993), 147–69.

KENT, C., 'Higher Journalism and the Mid-Victorian Clerisy', *Victorian Studies*, 13 (1969), 181–98.

KEYNES, J. M., 'The End of Laissez-Faire' (1926), in J. M. Keynes, *Essays in Persuasion* (London, 1931; repr. 1933).

KROUSE, R. W., 'Patriarchal Liberalism and Beyond: From John Stuart Mill to Harriet Taylor', in J. B. Elshtain (ed.), *The Family in Political Thought* (Brighton, 1982), 145–72.

KURER, O., 'John Stuart Mill on Government Intervention', *History of Political Thought*, 10 (1989), 457–80.

LEATHERS, C. G., and RAINES, J. P., 'Adam Smith on Competitive Religious Markets', *History of Political Economy*, 24 (1992), 499–513.

LITTLEWOOD, B., and MAHOOD, L., 'Prostitutes, Magdalenes and Wayward Girls: Dangerous Sexualities of Working-Class Women in Victorian Scotland', *Gender and History*, 3 (1991), 160–75.

MANDLER, P., 'The Making of the New Poor Law *Redivivus*', *Past & Present*, 117 (1987), 131–57.

MANDLER, P., 'The Making of the New Poor Law *Redivivus*: Reply', *Past & Present*, 127 (1990), 194–201.

—— 'Tories and Paupers: Christian Political Economy and the Making of the New Poor Law', *Historical Journal*, 33 (1990), 81–103.

MARLAND, H., 'The Medical Activities of Mid-Nineteenth Century Chemists and Druggists, With Special Reference to Wakefield and Huddersfield', *Medical History*, 31 (1987), 415–39.

MIDGLEY, C., 'Anti-Slavery and Feminism in Nineteenth-Century Britain', *Gender and History*, 5 (1993), 343–62.

MORRIS, R. J., 'Samuel Smiles and the Genesis of *Self-Help*: The Retreat to a Petit Bourgeois Utopia', *Historical Journal*, 24 (1981), 89–109.

—— 'Voluntary Societies and British Urban Elites, 1780–1850', *Historical Journal*, 26 (1983), 95–118.

MUNTING, R., 'Betting and Business; The Commercialisation of Gambling in Britain', *Business History*, 31/4 (1989), 67–85.

—— 'Social Opposition to Gambling in Britain: An Historical Overview', *International Journal of the History of Sport*, 10 (1993), 295–312.

PARRY, N., and PARRY, J., 'Social Closure and Collective Social Mobility', in R. Scace (ed.), *Industrial Society: Class, Cleavage and Control* (London, 1977), 111–21.

RASHID, S., 'Richard Whately and Christian Political Economy at Oxford and Dublin', *Journal of the History of Ideas*, 38 (1977), 147–55.

—— 'Adam Smith's Rise to Fame: A Reexamination of the Evidence', *Eighteenth Century Theory and Interpretation*, 23 (1982), 64–85.

—— 'Dugald Stewart, "Baconian" Methodology and Political Economy', *Journal of the History of Ideas*, 46 (1985), 245–57.

RAVEN, J., 'The Abolition of the English State Lotteries', *Historical Journal*, 34 (1991), 371–89.

REED, J. R., 'A Friend to Mammon: Speculation in Victorian Literature', *Victorian Studies*, 27 (1983–4), 179–202.

REID, A., 'Intelligent Artisans and Aristocrats of Labour: The Essays of Thomas Wright', J. Winter (ed.), *The Working Class in Modern British History* (Cambridge, 1983), 171–86.

RICE, C. D., '"Humanity Sold For Sugar!": The British Abolitionist Response to Free Trade in Slave-Grown Sugar', *Historical Journal*, 13 (1970), 402–18.

RICHARDS, E., 'Darwin and the Descent of Women', in D. Oldroyd and I. Langham (eds.), *The Wider Domain of Evolutionary Thought* (Dordrecht, 1983), 57–111.

ROBERTS, D., 'How Cruel Was the Victorian Poor Law?', *Historical Journal*, 6 (1963), 97–107.

ROMANO, R. M., 'The Economic Ideas of Charles Babbage', *History of Political Economy*, 14 (1982), 385–405.

ROSENBERG, N., 'Some Institutional Aspects of the *Wealth of Nations*', *Journal of Political Economy*, 68 (1960), 557–70.

—— 'Adam Smith and the Stock of Moral Capital', *History of Political Economy*, 22 (1990), 8–11.

RUBINSTEIN, D., 'Millicent Garrett Fawcett and the Meaning of Women's Emancipation, 1886–99', *Victorian Studies*, 34 (1991), 365–80.

RUSSELL, N., '*Nicholas Nickleby* and the Commercial Crisis of 1825', *The Dickensian*, 77 (1981), 144–50.

RYAN, C. C., 'The Fiends of Commerce: Romantic and Marxist Criticisms of Classical Political Economy', *History of Political Economy*, 13 (1981), 80–94.

SAGER, E. W., 'The Social Origins of Victorian Pacifism', *Victorian Studies*, 23 (1979–80), 211–36.

SALTER, J., 'Adam Smith on Feudalism, Commerce and Slavery', *History of Political Thought*, 13 (1992), 219–41.

SANTURRI, E. N., 'Theodicy and Social Policy in Malthus' Thought', *Journal of History of Ideas*, 43 (1982), 315–30.

SEED, J., 'Unitarianism, Political Economy and the Antinomies of Liberal Culture in Manchester, 1830–1850', *Social History*, 7 (1982), 1–25.

—— 'Theologies of Power: Unitarianism and the Social Relations of Religious Discourse, 1800–50', in R. J. Morris (ed.), *Class, Power and Social Structure in British Ninteenth-Century Towns* (Leicester, 1986), 108–56.

SHANNON, H. A., 'The Limited Companies of 1866–1883', *Economic History Review*, 4 (1933), 290–316.

SIGSWORTH, E. M., and WYKE, T. J., 'A Study of Victorian Prostitution and Venereal Disease', in M. Vicinus (ed.), *Suffer and Be Still* (Bloomington, Ind., 1972), 77–99.

SMITH, R. G., 'The Development of Ethical Guidance for Medical Practitioners by the General Medical Council', *Medical History*, 37 (1993), 56–67.

SPALL, R. F., JUN., 'Free Trade, Foreign Relations, and the Anti-Corn-Law League', *International History Review*, 10 (1988), 405–32.

STANLEY, B., ' "Commerce and Christianity": Providence Theory, the Missionary Movement, and the Imperialism of Free Trade, 1842–1860', *Historical Journal*, 26 (1983), 71–94.

STORCH, R. D., 'Police Control of Street Prostitution in Victorian London: A Study in the Contexts of Police Action', in D. H. Bayley (ed.), *Police and Society* (London, 1977), 49–72.

SUMMERS, A., ' "In a Few Years We Shall None of Us that Now Take Care of Them Be Here": Philanthropy and the State in the Thinking of Elizabeth Fry', *Historical Research*, 67 (1994), 134–42.

TEMPERLEY, H., 'Capitalism, Slavery and Ideology', *Past & Present*, 75 (1977), 94–118.

THOMAS, K., 'Cases of Conscience in Seventeenth-Century England', in J. Morrill, P. Slack, and D. Woolf (eds.), *Public Duty and Private Conscience in Seventeenth-Century England: Essays Presented to G. E. Aylmer* (Oxford, 1993), 29–56.

THOMPSON, F. M. L., 'Private Property and Public Policy', in Lord Blake and H. Cecil (eds.), *Salisbury: The Man And His Policies* (Basingstoke, 1987), 252–89.

TOSH, J., 'Authority and Nurture in Middle-Class Fatherhood: The Case of Early and Mid-Victorian England', *Gender and History*, 8 (1996), 48–64.

—— 'New Men? The Bourgeois Cult of Home', *History Today*, 46 (1996), 9–15.

TURNER, F. M., 'The secularization of the social vision of British natural theology', in id., *Contesting Cultural Authority: Essays in Victorian Intellectual Life* (Cambridge, 1993), 101–27.

TURNER, M. J., 'Before the Manchester School: Economic Theory in Early Nineteenth-Century Manchester', *History*, 79 (1994), 216–41.

TYRRELL, A., 'Class Consciousness in Early Victorian Britain: Samuel Smiles, Leeds Politics, and the Self-Help Creed', *Journal of British Studies*, 9 (1970), 102–25.

—— ' "Woman's Mission" and Pressure Group Politics in Britain (1825–60)', *Bulletin of the John Rylands Library*, 63 (1980), 194–230.

WACH, H. M., 'A "Still, Small Voice" from the Pulpit: Religion and the Creation of Social Morality in Manchester, 1820–1850', *Journal of Modern History*, 63 (1991), 425–56.

Bibliography

WADDINGTON, I., 'The Development of Medical Ethics—A Sociological Analysis', *Medical History*, 19 (1975), 36–51.

WALSH, S., 'Bodies of Capital: *Great Expectations* and the Climacteric Economy', *Victorian Studies*, 37 (1993), 73–98.

WALVIN, J., 'The Public Campaign in England against Slavery, 1787–1834', in D. Eltis and J. Walvin (eds.), *The Abolition of the Atlantic Slave Trade: Origins and Effects in Europe, Africa and the Americas* (Madison, Wis., 1981), 63–79.

WATERMAN, A. M. C., 'The Ideological Alliance of Political Economy and Christian Theology, 1798–1833', *Journal of Ecclesiastical History*, 34 (1983), 231–44.

WINCH, D., 'Adam Smith: Scottish Moral Philosopher as Political Economist', *Historical Journal*, 35 (1992), 91–113.

YEO, R., 'The Principles of Plenitude and Natural Theology in Nineteenth-Century Britain', *British Journal for the History of Science*, 19 (1986), 263–82.

YOUNG, R. M., 'Malthus and the Evolutionists: The Common Context of Biological and Social Theory', *Past & Present*, 43 (1969), 109–45.

Index